for

John Rubel

Making Weapons, Talking Peace

with

fond ~~materials~~ memories*

and

great affection

for

New York
La Jolla
2007

* oop!

BOOKS IN THE ALFRED P. SLOAN FOUNDATION SERIES

THIS BOOK IS PUBLISHED AS PART OF AN ALFRED P. SLOAN FOUNDATION PROGRAM

MAKING WEAPONS, TALKING PEACE

A Physicist's Odyssey from Hiroshima to Geneva

HERBERT F. YORK

Basic Books, Inc., Publishers

NEW YORK

Library of Congress Cataloging-in-Publication Data

York, Herbert F. (Herbert Frank)
  Making weapons, talking peace.

  (Alfred P. Sloan Foundation series)
  Includes index.
  1. Nuclear arms control—History.   2. Nuclear
weapons—History.   3. Arms race—History—20th century.
4. United States—Defenses—History.   I. Title.
II. Series.
JX1974.7.Y575   1987   327.1'74   87–47515
ISBN 0–465–04338–0

To Herbert, Nellie, and Sybil

CONTENTS

Illustrations follow page 178

PREFACE TO THE SERIES

T HE Alfred P. Sloan Foundation has for many years had an interest in encouraging public understanding of science. Science in this century has become a complex endeavor. Scientific statements may reflect as many as four centuries of experimentation and theory, and are likely to be expressed in the language of advanced mathematics or in highly technical terms. As scientific knowledge expands, the goal of general public understanding of science becomes increasingly difficult to reach.

Yet an understanding of the scientific enterprise, as distinct from data, concepts, and theories, is certainly within the grasp of us all. It is an enterprise conducted by men and women who are stimulated by hopes and purposes that are universal, rewarded by occasional successes, and distressed by setbacks. Science is an enterprise with its own rules and customs, but an understanding of that enterprise is accessible, for it is quintessentially human. And an understanding of the enterprise inevitably brings with it insights into the nature of its products.

The Sloan Foundation expresses great appreciation to the advisory committee. Present members include the chairman, Simon Michael Bessie, Co-Publisher, Cornelia and Michael Bessie Books; Howard Hiatt, Professor, School of Medicine, Harvard University; Eric R. Kandel, University Professor, Columbia University College of Physicians and Surgeons and Senior Investigator, Howard Hughes Medical Institute; Daniel Kevles, Professor of History, California Institute of Technology; Robert Merton, University Professor Emeritus, Columbia University; Paul Samuelson, Institute Professor of Economics, Massachusetts Institute of Technology; Robert Sinsheimer, Professor of Biophysics, California Institute of Technology; Stephen White, former Vice-President of the Alfred P. Sloan Foundation; and Steven Weinberg, Professor of Physics, University of Texas at Austin. Previous members of the committee were

Daniel McFadden, Professor of Economics, and Professor Philip Morrison, Professor of Physics, both of the Massachusetts Institute of Technology; Mark Kac (deceased), formerly Professor of Mathematics, University of Southern California; and Frederick E. Terman, Provost Emeritus, Stanford University. The Sloan Foundation has been represented by Arthur L. Singer, Jr., Stephen White, Eric Wanner, and Sandra Panem. The first publisher of the program, Harper & Row, was represented by Edward L. Burlingame and Sallie Coolidge. This volume is the third to be published by Basic Books, represented by Martin Kessler and Richard Liebmann-Smith.

—ALBERT REES
President
Alfred P. Sloan Foundation
August 1987

AUTHOR'S PREFACE

MY EARLIEST memories of public affairs include the election of Herbert Hoover, the Great Depression, the election of Franklin Roosevelt, the rise of Adolf Hitler, the Japanese invasion of China, and the Italian invasion of Ethiopia, all of which took place while I was still in grade school. They continue with the Spanish civil war, which occurred when I was in high school. The European branch of World War II started in the same month that I entered college at the University of Rochester.

Soon after that Pearl Harbor came along, and my professors began to leave in order to contribute their part to the war effort. I eventually joined them by going off to Berkeley and the Manhattan Project.

When the war ended, I was demobilized, so to speak, along with tens of millions of others all over the world, and I began what I hoped and thought was going to be a normal peaceful career in pure science. It was not to be. After only three and a half years, major external events, including the explosion of the first Soviet atomic bomb and the Korean War, brought me back into the nuclear arms race, and my life has been largely caught up in it ever since. This book chronicles my involvement, beginning with my work on the Hiroshima bomb and ending with my service as Jimmy Carter's chief negotiator at the Comprehensive Test Ban talks in Geneva.

In addition to participating directly in such events, I have from time to time had extended opportunities to stand back and reflect on them. This book, therefore, is also a memoir of the evolution of my understanding of what was going on and my thinking about what ought to be done about it.

In the course of preparing this manuscript, I have had the pleasure and good fortune to consult and reminisce with many of the people who have over the years been my close associates in these matters. They include

Harold Brown, Gerald Johnson, Michael May, James Killian, Jack Ruina, John Rubel, John Galbraith, Bill McGill, Roger Revelle, Marvin Goldberger, Freeman Dyson, Robert Buchheim, and Edward Giller. They did their best to correct my more egregious errors of recollection, and the final result benefits much from their efforts. I also received invaluable help from my current academic colleagues, especially Allen Greb, Gregg Herkin, Eleanor Hodges, Sanford Lakoff, William Mahedy, Christopher Canole, and James Skelly.

I wrote this book out in longhand scribbles on ruled yellow paper and then read it all word by word to Sybil, who put it on our word processor. Her editorial comments and corrections as we edited the manuscript were equally invaluable.

Hong Kong
1986

ABBREVIATIONS

ABM   antiballistic missile
ABMA   Army Ballistic Missile Agency
ACDA   Arms Control and Disarmament Agency
AEC   Atomic Energy Commission
AFPC   Armed Forces Policy Council
ALCM   air-launched cruise missile
ARPA   Advanced Research Projects Agency
ASAT   antisatellite
AWRE   Atomic Weapons Research Establishment
BMEWS   Ballistic Missile Early Warning System
CIA   Central Intelligence Agency
CTB   comprehensive test ban
DDR & E   director of defense research and engineering
FAS   Federation of American Scientists
GA   General Atomics
GAC   General Advisory Committee
IAEA   International Atomic Energy Agency
ICBM   intercontinental ballistic missile
IDA   Institute for Defense Analyses
IGY   International Geophysical Year
JCAE   Joint Committee on Atomic Energy
JCC   Joint Consultative Commission
JPL   Jet Propulsion Laboratory
MAD   mutual assured destruction

MIRV	multiple independently targeted reentry vehicles
MTA	Materials Testing Accelerator
NACA	National Advisory Committee on Aeronautics
NASA	National Aeronautics and Space Administration
NORAD	North American Air Defense Command
NPT	Nonproliferation Treaty
NSS	national seismic station
ODDR & E	Office of the Director of Defense Research and Engineering
OSD	Office of the Secretary of Defense
OSI	on-site inspection
PSAC	President's Science Advisory Committee
R & D	research and development
RDT & E	research, development, test, and evaluation
SAB	Science Advisory Board
SAC	Strategic Air Command
SALT	Strategic Arms Limitation Talks
SCC	Special Coordinating Committee
SDI	Strategic Defense Initiative
SIO	Scripps Institution of Oceanography
SIOP	Single Integrated Operational Plan
SMEC	Strategic Missile Evaluation Committee
START	Strategic Arms Reduction Talks
SVA	Separate Verification Agreement
TTBT	Threshold Test Ban Treaty
UCSD	University of California at San Diego

Making Weapons, Talking Peace

CHAPTER 1

The Manhattan Project

(May 1943–August 1945)

The War and the Bomb

I T WAS, as the Russians would say, no accident that the destruction of Hiroshima and Nagasaki by nuclear bombs marked the end of World War II. The histories of the war and of the bomb had been tightly intertwined from the beginning.

In 1931 Japan invaded China and set up a puppet state in Manchuria. In 1932 the English physicist James Chadwick discovered the neutron. In 1933 a French team headed by Frédéric and Irène Joliot-Curie discovered artificial radioactivity, Adolf Hitler became chancellor of Germany and Franklin D. Roosevelt president of the United States. In 1934 Leo Szilard arrived in England in the first wave of what became a flood of refugees from the Nazi terror. Almost immediately he conceived the notion that there must be some substance in which Chadwick's neutron would induce a nuclear chain reaction, which would in turn produce huge quantities of the Joliot-Curies' radioactivity and release enormous amounts of energy, but he did not (and indeed could not) know what substance would support such a process. Even so, he managed to take out two British patents—a public one sketching out his ideas for constructing what we would now call a nuclear reactor and a second, secret one outlining a possible means for producing an exceedingly powerful bomb.

In March 1938 Hitler's troops marched into Vienna and accomplished the forced unification of Germany and Austria. In September 1938 Hitler and Prime Minister Neville Chamberlain of Britain met in Munich and signed a pact designed to assure "peace in our time." The pact ceded the German-speaking border regions of Czechoslovakia to the German Reich and, contrary to its stated purposes, set the stage for a further series of disastrous events, including a temporary rapprochement between Nazi Germany and the Soviet Union. In December 1938 Otto Hahn and Fritz Strassmann, working in Germany, discovered that when a uranium nucleus was struck by a neutron, it split in two, releasing large amounts of energy and—possibly—producing additional neutrons, which could in principle go on and repeat the process in yet other uranium nuclei. Word of this discovery spread rapidly. The splitting process itself was soon named fission, and the possibilities inherent in the new phenomenon—a chain reaction and the release of the great store of energy known to be locked up in the nucleus—were quickly recognized by scientists everywhere. The world was primed for both the war and the bomb.

In March 1939 Germany annexed the rest of Czechoslovakia. Throughout that spring and summer physicists in many countries conducted experiments designed to elucidate further the process of neutron-induced fission and to determine its potentialities.

On August 2, 1939, Szilard, Eugene Wigner, and Edward Teller (all Jewish refugees from the Nazi terror) persuaded Albert Einstein (yet another) to write a letter to President Roosevelt to bring this novel and potentially ominous situation to his attention. After mentioning the prospects for nuclear power inherent in the new discoveries, the letter went on to say, "[I]t is conceivable . . . that extremely powerful bombs of a new type may thus be constructed."[1] He also noted that the Germans had recently taken over the Czech uranium mines, Europe's principal source of that uncommon element. The letter was not actually delivered into Roosevelt's hands until October 11, nearly two and a half months later. In the meantime the Hitler-Stalin "nonaggression pact" was signed, Germany invaded Poland, Britain and France declared war on Germany in response, and World War II was under way. On September 17 Soviet troops crossed the eastern frontier of Poland unopposed and in October moved into Estonia, Latvia, and Lithuania, ostensibly to keep the Germans from later doing the same. In November, Stalin's armies attacked Finland, where they were halted by surprisingly strong counterresistance.

Experiments in Britain and the United States (in the latter mainly at Berkeley, Chicago, and Columbia) continued throughout 1940 and 1941, now almost entirely in secret. It gradually became apparent that a new type of bomb of enormous destructive power could probably be constructed if sufficient amounts—then estimated to be tens or even hundreds of kilograms—of either of two very exotic materials could be produced. One of these was uranium 235 (U-235), and the other was plutonium (Pu). Neither exists in nature in suitable form, and neither had ever been produced before, except in submicroscopic quantities. The ideas and the experiments were followed closely by a special committee of scientists reporting directly to Vannevar Bush, Roosevelt's chief scientific aide.

In the spring of 1940 Hitler attacked and occupied most of northwest Europe, save only Britain and Sweden. A year later he turned east and attacked Russia, thus launching the most murderous phase of the war. Only days before Japan attacked the American fleet at Pearl Harbor, Bush signed a report to President Roosevelt informing him that an atomic bomb appeared to be feasible and recommending a crash program for its development. During the first half of 1942, while exploratory experiments continued at a number of different centers, detailed plans were advanced for organizing work both on the bomb itself and on the means for producing the special materials needed to make it. Finally, in the second half of the year, the Manhattan Project was formally instituted and set in motion.

The work of the Manhattan Project, as the totality of the effort came to be called, was dispersed over a number of laboratories and industrial sites. Research on the nuclear properties of U-235 and plutonium and on the design of the bomb itself was carried out at the Los Alamos Scientific Laboratory under the direction of J. Robert Oppenheimer. This laboratory, known during the war as Site Y, was specifically established for those purposes in 1942 by the regents of the University of California on a remote mesa high above the Rio Grande River. Major research centers whose goal was to develop the methods for producing adequate quantities of U-235 and plutonium were set up at the University of California at Berkeley, the University of Chicago, and Columbia University. The construction of huge plants making use of the methods to be developed at those places was undertaken even before the methods were fully elaborated. The largest scientific project by far in the history of the world was getting fully under way. The nuclear arms race—not yet called that—was entering its first phase.

It was inevitable that I would be drawn into this great effort. The new projects and organizations required lots of new talent, and they sent their recruiters out to comb the graduate schools to find it. In November 1942, just before my twenty-first birthday, a recruiter from the Berkeley laboratory found me at the University of Rochester, where I was a first-year graduate student in the Department of Physics. Sidney Barnes, a Rochester physics professor who had gone to Berkeley in early 1942, had given my name to their recruiter, and so when he came our way later that year, he was looking for me specifically.

I could not have remained a graduate student any longer even if I had wanted to, and I did not. Like most of my contemporaries, I wanted to go out into the world and do my part to win the war. I flirted briefly with other war projects—at MIT, Columbia, and McGill—but the lure of Berkeley was by far the strongest. Barnes and Joe Perry, until a few months earlier a fellow graduate student and roommate but now also on the Berkeley staff, reported that they found their jobs interesting and worthwhile. On top of that, Berkeley was in California, near San Francisco and Yosemite, all places I had read about as a boy and dreamed of seeing ever since. Most important, I had recently started doing research using a special machine called a cyclotron, which Ernest O. Lawrence, the director of the Berkeley laboratory, had invented, and the idea of one day going there and joining him had been forming in the back of my mind for some time.

When Berkeley extended a formal offer, I grabbed it and arranged to go as soon as I could. That turned out to be one week after the term was over, and I delayed that long only so that my parents could attend my formal graduation ceremonies. Eager to get on with the future, I had wanted to leave even earlier, but I couldn't very well deny them that pleasure.

Roots

My roots are in upstate New York. My great grandfather York was, I think, born in Watertown. He identified himself as a Yankee and came from a family that had long been in America. My other seven great grandparents all came to the United States from the "old country"—

Germany, Holland, and Ireland—between 1830 and 1870 and settled variously in Oneida, Pittsford, and Rochester.

Grandfather Lang (De Lange) lined caskets with satin, carved velvet, and other fancy materials. Grandfather York was a railway express messenger and baggageman on the New York Central Railroad.

My mother, Nellie E. Lang, finished high school in Oneida and then moved to Rochester where she took one or two years of post secondary education at the Rochester Business Institute. She later worked as a secretary in the shipping department of the Eastman Kodak Company and there she met my father, then employed as a shipping clerk.

My father, Herbert F. York, was expelled from high school during his senior year for some sort of mischief. He later enrolled in a correspondence course on surveying offered by the International Correspondence Schools, but nothing came of it. Eventually, for the last thirty-five years of his regular working life, he worked on the railroad in exactly the same job his father had had. Both he and mother were serious Episcopalians and active members of the Masons and Eastern Star, respectively. Both of these associations provided them contact with higher economic and social strata than they otherwise would have had.

I was born in Rochester on Thanksgiving day, November 24, 1921, five years after my parents were married. After another five years my sister Helen came along. Before my voice changed, I served regularly as a choir boy in a large downtown church. I was paid about four dollars a month in this capacity, a princely sum for a nine year old during the Great Depression. Later, during my teens, I served as an acolyte.

Dad basically enjoyed his job, often saying that he could not understand how factory workers could stand it, working indoors all the time. Even so, from the earliest times, I remember his saying he did not want his son to be a railroad man. He made it clear that that meant I should go to college, even though he knew little about what that actually entailed.

There were always newspapers and magazines around the house, but we owned very few books except for the Bible which was always displayed on a side table in the living room. Early on I became an avid reader of the newspapers, and I closely followed the course of the Italian invasion of Ethiopia, the Spanish Civil War, and Roosevelt's struggles to get the economy going again, all of which occured when I was in my teens. While still in grammar school I also developed a great interest in books in the public library on exotic travel (Richard Haliburton in Tibet, Sven Hedin in Chinese Turkestan) and on astronomy. (Camille Flammarion's *Astronomy for Amateurs* was an early special favorite which I owned.) I soon progressed to a level such that the books I wanted could only be found in the central library downtown. The travel books, along with stamp collecting and an occasional trip in the baggage car with my father to some far-off place like Albany or Niagara Falls, led to an enduring interest in the world as a whole and a strong desire to see as much of it as possible for myself. The astronomy books led to (or, perhaps, reinforced) a deep interest in science and the natural world.

Despite these interests, however, I was a very poor student, receiving below average grades, especially in deportment. At one point during my freshman year in high school, the authorities decided to expel me and send me off to Edison Tech, the only trade school in the city at that time. Happily, my father, recalling his own similar experience, successfully intervened and I remained in an academic high school.

During my sophomore and junior years, my geometry teacher and my English teacher lectured me long and hard about doing better. Finally they got through to me somehow and during the last two years I was above average in everything. As a result of this sudden late improvement and an unexpectedly good showing on an aptitude test, I was admitted to the University of Rochester in the fall of 1939 and given a one-half tuition scholarship. I continued to live at home, commuting daily by bus. The ride took about an hour each way.

The first year in college provided some of the greatest thrills of my life. I still remember vividly the discovery of all manner of things I had previously been totally unaware of: the joy of learning how the world actually worked, the existence of such things as graduate students, Ph.D. degrees, and, above all, mature people who did what they were doing because they enjoyed it and not just to earn money to support their families. College, I found, meant a great deal more than simply not working on the railroad, and I was determined to become a part of this newly discovered world.

Most fortunately for me, the University of Rochester even then was an excellent school, ranking well above the other urban universities in upstate New York, and I met many very special people there whom I would otherwise never have encountered. In later life a persistent thought often passed through my head and sometimes over my lips as well: "If I had been born in Syracuse or Buffalo, I would not be here, in this particular place, today."

Westward Ho!

Railways were still the normal way to travel in the early forties. They were crowded because, as everyone said, "There is a war on," and millions of people of all kinds were being uprooted and moved somewhere else. J. Robert Oppenheimer, Rosie the Riveter, GI Joe, and I were all among them.

I boarded the train at the Rochester depot a little before dawn on May 2, 1943. It was snowing lightly, and an inch or so had already accumulated on the platform. My parents were there to see me off to join the war effort, to explore the West, and to begin life on my own. Just a couple of hours later, soon after daybreak, I was beyond Buffalo—farther west than I had ever been before.

Because of the routing I had selected, it took me six days to cross the country instead of the usual three. Although in a hurry to get to Berkeley and to start work, I was also very eager to see some of the spectacular scenery and high mountains I knew were out in the West, and so I had searched the timetables for a route and a train that passed through a national park during daylight hours. The only train that met those conditions was the Great Northern Railroad's Empire Builder, then running from Chicago to Spokane and Seattle by way of the southern boundary of Glacier National Park. We reached that stretch of track around noon on the third day out. I was not disappointed. The scenery was glorious. There the Rocky Mountains rise directly and suddenly out of the gently undulating prairie. The prairie was grassy and green and the mountains were high and snowcapped, as I had long imagined them, only better. It was just the right time of year and the right time of day to see them. After the passing the park, the train crossed the northern panhandle of Idaho and the Bitterroot Mountains, a handsome range previously unknown to an ordinary easterner like me.

In Spokane I changed to a train bound for Portland and made up of very old cars, still outfitted with gas fixtures for lighting. It was full of young soldiers going off to war. It followed the bank of the Columbia River, where I was somewhat disappointed by Bonneville Dam and delighted by Multnomah Falls, another unexpected discovery. After seeing Mount Hood and passing the night in Portland, I started the last leg to Berkeley on the Southern Pacific's California Daylight. It was an especially clear and beautiful day, and for many hours I was able to see the great white 14,000-foot-high cone of Mount Shasta, first from far to its north, then right up alongside, and finally from well down in California's Central Valley, a hundred miles to the south.

Late on a Saturday evening I arrived in Oakland. There, to add one last, amusing surprise to the day, I was advised to board a streetcar labeled Alcatraz in order to get to Berkeley, where I had managed to locate a room at the YMCA. Bright and early on Monday morning, May 10, 1943, I reported for work at the University of California Radiation Laboratory. The people in the personnel office, located right on the Berkeley campus, put me on a jitney that took me up through Strawberry Canyon to a large, round building with a red roof that housed the 184-inch cyclotron magnet (called that because its pole pieces were 184 inches in diameter), then by far the world's largest. The site was high on a hill overlooking the Berkeley campus and San Francisco Bay, with its Golden Gate opening on the Pacific Ocean and separating the city of San Francisco to its south from Marin County and Mount Tamalpais to its north. It was yet another magnificent and impressive sight, even after all the ones I had taken in during the preceding week of travels. I marveled at it then and many times later, especially in the early evening after the city lights had started to come on but while the outlines of all the land forms and bridges could still be easily seen in the twilight.

The natural side of things "out west" fully met my hopes and desires. As it would soon turn out, the professional and personal aspects of life in California would also meet or surpass my expectations. I was indeed a very fortunate young man. Through a happy combination of circumstances, I had landed in the right place at the right time.

Lawrence and the Rad Lab

Ernest Lawrence's Berkeley Radiation Laboratory was the only one of the major institutions making up the Manhattan Project that was actually founded by its director. All the other units were created at the time by official fiat, and all the other directors were appointed by higher authority. In marked contrast, Lawrence's lab was already more than a decade old when it joined the project to make the bomb. This unique situation gave Lawrence an extra measure of leverage in his dealings with higher government and university authorities both then and after the war.

Ernest O. Lawrence was a dynamic, self-confident, optimistic, and exceptionally inventive scientist. In 1929, shortly after he had become a member of the Department of Physics at the Berkeley campus of the

University of California, he invented a device that he named a cyclotron. It was a machine for accelerating protons and other nuclear particles to high velocities by means of an ingenious combination of oscillating electric and static magnetic fields. Its basic purpose was to probe the properties of the atomic nucleus and to investigate its constituents. There were other machines for accomplishing this purpose—all were popularly called atom smashers—but Lawrence's cyclotron proved to be the most powerful and the most effective. More important, his approach appeared to offer the potential for virtually unlimited further development and extension. In fact, more than half a century later, nearly all of the world's huge particle accelerators are based on concepts that, while different in detail and generally much more elaborate, are the direct descendants of Lawrence's original invention.

The potential of the new machine, combined with Lawrence's boyish enthusiasm and confidence, attracted others to his laboratory, and the group that gathered around him grew rapidly. A special new autonomous unit, the University of California Radiation Laboratory (UCRL), had to be established to support and manage Lawrence's activities. In the years immediately following, the laboratory continued to expand, but the main emphasis remained on building bigger and more capable versions of the cyclotron rather than on using what was on hand for nuclear research.

Many other physicists soon recognized the potential of the cyclotron and sought to build versions of it in Europe, the Soviet Union, and Japan as well as at other universities in America. Lawrence was always very generous and openhanded in encouraging these groups and in helping them to forge ahead with activities parallel to his own. He welcomed visitors from these institutions in his laboratory, personally visited many of them, freely gave advice and counsel, and sent some of his own staff to work at these other sites. In 1939 Lawrence was awarded the Nobel Prize in physics for his invention and for his pioneering work with it.

(The first cyclotron to be built outside Berkeley was the one at the University of Rochester. It was my good fortune to be employed to operate it during my third year in college and to use it for some very modest research during my fourth year. Of course, I learned a lot about nuclear physics and its tools in the process; even more important for me in the long run, I became aware of the great man behind it all and of the laboratory he headed.)

Like their colleagues everywhere, the physicists at Berkeley immediately realized that the discovery of fission was of transcendent importance. Lawrence's younger coworkers quickly confirmed the new discoveries and expanded on them. Among other things, they discovered and determined the properties of plutonium, one of the two materials suitable for the making of nuclear bombs.

Lawrence followed these events very closely, but he devoted his personal energies to three other activities. One of these was the promotion of his plans for still bigger cyclotrons. Another was the participation in the national-level committees whose job it was to follow developments in the expanding studies of uranium fission and to make recommendations about what should be done in the area. The third was the conversion of his laboratory from one engaged in peacetime research to one dedicated entirely to the uranium project.

From the beginning Lawrence played a leading role in determining the course of the uranium project, first as a consultant and later as a member of the top level "S-1 committee," established to oversee all work in this area. Of the scientists who operated at that level, Lawrence was generally the most enthusiastic, the most optimistic, and the most aggressive in his approach to the project. He pushed hard to focus attention on the possibility of building a bomb, rather than just on that of generating power for ship propulsion or similar purposes; he argued strongly that the production of both U-235 and plutonium should be pursued in parallel; and he very early on urged that the project be greatly expanded to bring in the large number of scientists and to build the institutions necessary to accomplish the task quickly.

On returning home after a meeting in the late fall of 1941, he wrote a letter to Arthur Compton—the S-1 committee's chairman—that said in part,

> In our meeting yesterday, there was a tendency to emphasize the uncertainties, and accordingly the possibility that uranium will not be a factor in the war. This, to my mind, was very dangerous. We should have fastened our attention on the fact that the evidence now is that there is a substantial prospect that the chain reaction will be achieved in the near future, one way or another, and that military applications of transcendental importance may follow.
>
> It will not be a calamity if, when we get the answers to the uranium problem, they turn out negative from the military point of view, but if the answers are fantastically positive and we fail to get them first, the results for our country may well be tragic disaster.[2]

Lawrence's sanguine views were incorporated in the final version of the committee's report, declaring "a fission bomb of superlatively destructive power" to be feasible. In mid-November 1941 Vannevar Bush submitted these ideas to President Roosevelt, who then, in effect, ordered what history knows as the Manhattan Project to commence.

Just six days after Pearl Harbor, Bush sent letters out to the men who would become the various project leaders and gave each of them their specific assignments. Lawrence got the responsibility for "small-sample preparation, electromagnetic separation methods, and 'certain experimentation [on plutonium].' "[3] In anticipation of this assignment Lawrence had already disassembled one of his smaller cyclotrons in order to use its magnet as the basic building block for a device capable of producing microgram quantities of U-235. In addition, he diverted the much larger magnet originally intended for his next and biggest cyclotron to the construction of a still larger device, later dubbed a Calutron, for producing multigram quantities of the same material. Similar devices, called mass spectrometers, had been around for some years, but previous versions had been much smaller and served strictly as research tools. In effect, Lawrence proposed to take a research tool, increase its size more than a millionfold, and turn it into a mass production machine.

In the summer of 1942 the great 184-inch magnet was turned on, and experimental prototypes of the Calutron, Lawrence's gigantic mass spectrometer, were placed in operation between its pole pieces. By that time much of Lawrence's senior staff had left the laboratory to help launch other war-related projects. They were always sent off with his blessing and, usually, at his urging. As a result, a largely new and mostly even younger group had to be recruited to carry out the work at Berkeley.

By the end of 1942 enough was known about Calutrons that the design could be "frozen" and construction of a separation plant at Oak Ridge, Tennessee, be authorized. The plant, known as Y-12, was to be built by the Stone and Webster Corporation and operated by the Tennessee Eastman Corporation.

But even after construction was under way back east, experiments with prototypes continued at Berkeley for the purpose of optimizing the process and improving both the quantity and the quality of the product. The staff continued to expand, and I was about to become part of that expansion.

At the Rad Lab

My first assignment was to work as a member of the crew of the R-1 Calutron, one of two prototypes sitting between the pole pieces of the 184-inch magnet. The cochiefs of the crew were Frank Oppenheimer— Robert Oppenheimer's younger brother—and Fred Schmidt. Our task was to study the operating characteristics of the R-1 and, by using the Edisonian cut-and-try approach, to maximize its ability to extract U-235 in as pure a form as possible from natural uranium.

The details of all this came as a complete surprise to me, even though I had been quite certain even before my arrival in Berkeley that the Radiation Laboratory was engaged in some way in making a nuclear bomb. Nobody had told me that in so many words, but the general idea of nuclear energy and nuclear bombs had been in the air for some time. More accurately, it was in the air that budding physicists breathed in the early 1940s. Given Lawrence's reputation in nuclear physics, it was easy to put two and two together and conclude that Berkeley was somehow involved in making uranium bombs.

As clearly as I can recall, the word *uranium* was breathed in my ear very soon but only once after my arrival. From then on, code words were used for everything of special relevance to the project. Uranium itself was called *tuballoy,* a code name I later learned had been invented by no less than Winston Churchill. The three natural isotopes of uranium were called W (U-234), X (U-235), and Y (U-238). Mixtures of isotopes, especially enriched in U-235, were called R, and the residue of material depleted in U-235 was called Q. The object of the whole enterprise was to produce R as fast as possible and to have it be as rich in X as we could make it.

I do not recall anyone's preaching to me or others about the need for secrecy. The need was explained just once—but firmly—and thereafter the whole atmosphere of the time strongly reinforced it. To my recollection, following my first day I never again heard the word *uranium* either in a normal conversation or in a confidential aside. This custom—this way of living, working, and thinking with code words—became deeply ingrained in me and everyone I knew. As a result, after news of the bomb burst upon the public two and a half years later, it was deeply shocking for me to read that forbidden word in the headlines and to hear people utter it out loud—with a certain awe, to be sure, but nonetheless as if it were just another, normal word. Hearing it was one of those things that caused a sudden, queasy feeling in the pit of the stomach.

Something was badly awry. I clearly recall that for me, saying *uranium* out loud had become equivalent to cursing one's mother—I could not possibly have done either.

I met Lawrence only a few days after I arrived at the lab. I remember the form and style of the occasion vividly, but not its precise date or substance. It was one of the regular staff meetings. The meeting room had the makeshift and temporary look common to all parts of the lab. The walls were some sort of fiberboard nailed to joists that were exposed in many places. The room held between fifty and a hundred folding metal chairs. Up front, but off to the right, was a large leather-covered easy chair, and there was, of course, a blackboard. After most members of the staff—happily, including me—were assembled, Lawrence made a grand entrance. He was a tall, heavyset man, with a cheerful round face, blond hair combed straight back, and thin-rimmed glasses. He marched down the center aisle with a long, firm stride, went straight to the front, turned, beamed at all of the assembled, and sat down heavily in the easy chair. He called for the discussion to be started but did not otherwise introduce or lead it directly. Several group leaders reported on what they were doing and finding; Lawrence asked occasional questions and made various, usually approving, remarks about what he heard. It was a scene I was to see repeated often. Like the mountains of the American West, Lawrence and his laboratory fully lived up to my expectations. I was instantly much impressed by him both as a physical presence and as the laboratory's director and intellectual leader.

I was very pleased with my situation. Not only was I at last making a contribution to the war effort, but I was doing so with people and in an institution that had already accomplished great things and would surely continue to do so.

To exaggerate only slightly, Lawrence's philosophy was that no one was too good to do any job that needed doing and, conversely, that no job was too hard or too esoteric for anyone to do, if only he tried hard enough. One result was that a haberdasher was recruited to head a group of accelerator technicians, a philosophy professor became the plant manager, a dendrologist became scientific staff recruiter, and so on. Another result was that when the area around the Calutron got a little messy, the newest physicist on the crew—I, for a time—was handed a large broom and assigned the job of cleaning it up. Another early task, besides learning to operate the R-1 machine, that I recall vividly was quickly learning enough carpentry to build and paint a set of wooden racks for holding various Calutron components while they were undergoing modification. On other occasions I found myself learning to hand make simple widgets that the stockroom was out of at the moment, such as a brass-and-plastic double-pole, double-throw electrical switch.

After a few months of that kind of work, I screwed up my courage and reminded Frank Oppenheimer that I had a master of science degree. I suggested that perhaps I might do something more closely connected with all those things I had learned at the University of Rochester the past four years. Frank, who was always understanding and gentle with people, asked me what, specifically, I would like to do. His response took me by surprise, and I found I couldn't answer his question. It was one of those small events that become engraved in one's memory. I went off and worked out an answer. Much more important, I took the whole matter to heart and determined that never again would I simply wait for a boss to tell me what to do.

On the next day, I told Frank that I had been thinking about our conversation and that I had some ideas about how to modify the Calutron product collectors in a way that might enhance the purity of the R material. He immediately let me go to work on those ideas, and I soon became one of the local experts on the design of that part of the apparatus.

At one point later on, I told Lawrence I could do a better job if I could know the trade-off between quality and quantity of product. After his next trip to Los Alamos, he handed me a small slip of paper on which was written the critical mass of enriched uranium (in arbitrary units) for four or five different levels of U-235 concentration (all, of course, in numbers only, without any of those forbidden words). Because of the compartmentalization of information, I was the only junior person in our part of the project who had this information. I did make use of it in designing product collectors in order to optimize the rate at which the plant approached the production of a critical mass.

After the war ended, I convinced myself that my efforts, while not at all profound or even particularly clever, had had a small effect on the outcome. I had helped either to make the Hiroshima bomb available a few days earlier or to make its explosion a little more powerful. I knew, of course, that hundreds of others could make similar statements about hundreds of other small contributions, but I was pleased with what I had been able to do.

At Oak Ridge

In the meantime, in the fall of 1943, six months after I had arrived at Berkeley and while I was still there, the first attempt to begin operations at the huge Y-12 production facility in Tennessee failed. The great magnets frequently shorted out, other components couldn't be made to work properly, and the operating staff—recruited largely from nearby towns—proved to be inadequate for the task. Operations, equipment, and techniques that seemed straightforward—even if unusual—under the conditions prevailing at Berkeley turned out to be much too exotic when transplanted to Appalachia. The whole Calutron project in Tennessee took on the shape of a real disaster.

Back in Berkeley I was only dimly aware of those problems. It was, I learned long after the event, very hard on Lawrence, but he bulled the project through. The magnets and the Calutrons were torn apart and rebuilt correctly in time for a second try near the end of the year. In order to get the whole plant restarted properly, Lawrence moved several hundred of his Berkeley staff, including me, back to Tennessee in a private railroad car. After only eight months in California, I was off to another unexplored locale.

The idea was that the crews of young physicists and others who had designed and operated the prototypes at Berkeley would initiate the operation of the production versions at Oak Ridge; then, as soon as that was smoothly under way, the operation would once again be turned over to the locally recruited crews, consisting mainly of young female high school graduates in blue jumpers. The scheme worked, though never well enough that we could all leave the machines wholly in local hands.

Lawrence visited Oak Ridge often. As was his custom in Berkeley, too, he visited all parts of the plant and asked whomever he came across what he or she was doing and how things were going. I enjoyed talking with him when he chanced on my part of the project, and I also occasionally sought him out to discuss some particular idea. I appreciated whatever attention he paid to me, and his obvious interest and enthusiasm always gave me a big lift.

Oak Ridge was, all in all, an exciting and interesting place. I had never been involved in anything of that scope or importance before, and I enjoyed the opportunity of seeing the project take shape and get under way before my eyes. There were disturbing elements as well, elements that seemed especially out of place in that futuristic context. Every building had four toilets, one each for white men, colored men, white women, and colored women. Drinking fountains also came in pairs: white water and colored water. The idea of a fountain yielding "colored water" seemed faintly humorous, but that was not its main impression on me. As a Yankee, I had never been so close to overt segregation before, and I was troubled by it. It also clashed with the religious side of my upbringing. Even as a youngster I had some problems with the mystical side of the church's teachings, but I took the ideas about the brotherhood of man very seriously. The fact that southerners seemed even more religious than northerners served only to confuse me further when it came to the matter of the "colored water."

The countryside was also new and different—the Great Smoky Mountains National Park was in easy driving range, even with gas rationing—and I met lots of new friends, both my age and older. But the most important thing I got out of Oak Ridge in the long run was what I absorbed simply from observing—largely unconsciously—how Lawrence went about running a large-scale high-tech enterprise.

His style was direct and bold. On one occasion soon after we had gotten the plant fired up the second time, Lawrence discovered we were being held back because the cooling towers could not quite handle the excess heat produced in the magnet coils when they were all turned on at once. He promptly arranged for the local fire department to come out and play their hoses on the towers continuously until additional cooling capacity could be placed in service. On another occasion he found that of the partially enriched uranium going into the second (Beta) of the two refinement stages, only about one-half was coming out as final product. He decided that the remainder must be tied up in the stainless steel plumbing in the chemical processing laboratory. He immediately ordered that whole laboratory torn apart and all the piping sawed in half. Sure enough, the lost uranium was there; it had been plated out on the inside of the pipes as the result of an unanticipated chemical process.

"Hold Your Water 'til We Tell Ya"

A few weeks before I left Berkeley for Oak Ridge, I went to the local Naval Recruiting Office to see about enlisting as an officer. I had discovered that a number of officers were already working on the project, and I thought I might be able to join up and be assigned to the project for the duration. As a young researcher on the Manhattan Project, I had almost automatically received an "occupational deferment" from military service, but since nearly every other healthy young man seemed to be in uniform, I felt some pressure to join them. Besides, I could expect to enjoy the benefits of being a veteran afterward. They checked me out superficially, discovered I was too color-blind, and told me nothing doing. Before I could explore the matter further, I was shipped off to Tennessee.

After some months at Oak Ridge, the idea of enlisting arose again. At that site, a number of young men and women in Army uniforms were doing things not very different from what I was doing. I added up their salary, their immediate extras (free room and board), and their expected postwar benefits from the GI Bill. I concluded that, economically speaking, I would be better off if I could become one of them. At the very least, the continuation of my education in the postwar period would be guaranteed.

I went to see Lawrence and told him about the idea. I asked him to help me with the arrangements needed to make the transition without losing too much time from the job. In explaining my way of looking at it, I emphasized the GI Bill. He approved of my ideas and said he would help.

The very next morning he sent for me before I could take any further steps. "Don't do it," he said. "You won't need that kind of help. Stand on your own two feet." He implied that I could count on continuing on at his laboratory in Berkeley after the war. I promptly dropped the whole idea.

Nevertheless, some months later, the Army suddenly summoned me to Fort Oglethorpe, Georgia, to take my preinduction physical. The clear implication was that the days of "occupational deferment" were coming to an end.

I arrived at Fort Oglethorpe in the evening and joined a large group of others in the same situation. The last thing they told us before we went to bed was "In the morning, hold your water 'till we tell ya." We got up at 3:00 A.M. and had a hearty breakfast, with lots of juice and coffee. At our first, preliminary interview session, while we are still following instructions and "holding our water" from the night before, a corporal asked each of us if we "wet the bed." The right answer was obviously no, and we all gave it, even those who did not want to join the Army.

At about noon they finally asked for a urine sample. Once they had it, they dipped a pipette into it and lifted out a few cc's. Letting the fluid flow out so the stream passed in front of a black card, they barely glanced at it and promptly recorded its density, sugar content, and albumin content on a sheet of paper I was carrying along with me. To no one's surprise, all the figures were precisely normal.

At the end of the day, a psychiatrist asked me if I "liked girls." Knowing that the right answer was yes, I gave it. He started to argue, saying, "You're a physicist. You don't have time for girls." I forget exactly what happened next, except that I was declared fit for service.

That night I returned to Oak Ridge; I never heard from the Army again. Whoever was looking after my occupational deferment carried the day.

The Bomb

One day in the late spring of 1945, word came that we were to shut down all Calutrons on a certain June date and take all the material in the collectors out for processing and shipment to Site Y (Los Alamos). Normally, once a Calutron received its input charge, it took about a month of continuous operation to process all of it; only then were its product collectors removed and their contents processed for shipment. To stop in the middle of a "run" was inefficient. This sudden change from the norm could, therefore, mean only one thing: the project was coming to its culmination. The authorities had evidently estimated that by that date enough material would be available to make a bomb. (Or could it be two? I knew how much we had produced, but not how much was needed for one bomb.)

The magic date came. We took all the product we then had, processed it, and sent it off. We then recharged the machines and started them up again. But things were different; something new was in the air. Suddenly, after having worked long hours steadily for more than two years, we didn't have quite so much to do.

Several of us took advantage of this lull to go off for a ten-day vacation in the Colorado Rockies. While we were there camping near the Arapahoe Glacier, and entirely unbeknownst to us, the first nuclear test—"Trinity"—took place in the neighboring state of New Mexico. The date was July 16 and the time well before sunrise. People all over New Mexico reported a false dawn that morning. We could have seen it, too, if we had been on the heights and looking in the right direction. But we were totally in the dark in more ways than one.

I returned "home" to Oak Ridge about the end of July. Soon thereafter, while I was on my way to work one morning, a friend said to me in whispered tones, "Did you hear? They dropped a biscuit on Japan." *Biscuit* was not, to my knowledge, a code word; to this day I don't know why he used it, but I knew instantly what he meant. I went out to the plant and found the place buzzing with rumors. Those of us from Berkeley knew full well what had happened, but the locals were puzzled by it all. The event we had long been striving toward and waiting for had finally happened on August 6, Japanese time. I was thrilled, and my heart sank at the same time. I had no doubt the war would soon be over. Later that day I heard President Truman's announcement on the radio:

> Sixteen hours ago an American airplane dropped a bomb on Hiroshima, an important Army base. That bomb had more power than 20,000 tons of TNT. . . . It was an atomic bomb. It is a harnessing of the basic force of the universe. The force from which the sun draws its power has been loosed against those who brought war to the Far East.[4]

I thought to myself, "We did it."

Everyone even remotely connected with the project was either very excited or totally dumbfounded, or both. The principal local newspaper, the *Knoxville News Sentinel*, was for one edition relabeled the *Knoxs Sentinelville New* by its bedazzled and befuddled typesetter, and it carried an article quoting one Luis Alvarez, a "professor of psycnics" as saying something important I can no longer recall. People who had never heard of physics or physicists before suddenly knew that something of very great moment had happened and that those unfamiliar words were somehow behind it.

Within a short time the Smyth report,[5] an unclassified document describing the whole Manhattan Project, arrived in the hands of our group. Because of compartmentalization, we had previously known very little about what was happening at Los Alamos or in other parts of the project away from Berkeley and Oak Ridge. The report was in mimeographed form and simply stapled together in one fairly thick volume. Since this was long before Xerox, there was no practical way to make further copies. We therefore carefully took apart the one copy we had and made a separate document out of each chapter. We passed these around all through the day and night for everyone to read. I was especially surprised to learn about the Alamogordo test. I had had no way of knowing about the remarkable coincidence by which the plutonium project came to fruition within just weeks of our uranium project and thereby generated the additional nuclear fuel needed for the test bomb and for the one dropped on Nagasaki.*

---

*The three main components of the Manhattan Project were uranium isotope separation, plutonium production, and bomb design. Uranium separation research was concentrated

We didn't have to wait long for further developments: the drop on Nagasaki came on August 9, and Japan surrendered unconditionally a few days after that. On V-J Day we all went wild and celebrated the great victory and our part in it.

A few weeks later, after more than a year and a half in Tennessee, I set out in my Ford coupe for Berkeley. It was fun to see the country from that new vantage point, but I didn't take the time to savor it properly. We were all in a hurry to get to our various destinations and start life over again.

How Did We Feel about It?

In recent years, in classes and special lectures, I've had many occasions to describe to younger people the project, the bomb, and its use. I've found that at the start a very wide gap separates us. The first thing most of my listeners learned about World War II is that we won it. That is, so to speak, the last thing I learned about it. The first thing they learned about the atomic bomb is that we dropped one on Hiroshima and another on Nagasaki. That is the last thing I learned about the project. For most people born after 1940, those events marked the beginning of the nuclear arms race with the Soviets. For those of us in the project, they heralded the end of history's bloodiest war.

The original stimulus in 1939–40 for our developing the atomic bomb was the fear that Germany might do so first. This fear was certainly reasonable: fission had been discovered in Germany, and Hitler's thirst for power apparently knew no bounds. Einstein's letter to Roosevelt and Lawrence's to Compton make this original motivation clear.

By late 1941, and especially after America's own entry into the war, the depth and horror of the disaster engulfing us all had become more obvious. A new objective was therefore added: get the bomb as quickly as possible not only to assure victory, but to achieve it at the earliest-possible date.

---

at Berkeley and Columbia and production at Oak Ridge. Plutonium research took place at Chicago and Oak Ridge and production at Hanford, Washington. Bomb design was the province of the laboratory at Los Alamos, New Mexico. In general, these three components of the project were kept well separated from each other. I was one of the relatively few young people in the uranium project who were even aware of the plutonium project. Even so, I was quite surprised when—purely fortuitously—they both turned out their first critical masses of product only weeks apart.

As the war dragged on through 1942–44, the worldwide death toll—mostly civilians—climbed toward the fifty-million mark, and the number of homeless and displaced persons was similarly huge. Millions of others clung to life in desperate conditions in prison camps. When Germany collapsed in early 1945, it became manifest that we were no longer in a race for the bomb and that victory was assured, but the suffering and the misery caused by the war in Asia and the western Pacific continued unabated. War-related deaths in China already numbered in the neighborhood of twenty million, and that number continued to grow as the Japanese expanded their holdings in that unfortunate country even while they were falling back in the Pacific. The goal of the project thus narrowed simply to ending the war at the earliest-possible moment. My own views, as well as I can recall them so long afterward, followed the same general course.

When the bombs were dropped on Hiroshima and Nagasaki, most people, including those working on the project, were elated. The war had suddenly been brought to an end, and everything we knew suggested that the bombs were the cause of that. Moreover, we had every reason to believe that without the bombs a bloody invasion of Japan would have been necessary, an invasion that would have resulted in perhaps a million American casualties and surely even more casualties among Japanese soldiers and civilians. Indeed, postwar studies of Japanese documents show that the public view was basically correct. True, Japan had already begun to totter, and there was a growing peace party; but until the bombs were dropped, the military was able to retain full control of the government. Despite tentative efforts by the peace party to explore the possibility of a negotiated surrender, plans and deployments for the defense of the home islands against a massive American invasion were proceeding without interruption and with public support. Only after the second bomb did Emperor Hirohito directly enter the political scene and use his personal authority to swing the balance toward those who wished to sue for peace.

The emperor's August 14, 1945, radio speech announcing to the Japanese people his decision to surrender made it very clear that it was the *two* bombs that had compelled him to act. The speech was often general and in places fuzzy. "We must endure the unavoidable and suffer the insufferable," he said. But regarding the bomb he was explicit:

> The enemy has begun to employ a new and most cruel bomb, the power
> of which to do damage is, indeed, incalculable, taking the toll of many

innocent lives. Should we continue to fight, it would not only result in an ultimate collapse and obliteration of the Japanese nation, but also it would lead to the total extinction of human civilization.[6]

Would one bomb have been enough? We cannot know. The fact is that the emperor did not move decisively to tip the balance in favor of peace until after the second had fallen. Perhaps the Japanese military would have argued that the first bomb was the only one we possessed. The quick use of a second showed we had only just "begun to employ a new and most cruel bomb."

Some have argued that we should have demonstrated the bomb to the Japanese authorities before exploding it over a populated target. Lawrence at one point urged that policy at the highest scientific levels. Along with Oppenheimer, Fermi, and some others, he was a member of the Interim Committee, a body of scientific advisers established late in the war to consider future courses of action. They touched briefly on the question of how to use the bomb, but the largest part of their effort was devoted to planning the role of nuclear science in the postwar world. Szilard and others at slightly lower levels also pushed the idea of a demonstration or a warning, but they got nowhere. The counterarguments were that the bomb might not work, that a demonstration might not impress adequately, and that the aircraft carrying it to the announced site might be intercepted. Given the strong desire to end the war at the earliest moment and the delay that such a chancy course might entail, a demonstration of this sort was never really a serious possibility.

Others have argued that we should have taken advantage of the feelers put out by the Japanese peace party, and negotiated a surrender even before the bomb, or that a blockade of the islands would have starved the Japanese into surrender. Very iffy, at best, these propositions also ignore the dying and suffering then still being caused by the Japanese in China and the grave plight of the other captive nations and, even more, of all the prisoners of war. And what conditions might the Japanese have sought to obtain for surrendering without an invasion? They might have held out for the retention of their imperial grip on Taiwan, Korea, and Manchukuo, all of which they had acquired many years before the attack on Pearl Harbor.

Nevertheless, in addition to sharing the general public elation in victory, many on the project simultaneously had a sense of foreboding and some even a sense of regret. These other thoughts and attitudes were most common among the scientific leaders of the project. They had all along been in touch with the higher political and military authorities. For that reason, and because of their generally greater maturity and sophistication, they were more aware of the bomb's implications both for the outcome of the war and for the future development of the total world situation. Many of them clearly foresaw a nuclear arms race with the Soviets, concluded that it could only be very dangerous for all of us in the long run, and tried to work out and suggest ways for avoiding or containing it. At some of the project sites, notably Los Alamos and Chicago, the leadership shared some of these thoughts with middle-level people. At Berkeley and Oak Ridge, however, that did not happen. Lawrence said that such matters were best left in the hands of the higher political and military authorities. While he also believed that scientists should give advice when asked, he openly discouraged voluntary staff involvement in such broader issues. Scientists, he said, especially young ones, should not waste precious working time on extraneous issues for which they had no special training.

At war's end my main feelings were elation and anticipation—elation because the war was over and because I had had a role in that; anticipation because I could now resume my education and go forward to a career in science. I also felt some twinges of foreboding and sorrow, but these last were pretty well submerged by my satisfaction, at age twenty-three, with what I had done and my enthusiasm for where I was going.

"We Had Made War Obsolete"

In the days immediately after the drop on Hiroshima and war's end, many persons older and much wiser than I said that the bomb had made war obsolete. Its destructive power, they observed, was so total that it would become obvious to our political leaders that war would no longer be a rational means for achieving political goals, no matter what those goals were. That notion certainly seemed reasonable to me. I and most other people fervently wanted to believe that the death, destruction, and dislocations of the last years would never be repeated, and if our bomb could be the instrument for not repeating them, so much the better.

A few weeks after it was all over, my father came down to Oak Ridge to visit me. It had finally become possible to tell him about the work I had been engaged in since I had left home on that snowy May day in 1943, and I was able to take him up on a hill overlooking the Y-12 plant so that he could at least see the exterior of the place for himself. I explained to him what I had learned from those wiser heads—that what we had done here had made war obsolete.

In the ensuing years, as I continued to grow up and become more sophisticated about such things, I gradually turned away from that simple notion. I learned that similar claims had repeatedly been made before. I read that when the crossbow was introduced, people thought it had made war so horrible that it was obsolete, and that this claim had also accompanied the introduction of gunpowder, the airplane, and other such wonders. Moreover, the early cold war came upon us and grew worse, and the initial attempts to contain the incipient arms race failed. The war clouds seemed to be gathering once again, and the spread of nuclear weapons to dozens of other countries seemed just over the horizon.

Lately, however, I've begun to wonder if perhaps we weren't right the first time, back then in 1945. It is now almost half a century since the last great war, and we have not really come near to having another one anything like it, despite occasional periods of tension and episodes of military confrontation. It seems that national leaders everywhere have developed a proper respect for the bomb, especially its most recent versions, and they avoid with far greater caution than before the kinds of tactics and adventures that set off great wars in the past.

I do not believe the claim that if it had not been for the presence of the bomb, the Soviets would have invaded Western Europe. But this last half-century has seen many small crises in Europe and elsewhere, one or more of which could have led to a general war if the existence of the bomb had not greatly dampened ambitions and inclinations toward adventurism. For better and for worse, the bomb has thrown a blanket of stability over many a tinderbox that in the prenuclear world might well have burst into full flame. It is not necessary to believe there is something special about either American or Soviet leaders to reach this conclusion. The easily observed changes in the historical behavior of all the Western European tribes and their obvious respect for and fear of the bomb is sufficient for that purpose.

Maybe, just maybe, we can count on that situation to persist until the time when we can achieve a real and permanent solution.

The Dilemma

Victor Weisskopf was another of the physicist refugees forced to flee Europe in the late thirties. Fortunately for him but even more so for me, he landed a post in the Department of Physics at the University of Rochester. I first met him in 1941, my third year as a student there. At the time he taught the upper-division courses that dealt with the mysteries of the atom and its nucleus. Earlier, he had been a part of Niels Bohr's group in Copenhagen, then the center of the physics universe, and he passed on to us not only some of the facts of physics but also an appreciation of the great adventure that doing science can be. He was the first "world class" person it was my fortune to know, and I was greatly taken by what he had to say both about physics and about the world at large.

Weisskopf left Rochester even before I did. He joined the Manhattan Project at Los Alamos, where he served as Hans Bethe's principal deputy in the Theoretical Division. After the war he became a leading figure among those most concerned about the long-range issues the bomb had raised. I did not at first pay particular attention to his (or other people's) ideas in this regard. Later in life, however, when I reestablished contact with him after a long time, I again found his thoughts and views highly instructive, just as I had back in 1941–42. In a retrospective written forty years after the bombing of Hiroshima, he summarized his thoughts this way:

> Whatever one may think about the wisdom of the American use of the bomb, it did end a murderous war, and most probably saved more lives than it destroyed. We meant so well; it served our country and we thought that such powerful weapons will make war between great powers unthinkable. Some of us thought that the existence of these dangerous power sources will lead to an international administration of military and peaceful applications and will end the age-old custom of organized mutual mass murder. We were naive and wrong; we should have known better. True enough, because of the existence of the Bomb we had no war between great powers for 40 years, an unusually long period. But during that time the great powers have found only one way to keep this state of affairs: to indulge in an ever-increasing arms race.[7]

There, in a nutshell, is one way of describing the great dilemma of our time. We have avoided large-scale war for an exceptionally long time, and the bomb has played an important—perhaps—essential—role in that. But it has done so by raising the price of a breach of the peace—by constantly and insistently threatening to punish a major misdeed by mutual annihilation and the end of all civilization, if not of all mankind. Ronald Reagan, whose worldview is in most respects very different from Weisskopf's, in 1983 described the same dilemma and expressed the same frustration in words that came in unstaffed form, straight from his soul:

> [T]o look down on an endless future with both of us sitting here with these horrible missiles facing each other and the only thing that prevents a nuclear holocaust is just so long as no one pulls the trigger . . . this is unthinkable.[8]

President Reagan called them "horrible missiles," not "peacemakers"; he said the prospect was for a "nuclear holocaust," not a "winnable" or "limited" war; and he warned that currently the only thing preventing a holocaust was that "no one pulls the trigger." No virile talk there about "standing tall" and facing down the "evil empire," and no ambitious strategic jargon about "prevailing" should deterrence fail.

In the years since Hiroshima, our military power, as measured by our ability to wreak death and destruction in an ever shorter time, has grown enormously. Since 1949 our national security, as measured by the combination of the Soviets' ability to wreak death and destruction on us and our inability to do anything about it, except threaten revenge, has greatly diminished. This great security dilemma is mutual—in that reality perhaps lies hope.

No sane leader or informed observer believes that peace can be maintained indefinitely in this way. At the same time, however, the relations between states are, at bottom, anarchic and lawless; responsible national leaders, in concert with their publics have everywhere found it necessary to maintain very substantial levels of military preparedness. Nuclear weapons are at least arguably the cheapest and most effective means of doing so.

Forty years of experience tell me that we are caught on the horns of a dilemma and that we have no quick or easy way to escape. Attempts to solve this dilemma by dealing separately with only one of its horns have so far only made things worse. Eventually, we must find a way to deal with both issues at once, to find a means of maintaining peace and supporting freedom that is based on something better than the threat of mutual suicide. So far, this has proved to be uncommonly difficult; it will evidently take much more time before we can work it out. In the meantime, we must learn how to live with this dilemma without either fully resolving it or having it degenerate into a universal catastrophe.

The rest of this book is the story of how I went about making my contribution to the search for solutions to this dilemma and how my thinking on this subject gradually—sometimes fitfully—evolved.

CHAPTER 2

Interlude

(1945–1949)

Demobilization

WHEN the war ended, the Manhattan Project, like the Army and the Navy, demobilized. Faculty and students sought ways to resume their prewar careers and, in most cases, quickly found them. Many returned to the places they had come from. Others found opportunities in new places, opportunities that often emerged from new relationships that had developed during the war. A few stayed on at Los Alamos, Oak Ridge, and other war-created institutions. Some of these did so because they enjoyed the work they were engaged in, some because no new opportunities beckoned, and some because even then they thought they detected signs of new international crises that would require further efforts along similar lines. Together, those who stayed on managed to keep the new institutions alive and well during difficult and uncertain times.

The case of the Radiation Laboratory at Berkeley was different. Unlike Los Alamos and other specially created laboratories, it had already been a solid and dynamic institution before the war. When the war ended, the Rad Lab simply turned its attention back to its original goals: building and using great nuclear accelerators. Some of those who had joined the lab during the war—happily including me—were invited to join in the renewed enterprise. Most of the senior staff members who had been sent off to other wartime projects returned—Luis Alvarez, Edwin McMillan, Robert Oppenheimer, Glenn Seaborg, and Emilio Segrè among them. Many had been generating ideas for new machines and better experiments even while working on their wartime tasks, and they were eager to start carrying them out. Work on the great 184-inch cyclotron resumed, and a grand assault on the frontiers of physics was about to begin. The air was full of new ideas and great expectations.

I made it back to Berkeley only a month or so after the war ended. My first paid job was operating the older 60-inch cyclotron (built just before the war), mostly in the wee hours of the morning and mainly to produce radioactive substances for use by others in research in chemistry and biology. At the same time, I resumed graduate studies with a regular load of classes and participated in colloquia and research seminars at both the campus Department of Physics and the Radiation Laboratory. I found it all very interesting, and physics absorbed most of my time and energy. The war, I thought, was over and behind us.

Classes

One especially interesting class was in quantum mechanics. The subject itself was fascinating, and having it taught by Robert Oppenheimer made it more so. I learned much about the subject, but my memories of the teacher are stronger. Oppie frequently arrived wearing the porkpie hat that had already become his trademark. He smoked as he lectured, and he punctuated his ideas with a little cough that came to be much imitated in later years by some of his students.

The course was not easy. Indeed, several of the best students were taking it for the second or third time, and he often seemed to be aiming his remarks mainly at them. His performance in general was a stimulating combination of real sophistication and elegance mixed with a soupçon of the intellectual arrogance that later contributed to his undoing. Good students could and did learn a great deal from him; he didn't care too much about the others, or at least so it seemed.

At the time when I was taking this course from him, he was heavily engaged in political activities at the highest levels in Washington and at the United Nations in New York. I was only dimly aware of that side of his life, but I do recall one large public lecture he gave on the Berkeley campus during that time on the seriousness of the incipient nuclear arms race and what might be done about it. I was impressed by what he had to say, but it did not then arouse my interest enough to make me spend any of my serious time on those issues.

A second case where I found both the teacher and the subject especially interesting was Emilio Segrè's course in nuclear physics. Segrè had become Enrico Fermi's first student in Rome in 1927, and he continued for many years to be one of Fermi's closest friends and collaborators. Segrè, like one or two others in the extraordinary group of Italians whom Fermi eventually gathered around him, was Jewish, as was Fermi's wife, and so when Mussolini finally tried to copy even the ugliest, racist features of Hitlerism, they both found it necessary to flee to America. Segrè's first job in the New World was in California with Lawrence, where he continued some of the work involving neutrons and radioactivity that he had begun back in Italy. Later, because of his special experience with neutrons and fission, he was one of the first to be recruited to go to Los Alamos to work on the physics of the bomb itself. Since he was technically still an enemy alien, questions arose about the appropriateness of these arrangements, but first Lawrence and later Oppenheimer were able to straighten matters out through personal intervention.

Segrè was personally familiar with nearly all the people who had performed the basic experiments and worked out the underlying theories of nuclear physics, and he himself had been a participant at many of the most seminal and interesting occasions, both in Europe and in the United States. In his class he would tell us stories about what it was really like during those great days in Rome, and he would now and then instruct us to read the reports on the work in the original Italian (a suggestion that didn't work out too well) as well as in more widely understood foreign languages. He would sometimes lose his way in a derivation or explanation, but that only made it seem all the more real and served to distinguish his lectures from the secondhand, canned ones a less involved person might have given. Years later, when I taught a similar course, I incorporated my experiences with Segrè and some of his stories about Rome into anecdotes of my own.

It was obvious even at the time that learning about all this from Segrè was something very special. He made it evident both that there was much yet to be learned and that it was realistic for a person like me to aspire to participate in similar novel and wonderful adventures someday. As luck would have it, I eventually became one of Segrè's personal students, and I did the work for my thesis and another major experiment under his general direction.

The stories continued, now as parts of private conversations. In one, he told me what he knew about Fermi's work in building the first successful nuclear reactor. Built in a squash court at the University of Chicago, it produced the world's first artificial chain reaction in December 1942. Soon after it started to operate, Fermi decided he needed a calibrated neutron source he knew Segrè had in Berkeley. He placed a long-distance telephone call to see what might be done. Shortly afterward, as Segrè told it, Lawrence (and then two colleagues) came in and said, "What have you been doing? We've just had a report from the FBI that you and some other Italian have been talking long-distance for half an hour in an *unknown language.*"

Segrè told me that he then explained what happened, adding that the connection was poor and that he couldn't understand very well, so he told Fermi, "Let's speak Italian." Since Segrè was at that time still officially an enemy alien, and since there was, as they said, "a war going on," it may be silly but not surprising that the FBI became concerned. In any event, Lawrence was able to contain any damage that might otherwise have resulted.

Research

The great 184-inch cyclotron began operation in November 1946, and I managed to get transferred to its staff. At first I was assigned the job of measuring the general level of radiation it produced when running, in order to learn something about its potential hazards to health. Shortly afterward, and largely on my own initiative, I began a series of experiments that took full advantage of the extraordinary situation I found myself in. There I was, a member of the staff serving the world's most powerful machine for doing nuclear physics, a machine that generated particles with energies almost an order of magnitude greater than those available before or elsewhere. On top of that, the laboratory had a large cadre of technicians, working in well-equipped shops and willing and able to make on request all sorts of special devices for detecting, measuring, and recording the phenomena produced by these beams of high-energy particles. And, surely most important, time on the machine was available even for graduate students working on projects of their own.

The professors and other senior staff were, so to speak, still tooling up in those first months, and lots of cyclotron operating time was going begging, especially in the evenings and on weekends. During the first couple of years after operation started, I and several other equally junior colleagues were able to obtain 10 percent, and occasionally as much as 25 percent, of the time available on this immense machine for our own experiments for weeks at a time. We were in exactly the right place at the right time; only a decade or so later, operating time on the biggest machines was available only to large groups of senior staff who had applied for it many months before. But back then, in the late 1940s, we graduate students could get on such machines on our own account, and we could go directly to the technicians and ask them to build us the apparatus we thought we needed. It was truly a rare opportunity; in order to exploit it, a student had only to be willing to work long hours and at night, and possess a certain minimum of curiosity, eagerness, and energy, but not much experience, reputation, or even talent.

As one result of this special situation, I was able, in the course of the three years leading up to my graduation, to be a major participant in three important experiments. The first of these, to use the jargon appropriate to work of this kind, concerned the "angular distribution of n-p scattering with 90-Mev neutrons."[1] Soon after I started to conduct these experiments with the help of two fellow students, I was informed that Segrè and his colleagues were gearing up to do the same thing. We solved what could have become a sticky problem by simply joining forces. The experiments were the first to be conducted at an energy high enough to reveal the details of the neutron-proton (n-p) interaction. In particular, we found that when protons and neutrons interact at very small distances, they often exchange their electrical charges.

The second experiment involved the first observation—or "discovery"—of the neutral pi meson, a particle whose existence had been postulated for the past several years but not yet verified. My involvement in this was a classic case of serendipity. By chance, a visitor from the University of Illinois described to me a new device for detecting and analyzing high-energy gamma rays called a pair counter. I immediately recognized its potential and within a week assembled one from bits and pieces of apparatus available in the laboratory. My colleagues and I used it to explore the gamma rays emitted from the target of the cyclotron when it was exposed to 350-Mev protons, and we found radiation consistent with no other known source except the postulated neutral meson.[2]

The third set of experiments led to my Ph.D. thesis. The published version was entitled "Secondary Particles from Various Nuclei Bombarded with 90-Mev Nuetrons."[3] Largely by chance, a technician working in one of the cloud chamber groups had observed that certain weakly bound lightweight nuclei—deuterons and tritons, in particular— were in the debris produced when 90-Mev neutrons collided with nuclei in general. This was a minor surprise at the time, and I was able easily to explore the phenomena in detail by means of the apparatus I had already assembled for the other two experiments. In addition to these three major experiments, I was also a coworker and coauthor of several other papers published while I was still a graduate student.

In addition to gaining direct experience and learning a great deal from the many very talented senior people on the staff, I also benefited from a singular stream of visitors drawn from the top ranks of world physicists. I particularly remember Fermi in this regard. He could explain anything—how the stars work or what the fundamental particles really are—in a way that seemed immediately understandable but that turned out to be not so easily reproducible when I went back to my office to think about it later.

Important people from other realms also came through. The first Russian I ever met was the distinguished physicist Dmitri V. Skobeltsyn, then an adviser to the Soviet delegation to the United Nations. Lawrence brought him through the 60-inch cyclotron control room one day in 1946 when I was operating the machine. Unfortunately, he spoke only Russian and French and I spoke neither, so we couldn't converse, but I knew I had just greeted someone from the other side of the moon, and I found that interesting and somehow important.

On another occasion the crown prince of Saudi Arabia visited the laboratory, accompanied by a huge retinue. The high double doors of the cyclotron building had to be opened to permit a proper entrance, and in they came in a broad phalanx, all wearing burnooses and otherwise dressed in proper desert style, most of them with swords or daggers tucked in their sashes. We were all thrilled just by the spectacle. Inside the door stood two workmen, equipped with jackhammers and engaged in breaking up the concrete flooring so that additional heavy blocks of radiation shielding could be accommodated. The workmen were startled by all this splendor, and I heard one say to the other, "Wow, they mus' be from Turkey!" Indeed!

Those were, in sum, the sorts of times and circumstances that are long afterward often called a golden age. Luckily for me, it was not only in retrospect that I knew how special they were; I was at the time at least moderately aware of the uniqueness of my situation, was pleased with myself for having had the good sense to go to work for Lawrence at

Berkeley, and was determined to make good use of the opportunity it afforded.

Private Affairs

In the spring of 1946 Frank Oppenheimer and his wife, Jackie, invited me to a semiformal Saint Patrick's Day party. I in turn asked Sybil Dunford to be my date. We had first met several years before, when she was a student employed as night operator on the university central switchboard and I was a lonesome young physicist looking for some diversion, but this was our very first big date. Things developed nicely from there. We were married in Berkeley's First Congregational Church in September 1947, and we have lived "happily ever after" ever since. I acquired a three-year-old stepson, David, in the process, and we all soon set up housekeeping in a small place near the Southern Pacific Railroad tracks immediately behind Spenger's Fish Grotto. Spenger himself owned our first mortgage, and my in-laws held our second. I had at last gotten under way the other side of life on my own, and that was working out quite well too.

Sybil's personality and aspirations fitted very well with my own. She was content with my work and study situation with its long hours at the laboratory, and we were both satisfied with the occasional short vacations we were able to take, usually somewhere near Tuolumne Meadows, high up in Yosemite Park.

These meadows are just below the timberline, occupying a wide, flat region in the upper valley of the Tuolumne River. Go down, and you are in deep forest; go up, and you are on the fringes of the great open, undulating granite domes that characterize the Yosemite region. Higher still are the granite peaks with deep blue lakes at their feet and summer snowbanks on their flanks. It was then and remains today my favorite place in all the world.

By a happy coincidence Yosemite was also Lawrence's favorite spot, but I didn't know that when I was still a graduate student. Later on he and I were able to share our interest in the park on a few, brief occasions when he arranged for national-level laboratory directors' meetings to be held there at the Ahwahnee Hotel. At that time I was director of the Livermore Laboratory, and he was both still my boss and a member of the board of directors of the Yosemite Park and Curry Company, then the operator of all the concessions in the park. As I recall, included among these was a Cadillac dealership, and it was from them that Lawrence got the new baby blue convertibles he favored.

Sybil and I thought we had timed the birth of our first child for soon after the date when I would turn in my thesis, but the thesis dragged on a bit, and those important events fell on top of each other. As it happened, I turned in the final version of my dissertation on about April 15. That was the day the baby was due, we thought, but nothing happened. Sybil and I went for a walk that evening to see if that might induce something. While walking along Shattuck Avenue, we chanced to see a copy of the *Berkeley Gazette* with a special front-page news item headed "Atomic Scientist Delivers Own Child." Closer inspection proved that story was not in anticipation of us, but about Glenn Seaborg delivering his own sixth and last child before he and his wife could get out the front door. A few days later I reluctantly flew off to Washington (Sybil claims she practically had to push me out the door) to give an invited paper at the national meeting of the American Physical Society on the discovery of the neutral pi meson. Rachel Dunford York chose the period I was away to make her appearance. The big day was April 27, 1949.

That June my parents came west by train to see their new granddaughter and to attend the ceremonies at which I was formally awarded my Ph.D. It was, of course, a very special occasion for them as well as for me. I was the first in my family to go on to higher education, and I did so in large part because, for as long as I can remember, my father made it clear that I ought to.

After first trying out chemical engineering and chemistry in my freshman and sophomore years, I eventually ended up in nuclear physics for three basic reasons. First, it was the field of the most interesting and inspirational professor I met at Rochester, Victor Weisskopf. Second, the huge numbers, great distances, and enormously long times that I had found so fascinating in astronomy had their counterpart in physics in the form of their reciprocals: exceedingly short distances and unimaginably short times. Third, as I saw it then, many more jobs were available in physics than in astronomy, and as a child of the Great Depression I could not possibly ignore that.

Now, in June of 1949, all of this was finally coming together, and my parents were with me to enjoy the day.

After the ceremony we had a small party to celebrate the occasion; Emilio and Elfrieda Segrè were there, in part so that my parents could meet them. At one point Sybil remarked that she was glad it was

finished; I had been very absorbed in my work and had often come home
tired from arguing with Segrè. Elfrieda said she was glad, too, because
Emilio often came home complaining about having had a difficult time
with "that student." And, indeed, I do recall more than one occasion
when Segrè suddenly said, "You think you have a pipeline to God," and
declined to discuss the matter any further.

Getting to Know Lawrence Better

Lawrence made it a regular practice to tour all parts of his laboratory.
He would usually start with the control room of the 184-inch cyclotron,
where he would greet his old friends among the operating crew and ask
them to tell him what was going on at that moment. Sometimes he would
briefly take over the controls of the machine himself. Then he would tour
the various experimental areas around the machine and chat with any
persons he found there, always asking them what they were doing right
then. After that he would march off to visit Alvarez's linear accelerator
and McMillan's synchrotron—two other new, special-purpose accelerators for which Lawrence provided a home after the war. He also visited
the drafting rooms and the mechanical and the electrical shops; there
he would ask the workmen to show him the various things they were
making. I suppose that when he was in town, he visited nearly every
nook and cranny of his domain about once a week. Later, when I became a laboratory director myself, I deliberately and fruitfully copied
this practice of his.

When I happened to be working in the 184-inch cyclotron's experimental area, Lawrence's regular tours would usually include my experimental setup. If that was in the evening or on a weekend, as it often was,
there would be less activity elsewhere, and so we would have more time
to chat about my particular project and, sometimes, about physics in
general. Typically, he would find me sitting in the midst of a bank of
electronic equipment, often with another young colleague, recording
data that were coming in over cables from various particle detectors
closer to the cyclotron itself. He might peer closely at one of the oscillo-
scopes displaying the signals produced by these detectors and then ask
me to explain what it all meant. After I did so, he might give some advice
or express an opinion; then he would leave, usually with a big smile and
some encouraging words.

One especially memorable visit took place on a Christmas Eve. I was
working after supper for some reason, and I was eager to get home.

Lawrence came by as if there were nothing special about that time, asked, as usual, what I was doing, and, after I told him, announced he was going up to the synchrotron to see what was happening there. Moments later he returned with a surprised look on his face and announced, "There's no one there!" We all left soon afterward.

On Saturday afternoons I often walked with him to the main laboratory door after we had finished our discussion. Typically, his blue Cadillac convertible would be parked just outside the door in a no-parking zone, and there would be a tennis racket and some balls on the passenger's seat. He would get in and wave good-bye, after reminding me that it is a good thing for students to work hard while they are still young.

Sometimes our discussions ranged well beyond the facts of the moment. Once—on learning that I had managed to transfer myself from an activity I found a bit dull to one I found more exciting, without consulting him first—he glared at me fiercely and, with his jowls quivering, said, "You had better learn which side your bread is buttered on if you want to remain in this laboratory." When I told Segrè about this and a similar incident in which Lawrence had told me to cooperate or get out, Segrè beamed and advised me not to worry about it. He himself, he claimed, had already been fired six times by Lawrence, and so he felt I must be doing something right. On other occasions when I might have complained about something in the lab, the university, or the world at large, Lawrence would frown and say, "People will say you're a spoiled brat." He didn't say I was one—just that people who didn't know me well would say I was. At other times he would praise me fulsomely. He might say, "You can do as well as anybody else in the country"—or even "in the world"—and then quickly add, "But don't let that go to your head." On one occasion, after Robert Millikan had happened to visit my work area, Lawrence told me about their own first meeting, years before. He was surprised to find that Millikan, who had won the Nobel Prize for his pioneering work on the electron, was not as smart as he had expected. Lawrence explained that then and there he had realized that he, too, could win the Nobel Prize, and he implied that I was capable of doing work of the same caliber.

If politics ever came up in these discussions, he made it quite clear that he thought physics students should work hard at physics and not let such extraneous matters divert them. Discussions about nuclear political issues, which I later learned were commonplace at some other laboratories, were frankly discouraged at the Rad Lab. And if the question of job titles arose, Lawrence would say that physicist in the Radiation Laboratory was the "best title in the world" and that there was no need for anything fancier or more definitive.

I believe it was the large difference in our positions and, even more, in our ages—twenty years, a full generation—that made the criticisms completely acceptable, the homilies welcome, and the praise not maudlin. Sometimes Lawrence would try to deal with people closer to him in status and age in a similar way, and they often resented it. However, I almost always enjoyed any attention he gave me, of whatever kind. I learned some physics from talking with him; much more important, I absorbed—largely without realizing it—a great deal of knowledge and lore about how to run a large scientific enterprise and how to get the most and best out of other people. It was this latter sort of knowledge that I eventually made the most use of in my own career.

On Frogs, Puddles, and Front Seats

After I finished the work on my Ph.D. degree, Lawrence invited me to stay on indefinitely as a member of the research staff. I also received a number of very attractive offers of employment elsewhere, usually involving some mixture of research, teaching, and administrative responsibilities, and often at a much higher salary than I was making. The opportunities at the Rad Lab had been so rich, and seizing them had been so easy and straightforward, that many students like myself developed reputations that went well beyond reality. Some of these fancy offers came through Lawrence himself, but even then he would advise me not to take them. After much careful thought, I decided to remain at the lab indefinitely, with the hope in the back of my mind that I might eventually join the Berkeley faculty as well.

Many of those other opportunities involved being a much bigger frog in a much smaller puddle. I came to conclude firmly that for me it would be much more interesting to be a frog of modest size in a very big puddle, and for a young experimental physicist the Rad Lab was clearly the biggest puddle in all the world. I decided I didn't particularly want to be in charge of the action, but I did want to be in on some of it and to have a good front seat from which I could easily watch the rest. I use these similes now because I used them then in thinking these matters over and in discussing them with Sybil and a few other intimates.

As fate would have it, I played the role of a pretty big frog in a pretty big puddle more than once in my life later on, but I never once actively sought such a role, and at no time did I ever consciously reverse my priorities in such matters. Later, when I worked in the White House, served as an under secretary of defense, or held some other fancy position, it was being there and having a front seat on the whole world that I found so strongly attractive, not whatever power and authority went with it. I think I can fairly say I never shirked authority, but neither did I ever seek it for its own sake.

CHAPTER 3

"But Now We Don't Know It on Much Better Grounds"

(1949–1951)

T The Cold War and the Soviet Bomb

HE PEACE did not turn out as people had hoped. The basic antagonism between the Soviet Union and what is generally called the West—an antagonism that had temporarily been overshadowed by the joint crusade against Nazism—reemerged. The early attempts to control the nuclear arms race—including the elaboration of the Baruch Plan by the U.S. government—failed.*

*The Baruch Plan was the formal U.S. proposal for preventing a nuclear arms race. Its technical substance was developed by a committee chaired by the David Lilienthal and including Robert Oppenheimer. The work of that group was modified somewhat by a higher-level group headed by Under Secretary of State Dean Acheson and adopted as formal U.S. policy by President Truman. Bernard Baruch, a New York financier with impeccable political credentials, was selected to present it to the newly created United Nations in early 1946. Baruch added a few further modifications, which made the proposal even more unacceptable to Stalin, who saw it as a threat to Soviet sovereignty. The Soviet UN delegate, the ubiquitous Andrei Gromyko, rejected it out of hand.

42

Winston Churchill, in a famous speech at Fulton, Missouri, summarized the situation only a year after the end of the war as follows: "From Stettin on the Baltic to Trieste on the Adriatic an iron curtain has descended across the continent."[1] Most people accepted these remarks as an accurate description of a generally harsh and unpleasant reality. Some others, however, saw such tough and frank talk as part of the cause of the worsening situation rather than as simply an analysis of it.

In 1948 the Berlin blockade marked a new and threatening turn in what was already known as the cold war. For the first time Soviet troops directly confronted Western forces, separated only by a thin veil of East German customs officials and border guards. American high technology, in the form of high capacity transport aircraft guided through darkness and bad weather by the then still novel and untested ground controlled approach (GCA) radar landing system, carried the day, and the Soviets eventually backed down. (GCA was another of the many inventions of Berkeley's Luis Alvarez. It derived from work he had done while at the MIT Radiation Laboratory during the war.)

In August 1949 came an even more ominous event: the Soviets exploded an atomic bomb, their first, in Central Asia. This event was not, in the fundamental sense, a surprise. Nearly all Western authorities had estimated that it would take about four years for the Soviets to make the bomb after the Americans had demonstrated its feasibility, and that is just what happened. To be sure, two especially important authorities—Vannevar Bush and General Leslie Groves, who had directed the Manhattan Project—estimated that it would take the "backward" Soviets much longer than it had taken us, decades at the very least. Nearly everyone else—veterans of the U.S. project, professional intelligence analysts, even Winston Churchill—estimated that four years would be enough for the Soviets to end the American monopoly. According to public opinion polls, even John Q. Public held the same beliefs. In 1947 the intelligence estimates still said the first Soviet atomic bomb would come in another two years—that is, in 1949—but at that point the estimating process got stuck in a rut. As more time passed, the estimate continued to be "two more years" rather than "in 1949." Thus, in August 1949, on the eve of the actual event, the latest estimate was still "two more years." In the context of this static prediction, the Soviet explosion was, literally speaking, a surprise.

Of course, the event was much more than just a surprise because of its timing. The Soviets, universally regarded as technologically backward, had matched our most advanced technological accomplishment. It was therefore not merely surprising but also an exceedingly unwelcome event, one widely seen as bringing serious new dangers of a kind totally different from any we had ever faced before. The Soviet atomic bomb, combined with the projected acquisition of very long-range aircraft, promised to end forever the historical invulnerability of the United States. Almost immediately, serious concern over the possibility of a devastating surprise attack on us rose within nuclear and military— especially Air Force—circles.

As if that singularly menacing possibility had not been enough by itself, only a few weeks later Chinese Communist forces captured Peking, and Chairman Mao proclaimed the establishment of the Chinese Peoples' Republic. He then promptly paid a two-month-long visit to Stalin in Moscow, after which the two Communist leaders proclaimed their eternal solidarity and their eternal hostility to the decadent ideas and political system of the West. As Mao himself put it,

> The unity of the great Chinese and Soviet peoples, sealed by this treaty, is indestructible, everlasting, and unshakable. This unity inevitably influences not only the well-being of China and the Soviet Union, but also the future of all humanity. It will lead to the ultimate victory of justice and peace on the entire planet. . . . Long live the teacher of revolution to all the world, the best friend of the Chinese people, Comrade Stalin.

The subsequent analysis by the Chinese News Agency added these clarifications:

> This cannot help but alter the world situation and strike a solid blow against the aggressive plans and policies carried on throughout the world by the imperialist bloc, led by American imperialism. In other words, the Sino-Soviet Treaty changes the balance of forces.[2]

Although I was generally faithful to Lawrence's admonitions to keep my "nose to the grindstone" and to "stick to my knitting" at this point in my career, these events simply forced themselves on my consciousness. Like the proverbial mule whose attention was gotten when his owner beat him on the nose with a two-by-four, I could not ignore the news when it spoke of such ominous and threatening things, and I necessarily found myself speculating about it on my own and with my young colleagues.

Lawrence Reacts

Ernest Lawrence's reaction to this series of developments, and especially to the Soviet atomic bomb, was easily predictable. Seven years
before, he had led the call for an active response to the possibility of
a German atomic bomb, and now he reacted similarly to the reality of
the Soviet bomb. A new nuclear threat seemed to call for a nuclear
response, and so he actively sought ways to reinvolve his laboratory in
the development of one. Shortly after the explosion in Central Asia,
Lawrence and Luis Alvarez set out on a trip to Washington to explore
the question of what the Rad Lab might do. They traveled east by way
of Los Alamos in order first to visit with the laboratory director Norris
Bradbury, Edward Teller, then a visitor to Los Alamos on leave from the
University of Chicago, and others who they believed had to be similarly
concerned about the new turn of events.

Teller told them that the hydrogen bomb was the proper answer to the
new challenge. This type of bomb, often also called the superbomb
because its power was estimated to be perhaps a thousand times that
of an "ordinary" fission bomb, had preoccupied Teller since the earliest
days of the Los Alamos project. He had wanted to push ahead with it
even then, but he was frustrated in this desire by Oppenheimer's insistence that all efforts be concentrated on the fission bomb. Oppenheimer
believed that a bomb of the latter type, based on a neutron chain reaction in uranium or plutonium, was much more likely to be produced in
time to be of use during the war. Besides, a fission bomb would be
needed as the trigger for a hydrogen bomb in any event; only a fission
bomb could produce the conditions necessary for setting off a hydrogen
explosion. Teller had only grudgingly accepted Oppenheimer's conclusions during the war, and ever since its end he had been trying to find
a way to get serious work going on his pet project. The challenge of the
Soviet bomb seemed to provide the previously lacking impetus, and he
used every means and argument he could think of to exploit it.

At the time it was still not known exactly how a hydrogen bomb might
be constructed, only that in principle a few barrels of liquid deuterium,
perhaps laced with tritium, would produce a prodigious amount of explosive energy if it could be heated to a high enough temperature for a
long enough time—that is, to a temperature of many tens of millions of
degrees for a fraction of a microsecond, quite a long time for such
extreme temperatures and pressures.

(Deuterium and tritium are the isotopes of hydrogen having, respectively, double and triple the weight of ordinary hydrogen. Deuterium exists in nature in ample quantities but in highly dilute form. Tritium does not exist in nature; it has to be artificially produced in a reactor. Moreover, it is radioactive and decays away in about twelve years. In brief, tritium is a much more difficult material to get and use than deuterium. Its potential utility stems from the fact that its nuclear properties happen to be such that a fifty-fifty mixture of tritium and deuterium is up to one hundred times as reactive as straight deuterium.)

No one at the time knew for sure whether large quantities of tritium would have to be added to deuterium to make it adequately reactive, but it seemed probable that some would be needed for that purpose, and so Lawrence and Alvarez began to focus on the problem of how to produce it in sufficient quantities—whatever those might ultimately turn out to be. Their first proposal for doing so involved the building of large nuclear reactors specifically designed for the purpose. They explored that idea with officials in Washington and decided to proceed. Before they could really get going, however, the Atomic Energy Commission, acting partly on the advice of Robert Oppenheimer and the General Advisory Committee, which he chaired, concluded that such reactors should be developed under the guidance of the Argonne National Laboratory, where there was much more pertinent experience.

Never daunted by such a turn of events, Lawrence and his colleagues turned their minds to a search for alternative, perhaps better, means for producing large quantities of free neutrons. These neutrons could in turn be used either for producing the tritium that might be needed to make hydrogen bombs or for making additional plutonium so that the production of the now familiar fission bombs could be expanded.

They soon hit upon the notion of doing so by building huge accelerators capable of producing very large quantities of free neutrons by "brute force." Lawrence independently asked Robert Serber, then the chief theorist at the lab, and me to make estimates of the efficiency of this process. Our estimates were slightly different, and so, after I submitted mine, Lawrence asked me to set up an experiment to determine the efficiency. Pleased, as usual, to be involved in something of direct interest to Lawrence, I put the basic research projects I was doing on the back burner and set up an experiment to get the data he wanted.

By chance, while I was still in the early stages of these experiments, Harold Brown, at age twenty-one the bearer of a brand new Ph.D. from Columbia University, showed up at the Rad Lab not quite sure about what he would do there. The professional personnel people suggested that he check with me to see if he could help out on my part of the new project. Fortunately, that's just what he did, and a lifetime of personal friendship and fruitful collaboration in projects neither of us could then have imagined in our wildest dreams flowed out of that chance recommendation.

Our experiments indicated that the overall process could be made adequately efficient if a suitable accelerator could be built. Lawrence settled on a giant version of the linear accelerator for that purpose. The machine itself was called the Materials Testing Accelerator, or MTA, that being essentially a cover name to disguise its true purpose from the world at large. The grand plan called for the construction of a full-scale model of the front end of such a machine—sixty feet in diameter and eighty-seven feet long—at a site near Livermore, California, on a section of land that had served as a minor naval air station during the war. The full machine, perhaps a third of a mile long, would be built near Weldon, Missouri (known to the younger project staff as "East Jesus"). As things finally turned out, the machine was not needed as an alternative means for producing large amounts of tritium or plutonium. The then well-established means for doing so—reactors—proved capable of supplying all of those substances that was really needed for the national security. More seriously, building the machine turned out to be much more difficult than had been anticipated; the necessary technology was really not as close at hand as had been estimated, and a series of major problems and delays arose. As a result of these factors, either of which would have been sufficient by itself, the project was abandoned after several years of hard work. For the first time Lawrence had, in effect, over-reached himself in a big way.

By the time it floundered, I had long since left the MTA project to do other things, but the choice of Livermore as the site for building the prototype front end would have a major influence on the future course of my life.

The H-Bomb Decision

Even while the Berkeley group was still tooling up to make its own contribution to the American response to the Russian bomb, a major secret debate about what the American response ought to be took place in the government itself. Many organizations were involved in it, including the National Security Council, the Departments of Defense and State, the Joints Chiefs of Staff, Congress's Joint Committee on Atomic Energy (JCAE), and the Atomic Energy Commission (AEC). The last of these had the primary legal responsibility for generating U.S. nuclear policies and programs, and so most of the proposals and arguments about what to do arose in its domain.

The Los Alamos Laboratory proposed to step up the pace of the nuclear weapons development program across the board, including research on the physical processes underlying the still hypothetical hydrogen bomb. Among other measures, the laboratory's director, Norris Bradbury, proposed that they go on a six-day week and expand the staff, especially in theoretical physics. Other elements of the AEC world were making similar proposals for expanding their pieces of the program. These included plans for further expansion of plutonium and U-235 production and for producing such quantities of tritium as might be needed in hydrogen bombs. There were also proposals to expand ore production from known sources in Colorado and Africa and to initiate immediately searches for new sources.

Meanwhile, Teller, Lawrence, and Alvarez at the laboratories; Robert LeBaron and David Griggs in the Pentagon; Senator Brian McMahon, chairman of the JCAE, and his staff chief, William L. Borden, on Capitol Hill; Lewis Strauss at the AEC; and certain general officers in the Air Force—all had come to focus on the H-bomb, or superbomb, as the one correct answer to the Soviet A-bomb. They began a concerted effort to bring the entire government around to their point of view as quickly as possible.

After a brief period of uncertainty, the search for an answer came down to a single, crucial issue: Was or was not a high-priority program for the development of the superbomb the appropriate American response and, if so, how should we go about conducting such a program?

As a result of all this churning about, the AEC called for a special meeting of its General Advisory Committee (GAC), to be held as soon as possible. The GAC had been established by the Atomic Energy Act of 1946 for the purpose of providing the AEC with scientific and technical advice concerning its programs. The members were all persons who had been leaders in major wartime projects. Robert Oppenheimer, the wartime director of the Los Alamos Laboratory, was elected to be its first chairman. He was not only the formal leader of the GAC but, by virtue of his personality and background, its natural leader was well. His views were therefore of special importance in determining the contents of its reports.

Throughout his service on the GAC, Oppenheimer supported the various programs designed to produce and improve nuclear weapons. At the same time, he was troubled by what he had wrought at Los Alamos, and he found the notion of bombs of unlimited power repugnant. His inner feelings about nuclear weapons were clearly revealed in an oft-quoted remark, "In some sort of crude sense which no vulgarity, no humor, no understatement could quite extinguish, the physicists have known sin." When Lawrence heard this later, he remarked, "I am a physicist and I have no knowledge to lose in which physics has caused me to know sin."[3]

The call for the GAC meeting, in addition to raising the question of a high-priority program to develop the super, also asked the committee to consider priorities in the broadest sense, including the question whether the commission was "now doing things we ought to do to serve the paramount objectives of the common defense and security."

The GAC responded positively to all the proposals before it, save the one dealing with the superbomb. In particular, the final report of the group's deliberations endorsed the plans for intensifying the search for more raw materials and for expanding the production of the various fissile fuels. It also recommended "an intensification of efforts to make atomic weapons available for tactical purposes, and to give attention to the problem of integration of bomb and carrier design in this field." In this connection the group added, "We strongly favor, subject to favorable outcome of the 1951 Eniwetok tests, the booster program."

("Boosting" is a process in which the great heat of a fission explosion is used to cause a very small hydrogen explosion, which in turn reacts back on the fission explosion and "boosts" it to produce a much larger total explosion. The basic purpose of this design concept is simply to make possible more efficient and physically smaller fission bombs.)

Having made all these strongly positive recommendations, the GAC turned to the issue of the superbomb. After briefly reviewing the status of the scientific work, the members of the committee remarked,

Although we are not able to give a specific probability rating for any given model, we believe that an imaginative and concerted attack on the problem has a better than even chance of producing the weapon within five years.

Then, after estimating that such a weapon would have "an explosive effect some hundreds of times that of present fission bombs," they noted,

It is clear that the use of this weapon would bring about the destruction of innumerable human lives; it is not a weapon which can be used exclusively for the destruction of material installations of military or semi-military purposes. Its use therefore carries much further than the atomic bomb itself the policy of exterminating civilian populations.

They concluded,

> Although the members of the Advisory Committee are not unanimous . . . with regard to the super bomb, there are certain elements of unanimity among us. We all hope that by one means or another, the development of these weapons can be avoided. We are all reluctant to see the United States take the initiative in precipitating this development. We are all agreed that it would be wrong at the present moment to commit ourselves to an all-out effort toward its development.
> . . . The majority feel that this should be an unqualified commitment. Others feel that it should be made conditional on the response of the Soviet government to a proposal to renounce such development.[4]

The atomic energy commissioners split over the issue. Chairman David Lilienthal and two others accepted the GAC's view. Lewis Strauss and one other recommended that the United States proceed with the development of the hydrogen bomb with "the highest priority." The responsible civilians in the Pentagon, including the secretary of defense, held views similar to those of Strauss, as did most members of the congressional Joint Committee on Atomic Energy, including its chairman and its staff chief. The Joint Chiefs of Staff, then chaired by General Omar Bradley, also favored going ahead with the super, but not with quite the same enthusiasm as many of its civilian supporters. Secretary of State Dean Acheson also sided with those who wanted to proceed forthwith, despite contrary advice from George Kennan, one of his senior advisers.

President Truman considered all these varying views and easily concluded that the majority was right. On January 31, 1950, he announced his decision to go ahead with the development of the H-bomb:

> It is part of my responsibility as Commander in Chief of the Armed Forces to see to it that our country is able to defend itself against any possible aggressor. Accordingly I have directed the Atomic Energy Commission to continue its work on all forms of atomic weapons, including the so-called hydrogen or Superbomb.[5]

At the time, I knew virtually nothing about the details of the discussions and debates described above, although many of the leaders of the Berkeley laboratory were deeply involved in them—Lawrence, Alvarez,

Seaborg, and Serber. The level of secrecy at which they took place was way over my head, and all I knew about the issue came from the occasional news leaks about them. When I later became personally engaged in carrying out some of the projects they had recommended—and some they had advised against—I did pick up bits and pieces about it all. However, even then most of that would come from conversations with Lawrence and Teller, and that was naturally flavored with their own perspectives on the matter. Only twenty-five years later, in 1974, would I finally see the full GAC report and obtain access to certain other key documents. When that happened, I reviewed the whole matter carefully and completely for the first time and wrote a book about it: *The Advisors: Oppenheimer, Teller, and the Superbomb.*

Even if I had known more about the debate described above, I would probably not have behaved very differently in the years that immediately followed. There is nothing surprising or special about me in that; all of the GAC members contributed at least marginally to the superbomb program after Truman overruled them and ordered it to go ahead, and some of the program's strongest critics later contributed to it centrally. And besides, within months of Truman's order the sudden onset of the Korean War confirmed our worst fears and made second thoughts on the subject moot.

It would, of course, have been a good thing if we could have avoided the superbomb development, as the GAC had urged. That, however, would probably not have happened even if Truman had followed its advice. As we later learned from their own reports, the Soviets had started a superbomb development program some months before Truman's decision. It did not come to fruition until about a year and a half after ours did, but that was not for lack of trying.

Project 3.1.1.8

The president's January 31 announcement was followed by a substantial increase in activity at Los Alamos, although not nearly as much as some of the promoters of the H-bomb wanted. That spring, at about the time I was finishing up my experiments for the MTA project, Alvarez paid another visit to Los Alamos to learn more about the program there. In sum, he found that it was moving ahead, that certain new tests were being planned, and that the project could use additional assistance. On returning to Berkeley, he reported all this to Lawrence, and the two of them suggested that Hugh Bradner ("Brad"), a postdoctoral research physicist working for Alvarez, and I pay a visit to Teller and the others involved to explore the matter further. We promptly did so.

We learned that in the forthcoming test series called Operation Greenhouse, Los Alamos planned to include two nuclear explosions in which a mixture of hydrogen isotopes would be caused to undergo "thermonuclear reactions," as they were commonly known. (The word *thermonuclear* denotes that the reactions between hydrogen nuclei take place only at extremely high temperatures, some tens of millions of degrees centigrade. For that reason hydrogen bombs are often called thermonuclear bombs. They are also sometimes termed superbombs, because they are much more powerful than even ordinary fission, or atomic, bombs.)

One of the tests, called Item, was designed to explore the booster concept mentioned above. The other, George, was intended to be a first, rather tentative step toward the super. The George device was not a prototype of the super in the usual sense; rather, it was an attempt to ignite a small thermonuclear explosion under nearly ideal conditions and to learn as much as possible about the course of such reactions, if they could in fact be produced.

The design of the George device was being elaborated by the laboratory's theoretical division, directed by J. Carson Mark, a longtime Los Alamos veteran. Teller had recently rejoined the regular staff, and there was a steady stream of visiting consultants who, from my point of view, made up a veritable *Who's Who* of American physics: Hans Bethe, Gregory Breit, George Gamow, Enrico Fermi, Emil Konopinski, John von Neumann, and John Wheeler among them. In addition to all these famous men, Fermi brought with him a very special student, Richard Garwin, with whom I would later have many profitable and interesting relations.

Brad and I also learned that Los Alamos needed no outside help in designing or building any of the explosive devices themselves but that the lab could use additional assistance in designing, constructing, and conducting certain key "diagnostic experiments." These are experiments whose purpose is to observe and "diagnose" the sequence of events that unfold during the very brief moments of the nuclear explosion itself. By the time of our visit, about a dozen such diagnostic experiments were being considered seriously. Work on most of them was already well under way in groups made up of scientists on the staff at Los Alamos, but several of the more complex experiments called for a greater effort than could be pulled together from the other essential work going on at the time. Of these additional experiments, two were eventually assigned to two separate groups at the Naval Research Laboratory, in Washington, and Brad and I agreed to take on another to be developed at, and staged out of, the Berkeley laboratory.

I was excited about our participation in the new project and eager to get on with it, for a number of different reasons. First, I felt that the steadily worsening international situation did call for some sort of American response. And indeed, when the Korean War broke out only weeks after I joined this new enterprise, that confirmed to me the need for a renewal of work on all kinds of defense-oriented projects. Second, when I had worked on the atomic bomb project during the war, I had been employed in a more or less peripheral area, back at Oak Ridge, rather than in the center of the action, at Los Alamos. This time around, I would have the opportunity to work at the very core of the enterprise. Third, and I think most important, I looked forward to associating with Teller and all those other physicists whom I had been reading about in books and hearing about in lectures for years but whom, with only minor and brief exceptions, I had not yet met face to face. All in all, it was heady stuff, and I was quite pleased with this unexpected turn of events. New horizons had suddenly opened up before me, and I was anxious to explore them.

In the jargon that goes with that sort of enterprise, we were known as Project 3.1.1.8. The "3" meant that we were part of Joint Task Force 3, an enormous organization made up of several thousands of men organized in units from each of the military services plus all of us civilians, and commanded by Lieutenant General Elwood R. ("Pete") Quesada. And yes, I do mean men, not persons. Unbelievable as it may seem today, women were absolutely prohibited at the test site on Eniwetok: no nurses, no secretaries, no waitresses, no women.

The first "1" stood for Task Group 1, made up of all the civilians in the operation, from Los Alamos and elsewhere, and headed by Alvin C. Graves. The second "1" stood for the sub–task group made up of all those involved in the various diagnostic experiments. It was headed by Los Alamos's Fred Reines, a very fine physicist who later achieved wide renown by being the first to make direct observations of the elusive neutrino. Experience with large-scale experiments carried out at remote sites of the kind we were all then engaged in at Eniwetok played an important part in preparing Fred for his later neutrino work. Finally, the "8" stood just for us, the group Brad and I put together at Berkeley.

Our particular task was to measure the temperatures at which the expected thermonuclear reactions would take place. These temperatures were estimated to be somewhere in the range of several tens of millions of degrees, and we proposed to measure them by observing during the explosion itself the thermal radiation emitted from the surface of the device containing the reactants. At those temperatures the thermal radiation would be in the form of X rays rather than the infrared and visible light produced by objects just ordinarily hot.

In the course of working out our approach to the problem, Brad and I found it necessary to make many visits to Los Alamos. I met frequently with Teller, Fermi, Garwin, Bethe, and the others named earlier, and those meetings proved to be every bit as interesting and exciting as I had anticipated.

I still recall with special wonder three conversations I had with Fermi. One of them was at lunch in the Lodge; Teller and Emil Konopinski, another of the theoretical physicists trying to invent the H-bomb, were also there. All of a sudden, seemingly apropos of nothing in particular, Fermi asked, "Don't you ever wonder where everybody is?" We all immediately knew his "everybody" meant visitors from other worlds. He proceeded to analyze his own question by estimating the number of Earth-like planets there must be, the probability that life in general and intelligent life in particular would arise on such a planet, and the probability that such beings would develop and use interstellar travel. He concluded by saying that if his string of estimates was right, we ought to have been visited many times over already; but we haven't been, so where is everybody? This question and these calculations were, as is well known, repeated by others some years later, but Fermi seems to have been the first to do so seriously.[6] On a similar occasion Fermi asked, "What would you do if you had $100,000,000 to spend on science, with no restrictions or conditions attached?" Again he immediately answered his own question, this time saying, "Dig the deepest-possible hole." He observed that we knew less about the deep earth under our feet than about most other easily accessible things, and he believed that such a project would be, to put it in today's terms, very cost-effective. This was more than a decade before a group from the National Academy and the National Science Foundation (NSF) made a well-publicized pitch for the same thing under the name Project Mohole.

Fermi loved to pose and answer such questions. In this way he explored what he would do if he were pope (!), and in a third such monologue he told me that he thought that Lawrence and his team—including me—should go to work on building a rocket to take man to the moon. He added that he would go even if the chances of getting back safely were only fifty-fifty. I said I didn't think I would, to which Fermi replied,

"That's because you're younger." But even Fermi wasn't all science. On one occasion, when Sybil and our one-year-old daughter Rachel accompanied me on a visit to Los Alamos during the summer before Operation Greenhouse, he poked his finger in Rachel's fat tummy and cooed at her just as any other mortal would.

No only did we see Teller in Los Alamos—always an interesting and stimulating affair—on one occasion he came to see us in Berkeley. In a meeting that also included Alvarez and Lawrence, Teller reported that he and the others at Los Alamos were making real progress on the super. Lawrence then asked him if that meant he now knew how to construct one.

"No," said Teller.

"Where's the progress? You didn't know that the last time I saw you," replied Lawrence.

"Yes," said Teller, "but now we don't know it on much better grounds."

Teller always approached such matters with a youthful enthusiasm that was for many, including me, infectious.

The experimental setup that we finally developed and constructed included a very large collection of electronic recording devices. Because no space was readily available at Berkeley for setting all of them up and checking them out simultaneously, we did so in the enlisted men's ward in the old, abandoned hospital that had served the Livermore Naval Air Station during the war. After we had successfully set up everything and had it all working at Berkeley and Livermore, we moved most of the group and all the equipment out to one of the small islets that make up Eniwetok Atoll in order to prepare for the George shot.

Eniwetok itself proved to be an interesting, even fascinating, place. It is an atoll about twenty miles in diameter, made up of a nearly circular coral reef surrounding a deep blue lagoon. The reef is dotted with islets, ranging in size up to perhaps a hundred acres, and is broken by only two or three deep channels connecting the lagoon with the Pacific. The reef itself is rich with a great variety of coral growths, giant clams, and other unusual shelfish. Fish of many different shapes and colors abound. At that time a few of the larger islets had coconut groves, but most were barren or covered with low scrub. We were very busy and worked most of the daylight hours, but we did find some spare moments to enjoy the special glories of nature that were all around us in that strange place, quite different from upstate New York or California.

Here and there on the reef were the rusting hulks of broken Army tanks and ships, casualties of the war in the Pacific. Operation Greenhouse was taking place only five years after that awful episode had been ended by two earlier atomic explosions, and so it was oddly fitting that those reminders of that conflict were still there.

We managed to get everything ready just barely in time for the main event. On May 8, 1951, the George device was exploded. For the first time ever a tiny thermonuclear flame burned on the surface of the earth. We participated in successfully making the measurements that determined when, how, and under what conditions it had happened. Nowadays experiments like the one we did are done with much more sophisticated equipment and techniques, and they produce more accurate and detailed results. Nevertheless, thirty years later, during a brief visit to Livermore, I was pleased to run across a theoretical physicist doing some work that made use of the data we had collected on that pioneering occasion.

Seeing the Bomb with the Mind's Eye

I saw two nuclear explosions while I was at at Eniwetok during Operation Greenhouse. One, George, by far the most powerful to that date, was more than ten times larger than the bomb dropped on Hiroshima. In subsequent years I would see many others, both in Nevada and in the Pacific, including some more than a thousand times as powerful as Hiroshima's.

Nuclear explosions are, as most everyone knows, visually impressive. At first there is just an intense sense of a great flash of light somewhere out there. Then a fireball forms—a sphere if the bomb bursts in the air, a hemisphere if it explodes on the ground. It has a smooth surface, white-hot and very bright. The heat on the face at that moment can be more impressive than the light. Very soon thereafter, the surface tends to darken as its temperature falls and dust and smoke mix in, and the whole thing starts to rise. A stem of dust lingers behind the rapidly rising main cloud, and the familiar mushroom takes shape. The upper reaches of the cloud, the cap of the mushroom, has fiery lighted areas mixed in with the dust—some bright white, some red, and some purple. Much later a rolling boom passes over.

It's an impressive sight, all right, but the setting completely undercuts the true horror of the bomb. In Nevada, in the days when bombs were tested there in the atmosphere, the explosions commonly took place over a dry lake bed in the middle of a great circular valley. Nothing was destroyed, except the tower supporting the bomb; nothing even burned, except for an occasional desert scrub. No one was killed or even seriously endangered. The whole operation took place in such a way as to guarantee that nothing unpleasant would happen. Safety was the rule. It was all totally antiseptic.

It was the same in the Pacific. The explosions took place on tiny islets in the middle of a great ocean. Nothing but test equipment was destroyed, nothing burned, no one was killed. If the explosion made a crater, it filled with water and sand before anyone could get a look at it.

Far more impressive to me are the photographs of Hiroshima and Nagasaki the day after. Even in reproductions of the kind presented in newspapers, the full horror of those events can easily be seen. And in the case of the multimegaton tests of the 1950s, observing the explosions themselves did not impress me nearly as much as seeing a map of Washington with the bomb crater laid over it, the circles indicating the reach of total destruction enclosing the entire metropolis. The grass-covered, pie-shaped segment that still remains unbuilt in Hiroshima is far more moving and impressive than any nuclear explosion I ever saw.

Some of my friends—Harold Agnew and Walter Munk, to name two who have much experience in these matters—have said that the leaders of the world should be required to watch a megaton explosion every few years. I can't agree. It is not the bright light and the great heat of a test bomb that should be printed on their memories; rather, it is the knowledge of what these bombs did and can do again to man and his works that they must bear in mind. Make the leaders look at pictures of Hiroshima after the bomb and let them hear the ongoing stories of the still-surviving victims. That will give them a much truer picture of what humanity is facing.

I believe Oppenheimer and the others on the Interim Committee were right when they rejected a demonstration in some safe place in Japan. It is the contemplation of the deaths, not of the glowing clouds, that can really move people. Bombs over deserts and oceans are spectacles; bombs over cities are history.

The Teller-Ulam Invention

About two weeks before the George shot took place, Teller arrived in Eniwetok to see for himself how things were going. Very soon thereafter I found an opportunity to meet with him alone to learn more about events back at Los Alamos. It was the usual, warm tropical evening. We were in one of the slightly corroded all-purpose aluminum buildings on Parry Island. A blackboard up front, a few folding chairs, and a simple working table made up the furnishings. Teller quickly sketched out his most recent ideas on how actually to construct a superbomb. It turned out that only a few weeks earlier he had come up with the final, capping idea needed to convert several years of searching into a concrete, workable idea of just how to do it. I instantly recognized that this was it; this was the idea that Teller and so many other brilliant minds had been groping for, these last ten years. Even at the time I saw it was an opening into a new and dangerous era, and I still shudder a bit when I recall those moments.

Teller had come upon this idea during the lull after all the experimental designs for Operation Greenhouse had been frozen, but before the actual tests could be accomplished. It was a time when the experimentalists—Hugh Bradner and I and others like us—were exceptionally busy, but when the theorists had time on their hands and a chance to ruminate about more general questions than just how these particular test devices should be built and how they might work.

Of course, Teller's idea did not come in a vacuum. Ever since Truman's announcement, many ideas had been tossed out: some absurd, some impractical, some close to the mark. Stan Ulam, a senior mathematician in the Theoretical Division, later wrote,

> . . . I thought of an iterative scheme, and after I put my thoughts in order and made a semi-concrete sketch, I went to Carson Mark to discuss it. . . . The same afternoon I went to see Norris Bradbury and mentioned such schemes. He quickly grasped its possibilities and at once showed great interest in having it pursued. Next morning, I spoke to Teller.
>
> At once Edward took up my suggestions, hesitantly at first but enthusiastically after a few hours. He had seen not only the novel elements, but had found a parallel version, an alternative to what I had said, perhaps more convenient and general. From then on pessimism gave way to hope.[7]

Referring to the same events, Teller put it a little differently:

> Two signs of hope came within a few weeks; one sign was in an imaginative suggestion by Ulam; the other sign was a fine calculation by [Frederic] De Hoffmann. . . . Since I had made the suggestion that led to his calculation, I expected we would jointly sign the report containing the results. Freddie, however, . . . signed the report with my name only and argued that the suggestion counted for everything and the execution for nothing. I still feel ashamed that I consented.[8]

These two descriptions are quite different, but not contradictory. The "suggestion" that Teller said he had made and that led to de Hoffmann's calculation is precisely the "parallel version, an alternative . . . , perhaps more convenient and general," of Ulam's recollection. The details of this idea, still highly classified, are set down in two reports. One, dated March 9, 1951, is signed by Ulam and Teller. The other report, which included de Hoffmann's calculations, was issued less than a month later. The idea in this latter paper is the one that Teller described to me on that memorable evening in Eniwetok.

In June 1951 the new design idea and the calculations supporting it were presented to a wider group in a meeting held in Oppenheimer's office at the Institute for Advanced Study at Princeton. In attendance were members of the AEC and the GAC, as well as Teller, Bradbury, Bethe, and other staff and consultants of the Los Alamos Laboratory, including me. This wider audience immediately recognized that this new idea was the way to go. Several years later Oppenheimer compared the ideas presented in June 1951 with those current earlier:

> The program we had in 1949 was a tortured thing that you could well argue did not make a great deal of technical sense. It was therefore possible to argue also that you did not want it even if you could have it. The program in 1951 was technically so sweet that you could not argue about that. The issues became purely the military, the political and the humane problems of what you were going to do about it once you had it.[9]

That summer, plans were developed at Los Alamos and approved in Washington for a series of test devices designed to verify and exploit these ideas. The program for the construction and test of what would be the first very large hydrogen bomb, the "Mike" device, was placed in the hands not of Teller but of Marshall Holloway and other longtime members of the Los Alamos Laboratory staff.

In the fall Teller left Los Alamos and returned to the University of Chicago. (More on this in the next chapter.)

Shortly after the George shot I returned to Berkeley, having been in the Pacific for nearly three months. My first aim was to analyze our data and prepare a final report on what they meant. Then I planned to think about what to do next—presumably, in the world of pure research, well removed from the classified, defense-related activities I had been engaged in for the last year and a half.

Sybil was in the last stages of pregnancy at the time, and late one evening, just before midnight, it became clear that our next child was about to arrive. Since our neighborhood was less than ideal and our children were so young—David six a and a half, and Rachel two—I felt we had to have someone come and care for them while we went off to the hospital. It is not easy to find a regular baby-sitter at midnight, so I immediately thought of turning to one of my young bachelor friends. Harold Brown was at the top of our list for the purpose; fortunately, he was at home and available. He arrived and took up his post sometime after we had already left for the hospital, and soon after that, in the early morning of June 8, 1951, Cynthia Dunford York, our second daughter and last child, was born.

In the meantime, Lawrence had wangled an appointment for me as an assistant professor in the Berkeley physics department at one-third time. The other two-thirds of my appointment would continue to be as "physicist in the radiation laboratory," the job title that Lawrence insisted was the "best in the world." For the first time since leaving my childhood home eight years before, I thought I was looking forward to a long period of stability and growth in that combination of appointments, and I began to think about making some of the other aspects of my life more stable and more closely geared to the life that seemed to lie before Sybil and me.

Suitable housing was high on our list of priorities. The house we were then living in down by the railroad had become much too small; thanks to my new position and salary, I could now contemplate making the monthly payments on something bigger and in a better neighborhood. When we found the place we wanted, it was clear we could easily make the monthly payments, but the down payment turned out to be a different matter. We simply didn't have enough money. I turned once again to my young colleagues, and Hugh Bradner and Harold Brown each managed to come up with about a thousand dollars, quite enough for us to swing the deal. Harold and I have done many other things for each other since then, but those were the two easy though critical ones I particularly want my children to remember.

That fall, established in our new house in north Berkeley, I began what I thought would be a long, more or less standard career as a member of the faculty of the University of California. One of my first teaching assignments was an introductory physics course, for which Michael May, then an advanced graduate student, was my teaching assistant. Although neither of us could possibly have guessed it at the time, Mike and I would continue to collaborate in a wide variety of ways for the rest of our careers. I also taught a graduate course in nuclear physics. In it I related some of the stories I had heard from Segrè as well as my own experiences in the last few years at the Radiation Laboratory. At the same time, I tried to reestablish a program of research in basic nuclear physics of the sort I had been doing before the diversions of the last two years had intervened. I was just beginning to make some headway in that direction when Lawrence asked me a new question and made me yet another proposition that drastically changed everything once again.

CHAPTER 4

"Do We Need a Second Laboratory?"

(January 1952–December 1957)

Lawrence Has a Question

A S WAS his custom in those years, Carl Helmholz, one of the members of the Berkeley physics faculty, held a New Year's Day reception at his home in Orinda, east of the Berkeley Hills. Many of the members of the department and the laboratory staff were there. During the course of the party, Lawrence in a brief aside asked me to drop in on him someday soon; he had, he said, something he wanted to discuss with me.

Eager, as always, to chat with my boss, I called on him in his office within a day or two. He asked me a simple question: "Does the United States need a second nuclear weapons laboratory?" One of the AEC commissioners, Thomas Murray, had recently put that question to him, and he wanted to know what I thought. Since I had spent a large part of the preceding two years participating in the superbomb program, it was logical for him to expect that I might have some useful thoughts on the subject.

I replied I really didn't know enough to have a firm opinion, so I proposed that I make an extended trip around the country to discuss the matter with others who might be expected to have helpful views on it. Lawrence approved my suggestion, and I soon set out on what turned out to be an extended series of trips to Los Alamos, Washington, Chicago, and Princeton.

I rediscovered the obvious: Teller was the prime mover behind the question, and the question itself was hardly new. Teller had never been satisfied with the management of the American nuclear weapons program or felt that the total effort devoted to it was adequate. His conflict with Oppenheimer during the war was notorious, as was his refusal to participate in the postwar continuation of the work at Los Alamos unless the government and the laboratory would both commit themselves to a substantial nuclear test program. More recently, in the fall of 1949, he had fought the GAC over the issue of whether the United States should initiate a high-priority program to develop and build superbombs, and he was even disappointed when, on January 31, 1950, Truman ordered the AEC to "continue its efforts on . . . the so-called hydrogen or Superbomb." Truman's use of the word *continue* rather than *charge ahead* had led Teller to feel—quite mistakenly—that his cause had been lost. Even after the Los Alamos Laboratory had accelerated and expanded its program in response to the president's directives, Teller continued to believe that the laboratory leaders—Norris Bradbury and Carson Mark, among others—were not doing enough to recruit new people and were not diverting a sufficient fraction of the laboratory's effort from fission bomb development to the search for the super.

In mid-1951 all this strife finally came to a head. That May the George shot had proved that a mixture of deuterium and tritium really would explode if the right initial conditions could be achieved. That showed that a superbomb could be built, and the Los Alamos Laboratory set about reorganizing itself to do so in the shortest-possible time. Bradbury, surely with Washington's concurrence, decided to put longtime senior laboratory staffers, and not Edward Teller, in charge of the program. In Bradbury's judgment, Teller was no manager, and now that the basic idea was in hand, people who could manage and orchestrate a complex effort involving many different technologies had to be put in charge. More important, Teller's strident complaints about the laboratory management had so poisoned the atmosphere that it was simply impossible to give him the kind of autonomous position within the laboratory that he was demanding.

For Teller this was the last straw. Soon after these new organizational arrangements were announced, he left Los Alamos and returned to the University of Chicago. His memoir on the subject made it clear that one of his several reasons for leaving was his desire to press his campaign for a second laboratory:

> The dissension with Bradbury crystallized in my mind the urgent need for more than one nuclear weapons laboratory.
>
> I knew that science thrives on friendly competition, on the fostering of different points of view, and on the exchange of ideas developed in different surroundings. I knew, too, that a single group of scientists working together can easily become fascinated by special aspects of a development—to the neglect of other hopeful approaches. My conviction grew that the safety of our country could not be entrusted to a single nuclear weapons laboratory, even though that laboratory were as excellent as Los Alamos.[1]

Of course, Teller did not wait until after he had left Los Alamos to press his views. Indeed, throughout the whole period since the first Soviet A-bomb test, Teller had been telling all who would listen of his dissatisfaction with how the project was being run.

Teller took this message to his friends on the congressional Joint Committee on Atomic Energy. There he found an especially sympathetic listener not only in the chairman, Senator Brien McMahon, but also in the chief staff aide, William L. Borden—the latter being the man who three years later formally accused Oppenheimer of being a Soviet agent.

Teller also received a very sympathetic hearing from Air Force Chief Scientist David Griggs, a Rand Corporation physicist on leave, and from General Roscoe Wilson, both of whom also later figured prominently as witnesses for the prosecution in the Oppenheimer hearings. As one result, the Air Force, partly for its own reasons, began to make moves toward the establishment of a second nuclear laboratory directly under its own aegis. However tentative these Air Force actions may have been, they increased pressure on the AEC either to do something itself or to see its monopoly in the field end.

While Teller was lobbying in the defense establishment and the Congress, he was also doing what he could within the Washington headquarters of the AEC itself. He found some support for his ideas from Gordon Dean, who had recently succeeded Lilienthal as chairman of the

AEC, and from Thomas Murray, one of the newer commissioners. Following the usual procedures in such matters, they referred the idea of a second laboratory to the GAC for consideration at its December 1950 meeting and again at several later meetings. Except for Willard F. Libby, a University of Chicago chemistry professor and personal friend of Teller's, the GAC members took a dim view of the idea of a new laboratory and recommended against establishing one. They were influenced in part by Norris Bradbury, who said it wasn't needed and would inevitably divert essential support away from Los Alamos. In addition, many of the members of the GAC had previously found themselves in protracted conflicts with Teller over related issues, and that probably influenced their attitudes toward his latest proposal. A year later, in December 1951, after the GAC had made its third or fourth negative recommendation on the matter to the AEC commissioners, Murray put in the call to Lawrence that in turn prompted Lawrence's New Year's query to me.

When I set off on my trips to sound out opinions on this question, I was aware of the general situation but largely ignorant of the details presented above. I therefore visited Los Alamos to learn the views of my new friends and colleagues there, and I traveled on to Chicago to have a thorough discussion with Teller about his. The balance in these two cases came out as one would suppose: the Los Alamos people felt they could do all that was required, and Teller was convinced they could not. I went on to Washington, where I met with the same AEC and Air Force officials Teller had seen. Everyone in the Air Force seemed to think that not enough was currently being done to exploit the recent breakthrough and that new institutional arrangements were needed to set things right.

I also visited John Wheeler at Princeton University. He had long been involved in nuclear weapons and the search for the super, and he had recently set up a small group of theoretical physicists, based in the nearby Forrestal Center, to help Los Alamos carry out some of the key calculations needed to convert the Teller-Ulam invention from a set of sketches and theories into a workable weapons system. I found Wheeler very much in agreement with Teller.

My early reports to Lawrence on the results of my travels confirmed his own preliminary conclusion that a second laboratory was needed.

In February, Teller visited Berkeley, and Lawrence took him out to Livermore to see his latest pride and joy, the Materials Testing Accelerator. During the visit Lawrence brought up the possibility of building the second laboratory on this same site, and asked Teller if he would be willing to come to California to help establish it. Teller said that he would, provided that it included work on thermonuclear weapons.

While these discussions and machinations were going on inside the nuclear establishment, international political developments gave every sign that the situation was going from bad to worse. The establishment of the Sino-Soviet bloc, the invasion of South Korea by North Korea, and the subsequent entry of massive numbers of Chinese "volunteers" into that war, all reinforced the notion that we in the West faced a long-term struggle with a monolithic, aggressive alliance of the two Communist giants. Thus, while it was actions and ideas inside the American nuclear world that guided the processes that led to the establishment of a second laboratory, the threats implicit in the Korean War drove the process more powerfully and decisively than any other factor.

Combining his own prejudgments with what Teller and I had told him, Lawrence informed his friends at the AEC that he would, if they wished, take on the task of establishing an additional weapons research center on the Livermore site as a branch of the Radiation Laboratory and that he could staff it, at least at first, largely with people already on the payroll. This proposal changed the situation radically. It clearly meant much less initial expense and an immediate, if small, cadre of people ready to go to work as needed. As Oppenheimer later recalled, the GAC and the AEC very quickly "approved the second laboratory as now conceived because there was an existing installation, and it could be done gradually and without harm to Los Alamos."[2]

Lawrence and Teller felt that Oppenheimer himself was still opposed to a second laboratory but that under the new circumstances he had no choice but to go along with it. Later that year I met with Oppenheimer at Princeton and discussed the plans for the Livermore Laboratory. He received me in a friendly fashion, but I cannot recall his being of any particular help. It turned out to be the last time I would ever see him.

Lawrence asked me to draw up plans for the new research center. In response I began to sketch out my ideas about how to go about it: the first elements of a research program, new facilities required, manpower, and the rest. After a few weeks of such work, Lawrence asked me if I thought I could "run it." After only an overnight hesitation, I told him it was worth a try, and he simply instructed me to do so. It really was that casual; no search committee or any of the other procedures to which we are now accustomed. In keeping with his standard style of operation, he gave me no new title, no immediate raise in salary, or any other change in status. He made no announcement about it, except an informal one to his immediate associates. These last, especially his longtime general manager, Wallace B. Reynolds, eagerly gave me all the help and advice I could possibly use in carrying out Lawrence's new charge.

The precise plans for the new laboratory, as I developed them during the next few months, primarily reflected Lawrence's ideas and deviated considerably from Teller's views of what should be done. In essence, Lawrence firmly believed that if a group of bright young men were simply sent off in the right direction with a reasonable level of support, they would end up in the right place. He did not believe that the goals needed to be spelled out in detail or that the leadership had to consist of persons already well known. Teller, on the other hand, was as usual deeply suspicious of the intentions of the AEC leadership. He wanted something closer to the 1942 plans for Los Alamos: a plan for a laboratory with a well-defined goal that would be led by a solid cadre of well-established—even famous—scientists. I had rather limited experience in such matters, but I favored Lawrence's approach.

To complicate matters, during that spring Lawrence, suffering from a chronic illness (ulcerative colitis), spent much time away from Berkeley on long rest trips. As a result, I was left pretty much on my own to draw up the specific plans for a second laboratory, with nothing except the most general guidance from Lawrence plus such ideas as I gleaned from my occasional visits with Teller in Chicago. However, thanks to nearly eight years of close association, I both clearly understood and firmly agreed with Lawrence's approach to "big science," and I generated plans that he always warmly endorsed when he had a chance to review them.

Finally, and in close accord with Lawrence's views of the matter, the AEC in June 1952 approved the establishment of a branch of the Berkeley laboratory at Livermore to assist in the thermonuclear weapons program by conducting diagnostic experiments during weapons tests and performing other, related research. The question of how soon, or even whether, the Livermore Laboratory would actually engage directly in weapons development was left open, however.

Lawrence felt that this approach provided an adequate base upon which to build a second weapons laboratory. I would have preferred something more concrete, but I was quite prepared to accept it as a place from which to start. Teller, on the other hand, was extremely dissatisfied with the vagueness of the AEC's plans for the new laboratory.

Finally, after mulling the matter over, Teller, in the course of a well-

lubricated reception held at the Claremont Hotel in Berkeley in early
July to celebrate the launching of the new enterprise, suddenly announced to Lawrence, Chairman Gordon Dean of the AEC, and me that
he would have nothing further to do with the plans for establishing a
laboratory at Livermore. Lawrence was prepared to go ahead anyway,
and he even suggested privately to me that we would probably be better
off without Teller. However, at the insistence of Captain John T. Hayward (then deputy director of the AEC's Division of Military Applications), intense negotiations were resumed among all concerned. Within
days this led to a firm commitment on the part of Gordon Dean that
thermonuclear weapons development would be included in the Livermore program from the outset, as well as to a renewed commitment on
the part of Teller to join the laboratory.

Getting Started

That first summer was a very busy time. With Lawrence's powerful
backing and with some important help from Alvarez and Seaborg, I
recruited to the project some twenty physicists and a few chemists in
less than a month. With only two or three exceptions, all were from
Berkeley. Some of them, including Harold Brown and Robert Jastrow,
had been with me on Operation Greenhouse. A few, including Roger
Batzel, who became the director of the laboratory twenty years later,
were already at Livermore working on the MTA project. Most were
either just finishing their degrees or had done so only very recently.
Nearly a hundred others—engineers, technicians, machinists, and business office staff—were seconded to Livermore by the corresponding
departments in Berkeley. Shortly after Labor Day 1952 we opened shop
at the Livermore site. Teller joined us just a few weeks later. At first we
were, of course, totally preoccupied with getting ourselves organized
and devising our plan for work. Only two months later, before we could
get very far with these efforts, an event occurred that not only literally
shook the world but also affected us in a very direct way.

   On November 2, 1952, local date, the United States exploded Mike, the
world's first very large thermonuclear device, on Elugelab Island at
Eniwetok Atoll. Its yield was 10.5 megatons, fulfilling the prediction of
many years' standing that the superbomb, if it could be made, would be
a thousand times as powerful as the bomb dropped on Hiroshima. On

the basis of ideas by Teller, Ulam, and others, it was built and tested by the Los Alamos Laboratory. Because his relations with the Los Alamos leaders were so severely strained, Teller did not accompany them out to the Pacific to observe it.

The AEC authorities, on instructions from the White House, clamped an extraordinarily tight curtain of security over the whole operation. They intended to allow no post test reports to be sent from the Pacific back to the laboratories or anywhere else until after there had been an on-the-spot analysis of what had happened. Even then, the first word would go directly back to Washington only, with no other addressees. The Task Force Command did, however, broadcast a coded signal that indicated the moment when the button had actually been pushed. Because of some experiments on long-range effects that we were doing at Livermore, we were given the means for decoding that message. The moment I received it—I was in my office at the lab—I noted the time and telephoned Teller, then standing by at the Berkeley seismometer, to tell him just when "zero hour" had passed. He kept a very close watch on the seismometer, and at the appropriate time, some fourteen minutes after zero hour, he saw it make a good jump. He called me back and said, "It's a boy!" I then telephoned someone in authority at Los Alamos—I'm now not sure who—and passed that word on to him. It was the first news anyone there would get for some time telling them that their experiment had been highly successful.

When I reflect back on that moment, as I sometimes do in preparing or giving lectures on the history of the nuclear era, a feeling of awe and foreboding always recurs. Even at the time, I thought of that moment and of that coded message as marking a real change in history—a moment when the course of the world suddenly shifted, from the path it had been on to a more dangerous one. Fission bombs, destructive as they might be, were thought of as being limited in power. Now, it seemed, we had learned how to brush even these limits aside and to build bombs whose power was boundless.[3]

Could the development of the H-bomb it have been avoided? Even in the full light of retrospection, I do not see how. Even if there had been no other reasons—and there were others—the almost total lack of communications between Stalin's Russia and the rest of the world would alone have made its avoidance impossible as a practical political matter.

In any event, the success of Mike led inevitably and immediately to a demand for developing practical versions of the new bomb. That settled, once and for all, Livermore's role in the program; there was obviously plenty of work ahead for both labs.

The success of Mike affected us in another serious but unexpected way. The same high level of secrecy that surrounded the explosion itself was extended to cover any discussion of the program that had led up to it. Nevertheless, Teller's special—and colorful—role in the matter was generally known to interested members of the press, and so it was only natural that they gave him full credit for it, and by extension to the new Livermore Laboratory, where he now was, as well. This did not sit well with the staff at Los Alamos, to put it mildly.

This unhappy situation continued for more than a year. It was not until after two reporters, James Shepley and Clay Blair, Jr., published a lengthy and biased account of the matter that Bradbury was finally allowed to hold a press conference giving his—correct—version of the history.[4] In the meantime, the relationship between Livermore and Los Alamos, which had been strained from the start, grew worse.*

One of the early questions we had to face that first fall was how to fit Edward Teller into the laboratory. There was never any doubt in my mind that I was in charge of the scientific program of the laboratory and that other young physicists were responsible for carrying out the various projects I had assigned to them. However, Teller was Teller and not just one more member of the scientific staff. He was by many years the oldest, and he was the only one who had a truly substantial scientific reputation. More important, he was the principal inventor of the new technology we were about to spend the next years in exploiting, and he had been the most vocal among those who had urged the establishment of our new enterprise. We could not very well assign to a person of his stature some minor fiefdom in the laboratory, and we were not willing to give him a top-level management position.

We solved this problem in a simple way. We established a small steering committee and made him a member of it without responsibility for any specific part of the laboratory or its program but with a personal veto authority, for the first year only, over all elements of the scientific program—a veto that, to my recollection, he never used. This arrangement enabled him to participate as he wished in whatever part of the

*Relations between Livermore and Los Alamos were also made worse by the Oppenheimer security hearings of 1954 because the most important part of the anti-Oppenheimer testimony came from persons associated with the new lab, in particular from Teller.[5]

program struck his fancy and made it equally possible for anyone any-where in the laboratory to go to Teller to discuss anything on his mind. In this capacity Teller contributed a great deal to the life and success of the laboratory. Everyone who went to see him, including myself, found the visit always fun and often inspiring. Full of intellectual energy, he brought a tone and zest to the place it would not have had otherwise. To my knowledge this arrangement worked very well and proved to be entirely satisfactory to all concerned, including Teller himself. Twenty years later Harold Brown told me he thought Edward occasionally chafed at this particular bit. If so, I was totally unaware of it.

In brief, all of us in the laboratory held Edward in high esteem and enjoyed working with him, but some of those he was closely associated with on the outside went far beyond simple admiration. An extreme, but not unique, instance is illustrated by a conversation I had with one of the Atomic Energy Commissioners in about 1960. It took place at a cocktail party, and the commissioner had already had several drinks. He was berating scientists in general, complaining that they were paid too much and too often tried to influence policies they did not under-stand. At the end of his remarks, he added "that doesn't apply to Teller, of course." Then with great force he continued, "I don't just admire Edward, I *worship* him."

I chaired the steering committee from the start. The other core mem-bers were Harold Brown, John Foster, Gerald Johnson, Duane Sewell, and Kenneth Street, each of whom was responsible for a major element of the laboratory program.

The Staff and the Program

From the start Harold Brown headed A-Division. It was at first made up of half a dozen other physicists, all just a little older than Harold him-self, then still twenty-four. Its job was to design thermonuclear weapons based on the Teller-Ulam invention, but lighter, smaller, and in other ways more suitable for practical military applications. (The first version of this invention, Mike, is commonly said to have "weighed many tens of tons and filled a small building.")

Brown's division set about doing its work with gusto. After an early false start, it succeeded in producing a number of different designs that subsequently became major elements of the U.S. stockpile, including the first Polaris warheads. Harold went about all this as he did everything else: brilliantly, seriously, and with great dedication. During the earliest years at Livermore, he and I collaborated especially closely in developing the lab's ideas and programs, and we often argued in voices that carried well beyond the thin walls of my office. That made my secretaries very nervous and sometimes brought someone from a neighboring office in to see what was going on. Then, as always, I found working with Harold stimulating, and I think he found it stimulating to work with me too.

John S. Foster, Jr., then just twenty-nine, directed B-Division, also made up initially of half a dozen other young physicists, all roughly the same age. This division's job was to build better fission bombs—meaning, usually, physically smaller and lighter—by exploiting to the maximum the then still new boosting principle and other novel design ideas. Johnny also turned out to be a very effective group leader, ever highly supportive of those under him if they worked hard and well. He was also ambitious and not a little aggressive—always eager to expand his responsibility and authority to include other, related technical activities and always successful when given the opportunity to do so. The work of Foster's division also paid off handsomely, and many of the ideas he and his group generated opened up new horizons in weapons design and later made their way into the American nuclear stockpile.

Kenneth Street was the first head of C-Division—the chemistry section. Another recent Berkeley Ph.D., he was recommended for that job by Glenn Seaborg, chief of chemistry at the Berkeley lab. Shortly before Ken joined us, he had been seconded from Berkeley to Livermore as part of the MTA project team, so he was already accustomed to working at the site. When he came over to our project, he brought another Berkeleyan, Roger Batzel, with him as one of his principal assistants. Ken later served as acting director for a brief period after I left in 1958, and Roger served longer than anyone else as laboratory director, for a period beginning in 1971.

Michael May, another in the earliest group to come to Livermore, was not initially among the leaders of the laboratory, but he soon became one and served as laboratory director from 1965 to 1971. In its first thirty-five years the laboratory had six directors, all of whom were there in that first year. Even though six different personalities were involved, we had all started out together and continued to share the same general approach to directing this kind of institution.

Gerald W. Johnson joined us about a year after we opened shop. He had previously worked in AEC headquarters. When we started the lab, he was on the staff of the Armed Forces Special Weapons Project, a residuum of the original Manhattan Project that had remained inside the

Department of Defense. Because of his government and military experience, we put him in charge of L-Division, whose responsibility it was to
carry out the field tests—in Nevada and in the Pacific—of the various
prototypes Brown and Foster produced. Already well into his early
thirties, Jerry had just enough more maturity and experience than most
of us to make him seem especially suitable for this position, which
perforce involved a great deal of collaboration with the outside world,
especially with the military.

For safety and security reasons these tests had to be conducted in
remote places: on the Nevada Test Site, near Las Vegas, and on various
islands and atolls in the mid-Pacific. When new types of nuclear devices
were detonated, various complex observations were made in order to
determine precisely how the reactions evolved and explosions un-
folded. These observations, or diagnostic experiments, were usually
complicated and involved the assembly of large systems of measuring
apparatus at the site of the test. The job of setting up and carrying out
these experiments, and not the final assembly and detonation of the
device per se, was the heaviest consumer of laboratory manpower in
these remote places.

Jerry Johnson's appointment also turned out to be a happy one for me,
both professionally and personally. He did a great job of running our
part of the U.S. test program from the very start, and he and I have
shared a lifetime of many other fine opportunities to work—and play—
together.

From the beginning Duane Sewell managed all the technical support
activities at the laboratory, including engineering, facilities, and shops.
He had worked as an assistant to Lawrence since the late 1930s, and
he and I had known each other since our work in closely related groups
on the Calutron project during the war. He remained in essentially that
same position longer than any of the others, not relinquishing it until he
went to work in Washington during the Carter administration.

We had a harder time getting the theoretical group, T-Division, organized. Two years after we opened shop, Mark M. Mills, a fine theorist
then at Atomics International, a subsidiary of North American Aviation,
agreed to join us. He would have been my successor as director in 1958,
but he was killed on Easter of that year in a helicopter crash while
traveling on a work trip between islets at Eniwetok.

The men who ran the laboratory's chief programs and made up its
steering committee turned out to be a much more remarkable group than
we realized at the time, especially in terms of what its members did later

in their careers. Brown became a member of Jimmy Carter's cabinet, and no fewer than four others—Foster, Johnson, Sewell, and I—served several other presidents in high subcabinet posts.

The group was remarkable in another way as well: Teller aside, the average age of its members was just thirty, and except for certain modest projects set up deeply in and supported solidly by the larger laboratory structure, none had ever directed or managed any very substantial free-standing enterprise. I feel certain that no one but Ernest Lawrence would have even considered putting so much responsibility in the hands of such people. He was truly unique in his ability to spot talent, to give it just the right amount of authority and responsibility to cause it to develop swiftly and effectively, and then to summon up the courage to let it all happen. Nor, for that matter, would higher authorities—in this case the regents of the university and the AEC managers in Washington—have permitted any other laboratory director to delegate so much authority and responsibility to such an untested group. Only Lawrence's forceful personality, natural optimism, and remarkable record of success enabled him to get away with such a daring deed.

His actions in promoting and supporting us were parallel to his wartime appointment of a hosiery salesman to handle all nonscientific personnel, his naming of an astronomer and a dendrologist to handle scientific personnel, and other such seemingly incongruous but in the end fully successful actions. At the time I was dimly aware of how unusual the whole situation was; now I am always amazed when I reflect on what he did with us and how he managed to get away with it.

Lawrence, as usual, wanted to keep the use of titles to a minimum, but the laboratory's rapid growth and its need to relate in an understandable way to outside organizations forced us to adopt a reasonably orthodox pattern of organization and titles. Thus, before the first year was out, all of the people with specific responsibilities had titles such as division head, group leader, or manager, except for me. In those days, whenever I wrote a letter to officials in Washington to propose some new element of the program, to arrange for the construction of a new facility, to ask for more money, or the like and whenever I wrote to officials at Los Alamos or Sandia* to arrange for cooperation on some

---

*The Sandia Laboratory was founded in 1946 as a separate corporation to do the ordnance engineering necessary to convert a nuclear explosive device into a deliverable weapon. Sandia was established and wholly owned by Western Electric in order, as they said, to bring "telephone reliability" to the nuclear weaponry. The original unit of Sandia is in Albuquerque, less than a hundred miles from Los Alamos. In 1953 a second unit was established, adjacent to the Livermore Laboratory.

project, I simply signed the letter with my name followed only by my address: UCRL, Livermore. And whenever I traveled to Washington, as I did approximately once each month for the next six years, to negotiate programs, nuclear tests, millions of dollars, or any other major issue, Captain Hayward would repeatedly ask me, "Who is Mr. Livermore?" (or, freely translated, "Tell me again why I should be listening to you?") I would always answer, "Lawrence told me to go out there and run the place," and leave it at that.

Finally, after we were about one and a half years into the project, Lawrence, at the end of one of his weekly visits, said out of the blue, "Herb, why don't you start calling yourself the director?" As soon as he left, I told my secretary to answer the next telephone ring with the words *Director's Office* and to add the title *director* after my name on my letters. She did so, and that was that, unaccompanied by any other fanfare.

Our working philosophy, which I set out at the very beginning and which everyone readily accepted, called for always pushing at the technological extremes. We did not wait for higher government or military authorities to tell us what they wanted and only then seek to supply it. Instead, we set out from the start to construct nuclear explosive devices that had the smallest diameter, the lightest weight, the least investment in rare materials, or the highest yield-to-weight ratio or that otherwise carried the state of the art beyond the currently explored frontiers. We were completely confident that the military would find a use for our product after we proved it, and that did indeed usually turn out to be true.

In keeping with this philosophy, I at one point proposed to the AEC that we build and explode a bomb considerably bigger—over twenty megatons*—than any other built before that time. According to procedures then in effect, the president personally approved or disapproved every test. In the case of this one, I was informed that when it was presented to Eisenhower he said, "Absolutely not; they are already too big." Years later, Andrew Goodpaster, who had been President Eisenhower's military assistant, told me that it was during this period that Eisenhower concluded that "The whole thing is crazy; something simply has to be done about it."

---

*The power, or "yield," of nuclear weapons is measured in kilotons and megatons. A bomb yielding one kiloton releases approximately the same amount of energy as would one thousand tons of a nominal chemical explosive—or, more exactly, one trillion calories. A megaton is one thousand times larger.

Two specific examples of the application of my development philosophy are the Polaris warhead and the Davy Crockett device. The Polaris warhead started out simply as the lightest-weight thermonuclear warhead we could figure out how to build. After work on it was well under way, the Navy requirement for a lightweight warhead for its first submarine-launched missile, the Polaris, came along. They were a perfect match.

The Davy Crockett similarly started out as the smallest nuclear weapon of any kind that we could build. Since it was under a foot in diameter and well under one hundred pounds in weight, I was able to take a full-scale wooden model on a regular flight to Washington in a flight bag to show what we could do. The Davy Crockett application as a mortar-delivered weapon came long afterward. That notion had its ups and downs, and I later came to believe that it was not a good idea, but the basic design idea eventually found application in other small and lightweight delivery systems.

In pushing this philosophy, I had in mind two complementary benefits. First, it seemed to be the best way to assure continuing American superiority in nuclear weaponry. Second, it provided the kind of intellectual stimulus and prospect for adventure that young scientists usually find only in basic research. Thanks to our origin as a part of Lawrence's Berkeley lab, we already had a nucleus of the sort of persons who react most favorably to such a stimulus, and we wanted to keep them and attract more besides. The philosophy served both of those purposes very well.

This approach meant that the laboratory leadership had to engage in a continual effort to sell its ideas, to anticipate military requirements, and to suggest to the U.S. military ways in which its new designs could be used to enhance preparedness and better support our general nuclear strategy. If we had waited for Washington to tell us exactly what was needed in terms of dimensions, yield, special output, or other technical parameters, such selling would not have been necessary, but that is not the way we went about our business at Livermore, nor did they do things that way at Los Alamos, especially not after we brought competition onto the nuclear scene.

Some observers have criticized the laboratories for engaging in this selling activity. They charge that it pushes the nuclear arms race further and faster than would otherwise be the case. That is certainly true, but it is also true that it resulted in better weapons for the U.S. military, and better in this sense does not usually mean bigger and more destructive, as is frequently charged. Better more often means better adapted to a given delivery system, more appropriate to some specific purpose and therefore frequently smaller and producing less collateral damage, safer against accidents, and so on.

In all this lies one of the many contradictions that our nuclear security dilemma necessarily fosters. The United States cannot maintain its qualitative edge without having an aggressive R & D establishment that pushes against the technological frontiers without waiting to be asked, and that in turn means a faster-paced arms race. That is the inevitable result of our continuing quest for a qualitative edge to offset the other side's quantitative advantages. Back in 1952 when we—the government, Lawrence, Teller, and our group of young scientists—created the Livermore Laboratory, the Sino-Soviet bloc was a fresh menace, proclaiming itself to be monolithic, and apparently aggressive in its intentions. A qualitative edge in nuclear weaponry seemed to be the surest, safest, cheapest—and perhaps even the only—way to maintain the security of our country and its allies. Since then, the Sino-Soviet bloc has come asunder, but in the meantime the Soviets have built a formidable technological infrastructure on top of a huge manpower base, and the maintenance of a qualitative edge has remained a national priority.

Although the main emphasis of the laboratory program was always on nuclear weapons development, it conducted research in certain other scientifically related areas as well. From the beginning this included work in basic physics, chemistry, biology, and computer science, plus advanced development programs in a number of other areas that are based at least partly on the same fundamental science. At first these included work on controlled thermonuclear reactors (the "Sherwood Program"), on the peaceful use of nuclear explosives (the "Plowshare Program") and on two varieties of nuclear propulsion reactors, one for rockets and one for ramjets. In the following decades the first of these— the thermonuclear reactor—greatly expanded, the propulsion programs were dropped, and other areas were opened up, including, above all, laser isotope separation and the development of various types of high-energy beams for possible use as defensive weapons. These last, in turn, included particle beams, bomb-driven X-ray lasers, and free-electron lasers, or FELs, as they are commonly called, two of the prospective building blocks of Ronald Reagan's "Star Wars" scheme. In the beginning such auxiliary activities accounted for 10 to 20 percent of the budget and personnel; in later years this figure oscillated around 50 percent. My rationale for such programs always had two elements: they were intrinsically useful, and they added variety and interest to the laboratory program. The latter was of particular value both in retaining and in recruiting the kind of scientist the laboratory needed for its central program.

Lawrence at Livermore

Throughout the five years plus that I was director, Ernest Lawrence visited the laboratory once every week when he was in California. Typically, I would spend an hour telling him what we were doing and planning, and then he and I would make an extensive tour of the laboratory, visiting chemical and physical laboratory areas, the machine shops, the computer, and various other facilities. Sometimes he would also call on Brown, Foster, Sewell, or someone else to see what they were doing at the moment. He never gave me any programmatic instructions, but he made clear what parts of the program he thought were most promising and potentially valuable. Once each year I would sit in lonely glory and ponder and set the salaries of the top ten or so of my associates and then show these figures to Ernest at the next opportunity. He would then set my salary and, on rare occasions, change one or two of the others, always upward.

A major deviation from this pattern occurred in the spring of 1954. At that time our first attempt to build a new version of the superbomb resulted in a fizzle, the first such failure in U.S. testing history. (This was the "false step" I referred to earlier, in the paragraph about Brown.) The trouble with the U.S. reactor program, Fermi had earlier charged, was that no reactor ever exploded, and the trouble with the U.S. bomb program was that the bombs always did. In each case, he felt, this proved we were more cautious than necessary and proceeding more slowly than we had to. We had just taken care of one-half of his concerns. This fizzle was not, however—in terms of its details, at least—particularly educational. It had resulted from a simple design flaw that had in turn been engendered both by the novelty of the technology and by our inexperience.

An intensive review of what had happened and what had to be done next naturally took place in Livermore. During that study Ernest came out all day every day to sit in the back and listen intently to the discussion. Those who were there report that he had little to say, but they found his interest and obvious concern comforting and steadying. I was in Bikini at the time, on the other end of the Teletype line, and also busily engaged in trying to figure out what to do next. Ernest's personal support then and in the period immediately following gave us all a big lift.

Later that same year I developed an illness whose main symptom was a low-grade fever every afternoon and evening. An X-ray examination also showed swollen lymph nodes in the region of my heart. It persisted for more than two months. Senior staff frequently visited me in my home, but I was unable to go to my office during that entire period. Although I was in and out of the hospital several times, the cause was never officially pinned down. John Lawrence, Ernest's physician brother, saw me several times and concluded that I had an atypical mononucleosis, but tests designed to discover that disease never checked out positively. In mid-January 1955 I recovered suddenly, and I have never suffered a recurrence of that problem, whatever it was. During one of my stays in the hospital, Teller brought his old buddy Leo Szilard in to see me. I knew about him, of course, but I had never had the opportunity to meet him. He had recently recovered from a serious bout with cancer. His telling me about it was supposed to cheer me up, and it did.

As a result of this episode, Ernest Lawrence became concerned about my health. Himself a sufferer from chronic colitis and frequent colds and flu, he was painfully aware of how something like that might undermine my work and role at the laboratory. Moreover, I had been working hard and steadily, essentially without breaks, for several years, so some rest and recreation did seem in order. Together we worked out an arrangement for a combination business and pleasure trip for the following summer. I would visit various nuclear and research centers in Western Europe, and Sybil would accompany me so that we could both do the usual sight-seeing too. We had never been abroad before, so I spent some time studying airline timetables and the like. A line at the bottom of a page in the Pan American timetable flashed out at me. "Not everyone has been around the world," it said. The around-the-world fare it offered was only a few hundred dollars more than a round trip to and through Europe, and when would such an opportunity arise again?

The result was a trip around the world in six and a half weeks for the two of us, which Ernest paid for from a special fund he controlled through the laboratory. Nowadays such an arrangement might not be possible, given all the various university rules and IRS regulations that would apply, but it was, thank heaven, a simpler world back then. We both enjoyed the trip enormously.

I visited the major nuclear installations in Europe, including the huge Conseil Européen pour la Recherche Nucléaire (CERN), which straddles the French-Swiss border near Geneva. CERN, which eventually became the leading center for high-energy physics research in Europe, and perhaps in the entire world, had been organized only months before I arrived at the site on which all those great accelerators were one day built. More important, perhaps, Sybil and I both got our first real look at the world we live in—"the only one we've got," as my father-in-law used to remind me.

Also in 1955 Simon Ramo offered me a job as one of his principal assistants at the fledgling Ramo-Wooldridge Corporation, now TRW. (More on my earlier relations with Ramo in the next chapter.) It involved building the first generation of really big rockets, great machines then planned for use first as intercontinental missiles and later as the giant boosters needed to take man into space. The latter was something I had dreamed about since I was a boy. The salary was about double what I was making at the lab, and the offer also included a very nice stock option, which I believed—correctly—would eventually be worth a great deal. Sybil and I flew down to Los Angeles just to have supper with Si and Virginia Ramo, an act that in the mid-1950s and for people in our circumstances seemed big and bold. I could not readily resist that combination of opportunity and money, and so I told Lawrence at the next opportunity that I planned to accept the offer.

"Everything here is now in good shape," I said, "and it will continue to be so after I leave."

Ernest looked me in the eye and said, "You can't do that to me."

And indeed I couldn't. On reading his biography many years later, I learned that Lawrence himself had earlier entertained several invitations to leave Berkeley and go elsewhere, and had on occasion used them to better his position. However, I didn't know that at the time. Even if I had, I think I could not have left; the lab really was still not mature and the time not really ripe for me to depart.

Visitors from Another World

Lawrence's laboratories attracted an interesting stream of special visitors. All of them in one way or another added to the scientific life of the laboratories; some contributed in other ways as well. I particularly recall three visitors from the USSR. Given the nature of our work, their visit, though limited to Berkeley, seemed remarkable at the time.

All during the early postwar years, a resurgence of the worst features of Stalin's tyranny cut off almost all communication between Soviet citizens and the outside world. American scientists, including some who were foreign members of the Soviet Academy, tried to penetrate this "iron curtain," but to no avail. Then, in 1953, Stalin died. After a period of uncertainty, Khrushchev assumed power, and a genuine thaw in relations ensued. Gradually, a few Americans, many of them scientists, managed to visit the USSR. When they returned, they were treated with the special awe due those who had just returned from a distant and forbidden land, and they usually presented slide shows and lectured to their colleagues, students, and friends on what they had seen.

Soviet scientists also began tentative visits to the West. One of the earliest instances involved a group of physicists who came to the United States to attend the Sixth Rochester Conference on Nuclear Physics, in April 1956: Vladimir Veksler, a Nobel laureate, Moisey Markov, and A. P. Silin, all from the Lebedev Physics Institute.

Lawrence invited the three of them, plus Vasily Emelyanov, from the Soviet nuclear energy establishment, also then visiting the country, to visit Berkeley after the conference. As was his custom with distinguished visitors, Lawrence planned to entertain them at Trader Vic's in San Francisco, a restaurant widely known for its gourmet food and generous, if flamboyant, drinks. For some reason, the Washington authorities had placed San Francisco off limits to Russians. Lawrence was undaunted by such rules and placed what turned out to be a series of calls to ever higher officials in the State Department. Each time when he was told the problem couldn't be handled at the speaker's level, Lawrence asked to speak to that person's supervisor, threatening ultimately to call his good friend Vice-President Nixon. The calls finally worked their way up to someone who was able to approve the trip across the Bay Bridge to San Francisco.

As he often did, Lawrence included me in this expedition to Trader Vic's. For security reasons, I was not permitted to go to Russia myself, so the whole affair had something of the attractiveness of forbidden fruit for me. Coming off the bridge on the San Francisco side of the bay, we had to swerve suddenly to avoid a collision with another car. One of the Soviets (Veksler?) made a brief comment in a low voice. I asked the interpreter (Professor John Turkevich, a Princeton chemist) what he had said. "Woman driver!" was the answer. "The world is the same everywhere" was the not so profound thought that passed through my mind.

Trader Vic's seemed to both titillate and baffle our guests. They were used to alcohol, all right, but not served in a coconut shell and with a gardenia floating on top. I can't remember any details of the conversation, but I do recall being impressed by the fact that they were not, after all, very different from us. The next time I would meet a Soviet, the strangeness and distance would not create as high a barrier as it had that first time, and it would be easier to get down to substance. It was therefore a very useful meeting from my point of view.

Three of these Soviets, Emelyanov, Markov, and Silin, later became active in the Pugwash movement at about the same time I did, and I eventually met each of them again on a number of interesting occasions. Of the three only Silin was overtly doctrinaire. On one later occasion, when an American colleague was bemoaning the fact that "young people these days lack a sense of goals," Silin replied, "That's not so with us. Our young people are all devoted to the goal of building communism."

First Peek at a New Dimension

Throughout this period my attention was focused almost exclusively on reinforcing our military preparedness, particularly in its nuclear dimension. The only exception came as a result of the involvement of Lawrence, Teller, and Mark Mills as advisers to Harold Stassen, then Eisenhower's special assistant for disarmament.

Eisenhower, as I later learned from close up, had long been concerned about the nuclear arms race and where it was leading us. As a result, soon after he became president, he invited Harold Stassen, formerly governor of Minnesota and a perennial candidate for the Republican presidential nomination, to examine various possible ideas for containing it. Most of the ideas, including a cut-off of nuclear production and a ban on further weapons tests, had been in the air for some time. Eisenhower and Stassen felt that the whole matter, including the vexing question of monitoring compliance, needed to be reexamined by experts, and Lawrence, with the help of Teller and Mills, was invited to do so.

As the review proceeded, I had many opportunities to discuss it privately with each of my three colleagues. In general, Ernest and Mark were pessimistic about the possibility of doing very much but seemed willing to consider it. Edward was always unabashedly hostile to the whole idea. If we were behind, we had to test to catch up, he said; and if we were ahead, we had to test to stay there. There was no circumstance under which a test ban could be in our interest. Then, as now,

Teller felt that the only way to maintain our qualitative advantage—if indeed we still had one—was by charging full speed ahead, not by protecting our secrets with rules about classification, and he was always honest and open about that view. To be sure, I too did not then see any political or strategic benefits in banning nuclear tests, but I did already feel there might be some benefit in mutual restraints of some kind, and I said so on occasion.

This is a slightly different aspect of the contradiction mentioned earlier. It is simply not possible to put together a large team of scientists that would, on the one hand, assure the United States the technological edge that then, as later, was regarded as essential to counterbalance the Soviets' quantitative advantages and that would not, on the other hand, have a substantial number of its members actively, forthrightly, and honestly oppose any political action designed to inhibit them in going about the job of fulfilling that need. Higher authorities have to be ready and able to overrule such opposition; they cannot simply repress it or hope to convert it.

A stark example of how this works arose in the spring of 1957. In June of that year Eisenhower told a press conference that he was considering the possibility of a test ban, partly as a means for cooling the arms race, partly because of public concern about the radioactive fallout that tests produced. By chance, Lawrence, Teller, and Mills were in Washington meeting with Senator Henry M. Jackson, a strong opponent of any negotiations that might place restraints on our nuclear program. Jackson and Lewis Strauss, the AEC chairman, were concerned about where Eisenhower might be headed, so they arranged to have the three scientists meet with the president and tell him about their ideas for future tests. They explained we were on the verge of perfecting a "clean bomb"—that is, a bomb that would produce substantially less radioactivity—and they urged that testing be continued in order to accomplish it. Moreover, they said, by conducting future testing underground, we could do away with the problems produced by fallout. A few days later, at a second press conference, Eisenhower referred to these "important new possibilities" and drew back from his earlier expression of interest in a possible test ban.[6]

Later that same year, on October 4, 1957, the Soviets launched Sputnik, the first artificial satellite. Given my long interest in space flight, I became at least as excited about it as everyone else. And, like most other leaders of high-tech institutions, I used the climate it created to argue for increased support for our program. When General Fields, by then promoted to general manager of the AEC, visited Livermore soon after Sputnik, I played a recording of its radio signal as background music while I made my pitch.

I didn't know it at the time, but Sputnik would soon bring about my departure from the Livermore Laboratory. Except for my brief flirtation with Simon Ramo in 1955, I had not thought about leaving or otherwise considered my long-range future, but all that was about to change once again. Before going into that, though, I will first take up a different, and broader, aspect of my life as director of the Livermore Laboratory.

CHAPTER 5

John von Neumann and Other Martians

(1953–1957)

The Advisory Structure

THE SAME, crucial events that had brought about the development of the H-bomb and the establishment of the Livermore Laboratory—the first Soviet A-bomb test, the proclamation of the monolithic Sino-Soviet bloc, and the Korean War—also stimulated wide-ranging efforts to review and rethink where America stood in other areas of military technology. On top of all that, information about the existence of major Soviet R & D programs in long-range aviation and long-range rocketry began to surface. By modern standards, most of this information was vague and uncertain, but it nevertheless served to reinforce interest in certain technologies, especially those relating to air defense, intelligence gathering, and long-range nuclear delivery vehicles.

The reviews and studies that flowed from these new concerns and perceptions were beyond the capability of the existing institutions. In some cases ad hoc groups had to be created to carry them out. In others existing institutions, such as the Air Force Science Advisory Board, were expanded and their charters broadened.

The election of Dwight D. Eisenhower in 1952 brought further changes into this already fluid situation. It was the first real change in national administration in twenty years, and a thoroughgoing review of the national military posture would have been likely even without such special stimuli. In the Defense Department the military authorities produced the "new look" study, and the new civilians worked out a far-reaching reorganizational plan. John Foster Dulles, the new secretary of state, unveiled the doctrine of "massive retaliation." Taken together, these ideas and actions added up to a change in U.S. military posture designed to avoid further Koreas.

In Korea, it seemed, the enemy had chosen the time, the place, and the means of fighting, and as our authorities saw it, all of these choices had been to his advantage. In the future, whatever aggression he might commit, we would respond in a place and with a means of *our* choosing, means that would make optimal use of our strongest suit, high technology, rather than his, then taken to be raw manpower. As if all those stimuli were not enough, the successful detonation of the first, and seemingly revolutionary, superbomb—Mike—only days before Eisenhower's election reinforced both the idea that technology could provide us with the answer to our security problems and the idea that a thorough rethinking of how to go about exploiting it was needed.

Given my position as head of one of America's two nuclear labs, it was natural that I would be drawn into the broader process of rethinking the U.S. approach to national security. The first instance was an invitation to join the Air Force Science Advisory Board and its newly formed Nuclear Panel. Eventually, I would serve on literally dozens of ad hoc and standing committees dealing with various elements of the problem.

Writing and reading about committees can be a bit of a bore. Not for naught was it once said, "A camel is a horse designed by a committee." Even so, it was my good fortune in the 1950s to serve on a succession of committees chaired by exceptionally brilliant and influential men, committees that would have profound effects on the course of events as well as on the development of my own career.

Participation in these committees led to a remarkable and important synergism. I and leaders of other laboratories—both nonprofit and industrial—brought to them fresh information about what we were doing and reliable projections of where it might lead. In return we developed an understanding of the likely characteristics of future military requirements that was far more accurate and timely than it would otherwise have been. Equally important, we also acquired a firsthand working knowledge of the doctrines and strategies underlying our development and procurement plans, a knowledge we could have obtained no other way, a knowledge each of us used to guide the programs for which we were responsible. This two-way flow of information and ideas could, in theory, have taken place without the committee structure, but in that case the many horizontal layers within government units, and the vertical barriers between different units, would have required years to penetrate, and even then what finally came through would have been greatly attenuated.

The upside of this arrangement is that it helps assure the continuation of our technological edge over the Soviets. The downside is that it makes it possible for the most exuberant and persuasive of our technologists to promote ideas and sell hardware that often take us far beyond the point that mere prudence requires.

Von Kármán and the Air Force Science Advisory Board

I was invited to join the Air Force Science Advisory Board, or SAB, in the spring of 1953, toward the end of my first year at Livermore. My initial assignment was to serve as a member of its newly formed Nuclear Panel.

The SAB itself had been created in 1944. It grew out of both a recognition of the Air Force's need for scientific advice and a long-standing special relationship between General H. H. Arnold, then chief of the Army Air Force, and Theodore von Kármán, the man who would serve as its first chairman.

Von Kármán was another of the remarkable Hungarians who wielded so much influence over American high technology in the postwar period. Born in 1881, von Kármán was a generation older than the other four. He served as science adviser to the Austro-Hungarian air force, such as it was, during World War I. After the collapse of the Central Powers, he served briefly as under secretary of education in the Hungarian Communist (Béla Kun) regime that followed. When that regime fell as suddenly as it rose, he played it safe and returned to Aachen, Germany, where he had previously held a professorship.[1] There he pursued research on gliders and unwittingly helped lay the foundation of the *Luftwaffe,* the German air force of World War II. Junkers, Heinkel, and

Fokker, all German aircraft developers, were among his friends and associates.

In the late 1930s von Kármán moved to Caltech, where he trained many of the early aerodynamicists and aeronautical engineers who made the southern California aircraft industry possible. He founded both the Jet Propulsion Laboratory and the Aerojet General Corporation, one of the giants of the aerospace industry. On one occasion, when I told Teller I had heard a rumor that he and the others were not Hungarians but Martians, he immediately replied, "Kármán must have talked."

Even before World War II von Kármán's research in aerodynamics and rockets brought him into close contact with Henry H. Arnold, then a relatively young Army Air Corps officer stationed at March Field, in nearby Riverside, California. The two men took an early liking to each other, and when years later Arnold, then chief of the air staff, decided he needed organized scientific advice, it was natural for him to turn to von Kármán for help. Together, they established the Scientific Advisory Board, which held its first meeting on June 17, 1946.

Shortly after I joined the SAB, von Kármán—already seventy-two years old—resigned as chairman. Even so, I continued to see and work with him on other projects for more than another ten years, until he was well into his eighties.

Lieutenant General James H. Doolittle, USAF ret., succeeded von Kármán as chairman after a brief interregnum. Doolittle had earned a Ph.D. in aeronautical engineering from MIT, had been a pioneering test pilot, and was a genuine war hero. (On April 18, 1942, four months after Pearl Harbor, he led the first bombing raid on Tokyo.)

Doolittle was also a close personal adviser to the Air Force chief of staff, and he had a small office that gave him easy direct, personal contact with the chief. On one of our first meetings, when I was exploring the need for a second weapons laboratory, he explained that the important thing in Washington was not how big your office was but whom it was close to. I have always remembered that comment, and I add on the basis of my own experience that it is not whom the line on the organization chart says you report to, but how often you see him and how easily you relate to him. Jimmy carried much more weight in Air Force affairs after he retired than the titles he held would indicate, and the reasons, as is usual in such cases, were his reliability and his credibility, as those in power gauged them.

John von Neumann

When I joined the Air Force SAB in 1953, John von Neumann, another of the Hungarians, was chairman of its Nuclear Panel. Other smart people commonly said that John von Neumann was the smartest person they had ever known. Although I worked with him for only five years—1952–57, and even then on just an occasional basis—I came to know him well enough to feel the same way. His accomplishments generally confirmed this view; he developed the first complete, fully rigorous mathematical theory of the new quantum mechanics in the mid-1920s, he did original work in economic theory at about the same time, he founded game theory, and he invented the "von Neumann architecture," which underlies all modern digital computers.

Oddly enough, perhaps, although I frequently discussed strategic issues with him, I never once heard him use any of the jargon that game theorists and operations analysts are wont to use—"zero sum game," "prisoners' dilemma," and the like—nor did he ever seem to use such specialized notions in his own thinking about strategy. In discussing strategy with me, he always employed the same vocabulary and concepts and made the same connections as those that were common in the quality public press at the time. To be sure, he usually expressed his ideas more clearly than most other politically alert people did, but he did not couch them in a different language and they never seemed to me to involve different underlying theories or principles.

Von Neumann was pleasant and plump, smiled easily and often, and enjoyed parties and other social events. He practically always dressed formally, wearing a three-piece business suit and tie even in the warmest weather and, on one notorious occasion, even while riding muleback down into the Grand Canyon. His home base since the thirties had been the Institute of Advanced Study in Princeton. He was an active consultant at many public and private institutions, including Los Alamos, where he had spent the war years.

Johnny followed the events taking place in Europe and Asia closely. By the end of the 1940s, he had become very pessimistic about what they portended. In late 1951, in a letter to Lewis Strauss, Johnny wrote, "I think that the US-USSR conflict will very probably lead to an armed 'total collision' and that a maximum rate of armament is, therefore, imperative."[2]

In the early 1950s, as the studies of the proper role of high technology in the U.S. defense program intensified, Johnny became a member of both the Air Force's SAB and the Atomic Energy Commission's GAC. In those two positions he served as a superb channel for the transmission of ideas, plans, and hopes between the two organizations.

He liked high-ranking military officers and got along very well with them. If anyone during that crucial period in the early and middle-fifties can be said to have enjoyed more "credibility" in national defense circles than all the others, that person was surely Johnny. Both Jimmy Doolittle and General Bernard A. Schriever, at that time deputy chief for advance planning, made it clear to me that it was Johnny's personal projections about the future of thermonuclear weapons, and no other individual or institutional source, that first convinced them of the new possibilities and caused the Air Force to initiate the actions that eventually led to a high-priority program to build intercontinental ballistic missiles.

I had met and talked with Johnny several times during 1952 in connection with establishing the Livermore Laboratory. Therefore, when in 1953 he was asked to organize the SAB's new Nuclear Panel, created specifically to deal with the flood of ideas following the successful test of Mike, the first superbomb, it was natural for him to invite me to join it.

The SAB Nuclear Panel

The immediate purpose of the Nuclear Panel* was to assess the nuclear situation, particularly with regard to the new thermonuclear weapons. Even though the first truly practical version of a hydrogen bomb had not yet been built and tested, our panel was entirely confident that such bombs would be successful. In our final report we said that twenty megatons seemed like a "quite conservative" estimate for the maximum power of the largest bomb that could be accommodated by a B-52, a bomb then assumed to weigh between thirty thousand and fifty thousand pounds. And in the case of the lighter and smaller bombs in the "one- to two-megaton class" that the panel believed would be useful as warheads for long-range missiles, we opined, "We will get these weapons to weigh three thousand pounds, and probably even somewhat less."

*In addition to von Neumann, the panel included Hans Bethe, who had been the wartime head of theoretical physics at Los Alamos; three persons from the current staffs of the laboratories, Norris Bradbury, Edward Teller, and me; two persons from the technical staff of the Rand Corporation, David Griggs and L. Eugene Root; and one scientist from the Pentagon staff, Herbert ("Pete") Scoville.

After noting that the current Air Force requirements for "the long-range missile (Atlas) are a payload of three thousand pounds" and an accuracy of "fifteen hundred feet at the target," we went on to assert that "these two qualifications do not belong together," because a two-megaton bomb has a "significant destruction radius of 3.2 to 4.5 miles, probably the latter." Our report concluded by saying, "One or the other, perhaps both of these requirements should be relaxed in order to strike an optimum compromise." This is just what eventually happened. The exact values of these two parameters were not finally set until another year had passed and two more committees, both chaired by von Neumann, had had a hand in massaging the program plan, but eventually the payload was reduced to fifteen hundred pounds—enough for a yield of one megaton, we thought—and the accuracy was relaxed to two miles.

These paired changes in the requirements turned out to be more critical than we could know at the time or than a reader would guess so long after the fact. If the original requirement for a three-thousand-pound payload had not been cut in half, the rocket necessary to loft it would have had to be twice as heavy as the Atlas and Titan missiles we actually built and correspondingly more expensive. More important, the time to achieve such missiles would have been a year or two longer than it actually was. That, in turn, would have meant that the missile gap furor of the late fifties would have been more intense and the overreaction to it more serious than these actually turned out to be.

The same can be said of the accuracy requirement. If the fifteen-hundred-foot requirement ever made sense, it was in the earlier situation in which such missiles were supposed to deliver Hiroshima-type weapons, not the superbombs that we all were so sure were coming soon. More important, the technology of the time could not have provided such high accuracy; indeed, another twenty years passed before precision like that became possible in a fielded missile. Sticking with this outdated requirement would also have brought about further delays in getting the missiles built, and along with that would have come the unknown but probably bad consequences of those delays.

At the full SAB board meeting the following March, von Neumann, speaking extemporaneously, brought out the fact that another, more subtle revolution in nuclear weaponry was also under way:

> In addition to the extensive technological development which took place during these past eight years, there has also been a complete change in the underlying economic-political-strategic position: nuclear weapons are no longer expensive, they are no longer scarce, and they are no longer a

monopoly of the US. These things are known, but they still need to be repeated—I do not think that our thinking has assimilated them to the extent to which it should. . . . In other words, one must no longer consider the nuclear component as the hardest part of the problems involved in the weapons systems of which they form part—they are now among the least difficult and most flexible parts of such systems.[3]

The loss of the monopoly was obvious in 1949, and that the introduction of the superbomb would lead to great changes was also clear enough in 1953, but the transition from extreme scarcity to relative plenty was neither easy to recognize in the first instance nor easy to deal with after it was recognized. During the war, when we had yet to make the first bomb, and then for the next ten years, while the stockpile built up very slowly and secretly, we had, as Johnny said, become totally accustomed to thinking of bombs as being extremely scarce and extremely expensive. In the early fifties that situation was beginning to change, but we didn't recognize that reality at first; when we did, it indeed took an effort to assimilate it into our thinking.

Confirmation of this same situation is found in some retrospective remarks Hans Bethe made forty years after Hiroshima. "Nobody at Los Alamos," he said, "would have dreamed of ten thousand atomic weapons."[4]

A few weeks after the Nagasaki bombing, there was enough material for another bomb. Since it wasn't needed for the war, I presume it went into the stockpile as unit no. 1. Somewhere around the time Johnny addressed the SAB, back in 1954, the U.S. stockpile passed the one thousand mark. But in 1985, when Bethe spoke those words, we had more than twenty-five thousand of them, the majority of which were much more powerful than those first two. In trying to assess or understand so long afterward how we thought about nuclear weapons in those early days, it is necessary to bear in mind that none of us then "dreamed of ten thousand" of them. We thought of them as very rare, very expensive, special-purpose instruments—not at all as the widely available, general-purpose weapons they later became in the minds of many analysts and, unhappily, in the view of some officials as well.

The Strategic Missile Evaluation Committee

Trevor Gardner, assistant secretary of the Air Force for R & D, was a critical part of the Eisenhower administration's "new look" at, and reorganization of, our defense posture. Bright, brash, aggressive, and relatively young for the post, he was brought in specifically to stir things up, and he did.

Even while von Neumann was still in the midst of the above-mentioned review of nuclear explosives, Gardner invited him to head yet another study to review and evaluate all of our plans and programs for the development of the missiles intended to deliver those nuclear weapons. The ad hoc committee set up to do so was called the Strategic Missile Evaluation Committee, or SMEC. Except for von Neumann himself, there was at first no overlap with the membership of the SAB Nuclear Panel.

The SMEC published its recommendations in a report dated February 10, 1954, still three weeks before the first tests of fully practical versions of the superbomb, but based on a full confidence in their successful outcome. The technical conclusions concerning reducing payload and relaxing accuracy were, in essence, the same as those of the SAB Nuclear Panel. In addition, the SMEC urged that further study be given to the vulnerability of bases, readiness of missiles, and quick response.[5] The report includes a statement, carefully crafted by von Neumann personally, giving his reasons for approaching this matter with "unusual urgency":

> Unusual urgency for a strategic missile capability can arise from one or two principal causes: a rapid strengthening of the Soviet defenses against our SAC manned bombers, or rapid progress by the Soviet in his own development of strategic missiles which can provide a compelling political and psychological reason for our own effort to proceed apace. The former is to be expected during the second half of this decade. As to the latter, the available intelligence data are insufficient to make possible a precise estimate of the progress being made by the Soviets in the development of intercontinental missiles, but evidence exists of an appreciation of this field on the part of the Soviet, and of activity in some phases of guided missiles which it is natural to connect with the objective development by the Soviet of intercontinental missiles. Thus, while the evidence may not justify a positive conclusion that the Russians are ahead of us, a grave concern in this regard is in order.

There can be little doubt that Johnny knew everything that could be known about the Soviet program. What intelligence we had came mainly from German missile technicians who had been captured at Peenemünde in 1945, taken to Russia as war booty, and allowed to return to Germany a few at a time beginning in about 1951. In addition, there were some high-level defections from the Soviet program, the best-known being Colonel Grigory Tokaty-Tokaev.[6]

The available information was indeed sparse and ambiguous, compared with what we later became accustomed to, but it was obviously enough to enable von Neumann and others to arrive at the correct conclusion. The Russians were, as von Neumann and others suspected, somewhat ahead of us, and even though we instituted a "highest priority" program soon after the SMEC submitted its report, the Soviets did indeed succeed in launching an intercontinental-range ballistic missile about one year before we did. In later years we so often beat the Russians to the punch in high-technology accomplishments that it became easy to forget that they did for a time pace us in the development of large rockets and long-range ballistic missiles.

All this points up another of the many paradoxes we meet in dealing with the nuclear confrontation.

On the one hand, von Neumann's conclusion that we should be "gravely concerned" about the possibility that the Russians were ahead of us is a good example of what is called worst-case analysis. As he himself says, "the evidence may not justify a positive conclusion." The historical record clearly shows that analyses of that kind have on many occasions driven us to take actions and build weapons we didn't need, in order to be absolutely certain we would be safe rather than sorry, and as a result the pace of the nuclear arms race has been substantially faster than common sense and ordinary prudence required.

On the other hand, in this case Johnny was right: had we brooked further long delays in getting ourselves moving in this area, the Russian lead would have been greater, and the missile gap furor of the late 1950s and the relatively modest excesses that flowed from it would both have been much worse.

Turning to the matter of organization, the committee said, "[I]t is the conviction of the committee that a radical reorganization of the IBMS [*sic*] project considerably transcending the Convair framework is required if a militarily useful vehicle is to be built in a reasonable span of time."*

This last radical conviction corresponded very closely with views already independently held by Trevor Gardner and some key senior Air Force officers. The eventual result, after some additional months of shoving and hauling, was the establishment of a three-element organi-

---

*A relatively modest program to develop a ballistic missile of intercontinental range had been under way at the Convair Corporation in San Diego for several years. Called the Atlas, it had never enjoyed a particularly high priority with the Air Force and, for this and other reasons, had not progressed very far.

zational structure to run the Atlas ICBM program. One element was a special, new Air Force unit, the Western Development Division, commanded by Brigadier General Bernard A. Schriever. The second element was a project division within the brand-new Ramo-Wooldridge Corporation to work directly with the Air Force in providing systems engineering and technical direction for the entire project. (It was this second organization that Si Ramo invited me to join toward the end of its first year.) The third was another new and expanded von Neumann committee; this time I and some of the other SAB Nuclear Panel members were added to it.

The Scientific Advisory Committee on Ballistic Missiles

The expanded and renamed von Neumann committee met for the first time on July 20–21, 1954, in an abandoned church school on Manchester Boulevard in Inglewood, California. The main purpose of the meeting was to nail down all these changes in goals and organization as quickly and firmly as possible.*

In addition to the regular members of the committee, Assistant Secretary of Defense Donald Quarles, Assistant Secretary of the Air Force Trevor Gardner, General Schriever, Simon Ramo, and, for a brief period, representatives of the Convair Corporation were also present.

Such a mix of government, industrial, and academic people present at that meeting, combined with its subject matter—especially the question of how to organize the project—would have been impossible in later years because of the obvious potential conflicts of interest among the parties. At that time, though, there was a feeling of real urgency, the situation was full of unexplored novelties, and an extraordinary approach to such questions seemed justified so long as it promised to be the best way to get the right answers. Even in retrospect, I still regard the way we went about deciding these issues as both necessary and proper at that time.

In addition to redesigning and reorganizing the Atlas program, our

---

*The members included Jerome Wiesner and George Kistiakowsky, both of whom were later special assistants to presidents of the United States; Charles Lindbergh, the hero of the first transatlantic flight; Charles Lauritsen and Clark Millikan, both Caltech professors and longtime close associates of von Kármán (and Millikan also the son of the founder of the institute); Darol Froman, deputy director of Los Alamos, acting for Norris Bradbury; Frank Colbohm, founder and president of the Rand Corporation; Lawrence ("Pat") Hyland, then president of the Bendix Aviation Company, and soon to be president of Hughes Aircraft; Hendrick Bode of the Bell Laboratories; and me.

expanded committee in its next several meetings helped set in motion a second ICBM, the Titan, and called for the establishment of a complete set of alternative sources for all of its major components. Moreover, it successfully urged the president to give each of these development programs "the highest national priority second to no other."

We also periodically reviewed the several long-range cruise missile programs then under way (the supersonic Navajo and the subsonic Snark) as well as various missiles of intermediate range (Thor, Jupiter, and Polaris) and made recommendations with respect to all of them.*

In the spring of 1955, about the time the third von Neumann panel had finally managed to get almost all the main elements of the U.S. strategic missile programs in hand and only six months after he had been appointed one of the five atomic energy commissioners, it was discovered that Johnny had cancer. For a while, he was determined to continue his role in the work of the committee, and the Air Force authorities were at least as anxious for him to do so.

I recall several more meetings of the committee in which, after the rest of us were present and seated, Johnny arrived in a wheelchair propelled by a military aide. At first he seemed his normal self, smiling and cheerful, and the meetings proceeded in the customary way with Johnny dominating them intellectually, without being at all argumentative or overtly domineering.

Later, when he came to see that his condition was hopeless, he grew more despairing and turned back to the Roman Catholic church for solace. The son of a wealthy Hungarian Jewish banker, he had attended Lutheran high school and had then become a Catholic in connection with his first marriage. For most of his life he ignored religion, but now he returned to it. During that final period, I paid a last visit to Johnny. I went to Walter Reed Hospital with Lewis Strauss, then chairman of the AEC and a frequent companion to Johnny in his last days. Johnny was in a bed with high, criblike sides intended to keep him from falling out or otherwise getting up on his own. I tried to start a conversation about some technical topic I thought would interest and divert him, but he would say no more than a simple hello before turning to Strauss to

---

*Other groups were also active in studying these same questions. The most important, in terms both of its status and its effect on the program, was the Technological Capabilities Panel (TCP), chaired by James R. Killian, Jr., president of MIT, and set up as an ad hoc element of the White House advisory apparatus. In areas where the work overlapped, the recommendations of the two committees were essentially the same. In addition, both the U-2 and the reconnaissance satellite programs owe their origins largely to recommendations by the TCP.

discuss some detail of his will. I left the room after only a few, brief minutes.

Some weeks later I attended Johnny's funeral mass. Many dignitaries, fellow scientists, and mutual friends were there. I recall driving away in a crowded car with Norris Bradbury and others from the nuclear weapons world. At one point Norris turned to me and said, "If Johnny is where he thought he was going, there must be some very interesting conversations going on about now."

The passing of von Neumann marked the end of an era. In my more than thirty years of further intimate connections with the Department of Defense, I never again saw an advisory committee composed of part-time outsiders that enjoyed such high credibility and exercised such decisive influence as those chaired by von Kármán in the 1940s and by von Neumann in the 1950s. Later there were situations of that kind in the White House—the next chapter describes one such: Killian's PSAC—but never again to my knowledge in the Defense Department.

The Gaither Panel

On April 4, 1957, Eisenhower's National Security Council created another ad hoc group to study the rapidly changing defense scene. Officially called the Security Resources Panel, it is better known by the name of its first chairman, Rowan Gaither, a San Francisco attorney and good friend of Ernest Lawrence, who had a longtime interest in nuclear matters. Its main assignment was to study both active and passive means for protecting the civil population. In addition, it was asked to consider the deterrent value of our retaliatory forces, and the economic and political consequences of any major shift in our defense programs.*

It proved to be a hot summer in more ways than one. On August 7 the Soviets succeeded in making the first launch anywhere of a rocket with

*When Gaither became mortally ill, Robert Sprague, a Massachusetts industrialist, became chairman, but the committee has always been known by the name of its first chairman. The panel was unusually large and had a correspondingly complex structure. There was a steering committee of eight members, including Jerome Wiesner of MIT and the von Neumann committees; an advisory panel of nine members, including my boss Ernest Lawrence and Jimmy Doolittle; and a committee made up of special representatives from the White House Science Advisory Committee, including I. I. Rabi and James Killian. In addition to these high-level groups, there were some sixty-seven "project members," including me and a number of others with whom I later worked in a variety of guises—the most important being Richard Bissell of the CIA, Spurgeon Keeny of the Defense Department, and Paul Nitze of the State Department.

intercontinental range, from Tyuratam all the way across Siberia. On October 4 Sputnik went up. On November 7 the committee's final report was issued.

The report presented what can only be called an alarmist view of the situation. In effect, it urged a much more aggressive approach to the construction of both passive and active defenses, and it called for a speedup in the acquisition of offensive forces as well.

Eisenhower didn't like the tone of the report and didn't agree with its conclusions. The fact that it came out amid the furor over Sputnik only made things worse. Senator Lyndon Johnson and other congressional leaders demanded that it be made public in connection with their reviews of why Sputnik had happened and what it portended. Eisenhower claimed that it was a matter of executive privilege, and he refused to hand the report over. An extended political scuffle followed, but Eisenhower stood his ground.

When invited to become a project member, I was at first reluctant to do so. Sybil and I were planning a trip to Mexico that summer. It would be the first real vacation since our trip around the world two years earlier. As a special lure, one of the organizers of the panel offered to get us tickets to two major musicals playing in New York that summer. Frank Stanton, one of the members of the advisory panel, was president of CBS, and CBS owned the musicals, so it was easy to arrange. The upshot was a pair of front-row center seats at performances of *My Fair Lady* and *Damn Yankees,* no vacation in Mexico, and several weeks of intense work that summer in the Executive Office Building, next door to the White House.

My principal substantive recollection involves my working with Jerry Wiesner on the question of how many ICBMs the USSR could produce in the immediate future. The issue was both real and hot. We took the best data there were on the Soviet rocket development program, combined them with what we could learn about the availability of factory floor space needed for such an enterprise, and concluded that they could produce thousands in the next few years.

That estimate was quite wrong. I don't know what role it played in setting the tone of the final Gaither report. I recall discussing the matter with Robert Sprague, and I don't remember his arguing with our views. The problem was simple enough. Although I did by then know a fair amount about the American rocket programs and the American aerospace industry and its capabilities, I knew only a little about the Soviet missile development program and nothing at all about Soviet industry. In making this estimate, I was thus combining two dubious analytical procedures: worst-case analysis and mirror imaging. My alibi is that I was new to the subject and that, like the rest of the panel, I was an easy victim of the extreme degree of secrecy the Russians have always used to conceal what they are doing and, just as important, what they are not doing.

In any event, the final report of the panel did not mention such numbers, nor did it refer directly to either the August ICBM or the October Sputnik. It simply asserted, "The USSR will achieve a significant ICBM delivery capability with megaton warheads by 1959." It added, "The next two years seem to us critical. If we fail to act at once, the risk, in our opinion, will be unacceptable."[7]

Despite Sputnik, the president did not carry out any of the main recommendations of the report except for one or two involving things that were already under way. And "unacceptable" risk to the contrary, nothing happened.

My membership on these committees provided me my first opportunity for meeting most of the other members. In the future I would have further opportunities to work closely with many of them on other projects—including Killian, Kistiakowsky, and Wiesner. For all of us these committees served as an effective springboard to other interesting events and relationships. It proved to be an especially good way for me to learn more about both defense technology in particular and national security issues in general, and what I learned there gave me a big head start when I later took on full-time responsibilities in the White House and the upper echelons of the defense establishment. I also got my first lessons in how to assess "the threat" and, to a lesser degree, how *not* to assess it.

Most important of all for me was my meeting James R. Killian, Jr., who in just a few months would bring about the biggest change in my life since I had gone to work for Lawrence in Berkeley fourteen years earlier.

CHAPTER 6

Eisenhower and His "Wizards"

(1957–1961)

Sputnik

ON OCTOBER 4, 1957, the Soviets launched what they proudly called the "the first-in-the-world artificial satellite of the earth," or *Sputnik I,* for short. Weighing 184 pounds and measuring twenty-three inches in diameter, it contained two radio transmitters that broadcast a steady "beep, beep, beep" that could be picked up easily by radio receivers all over the world. This achievement greatly surprised and profoundly shocked almost everyone in the West, from chiefs of state on down. In its wake it brought about deeper and more far-reaching changes in American government programs and organizational arrangements than any other single peacetime event in modern history. And on a personal level the launching of Sputnik led to profound changes in my life and career and brought me into intimate contact with a group of men whose views about the world in general and national security in particular were considerably broader and more complex than those of the people I had previously been close to.

In America and Europe the initial surprise was quickly followed by a wave of apprehension. Newsmen, television commentators, the man in the street, and a variety of instant experts from many walks of life all expressed dismay that the "backward Russians" had beaten the United States to what was universally seen as one of the most spectacular and portentous technological achievements of all time. Most informed people realized that Sputnik itself was not a direct threat, but they did believe—and rightly so—that it meant the Russians were on the verge of producing long-range nuclear-tipped missiles, and perhaps other weapons, that would for the first time bring our cities and our civilization under the threat of nuclear bombardment.

Sputnik II was launched on November 3. It carried a dog, named Laika, into orbit and weighed in at an incredible 1,120 pounds. Our own Vanguard satellite, long anticipated but yet to be launched, was not only still merely a future hope but was projected to weigh only 3.5 pounds! Many people, including some scientists and engineers who should have known better, came to believe that the Soviets knew some "secret" about rocket propulsion that still eluded us, and even that Russian science in general was about to surpass American science.

Those who knew the facts about the American missile and satellite programs were not as surprised in the literal sense as the general public was, but most of them were every bit as dismayed. Herbert Scoville, deputy director of the CIA, made a speech before an open scientific meeting on October 4 in which he said the "Soviets could launch a satellite this month, this week, or even today."[1] Nevertheless, when he learned only hours later that it had actually happened that very day, he was as dumbfounded as the rest of us.

The roots of this situation reach back to the 1930s. At that time both the United States and the Soviet Union had very modest programs whose objective was to develop small liquid propellant rockets for military and other purposes. In marked contrast, the Germans were already pushing ahead with a major effort to produce a rocket weapon capable of carrying out some of the functions of military aircraft, the latter being forbidden to them by the Treaty of Versailles. In those and other countries small, organized groups of enthusiasts dreamed about the day when rocket-propelled spacecraft would become a reality. However, it was only after the Germans actually employed the V-2 rocket as a terror weapon during the waning days of World War II that the government of either of today's superpowers took large, long-range rockets seriously.

When Germany collapsed, the top leadership of the project, which was based at Peenemünde, in northeast Germany, managed to make its way west to surrender to the Americans. The Red Army overran the main facility and captured some thousands of lower-level engineers and technicians who had been left behind. The Soviet government decided—unknown to us at the time—immediately to push ahead with the development of large rockets capable of hurling nuclear or other large warheads over intercontinental distances. We, on the other hand, largely demobilized the great military technology establishment we had created during the war. We did not initiate a large-scale program to develop long-range ballistic missiles until 1954, several years after the Korean War had brought about a partial remobilization of American technology and even then only after we had become aware of the Soviet program through occasional Soviet defectors and German returnees. Nevertheless, because of our generally larger and superior technological base, we had been able to reduce the multiyear gap in program initiation to only about one year by the time Sputnik was launched. The result was that the Soviets made their first test launch of an intercontinental ballistic missile (ICBM) in August 1957 and that we made our corresponding first launch in August 1958.*

The first satellites owed their origin to a worldwide cooperative scientific program, called the International Geophysical Year (IGY) and scheduled for 1957–58. When plans for this program of international scientific activities were being developed, scientists in both countries were generally aware of the military rocket developments then under way, and in 1954 it was recommended that an attempt be made to launch a scientific satellite as part of the overall program. In 1955 a decision to do so was made at the highest levels of government in both the United States and the Soviet Union, but the paths chosen were very different in the two cases.

The Soviets chose to combine their scientific program with their military long-range missile program, and they thus used the same rocket booster for each of these two different ends. Between the initiation of the program and the actual launching of Sputnik I, the Soviets made half a dozen public statements to the effect that they would soon launch a

*The range of this flight was twenty-five hundred nautical miles. Not until December did we achieve truly intercontinental distances.

satellite. However, only those people who were interested in this sort of thing noticed these straightforward but terse announcements or remembered them when the day came.

In the meantime President Eisenhower, with the advice and support of most scientists and defense officials, opted to keep the scientific and the military programs completely separate. This decision led us to develop a largely new, special-purpose, and necessarily much smaller rocket system, the Vanguard, for launching our IGY satellite. As a result, our first attempt to do so could not be scheduled before early December 1957, a date that turned out to be two months after *Sputnik I*. When we finally did make that try, we failed. As if that were not bad enough, the weight of our satellite would have only been one-fiftieth of the weight of *Sputnik I* and one three-hundredth of the weight of *Sputnik II*. Even when, on January 31, 1958, we finally did get a satellite successfully into orbit, using an entirely different booster system (the Army's Jupiter C, renamed the Juno I), it was six and a half inches in diameter and weighed only thirty-one pounds, still far less than its Soviet predecessors. This huge difference in weight, combined with the "shocking" time gap, exacerbated an already difficult situation.

At the same time and in addition to the widely publicized scientific satellite program and the just-plain-secret ballistic missile program, the U.S. Air Force was conducting a supersecret project to develop a satellite for a variety of military purposes, especially for intelligence gathering. Even the existence of this effort was known to almost no one outside the project itself. A proposal to build such a satellite had first seriously been put forward in 1946 by the Rand Corporation, but it was not finally approved as a funded Air Force project until 1956—still a year and a half *before* Sputnik—but only after it had become evident that our ballistic missile program would result in boosters capable of launching such satellites. The performance goals and the scheduling of this project were, of course, determined by considerations entirely separate from those that guided the IGY scientific satellite program. As of the summer of 1957, the schedule called for the first launch of a military satellite in late 1958 or early 1959, about a year after the actual launching of *Sputnik I*. Several versions were planned, variously weighing from 1,500 to 5,000 pounds, substantially larger even than *Sputnik II,* and about the size of the third Sputnik (2,926 pounds), launched by the Soviets in early 1958. But because neither the general public nor the scientists and engineers engaged in the IGY program knew anything about this supersecret project, its existence played no role in the formation of public opinion or even of public policy at the time. (The name of this project changed several times. At the end of the 1950s, the project was designated WS117L, the booster was called the Atlas Agena, and the most important satellites were named Samos and Midas.)

President Eisenhower knew all of the pertinent facts about the American programs, and he had a good grasp of the Soviet effort, but neither he nor his top advisers appreciated how less well informed persons would interpret the events surrounding the launching of the first Sputnik. He was therefore stunned and surprised by the intense concern expressed by most of the American people and much of the world press. His first public reaction was to reassure the American people, to explain to them that the Soviets did not possess some special secret, to express his confidence in American science, and to assert the overall adequacy of our military posture.

In the minds of many this seemed to prove not only that things were bad but also that the current leadership could not understand that simple fact. Leading Democratic politicians, Senators Stuart Symington and Henry Jackson prominent among them, saw all this as an opportunity to defeat the Republicans in the next general election, and they spoke out accordingly.

But even though Eisenhower knew that things were not as bad as they seemed on the surface, he did share the general concerns about what Sputnik portended. These concerns were reinforced by his knowledge, gained through intelligence channels, of recent Soviet successes in developing powerful thermonuclear weapons. The development of these new warheads, which could be hurled intercontinental distances by boosters identical to those that launched the Sputniks, did indeed mean that we were about to enter a new and potentially dangerous era, and Eisenhower was determined to find a suitable way of coping with the situation.

Killian and the President's Science Advisory Committee

On November 7, four days after the launching of *Sputnik II,* the morning papers reported that Premier Khrushchev was now predicting Soviet victory over the United States in the building of heavy industry and the production of consumer goods. That evening President Eisenhower delivered the first of several nationwide talks on science and defense.

In this talk he first presented various facts about American military technology. In his memoirs he recalled,

There were the facts—as many as could be disclosed—as hard and clearly as I could state them. On them rested this conclusion: "It is my conviction, supported by trusted scientific and military advisers, that, although the Soviets are quite likely ahead in some missile and special areas, and are obviously ahead of us in satellite development, as of today the over-all military strength of the Free World is distinctly greater than that of the Communist countries."

But such facts, formidable as they were, were no reason for self-congratulation. Unless we moved further, I said, we could fall behind. As spurs to action I announced a number of specific decisions, among them:

(1) I was appointing Dr. James R. Killian, president of the Massachusetts Institute of Technology, as Special Assistant to the President for Science and Technology, a new post. He would be aided by a staff of scientists and by an advisory group—the existing Science Advisory Committee of the Office of Defense Mobilization, now enlarged, reorganized, and elevated to the White House.

Looking back on these events five years after he retired from the presidency, Eisenhower remarked,

The appointment of Dr. Killian, and later Dr. George B. Kistiakowsky of Harvard, worked out wonderfully. In character and accomplishment they could have had no superiors. Whatever the task—to build an airframe for the enormous B–70, or solve the metallurgical problem of ways to dissipate heat for nose cone re-entries into the earth's atmosphere—the scientific adviser kept me enlightened. My "wizard" helped me to keep the subject of space away from becoming a "race" and from deteriorating into a series of stunts. He helped to make certain that the government was supporting both basic and applied research. Without such distinguished help, any President in our time would be, to a certain extent, disabled.[2]

Killian proceeded swiftly in establishing the new President's Science Advisory Committee, or PSAC ("pea-sack"). On November 29 the White House announced the completion of that task and presented the names of the new members of the enlarged group. By a totally unexpected stroke of good luck, I was among them. Why me? Evidently they wanted someone from inside the current nuclear weapons establishment. Edward Teller might perhaps have been considered, had he not been persona non grata with many of the other members because of his earlier role in the Oppenheimer hearings. Also, when forming a new committee it is typical to call for "a younger person," "someone with a new perspective," and since I was only thirty-five, I fit that criterion as well. The other new members were George B. Kistiakowsky, General James H. Doolittle, Robert F. Bacher, and Edward M. Purcell.*

Ten days later, on December 9, the full committee met for the first time, in the Old Executive Building, inside the White House perimeter at the corner of Pennsylvania Avenue and Seventeenth Street. That magnificently ornate and sturdy nineteenth-century building had housed the State Department, the Navy Department, and the War Department up until the beginning of World War II, all at the same time. The ceilings were high and the walls thick. The fancy molding around the inside doors and windows was of cast iron with such a heavy coat of white paint that it looked like plaster. All the office doorknobs carried the seals of the cabinet departments the rooms had earlier housed. I often thought of taking one as a souvenir, but good sense always prevailed. The anteroom of the larger room we commonly used for our meetings was the very place where Secretary of State Cordell Hull had chewed out the Japanese ambassador immediately after the attack on Pearl Harbor. The meeting room itself had been Hull's personal office. After the war President Truman firmly resisted proposals to tear the building down and replace it with something more modern and, supposedly, more useful. The history of the place and its conservative magnificence made our purpose for being there seem all the more important. When I had a chance to stop and think about it—which wasn't all that often—I became deeply aware of having somehow fallen into at least an important eddy in the mainstream of American history.

Jim Killian, serving both as special assistant to the president for science and technology and as our chairman, started that first meeting by explaining just what it was that the president wanted from us. He did so with the exceptional clarity and precision that were his personal hallmark. He was truly extraordinary in his ability to understand what the president wanted and to convey that to us. Then, when we finally had some conclusions to report or some advice to give, he could present it to Eisenhower in a fashion perfectly suited to the president's needs. Killian provided a superb match between the president and his committee, and it was this feature of his chairmanship that, more than anything

---

*The holdover members of the committee were Detlev Bronk, president of the National Academy of Sciences, Lloyd Berkner (Associated Universities, Inc.), Caryl Haskins (Carnegie Institution), Jerrold Zacharias (MIT), William O. Baker (Bell Labs), Hans Bethe (Cornell), H. P. Robertson (Caltech), Edwin Land (Polaroid), I. I. Rabi (Columbia), James Fisk (Bell Labs), and Jerome Wiesner (MIT).

else, led the president to say in his memoirs that it had all "worked out wonderfully."

Our chairman next outlined a work program that called for one two-day meeting of the full committee per month, he announced the formation of special panels to deal with specific questions, and he said he hoped that some of us would be able to devote additional time to them and other matters. As it turned out, George Kistiakowsky and I had working situations that allowed us to devote full time over an extended period to the tasks before us, and several others were able to spend half time or more on the committee's work. In my case, the Livermore Laboratory was then more than five years old, and the job of directing it had become fairly routine. More important, I was fortunate to have a number of key associates easily capable of carrying on without any supervision from me, including Harold Brown and John Foster. During the next four months I found myself going home to California only every other weekend for three days, one at the lab and two with my family.

I was soon working on five panels. One I chaired; its task was to assess the current U.S. space program. The purposes of the other four were (1) to assess the U.S. missile program, (2) to draw up a plan for the future U.S. space program in terms both of goals and of organization, (3) to review and advise on the problem of nuclear arms control, and (4) to monitor and advise on the classified space programs.

The Space Assessment Panel

The Space Assessment Panel, made up of myself as chairman plus Kistiakowsky and Emanuel Piore (chief scientist of IBM), began its work immediately after the first meeting of the parent PSAC. Its task was to review all elements of the U.S. space program, particularly those relating to the IGY, and to assess the prospects for making an early successful American response to the Sputniks. I quickly discovered the special power of an invitation from the White House and summoned the leaders of the two primary candidate programs for launching the first U.S. satellite. One of these was the Vanguard program, a Navy project under the direction of John P. Hagen. The other was the Army's Jupiter C program, directed by Wernher von Braun.

The Vanguard program had been set in motion in 1955 as the chosen instrument for putting up a scientific satellite as a part of the U.S. contribution to the International Geophysical Year. It quickly ran into a series of technical and budgetary problems. The first launch attempt could not be made before December 6, 1957, two months after Sputnik I and three days before the first PSAC meeting. And when it was tried, it failed before a television audience of millions. Hagen and his colleagues briefed our panel about what went wrong and what they proposed to do next. In the evening we spread out huge blueprints of the rocket system on the floor in the halls in the Old Executive Building; they were much too big for the tables in our offices. After a few days of intensive study, we were able to develop an understanding of what was going on and what the prospects were for the next attempts.

The other candidate program—the Jupiter C—was under the direction of Wernher von Braun, then the technical leader of ballistic missile development at the Army Ballistic Missile Agency (ABMA), in Huntsville, Alabama. Immediately after the 1955 decision to launch an IGY satellite, his group proposed building a satellite launcher based on the Redstone, a tactical ballistic missile with a range of some two hundred miles. Generally speaking, it was a lineal descendant of the V-2 rocket von Braun had earlier designed and built for the Nazi war machine in the 1940s. The basic design proposal called for placing three additional stages of small solid rockets atop the much larger liquid-fueled Redstone. The total velocity increment attainable by such a system would be enough to place a thirty-one-pound satellite into orbit. A virtually identical system, differing only in that the final, fourth-stage rocket had been filled with "sand instead of powder," was successfully fired from Florida to a point thirty-four hundred miles down the Atlantic Missile Range on September 20, 1956, about thirteen months before the first Sputnik. The ostensible purpose was to check out the technology proposed for making possible the successful reentry of missile warheads ("nose cones") into the atmosphere, but it was widely understood to be a bootleg attempt by von Braun and his boss, Army General John B. Medaris, to make an end run around the earlier decision assigning the first satellite launching to the Navy's Vanguard project. As General Medaris later told Secretary of Defense Neil McElroy, "It would have gone into orbit without question if we had used a loaded fourth stage,"[3] and in that event it would have been the "first-in-the-world" satellite more than a year before Sputnik. How different things might have been if it had! Now, more than a year later and in the wake of Sputnik and the public reaction to it, McElroy on October 8 ordered the Army to reactivate this project and get ready for a launch at the earliest-possible time, then estimated to be in January or February 1958. Our panel went over this project in great detail with von Braun and his colleagues.

We also took a look at yet a third possibility, based on the supersecret

Air Force program to place reconnaissance satellites in orbit. We concluded that nothing much could be done to advance its already long-
scheduled first launch, still over a year away.

We completed our investigation in just a couple of weeks, finishing
before Christmas, and wrote a report about it for James Killian. When
I compare this report to the many other government (and university)
committee reports I have written or helped write since then, I remain
especially proud of it. It was done in record time, it was extraordinarily
brief (only one and a half pages), and its predictions were right on target.
In sum, we wrote that the Vanguard had only a fifty-fifty chance of ever
working successfully during the next year, while the Jupiter C had a
fifty-fifty chance of working on the very first try, which we agreed could
be made in about six weeks. We recommended that "there should be
no expansion of the Vanguard Program for the IGY but that additional
resources be made available to the Jupiter C in order best to insure
successful launching of satellites."[4]

Even before that report was written, Killian took me across the alley
to the Oval Office, in the west wing of the White House, to tell the
president what we were finding. I had never talked with or even met a
real live president of the United States before, and, to put it simply, I
was thrilled. When we walked in, he was sitting at his desk looking
away, but he quickly rose and gave us both a warm smile and a firm
handshake. The election campaigns in 1952 and 1956 had used "I like
Ike" as a rallying cry, and I felt the same way, even up close. I found
him then, as on many other occasions later, to be very much interested
in what we had to say and quick to understand it. In effect, we
reaffirmed the good sense of McElroy's decision of two months earlier
to place the country's bet on Jupiter C, and he was pleased by that.

In a second conversation with the president I remarked that Sputnik
weighed 1,120 pounds.

"How do you know that?" he asked.

"The Russians said so," I replied.

"That's the first time I ever heard anyone say you could take their
word on a thing like that!"

"Oh, in my experience, the Soviet Academy always either tells the
truth or says nothing at all on factual matters like that."

The substance was correct, but the argument was weak. My "experience" was pretty small. I was really arguing on the basis of plausibil-
ity, not experience, and that's not a sound basis even if it does produce
right results. The president probably forgot this brief interchange, but I
didn't.

The Ballistic Missile Assessment Panel

The Ballistic Missile Assessment Panel was chaired by George Kistiakowsky, and its other two members were James McCrae, then president of the Sandia Corporation, and I. In this instance, six missile programs were involved: the Air Force's Atlas, Titan, and Minuteman ICBMs and its Thor IRBM; the Army's Jupiter IRBM; and the Navy's Polaris SLBM.* We reported our findings to Killian right after Christmas, and he combined them with our assessment of the space program in the single "Memorandum for the President" dated December 28. This report was also exceptional for both its brevity and the accuracy of its predictions. Excerpts follow:

THE MISSILE PROGRAMS

It is our judgment that *technically* our missile development is proceeding in a satisfactory manner. Although it is probably true that we are at present behind the Soviets, we are in this position largely because we started much later and not because of inferior technology. Our technological progress in the missile field, in fact, has been impressive.

The so-called failures of flight test vehicles, to which much publicity has been given, are normal and unavoidable occurrences in the development of complex mechanisms, many functions of which can be tested only in flight. . . .

At present, the development programs of the IRBM are moving ahead very rapidly. There have been flights of both the JUPITER and the THOR which were complete technical successes. The regular production of IRBMs is soon to begin. In the development of ICBMs, the progress is also good and the recent successful flight test of the ATLAS gives confidence in the future of this missile. Another more advanced ICBM, the TITAN, is reaching the stage where initial flight testing will begin in 1958. We are confident that the U.S. has ample technical competence in our ballistic missile technical groups to achieve satisfactory operational missile systems at an early date.

. . . For the longer-range future, our basic research and development of entirely new methods and techniques for missiles must be vigorously and imaginatively pursued. We attach great importance to boldness in our planning for these future missiles and the initiation and successful carrying through of fundamental and exploratory work.[5]

---

*The acronyms stand for intercontinental ballistic missile, intermediate-range ballistic missile, and sub-launched ballistic missile.

Killian personally presented these conclusions to the president on New Year's Eve. Our views jibed very well with Eisenhower's own view of the matter, but our detailed judgments and estimates reassured him and enabled him to act with greater force and conviction. Things were not nearly as bad as his political opponents in the Congress claimed and as the general public believed. In his State of the Union Message given ten days later, he was pleased to be able to say,

At this moment, the consensus of opinion is that we are probably somewhat behind the Soviets in some areas of long-range ballistic missile development. But it is my conviction, based on close study of all relevant intelligence, that if we make the necessary effort, we will have the missiles, in the needed quantity and in time, to sustain and strengthen the deterrent power of our increasingly efficient bombers. One encouraging fact evidencing this ability is the rate of progress we have achieved since we began to concentrate on missiles. . . . When it is remembered that our country has concentrated on the development of ballistic missiles for only about a third as long as the Soviets, these achievements show a rate of progress that speaks for itself.[6]

Three weeks after that, on February 4, Jim Killian, Kisti, and I met again with the president to present our latest conclusions in the matter. By then we were able to tell him that "there were grounds for real confidence that both liquid and solid propellant missiles would perform satisfactorily, that technical progress was all that could be expected and more and that there were no more problems remaining with the first generation of missiles." Regarding the ICBM, specifically, we estimated on the basis of all the intelligence then available that the Russians "were probably one year ahead of us in propulsion, one year behind us in warhead development, and somewhat behind us in guidance."[7] In retrospect, it is clear our net position was substantially better even than that estimate, but it was reassuring as it stood.

Blueprint for Space: Substance and Organization

The third PSAC panel was set up on February 4, 1958, shortly after the first two panels completed their work. Its task was to prepare a master plan that would include both a program of work and an organization capable of carrying it out. The panel was chaired by Edward Purcell, a Nobel laureate in physics and professor at Harvard University. The other three members were Jimmy Doolittle, Edwin Land, a prolific inventor and founder of the Polaroid Corporation, and I. Its scope included all aspects of space flight: practical applications, science, and the direct exploration of the solar system. The only area excluded was the military's reconnaissance satellite program. That came under the purview of the Land panel, which also included Purcell and me.

Since boyhood I had had a strong, serious interest in astronomy, especially the astronomy of the solar system, and I had also been fascinated by the idea of space travel as it was presented in science fiction, including the *Buck Rogers* and *Flash Gordon* strips in the Sunday comics. Now I was being asked to help plan the real thing, to work out a program for making fantasies come true. I was very interested in, and excited by, all the things the PSAC was doing, but I approached this panel with special enthusiasm.

We interviewed many people from the the military, private industry, and the world of science. We found that there was a huge reservoir of ideas and proposals out there, most of them straight but some pretty kooky. Surprisingly, perhaps, nearly all of the good ideas had been around for some years. However, Sputnik had excited everyone and stimulated a lot of thinking, and so even mature ideas were presented with fresh vigor. Many proposals were obviously self-serving. Corporation X proposed that we should push ahead with what corporation X was good at, and the same was true for each of the military services and many individuals as well. But in the main, and even including the self-serving ideas, the proposals were inspired largely by a spirit of intellectual adventure born of the obvious opportunities the flights of the Sputniks had brought with them.

We reviewed many practical applications for satellites: communications relay systems, man-made constellations for improving navigation, meteorological satellites that could monitor the weather in the remotest places, systems for surveying natural resources, and systems for greatly improving mapping and geodesy.

We heard many proposals for doing science from a space platform. These included looking down to study the earth, looking around to investigate the not so empty space environment itself, and looking out to learn about the cosmos. The last was the most fascinating. The coming opportunity to see the universe in "full color," instead of merely in those wavelengths the atmosphere happened to let through, augured a great intellectual adventure just ahead.

And then there was the moon. When I was ten, I went there frequently in a spaceship that other people might have identified merely as a cherry tree in Henry Senke's backyard. (Cherry trees are especially easy for awkward boys to climb.) When I was twelve, I somehow arranged for my Boy Scout troop to peer through the ten-inch refracting telescope on the roof of Bausch & Lomb's main Rochester works, and we all got a good look at the real thing, and at Saturn and some great globular star clusters as well. Later, when I was director of the Livermore Laboratory, I visited the nearby Lick Observatory and brought back some great pictures of the moon, and Sybil surprised me by having several framed and hung on the walls of our home. Now I suddenly and unexpectedly found myself in a situation in which the "highest authorities"—as they say—actually wanted me to think about how it might really be done and to advise them about it. Needless to say, I concentrated on the question of how to send not only instruments but MAN himself to the moon and back.

The panel met with many persons who had something particular to say about this matter. I spent added hours on my own in pressing further. I was still the only member of the group able to devote full time to these issues. I went over various elements of the problem with Bill Pickering of the Jet Propulsion Laboratory, Bob Gilruth of the National Advisory Committee on Aeronautics (NACA), Wernher von Braun and Ernst Stuhlinger of the ABMA, and several Air Force officers, including the director of the space medicine laboratory. I drew up a plan for getting to the moon that involved the use of a low earth-orbit rendez-vous, and I tried to estimate time and cost. My estimate for cost was three billion dollars, and that figure actually showed up in the PSAC's final report on the subject. The actual cost was nearly ten times that.

My estimate for how long it would take was between ten and twenty years, and it actually took eleven and a half. However, the PSAC as a whole thought that in 1958 it was premature to make a concrete plan and to set a schedule for getting a man to the moon and back. Too many intermediate steps remained to be accomplished, including the develop-ment of rocket engines with adequate thrust, the necessary huge, multi-stage boosters, and all of the techniques needed to enable humans to live and work in the space environment. The final report of the commit-tee does not, therefore, mention my time estimate; it merely says that various things will be done "early," "later," "still later," and "much later still," and it puts man on the moon in the third category. President Eisenhower felt the same way.

It is often said that the goal of going to the moon was set by President Kennedy. That is true in the limited sense that it was he who first set it out as a specific goal to be accomplished "before the end of the decade." But Eisenhower was fully aware that the projects his administration was about to set in motion would one day take us to the moon. Moreover, he thought that ought to happen in due course, but he believed it was worse than useless to proclaim a specific plan and schedule for it when the largest U.S. satellite weighed only thirty-one pounds. His views on this matter were very much influenced by certain recent experiences in which various spokesmen had made predictions or promises about some missile launch, only to have the result be a spectacular public failure.

A related incident occurred later that year, after I had left the White House to take up full-time work in the Pentagon. On that occasion the president was presiding over a small meeting in the Cabinet Room that included the secretary of defense, the secretary of the Air Force, the chief of staff of the Air Force and his vice-chief, and me. At a point early in this meeting, the president pounded the table and said, "Why don't *they* make those two generals shut up?" He was referring to two Air Force generals down at Cape Canaveral who had recently made some public predictions about upcoming launches, and in too many previous cases such predictions had simply led to embarrassment and letdown. I was amazed by the president's remark. Here *they* were, sitting around this very table, the superiors of those two generals five layers deep and extending all the way up to the commander in chief himself, and yet this *they* wanted some other *they* to take care of the problem. It was one of those special moments that leave a vivid memory trace even thirty years later. I think the lesson buried in there is that in our society there really is no *they* in any final sense. The commander in chief and his deputies four deep could not "make them shut up," because the Congress, the press, and, ultimately, the people simply wouldn't permit it.

Years later, during the Carter administration, I spent some days with the highest-ranking chief master sergeant of the Air Force. We were working together on the President's Commission on Military Compensation. He remarked that it had long been his goal to meet *them* and to see the *big picture* before he retired from the service. I told him I had found there were no such things.

After the space panel was well along in defining a national program, it turned to the matter of organization. Here, too, there were many conflicting hopes and ideas. Each of the military services proposed that it should run the whole show, or at least most of it. The Navy said, "They call them space ships, don't they?" The Air Force asserted that air and space were simply two parts of a continuum, and it proposed renaming itself the U.S. Aerospace Force. The Army exploited the fact that it had Wernher von Braun on its team, and it sent him out on a barnstorming tour to present the Army's ideas and hopes to anyone who might listen and then write his congressman about it. Some suggested an AEC-like agency or even the AEC itself. And finally it was proposed that the existing National Advisory Committee on Aeronautics (NACA) be expanded and upgraded to take over the job of carrying out all elements of the national space program except those having direct military application. (Despite its name, NACA was an operating organization that included several very large laboratories.) We quickly settled on this last idea as the way to go. The president himself had definite views on the matter, and this was also his favorite solution. In particular, he didn't want any of the services to be given the entire task. In part this was because he felt it would interfere with their other essential missions. More important, he was "fed up" with the way interservice rivalry had played out over the last several years in the closely related long-range missile programs, and he was not about to permit that to happen again.

We thought it was especially important that the man-in-space program be placed under the authority of this new National Aeronautics and Space Administration, or NASA. Both the Army and the Air Force had made strong pitches for this element of the program, but the rationales they presented were either too vague or too nonsensical. Notions such as the moon's being "high ground," transporting troops in ballistic missile nose cones, and the like kept popping up. We felt that the main reason for sending man himself out into space was to explore in the old-fashioned sense, to confront the unexpected and cope with it as no automata could, and not simply to extend armed combat to yet another dimension. It thus seemed clear that the general rationale for creating a civilian space agency applied with special force to this particular project.

We did leave some loose ends, the most important being the question of what agency should develop the large boosters we knew were necessary. This question was to remain open and troubling for another year and a half. I will take up its final resolution in chapter 7.

The panel's ideas concerning organization were reviewed further by an ad hoc committee consisting of Killian, Director of the Budget Percy Brundage, and Nelson Rockefeller. That group endorsed them in full and passed them on without change to the president in March. They became the basis for the actions that ultimately led to the Space Act of 1958 and to the establishment of NASA that same year.

Purcell and I presented the panel's ideas to the National Security

Council. They were well received and became in effect the blueprint for America's civil space program.

Early in the course of the Purcell panel's work, I arranged a visit to the Pentagon to brief Secretary of Defense McElroy. A date to do so was set up for Monday, February 17. That weekend fourteen inches of snow fell on the nation's capital, and all traffic came to a standstill. The administration issued an order saying that only those in essential positions should report to work. An editorial wag wrote that even the director of national monuments stayed home and let his charges shift for themselves unprotected. I made my way with difficulty across the river to the Pentagon and did a lot of walking in deep snow in the process. Perhaps I managed to take a cab to the Marriott Hotel on the Virginia side of the Fourteenth Street Bridge and then walked the rest of the way from there; I'm not sure. In any event, the secretary of defense did report for work that day, but most of his minions did not. The result was a pleasant, unhurried, hour-long, one-on-one conversation that I could not have had with the secretary on an ordinary, busy business day. I told him about our ideas for the substance and organization of the civil space program. I also presented at length my thoughts about the defense space program. I was already aware of some of his own thinking on the subject, including his plans to establish a new Advanced Research Projects Agency to handle the military space programs, and I discussed those ideas as well. He evidently liked what he heard. I believe it was this chance, extended conversation that, more than anything else, led him to appoint me the first chief scientist of the new agency a few weeks later.

A Moratorium on Nuclear Tests

The fourth PSAC panel dealt with arms control in general and a possible nuclear test ban in particular. It was chaired by Caryl Haskins, the director of the Carnegie Institution of Washington, and its other members were Hans Bethe, I. I. Rabi, Herbert Scoville, and I. At first I did not approach it with anything like the enthusiasm I had for the space and missile panels. Indeed, I cannot today recall anything about the early meetings of this panel. Then, on April 8–10, 1958, there occurred another one of those sharp turning points that I encountered so often during the years immediately after Sputnik. The PSAC held a special meeting of the full committee devoted specifically to a possible nuclear test ban. It took place at Ramey Air Force Base, in Puerto Rico. We chose that location to minimize all outside interferences, including long-distance calls from the home institutions of the members.

The president had long been concerned about the nuclear arms race. He was convinced it was leading us somewhere we had better not go, and he looked for ways of getting it under control. The proposals presented in his "Atoms for Peace" speech had been an early stab at the general issue. Later he proposed "open skies" over Russia and America as a means for reassuring each country that no grand surprises were being prepared deep inside the other's territory. And ever since the "Bravo" nuclear fallout accident in the Pacific in 1954 had raised world consciousness about nuclear tests, he had mulled over the possibility of a nuclear test ban both as a solution to the fallout problem and as a means for slowing down the arms race.* Adlai Stevenson had raised the issue of fallout during the presidential campaign of 1956 in a way that Eisenhower took as a personal attack, and he backed off from his own, tentative thrusts in order not to be seen as acquiescing in Stevenson's charges. By mid-1957 he was again considering the possible merits of a nuclear test ban as a "first step" on the way to a more comprehensive arrangement. Fortunately, Premier Khrushchev apparently was thinking along similar lines independently. Thus, even before the furor over Sputnik had faded, Eisenhower turned to his new PSAC to give him advice on this already mature notion.

During the period immediately prior to Sputnik, the scientific advisers who had the most impact on this issue—Strauss, Lawrence, and Teller—were all participants in the nuclear weapons program. It was their ox that was about to be gored, and they were unenthusiastic. The members of the new PSAC, except for me, had no such current involvement; indeed, some of them regarded nuclear testing as pernicious. As a result, the whole approach to the question underwent a sea change at the White House level.

There were two questions before us in Puerto Rico. First, would a nuclear test ban be in the best interest of the United States and, second, could compliance with a ban be monitored adequately? We discussed these questions thoroughly, and then the chair called for a vote. Nor-

---

*On March 1, 1954, the world's second very large thermonuclear explosion took place at Bikini Atoll. Insufficient experience in predicting the fallout patterns produced by such huge and unprecedented explosions led to serious errors in the projections of just where the radioactive fallout would come down. As a result, some hundreds of Marshall Island natives at nearby atolls received very large, but sublethal, doses of radiation. A Japanese fishing vessel, the *Fortunate Dragon*, was in the vicinity, and its crew also received very high doses of radiation. The captain eventually died as a result.

mally we talked things out at length, and usually a consensus emerged, but this time we actually voted. Everyone except me responded "yes" to both questions. I felt slightly overwhelmed by all of my seniors' voting that way, but I screwed up my courage enough to vote "abstain." Given my recent responsibilities, I might well have responded "no," but "abstain" was the most I could do under the circumstances. I argued that the matter before us was essentially a political and strategic issue and that a group made up entirely of scientists wasn't appropriate for deciding such questions. There must be, I felt, some other group somewhere else in the government better suited for dealing with such matters. After the meeting, Jerry Wiesner took me aside and patiently explained several things to me. One was that the president could ask anyone any question he wished. Another was that there really was no one else; it was us or no one, be that plausible or not. Besides, he and others seemed to imply, scientists could indeed do as well in handling this novel question as any other collection of experts. I quickly came to realize that he and the others were right about this peripheral issue, and I approached the substantive questions with a new seriousness. I later learned that Wiesner himself actually did have doubts about the appropriateness of our group's answering such questions. In a speech made two years later, in 1960, he said,

> I've been billed as an expert on arms control, and I think I'm an example of what's wrong with the American posture in this field. . . .
> My background is primarily in the field of military technology. . . . I come to the arms control field with all the biases, prejudices and skepticism to be expected of someone who has been working very hard on military weapons.[8]

There is a real paradox here. It is a historical fact that for forty years now scientists, especially those with weapons development experience, have taken the lead in sounding the alarm about nuclear war. The existence and actions of a number of public interest groups that toil in this vineyard attest to that: the Federation of American Scientists, the Union of Concerned Scientists, the Physicians for Social Responsibility. Surely, this concern is not simply a matter of guilty feelings derived from the fact that "the physicists have known sin." It stems mainly from special knowledge; physicists and physicians understand better than others the thermonuclear horror that is always only thirty minutes away from happening.

The warnings of these public interest groups are correct and soundly based. Their prescriptions of what to do about the problem, however, are often naive and based on false notions of how things are and why they are that way. Scientists and engineers do not in fact understand the political and strategic elements of this issue as well as do political scientists, Sovietologists, historians, strategists, statesmen, and certain others. Unhappily, these other experts seem often not to grasp just how serious, how total, the nuclear threat is. To paraphrase an old saw, some of these groups are naive all of the time; all of them are naive some of the time.

The solution used to solve this paradox over the past twenty years has been to "bureaucratize" it. Bureaucracies—the Arms Control and Disarmament Agency in the case of the United States—have been created whose mission is to solve the problem of controlling the nuclear arms race without undermining the military balance. They have brought together scientists, statesmen, military experts, and diplomats, all in a single bureaucratic unit. The controversial and complex nature of the problems involved and the large number and variety of people needed to solve them make such an approach both necessary and inevitable. The question of whether this approach works depends not on the mechanism but on how much force the president personally puts behind the process. Hawks and doves, liberals and conservatives, all become very concerned about decision making in this area, about whether proposed actions will help or harm our security. As a result, the responsibility for deciding what to do and then doing it cannot be delegated to anyone else.

Following the Puerto Rico meeting, a panel chaired by Hans Bethe delved more deeply into the various technical issues involved. I participated as much as I could, but I had begun working full-time in the Pentagon even before the meeting at Ramey Air Force Base, and so my availability had become limited. Clearly, there could be national purposes that required that nuclear tests be banned, and such purposes might override the reasons for nuclear tests. However, these latter reasons had to be taken into account in any serious consideration of the issue, and I was the PSAC's current resident expert on what they were. Even so, over a period of several months of participation in these studies, I gradually came to realize that the president was right to pursue these new-to-me goals, to believe that a nuclear test ban was in the best interests of the United States—and of all mankind—and to think that such a ban could probably be adequately monitored.

Just two weeks after the Puerto Rico meeting, on April 20, Eisenhower acted. In his memoirs he remembered,

... I formally proposed to Chairman Khrushchev a measure we had been considering—a meeting of experts whose technical studies would precede any political conference.

The Chairman, eleven days later, sent an acceptance. Details of the meeting to be held during the summer were soon worked out. To represent the United States I appointed Dr. James Brown Fisk head of the delegation, and Drs. Ernest O. Lawrence and Robert F. Bacher.[9]

The experts met in Geneva in the summer of 1958. Their conclusions showed that the prospects were good. The final result was a matched set of unilateral statements that led to a moratorium on all nuclear testing, commencing on November 1, 1958. (More on the moratorium and how it ended in chapter 11.)

During my period of full-time service in the Pentagon, first as the chief scientist of ARPA and later as the director of defense research and engineering, I became more and more committed to the view that the nuclear arms race must somehow be brought under control and that a nuclear test ban would make a good first step. The general climate on that side of the Potomac ranged from dubious to hostile, though I was not, of course, the only person sympathetic to the president's views. As a result, I found myself in the unusual and faintly amusing situation of being a member of a rather special minority in the national security establishment, one that included the commander in chief himself.

This situation had its dark side as well. On a memorable occasion in early 1960, a meeting between Secretary of Defense Thomas Gates, Chairman John McCone of the AEC, myself, and one or two others took place. At one point the discussion turned to the question of whether the Soviets were cheating on the nuclear test moratorium then still in effect. McCone had been arguing for some time that they were, and one of his purposes at this meeting was to persuade Gates to join him in putting pressure on the president to end his policy of continuing the de facto moratorium. I said that I had just gone over every shred of intelligence we had on this matter and had found no evidence whatsoever supporting such a claim. McCone replied that my saying that was tantamount to treason. I was flustered by that awful charge, but I reasserted my position. Although the meeting ended inconclusively, I have never forgotten it. I believe that history fully confirms I was right. When the Soviets unilaterally ended the moratorium, they did so with a huge bang, not a secretive whimper. They did deceive us about their preparations during these many months they needed to get their extensive test series ready, but there remains to this day no reason to believe they conducted any clandestine tests before they suddenly did so openly.

Very little of what I found myself doing in the Pentagon in those years had any direct connection with this issue, but I did what I could. For instance, I arranged for the development and deployment of various remote means, collectively called the Vela program, for monitoring a test ban and other arms control measures. During these last Eisenhower years I also often attended meetings of a group known as the Committee of Principles, as the deputy or alternate to the secretary of defense. This committee's purpose was to advise the president on all matters relating to nuclear arms control. Its members were his top official advisers, the secretaries of state and defense, the director of the CIA, and his special assistant for science and technology.

A Little R and R

It wasn't all work even in those busy early days. The president invited some fifty scientists and their wives to a reception and state dinner on February 4. He included some PSAC members, and since I was spending so much time away from home in Washington, Killian arranged for Sybil and me to be among them. When the moment came, another snowstorm was in progress. The only hat I happened to have with me was a red baseball cap. I arrived at the White House guard gate in white tie, tails, and red cap. About five years later, on a totally unrelated White House visit, I met the same guard. He immediately passed me, saying, "I know you. You came here one day in a red baseball cap." The White House police really are a cut above average.

Jimmy Doolittle and his wife were among the first arrivals, as were we. Sybil had been gently chiding me for some weeks about how little time I was home. I knew Jimmy traveled even more than I did, so I cleverly thought to ask Mrs. Doolittle in Sybil's presence how she managed to put up with it. "Oh," she said, "I always go with him." That was a great idea, but with three small children at home we couldn't use it. Roger Revelle, whom I had not yet met but who later became a close friend and colleague, was also there. Sybil recalls that she had a great time at dinner, sitting between George Kistiakowsky and Dr. Michael E. De Bakey, famous for his "blue baby" operation. We both remember it as a truly grand occasion.

Linking the White House and the Pentagon

After only four months of full-time service in the White House, I moved over to the Pentagon, and that became my institutional home for the next three years. During that time I maintained a relationship with the White House that was very unusual for someone in my position in the defense hierarchy. My calendar and George Kistiakowsky's diary for those years show that I visited the White House and the old Executive Office Building about once a week throughout that period. All of this was done with the full knowledge of the three secretaries of defense I worked for in succession: McElroy, Gates, and Robert McNamara. I had a superb working relationship with all of them. They trusted me to deal directly with the White House on my own, and I behaved in accordance with that trust.

Among other things, I frequently acted as the de facto link between the Office of the Secretary of Defense and the White House on a number of intelligence matters. These included both intelligence about Soviet technical developments and the use of technology for producing such intelligence. The first included the Soviet nuclear program and missile program. The latter in turn included such things as the programming of the U-2, the development of the new reconnaissance satellites, and the monitoring of the nuclear test moratorium.

The Missile Gap and the U-2

One of the issues that absorbed much of my attention throughout my years in Washington was the so-called missile gap. I first became involved with it a few months before Sputnik as a result of my service on the Gaither panel in the summer of 1957. As I reported earlier, that committee, with some modest help from me, took an extreme view of the situation. It was not alone. That fall, after Sputnik, Secretary of Defense McElroy and many others began to talk about a coming "gap" favoring the Soviets, and the term *missile gap* entered political discourse with great force and frequency.

After I joined the PSAC, and even more after I became a defense official, I learned how we obtained the intelligence we had, and I also became more sophisticated in interpreting it. A large part of what we knew then came from the flights of the U-2 "spy plane" over the USSR, particularly in the region of the missile test range near Tyuratam, in

Kazakhstan. The more flights we made, the more we learned about the Soviet development program. And what we learned gave us pause. The Soviets had in fact successfully accomplished the development of a huge ICBM, several times as big as the Atlas and Titan we were working on. It was capable of delivering very large and powerful thermonuclear warheads to targets in our country in less than thirty minutes. But we saw no deployments of such rockets. The only launch facilities we found were those at Tyuratam. We continued to hunt and continued to come up with nothing.

Many of those privy to these facts, including the president, began to suspect that the most probable explanation of why we found none was that there were none, or at most only a few. Secretary of Defense Gates and I came to share this view. At the same time, important Democrats in the Congress, especially those eyeing the forthcoming 1960 presidential elections, became steadily more strident in their insistence on the reality and importance of the missile gap. It was a difficult situation. We on the inside grew more convinced that there was no missile gap, but we couldn't prove it, not even to ourselves. The Soviet Union was, after all, the largest country on earth, seven million square miles in all, and the U-2 flights had covered only a tiny fraction of it. We were in effect trying to prove a negative on the basis of a very small sample.

By the spring of 1960 we were all the more determined to settle this question if we could, not just in order to be able to put down those making exaggerated claims and strident charges but also because we in the administration really weren't certain ourselves, and it was, in truth, a most important matter. Since intelligence about technology acquired by technological means was at the heart of the matter, I was the de facto, though not the de jure, link between the Office of the Secretary of Defense and the science adviser—and sometimes the president—on the matter. In particular, it was at a special meeting with the president that spring that Richard Bissell, the CIA's man in charge of the U-2 program, and I briefed the president on why we thought Francis Gary Powers's fateful flight should go when it did and where it tried to go. We had to search new areas, and the flight path chosen passed over never before seen but likely places where ICBMs might be deployed. In late April, Powers took off in his U-2 from Pakistan and was shot down near Sverdlovsk, in the Soviet Union.

The Soviets had repeatedly tried to bring down these U-2s in the past, and now they had finally succeeded. We always knew they would one day, but we had gotten away with it so long that we weren't really prepared for it when it happened. When Eisenhower got the word about

it, his first reaction was to assume the pilot was dead. His memoirs give
the following description:

> On the afternoon of May 1, 1960, General Goodpaster telephoned me:
> "One of our reconnaissance planes," he said, "on a scheduled flight from
> its base in Adana, Turkey, is overdue and possibly lost." I knew instantly
> that this was one of our U-2 planes, probably over Russia. Early the next
> morning he came into my office, his face an etching of bad news. He
> plunged to the point at once. "Mr. President, I have received word from the
> CIA that the U-2 reconnaissance plane I mentioned yesterday is still miss-
> ing. The pilot reported an engine flameout at a position about thirteen
> hundred miles inside Russia and has not been heard from since. With the
> amount of fuel he had on board, there is not a chance of his still being
> aloft." . . .
> There was, to be sure, reason for deep concern and sadness over the
> probable loss of the pilot, but not for immediate alarm about the equipment.
> I had been assured that if a plane were to go down it would be destroyed
> either in the air or on impact, so that proof of espionage would be lacking.
> Self-destroying mechanisms were built in.[10]

Aides were waiting to tell me about it the moment I got to my Pentagon office that morning, and my immediate reaction to it was the same
as the president's. Soon afterward the Soviets announced they had
downed a spy plane, but they did not at first let on that they had
captured the pilot alive. We tried to bluff. Our spokesmen claimed it was
a weather reconnaissance plane that had somehow strayed off course
and was presumed lost.

That evening I attended a cocktail reception at the Australian embassy. The Soviet claim that it had shot down a U.S. spy plane deep in
its territory was the talk of the party. The Luxembourg ambassador,
another guest at that party, chanced to say to me that he knew it couldn't
be true, that the United States would never do a thing like that. I had
had nothing to do with the original plans to build and use the U-2 in this
way, but I fully approved of the policy after I became involved, and I
continue to believe it was a necessary and therefore proper part of
Eisenhower's approach to the problems of the time. We were otherwise
in the dark about what the Soviets were doing, we really had to know,
and knowing eventually prevented us from overreacting to mere possibilities even more than we actually did. The Luxembourger's remark,
however, showed that even this program of essential but formally illegal
actions had its costs, its negative side. The ambassador's implicit trust
and confidence that the United States would not do something of that
nature was, by itself, something positive that was eroded in the event.

Next time, when the charges might be totally false, they would be easier to believe. (Years later, after he had retired from the presidency, I had a good opportunity to discuss the U-2 incident with Eisenhower. He mentioned that when Khrushchev visited him at Camp David shortly before the incident, he was concerned that the latter might bring up the subject of the U-2 flights, but he never did. Eisenhower went on to emphasize that he really did not know what he would have done had Khrushchev mentioned it.)

Afterthoughts on the White House

After I left full-time Washington service in 1961, I continued to visit the White House for various official purposes throughout the rest of my career. Sometimes these visits would be several per year; sometimes a few years would go by between visits. During the later visits, the earlier ones would return to my mind. At one of the earliest meetings I attended in the Cabinet Room, an irrepressible question popped into my mind: What on earth am *I* doing *here?* I have never since been present in either the Cabinet Room or the Oval Office without having the same question recur. I know perfectly well why the person with my title is there, but I'm puzzled about why the person with my name is. I am fully aware of the importance of whatever purpose brings me there, but I also know it could be carried out just as well or better by many others. This never happens to me anywhere else.

The Military-Industrial Contradiction

President Eisenhower's farewell address is justly famed for its twin warnings about the "military-industrial complex" and the "scientific-technological elite." I was not surprised by his remarks, but, like many others, I wanted to know more about them. I had the opportunity to do so just a few years later.

After leaving the presidency, Eisenhower spent his winters in Palm Desert, California, a town less than one hundred miles from my home in La Jolla, and I called on him there on several occasions to pay my respects. Our conversation sometimes turned to the two warnings. I asked him to explain more fully what he meant by the warnings, but he declined to do so, saying he didn't mean anything more detailed than what he had said at the time. I understood what he meant: the warnings were not the result of a methodical analysis; rather, they were the product of a remarkable intuition, whose power has generally been underestimated.

What, then, was the context of these remarks? What annoyed and irritated him? Whom are we to be wary of?

The context spanned the forty months from the launching of Sputnik to the end of his administration. The people who irritated him were the hard-sell technologists who tried to exploit Sputnik and the missile gap psychosis it engendered. We were to be wary of accepting their claims, believing their analyses, and buying their wares.

They invented all sorts of technological threats to our safety and offered a thousand and one technical delights for confronting them. Anyone who did not agree with their assessments and proposals was either unable to understand the situation or trying to put the budget ahead of survival.

In the months after Sputnik, their claims that they could solve the problem if only someone would unleash them carried a lot of weight with the public and some segments of the Congress and press. Other scientists and technologists had performed seeming miracles in the recent past, and it was not unnatural to suppose that they could do it again. It appeared that radar had saved Britain, that the A-bomb had ended the war, and that the H-bomb had come along just in time to save us from the Russian A-bomb. A large part of the public was ready to accept the hard-sell technologist's view of the world and to urge that the government support him in the manner to which he wanted to become accustomed. It seemed that the pursuit of expensive and complicated technology as an end in itself might become an accepted part of America's way of life.

But it was not only ordinary citizens who believed that the technologists understood something the rest of the world could not. Many of the technologists themselves thought that only they understood the problem and that it was their patriotic duty to save the rest of us whether or not we wanted them to. The Eisenhower administration, with the help of the PSAC, was able to deal successfully and sensibly with most of the resulting rush of wild ideas, phony intelligence, and hard sell. But some of these ideas did get through, at least for a while. Beyond that, dealing with self-righteous extremists who have all the answers—and there were many among the scientists and aerospace technologists at the time—is always annoying and irritating.

Eisenhower believed both in the necessity of having a military-industrial complex and in the problems and dangers it brought with it.

He was more aware than most Americans of the paradox later raised in Ronald Reagan's 1985 State of the Union Message: "We only have a military industrial complex until a time of danger, and then it becomes the arsenal of democracy."[11] A president must not only try to resolve paradoxes and contradictions but also learn to live with those that can't be fully resolved. He must both prepare for nuclear war and avoid it. He must simultaneously cope with the "Soviet threat" and avoid the holocaust inherent in the "nuclear arms race." Others can and often do solve these contradictions by simply disbelieving in one or the other of the elements that make them up. The president does not have that luxury, nor do those who would presume to be his advisers.

CHAPTER 7

"Space Is a Place, Not a Program"

(February 1958–December 1958)

Project Argus: One Unusual Reaction to Sputnik

WE AT the Livermore Laboratory reacted to Sputnik in the same way that most other Americans did. It excited us and provoked lots of ideas. We passed the best of these around and mulled them over in staff meetings and elsewhere. We speculated broadly about what Sputnik meant for the country, the laboratory, and ourselves individually.

Of the ideas that came to my attention in the first weeks, none could compare with one originated by Nicholas C. Christofilos, a physicist-inventor who had been with us for about two years. His idea was the most amazing and most original of all not only at Livermore but, to my knowledge, in the entire country. Nick was one of those rare people who sometimes made an invention requiring two new ideas at once. That ability is one of the hallmarks of true genius. Merely very clever people cannot do it.

Nicholas Christofilos was born in Boston in 1916. At the age of seven, after only two years of school, he moved with his parents back to their native Greece. He continued school there, eventually earning bachelor's degrees in mechanical and electrical engineering at the National Technical University. After graduation he worked in Athens for a firm that repaired and installed elevators. World War II caught him there. The Germans converted the elevator factory into a truck repair facility. Nick stayed on but had relatively little to do. To keep himself occupied, he studied German-language physics texts and journals, focusing his attention on the design of high-energy accelerators—cyclotrons and the like.

In 1948, three years after the war ended, Nick wrote a letter to the Radiation Laboratory at Berkeley purporting to describe a new invention. The letter was, apparently, not easy to decipher, but when its reader (I don't know who he was) did puzzle it out, he discovered that it was only another way of describing the synchrocyclotron, a device invented independently several years before by McMillan at Berkeley and Veksler in the USSR. Papers describing that invention had already been published more than a year before Nick's letter arrived, so it was set aside and forgotten.

Two years later, in 1950, a second letter arrived from Nick, still in Greece. This one appeared to describe another new type of accelerator. It was considerably more complex than the first, and whoever was assigned to read it could not make out what it was trying to say. Like the first, it was set aside.

Two years after that, Ernst Courant (a former roommate of mine at the University of Rochester) and two colleagues at the Brookhaven National Laboratory published an article describing yet another advance in accelerator design, one that would in due course provide the basis for building accelerators that could, for the first time, produce particles with more than one billion electron volts of energy.[1] Shortly after that, Nick was in the United States and happened to read their paper. He immediately got in touch with all involved and in essence said, "Hey, the invention by Courant et al. is the same one I described in my letter of two years ago, and I'm not getting proper credit for it!" People checked back and found that, sure enough, Nick had a clear priority of invention in this case.

Naturally, the discovery that a Greek elevator installer had priority in this very sophisticated invention produced a flurry of interest and reaction. In 1954 Nick was invited to join the staff of the Brookhaven National Laboratory, then actually engaged in building a huge accelerator, the world's most powerful, based on this new principle. He worked there for a while, becoming acquainted with the American version of big-league physics in the process.

Once on the Brookhaven staff, he lost interest in accelerator design and turned to other ideas, having to do with a device for the production of thermonuclear energy under controlled conditions, a device he later named Astron. A group of projects with that same goal, collectively known as Project Sherwood, were under way at a number of American institutions at the time, including Livermore. Brookhaven, however, was not one of them, and the leadership there didn't want to divert attention to yet another area of machine building at the time.

It was at about this time that I first heard the foregoing story. I found it fascinating. Since I had the authority and the money to put an interesting package together, I invited Nick to join us. The idea of moving Nick from Brookhaven to Livermore seemed like a good idea at each institution, but the security people had their doubts. They found it hard to believe that "an elevator mechanic" had accomplished all that Nick claimed. He must be, they thought, some sort of mole that the Russians, who also knew about accelerator technology, had pumped full of ideas not his own. Finally, it was agreed that Nick could come to Livermore to work on his ideas for a thermonuclear reactor but that he could not be given access to the nuclear weapons program.

Nick joined us in 1956 and continued to generate a stream of ideas relating to thermonuclear reactors. He might have been content doing that indefinitely had Sputnik not gone up and changed everything. Nick was more strongly moved by that event than anyone else I knew. He was convinced that the Russians were about to gain a decisive advantage over us, and he threw his entire energy into finding a way to keep this from happening.

His solution was an Astrodome-like defensive shield made up of high-energy electrons trapped in the earth's magnetic field just above the atmosphere. Only a few weeks after Sputnik, he came in to tell me all about it. In essence, he proposed to explode a large number of nuclear weapons, thousands per year, in the lower reaches of the earth's magnetosphere, just above the upper reaches of the atmosphere. These explosions would produce huge quantities of radioactive atoms, and these in turn would emit high-energy electrons (beta particles) and inject them into a region of space where the earth's magnetic field would trap and hold on to them for a long time. Nick could not easily estimate how long this time would be, but he thought it might be months or longer.

The number of trapped electrons, he believed, would be enough to cause severe radiation damage—and even heat damage—to anything, man or nuclear weapon, that tried to fly through the region. He expected that this region would extend over the entire planet, save only a relatively small region around each pole. Nick had, in effect, invented a version of the naturally occurring Van Allen belt, before it was discovered. (That discovery had to await the flights of the Explorer satellites, early in the following year.) His purpose was of epic proportions. He intended nothing less than to place an impenetrable shield of high-energy electrons over our heads, a shield that would destroy any nuclear warhead that might be sent against us.

To anticipate the end of the story, the idea didn't work out, but not because it was stupid or because it violated any fundamental laws of nature. It simply turned out, when all the facts and figures were finally in, that our earth's magnetic field is too weak to support an effective shield of this kind, and that processes then unknown further reduce the stability of the field in such a way that it will hold neither as many electrons nor for as long as Nick hoped. There could, however, be another earth, another planet with opposing superpowers, where such a shield might actually be possible and make a difference.

Nick was completely confident that he had found the answer to the new Soviet threat, and he was eager to work it out before it was too late. He knew, of course, that we had satellites of our own coming along soon, so he proposed an experiment, named Argus, to check it out. In it we would explode a nuclear bomb high above the atmosphere, after first placing in orbit a satellite with instruments on board suitable for observing the predicted injection of high-energy electrons into the magnetosphere.

A week or so after Nick first opened the floodgates on this stream of new ideas, he came in with an addendum. He had made a new calculation that showed there is already a "background" of electrons of natural origin trapped in the earth's magnetosphere, and he said we had to measure it before we did any experiments with a bomb. As luck would have it, the design of such experiments had already been completed by James Van Allen and Carl McIlwain of the University of Iowa, and they would soon actually be programmed to be carried into space by the first U.S. satellites, the Explorers, in early 1958. As is well known, these first U.S. satellites did discover what the world now knows as the Van Allen belts, and these belts were indeed found to contain the trapped electrons Christofilos had predicted some three months before their discovery.

At the time Nick presented these proposals, I could not conceive of a procedure for actually carrying them out. The experiments he wanted were on a grand scale and necessarily involved satellites. Such devices were coming along, but we had not yet flown any. Moreover, experiments relying on them were clearly beyond the purview of the AEC, at the time our sole sponsor. Projects of that scale were sometimes carried out in the military services, but they were always of an engineering nature and normally involved nothing more radical than the direct extrapolation of well-established techniques and technologies. Argus, to say the least, was a collection of far-out, untested ideas of the kind that make up basic research, utterly different from the sort of projects the services did well, such as Admiral Hyman Rickover's nuclear submarines or General Schriever's long-range missiles. Of course, the National Science Foundation did know how to judge and sponsor basic research, but the kind it was familiar with was normally carried out within the confines of an academic institution and for much less money than Argus would need. In addition, NSF projects tended to· involve work spread out over a period of years, and Nick was in a big hurry.

In sum, there was simply no place to take an invention like Nick's. Before such an invention and the experiments that supported it could be acted upon, a wholly new organization had to be created, one that could deal with projects of this grand scope and great novelty, projects that had to be taken seriously but did not fit into any existing niche.

Neither Nick nor I could possibly have anticipated it at the time, but it would be a document called "ARPA Order #4," elaborated by me and one or two other Pentagon colleagues I had not even yet met, that finally set in motion the events that led up to the actual Argus experiment. That order was directed to the Armed Forces Special Weapons Project in the spring of 1958, a mere four months after those first conversations.

Project 137: Another Unusual Reaction to Sputnik

In addition to those scientists specifically invited by high officials to give their views on how to respond to Sputnik, many others did so on their own. One key group in this category was made up of three professors at Princeton University: John Wheeler and Eugene Wigner, both physicists, and Oskar Morgenstern, an economist and coauthor with von Neumann of the seminal book on game theory. They proposed the creation of something they called the National Security Research Initiation Laboratory. It would be a place where "at the working level ideas from one field could be brought to bear on problems from another with the coils of inter-agency secrecy cast aside and with the duty to explore systematically and continuously the two areas of science and security."[2] In essence, they believed that new developments in science could contribute much more to the national defense than they currently did and that the major reason this wasn't happening was the lack of an appropriate mechanism for coupling active research scientists with those knowledgable about national security. Their proposed new laboratory would itself do preliminary work on new ideas, and then, if these showed promise, either existing laboratories would be "induced" to take them on or a new special-purpose laboratory would be created. As a first step, they suggested

> the formation of a study group of about 15 or 20 of our best scientists with a strong interest in the defense of the country. This group would assemble for about three weeks in Washington, it would be briefed for about three hours a day and then would start discussions and calculations both on the obvious ideas which present themselves for the problems and also on more adventurous methods of which the group might think.

Other scientists, younger and with fewer contacts and less experience in defense work, were also seeking ways to be more usefully involved. Marvin Goldberger, then chairman of the physics department at Princeton University, later told me,

> In 1957, Ken Watson, Keith Brueckner and I were consulting for a group at Convair that had a contract to study nuclear explosions. We were just getting into the defense community. We became depressed by two factors. First, we always saw only the same small group of people, and second, we did all the work, but Convair got all the money. We considered setting up our own consulting firm and proceeded some way down that road. However, we soon became uneasy about that approach, and began to search for other mechanisms.[3]

There were many others just like them, also able and interested, but with no notion of how to get involved.

Eventually, the "first step" part of the Wheeler-Wigner-Morgenstern idea took life and turned out to be unusually fruitful. A "study group" like the one they prescribed met in the summer of 1958. In addition to the three Princetonians who suggested it, Goldberger and Watson also attended, along with a dozen or so others like them. Beginning in 1960 the idea became institutionalized in the form of the so-called Jason group.

At the time all this was first proposed, in the fall of 1957, no official in the Department of Defense had either the authority, the breadth of interest, the inclination, or the money to sponsor such an activity. Worse, no one was really capable of understanding what Wheeler was driving at or what Goldberger wanted to do. Before these latent interests and enthusiasms could be properly exploited, a new organization had to be created, one capable of dealing with proposals like this one, with inventions like the one by Christofilos, and with many other larger-scale matters then either being handled inadequately or not at all.

The Department of Defense Reacts to Sputnik

The Soviet Union, generally considered to be a backward nation, had launched the first artificial satellites. Whatever the satellites themselves might mean, the technology used in launching them was obviously of enormous importance to national defense. A huge rocket, propelled by powerful engines and guided by modern electronic devices, all of the kind that made it possible to launch the Sputniks, could just as well send thermonuclear weapons from Siberia to the United States in thirty minutes. We had been striving toward that same goal for several years but had not quite reached it. The Soviet Union, our principal rival and antagonist on the world scene, had beaten us by at least one year, and many informed people believed our lag time was substantially greater than that.

Americans everywhere, including those in the Congress, demanded to know why it had happened and what it meant. More important, they wanted to know what the government, meaning the White House and the Defense Department in particular, intended to do about it. When they didn't get satisfactory answers, they began to produce their own.

By chance, it was on October 9, 1957, just five days after Sputnik, that Neil McElroy was sworn in as secretary of defense. Although in no way responsible for these shocking events, he was the man who had to respond to them, at least within the defense establishment.

McElroy had previously been president of Procter & Gamble. He was an intelligent, hearty, optimistic man with a pleasant and positive personality. He knew next to nothing about either defense policy or defense technology, but he had the reputation of being an excellent manager. Like many good executives, he was a good judge of people and usually could quickly distinguish between those who knew what they were talking about and those who didn't. He was sensitive to the public clamor, and he knew that his first order of business was to develop answers to the questions the American body politic was insistently raising.

What, in retrospect, was the matter, and what could the new secretary do about it? As I see it, the overall situation was characterized by three major factors.

The first factor was positive. The record of the times clearly showed that the military departments, when given adequate authority, instructions, and resources, could successfully carry out complex development programs. In the years before Sputnik the most important of these programs and the men who directed them were the Navy's nuclear submarine program, directed by Admiral Rickover, and its submarine-launched missile program, directed by Admirals William Rayborn and Levering Smith; the Army's missile program, directed by General John Bruce Medaris; and the Air Force's collection of long-range missile and space programs, all managed by General Schriever. Each of these programs was well managed and efficiently run. Each moved smartly toward its objectives and was manned by persons who understood what they were doing and who worked easily with outside experts who could fill in whatever the regular staff members didn't know.

They were all able to make good use of advanced technology, and they sometimes surpassed their original goals. Occasionally they pushed hard up against the frontiers of the "state of the art" and advanced it further in the process.

The second factor was negative. It involved that special set of problems commonly called "interservice rivalry" and the closely connected "unnecessary duplication." In brief, those elements of the missile and space program that fell unambiguously within a single military department were being handled reasonably well; those that transcended one service were not.

In particular, unnecessary duplication was rife, and vicious interservice struggles over roles and missions were creating confusion. In certain vital areas some essential work was being omitted and some programs were being done poorly. The Army diverted large sums from programs designed to improve its ability to fight conventional wars into missile and space programs whose purpose was to preempt Air Force activities in those areas. The Air Force, in turn, distorted its own programs in order to head off the Army in those same areas, again neglecting some other responsibilities in doing so.

The third factor was even more negative. In short, the staff of the

Office of the Secretary of Defense (OSD), which should have been capable of handling interservice issues and of discovering serious omissions in the total program, could not even begin to do so. And, of course, it could not handle radical new inventions like that of Christofilos or ideas like that of Wheeler and colleagues. OSD had been created in the first place in part so that there would be a home for those issues and ideas that did not fit within the purview of a single service, but it was not providing such a home. The organization chart of OSD seemed to show that it was staffed with people who could provide advice and counsel on such matters, but the reality was far different from the appearance. When it came to modern technology, the OSD that McElroy had inherited was, by and large, an intellectual desert.

Only a strong and well-informed OSD could have handled the situation facing McElroy when he took over his new post. Possession of formal authority by certain officials was not enough by itself. In theory, the secretary of defense, acting on behalf of the president, could have put things straight. On paper, he had the power to eliminate duplication, order an end to interservice struggles, and have omitted technologies be explored. The interconnections among high defense officials, senior military officers, members of the key congressional committees, and the defense-oriented press operated in such a way that formal authority had to be reinforced by intellectual authority if radical changes were to be accomplished. It was crucial that the senior official seeking to make such changes be seen as understanding in detail the essential elements of the matter either in person or, at the very least, through persons directly and intimately associated with him. Such a combined force— formal authority plus intellectual power and grasp—was largely lacking in OSD in the mid 1950s.

The Solution

The creation of the Advanced Research Projects Agency, or ARPA, was the new secretary's first answer to Sputnik. The establishment of the Office of the Director of Defense Research and Engineering, or ODDR & E, was the second. ARPA, and my role in it, is the subject of this chapter; the ODDR & E will be covered in the next.

As soon as he was sworn in, McElroy turned his attention to these problems. He consulted widely within the defense establishment and sought outside counsel and assistance. Foremost among the outsiders he turned to were James Killian and Charles Thomas.

McElroy had not previously known Killian, but given the latter's White House position and his review of similar problems, it was natural to consult him. Both men were deeply and seriously concerned, both were naturally amiable, and a positive and easy relationship developed quickly.

Charles Thomas, like McElroy, was chief executive of an industrial giant, the Monsanto Chemical Company. When McElroy asked him to come in and consult about the situation, Thomas asked to delay briefly his visit until he could arrange to bring along another special friend of his, Ernest Lawrence. Years earlier, during World War II, Thomas had been responsible for a key element of the plutonium project. In that connection he and Ernest had met each other. They saw eye to eye on a wide variety of issues and quickly became fast friends and mutual admirers.

Thus, by another of those remarkable chance events that blessed my life, two of the three outsiders McElroy turned to for special help were men who knew me and thought well of what I had accomplished so far. Both Lawrence and Killian advised McElroy to bring me into OSD in some high position where I could help build an in-house capability for coping with issues of high technology.

I was quite unaware of these interventions on my behalf, and I was certainly not seeking any such opportunities. I had my mind set on doing what I could as a member of Killian's PSAC and then getting back to my career at the University of California.

As a result of these important but unexpected interventions, and also because of the snowstorm-inspired private meeting I had had with McElroy in mid-February, I did indeed become deeply involved in building a capacity for handling high-tech issues in OSD.

ARPA

McElroy very early concluded that a new organization was needed within OSD. It must, he thought, be empowered to sponsor and manage research and development in certain key areas where things were not going right. He had in mind areas that were either being ignored by the military services or in which interservice rivalry was holding things back. He believed that the space program and the antimissile program were immediate candidates for such an approach, and he felt there would be others as well.

Many different organizational formats were proposed in those first few months after Sputnik. Since it was still only twelve years since World War II, a Manhattan Project for space was high among the analogies discussed.

The Wheeler-Wigner-Morgenstern proposal for the creation of a National Defense Research Initiation Laboratory was another. Wheeler apparently urged Lawrence to lead a delegation to make such a proposal to McElroy in person, but that never happened.

Others spoke of creating a "fourth service," devoted specifically to developing and producing new high-tech systems while leaving the operation and use of the existing military hardware to the other three services.

McElroy eventually settled on the idea of creating a new agency that would on his behalf promote, control, and manage a variety of "advanced research projects," including all those involving satellites, space flight, and missile defense. The agency, which he soon named the Advanced Research Projects Agency, or ARPA,* would be manned by a staff modest in size but made up of people who knew the relevant sciences and technologies and who had had direct experience in designing and building systems based on them.

Finally, on January 9, 1958, Eisenhower announced in his State of the Union Message the creation of ARPA "to concentrate into one organization all anti-missile and satellite activities undertaken within the Department of Defense."[4]

The Opposition

The proposal for a new agency was widely opposed in the military departments. The reason was simple: it would take away their authority over a number of programs they deemed especially important. Particularly in the Army and the Air Force, space technology was seen as the key to the future, to the acquisition of the roles and missions needed for their further development and expansion.

The most persistent opponent was Air Force General Bernard A. Schriever, then head of the Air Force Ballistic Missile Division. He strongly opposed ARPA while it was still an idea and continued to attack it after its creation; even years later, when it had been modified

*A few years later the word *Defense* was inserted at the beginning of this name, so the agency is now known as DARPA.

in ways that met most of his objections, he still called for its aboli-
tion.

Schriever had two main reasons for opposing ARPA. First, like all of
his associates, he believed that no new agency was needed. The services were perfectly capable of doing all that was required, if properly
supported and instructed by higher authority. More important, he opposed the new agency because its initial program would be made up
largely of projects already under his command. They were all going
well, and he saw any change in his authority over them as somewhere
between malicious and nonsensical. Perhaps even more to the point,
Schriever believed he and the Air Force could provide the total answer to Sputnik if only they were given the orders and authority to
do so.

There was a certain irony in this situation. Eventually Schriever's
basic notion about how properly to handle military space was adopted
and did indeed prove to be right. However, it was simply impossible in
the months immediately after Sputnik to arrange things that way, in one
step and by fiat. As I will discuss later in this chapter and in the next
one, it turned out to be necessary first to eliminate the Army–Air Force
rivalry over military space and then to sort out those projects that were
primarily related to the civilian space exploration role from those that
were intrinsically military in nature, before the final, sensible result
could be achieved. This sorting out could be accomplished only through
several intermediate steps, the first of which involved turning responsibility for all defense-related space projects over to the new agency,
ARPA.

The People

After a brief hassle with some key members of Congress, during which
McElroy had to assure them that the new arrangement would in no way
interfere with their prerogatives, ARPA got under way during February
and March 1958. Each of the four major general constituencies of the
defense establishment—civilian executive, military, science and technology, and financial administration—had a hand in making a key initial
appointment.

Secretary McElroy himself selected the director, Roy W. Johnson.
Johnson had just been executive vice-president General Electric, a position that had important parallels to McElroy's at Procter & Gamble.

They had known each other before, and apparently McElroy had reason to believe that Johnson was movable. Johnson himself was commonly described in the press as ebullient, enigmatic, private, religious, and frank. He freely acknowledged that he knew next to nothing about science and advanced technology. However, he claimed—often with force—that he "knew management," and, when aroused, he made clear his belief that scientists generally neither possessed nor understood this skill. His appointment was announced on February 9, 1958.

Admiral John Clark became deputy director and de facto military representative at the top of the ARPA hierarchy. He had previously been the director of guided missiles and before that commander of the Navy's missile test range at Point Mugu, California. Given the extreme rivalry between the Army and the Air Force in this area, a naval officer had to be selected for the position. Later, after the initial difficulties in establishing ARPA had been overcome, the post was held by senior officers from the other services, but it could not start out that way.

Lawrence Gise was nominated to be business manager by Wilfrid J. McNeil, defense comptroller. At the time, Gise was a high-level administrator in the AEC and was therefore already familiar with the problems inherent in financing and administering high-technology programs.

And I was the nominee of that part of the scientific establishment represented by Killian and Lawrence for the role of chief scientist. My appointment to that position was announced on March 17.

It fell to me to recruit the remainder of the initial technical staff, some dozens of scientists and engineers experienced in the relevant branches of high technology. But before that could be accomplished, we had to find a way around the problem created by the abysmally low salaries then being paid within the civil service structure to such persons.

A Special Role for IDA

Inspired by the feeling of "national emergency" that Sputnik had wrought, we worked out a special arrangement for solving the salary problem, an arrangement that under ordinary circumstances would not have been allowed. With the cooperation of OSD officials and the White House, and with the acquiescence of the Civil Service Commission and the Congress, we arranged to issue a contract to a private organization, the Institute for Defense Analyses (IDA), to hire all the scientists and engineers we needed. IDA then assigned them to work in the Pentagon as directed by ARPA management.* As one example, IDA hired me to be director of its Advanced Research Projects Division—newly established just for the purpose—and then assigned me to work for Roy Johnson on a "without compensation" basis. My formal employment date was March 16, but by then I had already been effectively at work for several weeks. All the other initial scientists and engineers were hired in the same way.

The organizations from which the first cadre of scientists and engineers came in that spring and summer of 1958 included five aerospace companies, Aerojet General, Convair, Douglas, Hughes, and Reaction Motors; three chemical companies, Du Pont, Rohm & Haas, and Union Carbide; four electronics companies, Bell Labs, GE, RCA, and Sylvania; and General Motors. Five came from within the government and seven (including me) from nonprofit institutions.

This arrangement, in which IDA acted as a "hiring hall" for the government, was unusual in itself, but the peculiarities did not end there. IDA and ARPA officials negotiated directly with a number of corporations, all doing business with the Pentagon, for assistance in the recruitment of its staff. We met with corporate presidents or vice-presidents, told them of our needs, and asked them to nominate rising members of their staffs to come and work with us for a year or two. We allowed them to make whatever arrangements they wished concerning the eventual return of the individuals to the company. We insisted only that while they were with us they could not receive any compensation from any source except IDA. This decidedly non–arm's length arrangement, which then as today would normally be considered both illegal and improper, was accepted by all concerned as the only means available for coping with the emergency we faced.

Soon after I was officially on board as chief scientist of ARPA, I asked Albert Hill, the vice-president of IDA, how I should address General Nathan Twining, then chairman of the Joint Chiefs of Staff. Al said, "I always call him General Twining, but you're a brash young Californian, so you can call him Nate." I continued to call him Sir or General Twining, but I was more relaxed about it.

---

*IDA, a private corporation, had been established two years earlier, in 1956. Its purpose was to recruit and manage a group of civilians to work directly in the Office of the Joint Chiefs of Staff in a special unit called the Weapons Systems Evaluation Group (WSEG). This unit, consisting of a mixture of IDA civilians and regular military officers, conducted studies of the kind commonly called operations research or strategic analysis. As in the period after Sputnik, it had at that earlier time proved to be impossible to get the right people under the civil service practices then in force, and this new corporation was set up to overcome that difficulty.

Even at the beginning, however, we did not think of these peculiar, ad hoc arrangements as being permanent. Sputnik had also inspired some new public laws that allowed high-tech agencies of the government a quota of above-grade salaries. With that as an extra attraction, we were able to build up a cadre of first-rate civil servants who were both attracted by the excitement of our program and already accustomed to living on government salaries. As a result, within less than two years, the central office of ARPA was staffed entirely by civil servants. From then on, IDA provided support to ARPA through study contracts, each encompassing a specific problem that IDA personnel could do independently rather than as direct staff provided by a "hiring hall."

The Initial ARPA Program

At the beginning the ARPA administration, working closely with McElroy and Deputy Secretary of Defense Donald Quarles, considered several schemes for managing its projects. These included contracting directly with industry, setting up new laboratories or taking over existing ones, and contracting for its projects through the military services. Very soon we realized that only the last concept was practical. Not only would this get us launched faster than any of the other schemes; it would also help alleviate some of the worst fears of the services about our long-range intentions.

Among the organizations that we briefly considered taking over were the von Braun section of the Army Ballistic Missile Agency, MIT's Lincoln Laboratory, and Caltech's Jet Propulsion Laboratory. For various reasons, including internal opposition in each case, the idea of incorporating any of them into a super ARPA was abandoned. Despite these early rebuffs, ARPA was able to maintain very good relations with each of these institutions at the technical working level.

The programs initially assigned to ARPA were space, ballistic missile defense, and solid rocket development. The last program was the smallest; it came about largely because George Kistiakowsky, then an active member of the PSAC and a chemist himself, thought that a concerted research effort would produce rockets with substantially higher performance than those currently available. Within ARPA, this program was headed from the start by John Kincaid, who had come from Convair.

The second program, ballistic missile defense, was intended to include all research and development on the subject except that specifically necessary for the Nike-Zeus project. The purpose of this last project, then under the supervision of General Medaris and the Army Ballistic Missile Agency, was to construct a defense against the current generation of Soviet missiles, using the current state of the art to do so. Originally, McElroy had considered assigning the whole Nike-Zeus project to ARPA, but managing such a large program would have swamped us and undercut our ability to do the other, more advanced projects. After a brief study, prudence prevailed, and we took on only work designed to develop more advanced components for use in future generations of ballistic missile defenses. Called the Defender Program, it worked out well. Many of the components of successor schemes to the Nike-Zeus—Nike X, Safeguard, Sentinel, Hi-ads, and Lo-ads—have come out of the ARPA Defender Program.

The main focus of our early efforts was on satellites and space flight. I maintained direct control over this aspect of our work. Our original activities in this field are best explained if they are divided into four separate categories.

The first category consisted of the development of satellites designed to perform clearly military functions: reconnaissance, surveillance, early warning, communications relay, navigation, military meteorology, and the like. Each of these functions was already being performed by earthbound means, including overflight by aircraft, but the new possibilities opened up by the adapting of satellites for such purposes seemed extremely promising.

The second category consisted of things generally called space science and exploration. It included such projects as the direct scientific investigation of the space environment, the making of astronomical and other observations with instruments unobscured by the earth's atmosphere, and, eventually, both manned and unmanned exploration of the moon and the planets.

The third category included the civilian aspects of the applications of satellites, such as relaying civil communications, predicting the weather, and exploring the earth's resources from space.

The fourth category included all projects intended to make it possible for man himself to travel and work in space, for whatever final purposes.

It was clear that the first category of projects, those involving the direct application of satellites to military purposes, would remain permanently with ARPA. It also seemed obvious that all or most of the projects in the second and third would eventually be transferred to NASA, which did not yet exist but which the White House and the Congress were working hard to bring into being.

The case of the fourth category was less clear. We in ARPA did know that President Eisenhower wanted such grand projects as the exploration of the moon to be under civilian control. He and his advisers not only felt they would get a better program that way but, more important, believed that if this supersexy sort of activity were assigned to either the Army or the Air Force, both of whom wanted it very badly, it would divert resources—money and nervous energy included—away from areas where they were more sorely needed. But knowing that didn't completely resolve the matter. There seemed to be direct military applications for man in space as well, or, at least, so highly placed persons in each of the services proclaimed.

Senior officers in the services, high executives in the aerospace industry, and editorial writers in the missile press all insisted that manned space vehicles would very quickly become essential elements of our defense posture. Intelligence experts pointed out that the Russians commonly spoke of the "conquest of space" (so did Buck Rogers, but no matter) and that we all knew what that meant, didn't we? Beyond this type of general argument lay yet another. Even sober analysts claimed that the incorporation of man into space systems would lead to greater flexibility, to a capacity for making decisions on the spot, and to the ability to take advantage of unexpected events and observations as only man can.

Our problem was that even after a year or so of fervent search and impassioned argument, no specific cases in which a military satellite needed a man *on board* as an essential component were uncovered. Most of the ARPA staff, especially Roy Johnson, believed such cases would soon develop. The space panelists of the PSAC, and I, had strong doubts about it, at least for the foreseeable future. However, given the uncertainties, the convictions of many senior officers, and the unpredictability of the future in such an unexplored area, I considered it prudent to assume for the nonce that it was essential to develop the capability for military manned space flight. I therefore joined with the rest of ARPA in promoting a long-term program of work to that end.

First Actions

Our first substantive actions were to review all the space programs then either under way or being seriously considered for funding in each of the services.

In the case of the Air Force, we found a series of well-run and fully justified projects in which satellites were to be used for reconnaissance, early warning, communications, and weather forecasting. We approved these essentially as they stood, included funding for them in the new budget we were responsible for, and turned them back to the Air Force for management by the people who had been running them all along.

We also considered several new Air Force proposals. The most important was for a satellite called Discoverer. As we always explained before congressional committees in open session, its purpose was to "develop all the various engineering techniques necessary to exploit fully the new ability to fly in space, including especially those needed for the recovery of satellites from orbit." We made some minor modifications in the project, returned it to General Schriever's operation for management, and gave it an especially high priority in our overall program. It resulted in the first successful recovery of a payload from space, in August 1960, just two years from the project's initiation.

Three other Air Force proposals in the military applications area were judged to be potentially interesting but much too far ahead of the state of the art for hardware development, and they were therefore approved for study only. They were SPAD, BAMBI, and Dyna-Soar. The first two were space-based antimissile systems, the acronyms standing for Space Patrol Air Defense (no kidding!) and Ballistic Missile Boost Intercept. The basic idea in each instance was to intercept missile warheads early in their course from Siberia to North America—even, if possible, during the first few minutes after they were launched and while they were still in the boost phase. They were very similar to some of the "kinetic energy" weapons in the Star Wars scheme promoted by President Reagan twenty-five years later. We concluded that their objectives were worthwhile but that the state of the art could not support those goals at the time. The case of the Dyna-Soar was similar. It was a device much like the space shuttle that came into use in the late 1970s. On further study, however, it was evident that this device, too, was way beyond the reach of current technology, so we did not provide funds for its development.

The Army was also promoting a number of military satellite projects. We approved those for relaying military communications over great distances. There were several different versions of these, and, as with the Air Force projects, we turned them back over to the Army for management after making some minor modifications. We rejected several other projects outright, including one that directly challenged the Air Force's role in building reconnaissance satellites. We also rejected a bizarre scheme for transporting troops from one spot on the earth to another in giant missile nose cones.

The only Navy proposal involved a satellite called Transit, a device that would act as a cooperative artificial star and thus help greatly improve the ability of ships and aircraft to navigate accurately. Again, we approved it, included it in our budget, and handed it back to the Navy for direct project management.

At the time, I thought Transit was a novel idea. All the other applications were versions of things I had heard of long before, either in science fiction or in more serious pre-Sputnik discussions of the possible future uses of space. Transit, however, was new to me. Later I learned that it is in fact the oldest of the ideas for satellite applications. The original version of the idea was set out in a story written in 1868 by Edward Everett Hale—famous for making the *other* speech at Gettysburg. Entitled "The Brick Moon," it was published in 1868 in *Harper's* magazine. Hale noted the difficulty of determining longitude (it being long before radio) and proposed to do so by launching an easily visible satellite into a polar orbit around the earth. He made his satellite out of brick so that it could withstand the great frictional heating it would encounter as it sped through the upper atmosphere on its way to orbit.

In the case of projects in category two—that is, those we knew would eventually go to NASA after they got under way—we received a diversity of proposals from the services and from private industry. Such proposals described things that would, it was claimed, both be useful in themselves and outclass the Russians in their public relations impact. Most were poorly thought through, and many were crazy, but some of them were good.

The first one we chose to support involved the construction of a small space probe that would pass by the moon and send back the first close-up pictures of that body—even including, we hoped, some of its mysterious "back side." The space probe itself was to be built by the Jet Propulsion Laboratory (JPL), and the launch would be provided by either a Jupiter or a Thor-Able rocket system. ARPA orders number 1 and 2 were issued to the Army and the Air Force, respectively, for this objective. Before the launch could be carried out, however, NASA came into being, with JPL as one of its constituent parts, and the project was transferred to them.

Unfortunately, in this instance we were reaching too far too soon, and the first several tries all failed. Rather than useful results and improved public relations, these failed attempts created only embarrassment. I recall one particularly poignant moment. I was down at Cape Canaveral to watch one of the later attempts to fly by the moon. At lift-off I was standing next to Keith Glennan, the first administrator of NASA and thus the man by then responsible for the project. Just before the rocket disappeared from sight, we saw a bright spark separate from the main body and fall slowly back to earth. We had no idea what it was, but we were both pretty sure something wasn't right. Later we learned that the aerodynamic shroud protecting the lunar flyby package had ripped loose and fallen off. When that happened, the uppermost stage and the more delicate lunar flyby package were destroyed.

Most of the foregoing decisions were worked out during ARPA's first three months. It took longer to elaborate a sensible program for the development of the rockets we judged would be needed for a sustained program of space flight, including manned and unmanned exploration. A great many proposals for building such rockets were submitted to us during early and middle 1958. They came in from almost every aerospace and rocket engine company then in business. At the time, when the largest Soviet satellites weighed thirty or more times as much as the largest American ones, even fairly well informed people held the widespread belief that some secret, known only to the Russians, was eluding us. That was, of course, not true. Our programs for the development of the Atlas, Titan, and other long-range missiles involved highly efficient, very large launch systems solidly based on excellent technology. However, those programs had been funded in a big way for only about two years prior to the launch of Sputnik, and it thus simply required another year or so to complete all the practical engineering steps before they could be launched. Even giving them a "highest priority" push could not do more than cut a few months off their schedules. Most Americans found it difficult to understand this, and they consequently felt there must be something fundamentally wrong. And even many who could have understood this matter if they had wanted to chose not to, for their own political or other selfish reasons. Unhappily, Eisenhower's response to Sputnik was fast becoming a partisan issue and remained so through the 1960 presidential campaign.

We in ARPA, of course, were fully aware of the status of these existing programs, and in most cases we based our future plans on them, rather than on the many proposals for wholly new rockets. As a result, we disappointed a lot of people and brought down some wrath upon ourselves, but we set in motion a series of projects that eventually produced an outstandingly successful series of space flights. These included the projects that used a modified Redstone missile as the booster for the suborbital Mercury flights of 1961 (Alan Shepard et al.), a modified Atlas for the orbital Mercury flights beginning in 1962 (John Glenn et al.), and a modified Titan for the Gemini flights beginning in 1965. All of these were under the aegis of NASA at the time they actually went into orbit, but all were based on plans ARPA had worked out and set in motion during those early months when only we were in a position to do so.

In addition to exploiting these existing rocket systems, we devised with the Army and von Braun a plan for the development of a very large rocket involving eight Atlas engines working in parallel—the Saturn IB. And, with such projects as manned flights to the moon in the backs of our minds, we also set in motion a high-priority project for the development of what we called the Nova engine, then slated for producing 1,000,000 pounds of thrust in a single chamber. That was six times the thrust of the largest U.S. rocket engine then operating and nearly twenty times the size of the largest the Russians were then using. (Sputnik had been launched by a rocket in which twenty engines, each generating 55,000 pounds of thrust, had been "ganged," or strapped together, and operated in parallel.) Developed by North American Aviation, Nova ultimately produced 1,500,000 pounds of thrust, and when ganged in a group of five, it powered the great Saturn V rockets that propelled the Apollo system to the moon only eleven years later, in 1969.

This last project, the development of an engine with a million pounds of thrust, was one of Senator Lyndon Johnson's favorite ideas, generated in the period after the first Sputnik but before ARPA was under way. It is a further illustration of an important point implicit in this account of the origins of ARPA. ARPA did not, in those first months, invent very much that was new. Rather, from the huge number of ideas coming in from all directions, we selected those few that seemed to be the most promising elements of the American response to Sputnik that everyone was demanding. In retrospect I think the record shows that we did that very well.

Project Argus after ARPA

Nearly all of ARPA's early projects evolved naturally from prior work and ideas. Most seemed new and astonishing to the general public, but insiders had been looking forward to nearly all of them for some years. Two, however, were genuinely new and grew directly out of the special intellectual ferment stimulated by the flight of Sputnik. One was Project Argus; the other was Project Orion.

Once in ARPA, I found myself with both the responsibility and the authority for carrying out the experiments Nick Christofilos and I had first discussed four months earlier. With the help of Nick himself, we were able to elaborate ARPA order no. 4, conveying fiscal authority and instructions to the Armed Forces Special Weapons Project, and thus to set in motion Project Argus, the experiment to explore Nick's ideas. As a result, between August 27 and September 6, 1958, three nuclear weapons were exploded above the atmosphere at an altitude of three hundred miles over the South Atlantic at a point approximately longitude ten degrees west and latitude forty degrees south. A satellite, *Explorer 4,* suitable for observing the high-energy electons produced by the explosion and trapped by the earth's field was in place. We found that electons were trapped as Nick had predicted but that they did not persist for as long as he had hoped.

Ten months from the germ of an idea to its actual execution in outer space was just short of fantastic even then; today, with more complex rules and regulations, it would be utterly impossible.

The bombs had been lofted by a rocket launched from a ship in the lee of Gough Island, an uninhabited British possession located in just the right place in the South Atlantic. For reasons having to do with the imperfect symmetry of the earth's field, the launch had to take place in either the South Atlantic or the North Atlantic somewhere near Iceland. I vividly recall poring over maps (something I've always enjoyed) looking for an appropriate site, discovering that Gough Island was in the right place, and then and there personally deciding on that location.

The results of the experiment showed that the earth's magnetic field is too small and too unstable for the scheme to work on this planet but that on some other world it just might. For this reason when I hear a good scientist firmly proclaim "(nearly) perfect defense is impossible"— as during the debate over Reagan's Star Wars—I think that he is very probably right, but maybe, just maybe, there is another Christofilos out there about to present a novel and unexpected solution to the problem that will fit the facts of our particular world.

At the time, naturally enough, we all wanted to keep the whole idea to ourselves, but it was Nick himself who showed the most concern about secrecy. He was deeply bothered when we talked about it in Pentagon offices with only an ordinary door between us and the main corridor where just anybody might be listening.

Eventually, Hanson Baldwin, a *New York Times* reporter who specialized in the Navy, got hold of the whole story. In the first week of January 1959, on my first or second day on the job as director of defense research and engineering, he came to my office and tried to strike a bargain. We will, he said, hold the story indefinitely if you will promise to give us twenty-four hours' notice of any release on this subject. I was totally inexperienced in such matters, so I immediately reported the whole thing to Quarles and Killian. They rejected his proposal. The White House joined the Pentagon in trying to persuade the *New York Times* to suppress the story.

After a few weeks' deliberation, the *Times* decided to publish, and the story occupied much of its front page on March 19, 1959. It included a profile of Christofilos and signed pieces by Hanson Baldwin and Walter Sullivan, the *Times*'s longtime chief science writer.

By a charming coincidence, ten years later Sullivan and I were sitting in the back of a bus traveling from Pitsunda, in Soviet Georgia, to Sochi, a Russian Black Sea resort, talking about this episode and how the *Times* on its own decided to defy the White House. We were there to attend a Pugwash conference, and the bus ride was part of a break from work about halfway through the five days of meetings. Most of the people near us were English-speaking Russians. They were fascinated by the whole idea and drank in every word Sully said as he described how the editors made their decision.

Project Orion

The only other really novel idea that we in ARPA approved for funding in those first months—in this case for study only—was Project Orion. Originally the brainchild of Stan Ulam, it had been taken up by Theodore Taylor, then at General Atomics, in La Jolla.

The idea was to propel a huge space vehicle by means of a large number of carefully timed, sequential nuclear explosions. In one version, the spaceship weighed about four thousand tons, more than a hundred times the payload of today's space shuttle, and more than two thousand times the weight of *Sputnik III,* the largest of the early lot. The explosions, some thousands in all, were to be produced by specially designed nuclear bombs, which would direct a substantial part of their energy and mass toward a large "pusher" plate. The rebound of the bomb mass off the pusher, plus whatever mass would be evaporated from the plate itself, would produce an impulse that would be transmitted through a massive shock absorber to the space vehicle proper.

Ted gathered a small group of original thinkers around him to elaborate the idea. One of them was Freeman Dyson, the author of *Disturbing the Universe.*[5] In it he also presents the story of Project Orion, but from a different point of view.

Freeman, quite an original thinker himself, was one of those who thought the project was a great and promising idea. I was the Washington bureaucrat, unnamed in Dyson's book, upon whose desk the project proposal finally arrived for action. I concluded that it could have a very large potential payoff if the many unexplored problems connected with it could be handled effectively. There were so many of those, however, that I estimated it had only an extremely small chance of succeeding.

After we had been supporting the project for about a year, I happened to have supper with Frank Pace, then chairman of the board of General Dynamics, the conglomerate of which General Atomics (GA) was a part. He asked me what I thought the prospects for the project were. I told him that, in the context of overall American objectives, it was worth a million or so a year in an overall defense research budget of several billions, but I added that if I were on his board, I would vote to deny it any company funds. The potential payoff was indeed very great, but the probability of payoff was so small that it was not a good investment, even at the million-dollar level, for anyone but the government itself.

The more the people at GA studied the problem, the more excited they became, but my assessment remained the same. The group at GA even adopted "Saturn by 1970" as its working motto. From our point of view in the Defense Department, not only did the whole project look dubious but expeditions to Saturn were not on the list of goals. In sum, it was a bold, novel idea, but one that, for the immediate future, seemed both impossible and unnecessary.

In 1959, following standard government practice, we appointed a committee to review the project. It was chaired by Ernest Martinelli, then at the Rand Corporation, but earlier one of our original group at Livermore. The committee report recommended that the project continue, but it also emphasized that great uncertainties still remained in all areas, especially with regard to the pusher and the shock absorber system.

The report also disputed GA's estimates of time and costs. Where GA thought it would take five years and one billion dollars to develop a 4,000-ton vehicle, the committee estimated it would take eleven years and fourteen billion dollars. My view was that both groups had grossly underestimated both time and costs, but by then yet other developments, outside the purview of either GA or ARPA, were working to block the project. For one thing, a nuclear test moratorium of indefinite duration was in effect, and the leaders of the United States and the USSR were trying to work out a treaty to make it permanent. Under these circumstances neither the test nor the operation of such a device would be permitted. For another, GA estimated that one megaton in fission explosions would be needed to loft Orion, and that, even in the absence of a treaty forbidding it, would have been highly unpopular. As a result of all these factors, ARPA lost interest in Orion in the early sixties. (The Air Force continued to support it until 1965.)

Orion, or something like it, may come back one day to fill some future, not yet foreseeable need, but in the late 1950s—and even the mid-1980s—it had to be judged as interesting but premature, at best.

Project 137 After ARPA

We in ARPA also picked up the Wheeler-Wigner-Morgenstern idea for a new national laboratory within weeks after we got under way. Before, there had been no one with the authority, interest, or money to move it forward, but now there was. Concrete plans for a special, one-time summer conference, now called Project 137, intended as a first step, were formulated, and the three authors of the idea, plus Marvin Goldberger, submitted a list of names of people to be invited.

In June I sent a letter to some thirty persons inviting them to "participate in a small Top Secret study and work group here in Washington, July 14–August 2, 1958." The format and purpose closely followed the proposal for a "first step" originally elaborated by Wheeler and his colleagues. IDA's Albert G. Hill and I worked out a program of briefings by high-level defense officials. They covered a wide spectrum of defense problems in which we thought the application of the most up-to-date science might be helpful. Approximately twenty scientists attended. Mostly young and academic, they were, by all the standard measures, an unusually able and productive group.

Among the matters they studied that summer were electromagnetic propulsion, small submarines, hydrofoils, nuclear airplanes, communications for the Polaris system, weather control, antisubmarine warfare, game theory applications, and automata. The ingenious Nicholas Christofilos was among the attendees, and the preliminary agenda showed that the group intended to discuss what the conveners quaintly called "the Greek problem: ARGUS."

The principal conclusion of the conference was that many useful projects were suitable either for study at another similar meeting or for making up the agenda of the new laboratory.

After the conference I explored the possible interest of some of its prime movers—Wheeler and Goldberger, in particular—in becoming the founding director of the laboratory they were promoting. It quickly became evident that none of them was willing to give up his current work to take on such a responsibility. All of them, however, clearly indicated great interest in follow-up conferences of a similar kind.

Two years later, in 1960, Charles Townes, then vice-president of IDA, took a new look at the idea. He, Goldberger, and others met with Marvin Stern, then one of my deputies in the defense research and engineering directorate. Together, they cooked up a plan for institutionalizing "Project 137" in lieu of a full-scale laboratory. They called for a long summer study every year, plus several additional, brief meetings during the winter, all devoted to the study of the sort of science and security issues that had engaged them that first summer in Washington. The group would be a special division of IDA, and its members would dedicate all their consulting time and effort to it. In exchange, the group would get unusually uninhibited access to information and high officials, as well as an opportunity to exercise more influence over the course of events than part-time advisers usually do.

The idea took. Under my sponsorship, IDA and ARPA adopted the idea that Townes, Goldberger, and the others had generated. The new unit was soon named Jason and has flourished ever since. (The IDA logo was reminiscent of a Greek temple. Mildred Goldberger leaped from that fact to the suggestion that the new unit be named Jason.)

Perhaps the most important and unusual characteristic of Jason has been its ability to involve first-rate basic researchers to work on problems of direct relevance to national security. Many summer study groups claim that their people fit that description, but only in the case of Jason is it really true. Of the some one hundred people who have seriously participated in Jason activities during its first twenty-five years, eight have been Nobel laureates, all of whom received that honor *after* they became associated with Jason. Any organization can invite people who already have such honors to become members, and some can actually get them. What makes Jason special and unusual is that it selected such people beforehand. (More on my later involvement in Jason in chapter 12.)

The Formation of NASA

ARPA could be created by an executive order of the secretary of defense, but the establishment of NASA, a wholly new independent agency, required legislation and hence took longer. It was not until October 1, 1958, that NASA opened shop, more than half a year behind ARPA, in what had been Dolley Madison's house, diagonally across Lafayette Square from the White House.

T. Keith Glennan, president of the Case Institute of Technology, and formerly a member of the Atomic Energy Commission, was appointed to be the first administrator. Hugh Dryden, who had long been the technical director of NACA, became the first deputy administrator.

Initially, NASA was made up of all of the old National Advisory Committee on Aeronautics plus about two hundred persons from the Naval Research Laboratory, largely John Hagen's Vanguard team plus a small group of upper-atmosphere researchers. In addition to taking on all the projects managed by those predecessor groups, the Space Act authorized transfer of many of the programs already initiated by ARPA and others in the Department of Defense. These included certain space probes, satellites, and rocket engine development programs, all of which had been initiated with the understanding that they would probably be transferred to NASA when the latter came into being.

The Space Act also provided for the transfer of such other government units to NASA as the president might deem necessary. In that connection, Glennan, like Roy Johnson before him, explored the possibility of acquiring both the von Braun group and the Jet Propulsion Laboratory. He soon discovered that the laboratory was willing but that the Army would fight, and fight hard, any attempt to take von Braun from them. Wilbur Brucker, the secretary of the Army, warned that "breaking up the Army missile team" would gravely damage the national security. As a young man, Brucker had been elected governor of Michigan as a "dry" candidate, and more recently he had performed as an occasional speaker on the evangelical circuit, so he knew how to make an impassioned plea when one was necessary. When Brucker said he would fight it everywhere, in the Congress, in the public press, and out on the hustings, Glennan took him seriously. Glennan concluded that his new agency did not need the extra burden of such a struggle at the time, and he backed off from that leg of his proposal. As a final result, the Jet Propulsion Laboratory became a part of NASA in December 1958, but the von Braun team remained part of the Army for another year and a half, until July 1960.

The transfer of the von Braun group eventually took place—logic demanded it—but it required a better-prepared assault on the system. That assault had to wait until after my authority was extended in December to cover all elements of research and engineering in the Department of Defense, including those managed by the Army. In the meantime the managers of the two new agencies, NASA and ARPA, had to work out suitable ad hoc arrangements in an imperfectly organized world.

The political maneuvers that finally resulted in rationalizing fully the U.S. space program, and that got von Braun out of the Army and into NASA, constitute one of the high points of my career. They will be described in the next chapter.

Testifying before the Congress

My new responsibilities in ARPA brought me into a much more intense and interesting relationship with the Congress than before. I found myself testifying before a variety of committees, in both the House and the Senate, about once a week and sometimes more often. Later on, after the whole situation had matured, ARPA officials testified on a more routine basis, less frequently and before fewer committees, but for now space was hot stuff and ARPA was new and controversial.

By chance I behaved in exactly the right way to make the best-possible impression on a congressional committee. Because of my great interest in the subject, I knew all sides of it very well: what could be usefully done in space, how it should be done, what the Soviets were most likely doing and what that meant, and—by definition, almost—what our Department of Defense was going to do in and about space. As a result, when I was called to testify, I took along at most one aide and seldom referred either to him or the notebooks he carried. I usually gave an ad lib summary of what we were planning to do and then answered questions easily and reasonably fully. I did not know it at the time, but most bureaucrats in similar situations normally read from carefully prepared statements and frequently turned for help to the numerous aides and notebooks they always brought with them.

After one such closed hearing, Chairman George Miller, a California Democrat of great seniority, who treated me like his own constituent

(Livermore was in his district), thanked me and made a little speech about how now that I was in place in the Pentagon, the Congress and the people could breathe more easily, knowing that the Republic would soon and surely be rescued from the menace posed by Sputnik. The other members followed suit, with only one exception, Daniel Flood, a Democrat representing a coal-mining population in the Eleventh Congressional District of Pennsylvania.

Flood was literally a colorful character. He had a narrow, heavily waxed black mustache that curled tightly at each end, making a more than complete circle in the process. He always wore a vest of some unlikely color—bright yellow, say—with a boldly patterned sports jacket over it. He often introduced his remarks by declaring that he was a member of the Holy Name Society and that it was therefore impossible for him to say what he really thought about the matter at hand, and then immediately launch into the most purple prose I think I have ever heard anywhere. (Much later, at the end of the 1970s, he retired from the Congress in the face of charges of "financial misconduct." He was different from his colleagues in more ways than one.) Despite these peculiarities, it was my impression that he cared as much about the country and its security as anyone on the committee, but he always approached these issues in his own, special way.

When I finished my testimony, Flood, too, delivered a good paragraph of fulsome praise. But then he suddenly looked me in the eye, wagged his finger at me, and added, "This guy is either real smart or real glib, and none of us can tell which."

I was quickly brought back to reality by his remarks. I thought then—and I still think—that he was closer to the truth than any of the others in that last round of pretty comments. In the course of the next several years, I had other bizarre brushes with Dan Flood, but this was the most educational.

At that hearing I could have been telling the whole truth or I could have been making it up right on the spot, and not one of them could be sure which it was. That is not typically the situation in the Congress. Senior members of committees commonly have more experience with the topic at hand than the witnesses before them, and they can as a rule easily distinguish between a real expert and a blowhard. In this case, however, space was novel and ARPA was new, and I was protected both by that novelty and by my own obvious political innocence. They really could not tell where I was coming from.

Most of my congressional appearances were, like that one, before closed sessions of the various interested committees. Some others were open. In some ways the open ones were more exciting; spectators were usually present and so were reporters. When TV cameras were present, there would be lots of handshaking and big smiles before the real work of the hearing got under way. I soon formed the impression, one reinforced by subsequent experience, that the congressional committees do their best work in closed sessions, like it or not, and no "sunshine laws" can effectively change that. Public sessions are full of posturing; closed sessions are generally not. In addition, public sessions are fraught with partisan behavior. To be sure, that also occurs in closed ones, but with much less intensity or bearing on the outcome.

In the open hearings of that period, after some good discussion of the real substance of the situation, the questions often turned to the basically partisan issue of whether President Eisenhower really understood the problem and was doing enough about it. "Dr. York, do you *really* believe the president is authorizing enough money in this area?" "Are you getting the support you need from the White House?" "Are we not in a life-and-death race with the Russians, and what are we doing to win?"

I always found it possible to give my honest views in such questions without ever coming close to criticizing the president. We in the executive branch all had our individual opinions, I would carefully and repetitiously explain, about what should be included and how much should be done, but only the president had full responsibility for the total picture, and only he could put the whole thing together in a way designed to serve America's best interest. Lyndon Johnson, then Senate majority leader, pushed hardest on this issue, but even he couldn't get me to denounce Eisenhower's approach.

Unfortunately, my immediate boss, the ARPA director, Roy Johnson, didn't always handle such questions properly, and relations between him and the White House, meaning both the President's Science Advisory Committee and the president, never warm to begin with, began to sour. Fortunately for me, however, my own political situation was sufficiently independent that my relations with people across the river remained good and undiminished by the problems my boss was creating for himself.

There were some lighter moments also. At one hearing I had said we were not going to support one outlandish project, because the state of the art would not permit it.

An elderly senator whose mind had been drifting off somewhere suddenly tensed and interrupted to ask, "What did you say?"

I repeated, "The state of the art won't permit it."

"Oh," he said, relaxing back, "I thought you said the state of New York!"

Relations with members of the Congress can sometimes get too good. On one occasion that first spring, Senator Henry Jackson called me up and explained that a certain good friend and colleague of his, one Jack Kennedy, had a kid brother, Ted, in law school down at the nearby University of Virginia, and that Ted in turn needed an expert to speak to his law class club on space, so how about it? A few days later I dutifully made my way to Charlottesville. Ted Kennedy picked me up at the airport in a yellow convertible and drove me off for supper and the after-dinner speech to the club. That sort of thing interfered with my work, but I enjoyed a certain amount of it, and in this particular case it led to a friendly and rewarding relationship, though not a close one, with Ted.

Retrospective on the Congress

From childhood, I had always had great confidence in the American government, in both its grand principles and its operating mechanisms. My years in Washington taught me a lot of details I hadn't known or even dreamed of before, but the net result was an even stronger confidence in its validity and in its ability to produce the right policies, given accurate inputs and enough time.

I learned all those things about both the Congress and the executive branch that Washington correspondents and political experts know in their bones and take for granted. I discovered that some congressmen and high officials are inadequate for their responsibilities. Some are dim-witted and lazy; some represent very narrow constituencies or special interests. A few are too far over the hill, and a few are too new and naive. Some drink too much or spend too much time in pursuit of personal pleasures. But a substantial majority are serious, intelligent, hardworking, patriotic, humane, and dedicated to doing what is right for the country. From time to time all of them tell themselves that in order to do good for the country, they must first get reelected, and that realization does color what they say and do during certain periods on the political calendar. But even that does not in most cases, or at most times, seriously interfere with the way they decide truly important questions.

A member of Congress faces many problems, but probably the biggest lies in the difficulty of getting the facts, in sorting out the good ideas and the quality information from the great and constant noise they live in.

They are at the center of a hurricane of ideas, proposals, and importunings, fed by constituents at home, lobbyists in the Capitol, officials and bureaucrats at many levels of the government itself, and their own staffs and colleagues.

Most of what they hear and read is inevitably self-serving. If it involves a national security issue, it usually comes in a package along with the pleader's private views of the Soviet Union and its purposes, as well as with his usually amateurish interpretation of the latest intelligence information. Most of what the members of Congress hear is pushed upon them, but they also seek information directly. This may be from friends, colleagues, or other confidants, but perhaps most comes from witnesses they interview either individually or at a hearing.

Despite all those problems and all that cacophony, it is my firm conclusion that "at the end of the day," as the British would say, the Congress will produce a reasonably correct result if, and only if, it gets good inputs from the responsible officers and bureaucrats in the executive branch. This rule holds in cases involving unfamiliar topics like science and technology as well as in those involving more familiar matters.

Advice from outsiders—even invited, high-quality advice—can help only in fine-tuning the result, and even then only if the information coming from inside the government is correct, reasonably complete, and based on a real understanding of the facts. And, of course, advice that is forced on the Congress, as by special-interest groups at public hearings, has almost no impact on the course of events. It may grab some local headlines, and the members of the committee can be skillful at making the witnesses think that someone is actually listening, but they really are not, except perhaps with a purely political part of their mind, and the influence on what happens is as one would expect.

In sum, my view of the Congress, developed then and reinforced since, is that it is a great institution and that its structure and rules can produce the results we need, given half a chance. The sine qua non, however, is quality information from the executive branch. Witnesses must understand the inner substance of the issues at hand, know how things fit together, and be able to assess their relative importance and priority in the larger scheme of things.

Public Relations

I also met frequently with the press in a great variety of formats and circumstances: one-on-one, in press conferences, in radio interviews, and on television news and talk shows. I soon discovered that a straightforward and honest, politically naive approach worked nearly as well with the fourth estate as with the Congress.

On Cynthia's seventh birthday, June 8, 1958, I made a half-hour live appearance on CBS's "Face the Nation." I still have the film of that broadcast, and I recently took the opportunity to review it for the first time in twenty-five years. I was fearful that I might not like what I saw after the passage of so much time and the intervention of so many other events, but I did.

In substance it was much like the open congressional hearings. John Finney, the *New York Times*'s man in the Pentagon, in effect asked me in several different ways, "Isn't it true that we are in a very serious race with the Russians and that the president isn't doing enough about it?" Again, I found an answer that was both honest and supportive of the president. "Things are not really as bad as they seem," I insisted, "and our own work in this area is much further along than a superficial view of the facts may indicate."

"What about the million-pound engine? Why hasn't it been contracted?" someone else asked.

"We in ARPA have only been formally in business about two months, and we will be issuing a contract for it soon after the beginning of the new fiscal year, on July 1, now just three weeks away. I don't know how soon you will hear a great swoosh as it takes off, but we are getting a major program in this area under way very soon."

The questioners persisted: "Why isn't the whole space program in one agency?" "Why is there both an ARPA and a NASA?" "Doesn't there simply have to be a single space czar if we are to have any hope of ever catching up with the Russians?" To answer this set of questions, which also arose on other occasions and came from many directions, I developed a simple aphorism as my constant answer, and I used it on that show: "Space is a place, not a program." To that I might add, depending on the precise circumstances, something like "And it is appropriate for any agency of the Department of Defense or the government to conduct activities and projects there if doing so can contribute to the conduct of its proper functions" or "We have to develop the large rockets for reaching space in a carefully planned, coherent, and unified way, but the satellites themselves can well be developed and operated by whoever can directly benefit from their use."

I suppose I used that phrase "Space is a place, not a program" literally hundreds of times during 1958, and eventually, I think, I actually sold that simple notion and the more complex reality behind it in the places it counted—in the Congress, in the PSAC, and in the higher reaches of the Department of Defense.

Last Talk with Lawrence

My new responsibilities in Washington were exciting and absorbed all the intellectual energy I could muster. I found little time to think about the people and times at Livermore and Berkeley, interesting and important as they had been to me. The only exceptions came when someone from California traveled east on business.

Sometime during that first spring in Washington, Ernest Lawrence dropped in to visit. It was the last time I would see him. If I'd known that then, the date and place would be engraved in my mind; but I didn't and they aren't.

We must have covered a wide range of topics: ARPA, Livermore, the forthcoming meeting of experts in Geneva, and the like, but I remember only two items, which still stand out clearly in my mind.

The first item concerned accelerators. The Russians were very active in this field, and for some time visitors had been going back and forth between various Western laboratories and Serpukhov, the Soviet accelerator center. Some Americans suggested that an "accelerator Sputnik" might somehow be in the offing—"We couldn't allow something like that to happen again, could we?" Self-serving predictions of Sputnik-like events that had nothing to do with either space or reality were quite common in those days, and nuclear physicists were, sorry to say, no exception to the general rule. For that as well as for other reasons, proponents of new accelerators were filled with great enthusiasm and held high hopes for still bigger—and more expensive—machines.

By then, accelerators in the ten-billion-volt range were already operating in America and in Eastern and Western Europe, and the next step was clearly in sight. Just as the particle energy rose with each new machine generation, so did the cost, and the next machines were being estimated to cost well over a hundred million dollars.

Lawrence had started this trend of ever onward and upward machine building in the early 1930s, more than twenty years before. Indeed, the quest for ever bigger machines had dominated most of his professional life, and, as we know, his enthusiasm for the next generation had inhibited him from fully exploiting the one in hand. One might have expected that he would have been enthusiastic about yet another round of bigger machines, but he wasn't, and, for whatever reason, he wanted to explain his views to me at this last meeting.

"When I was young I knew that if we were ever going to unlock nuclear energy, we would learn to do so through research with particles whose kinetic energy was in the range of the energies that bind the particles together in the nucleus. The early cyclotrons were precisely in that range, and I was therefore confident that they would produce a practical result. Today accelerators produce particles with energies a thousand times higher, and more factors of ten are in sight, but there do not appear to be any corresponding prospects for practical applications. I therefore doubt that it is today socially justifiable to invest such huge sums so fast in so many machines."

Those were not his exact words, but they were certainly his basic thoughts. They were quite surprising to me and are therefore engraved solidly in my memory. He didn't mean we shouldn't build any bigger machines at all, but he definitely did believe that the rates of expenditure then being discussed could not be justified by the potential value, in economic and social terms, of the likely results. It was not a question of whether there was more to learn—I have no reason to believe he had any doubts about that. Rather, it was a question of the benefits of such expenditures to humanity as a whole. Lawrence was a pure scientist, as were most of his colleagues, and he believed that doing physics was a worthy and proper human activity in itself; but he also had a strong practical orientation and always kept in mind applications of the machines and techniques of science, and he saw that side of it gradually fading in importance as the machines got bigger and more expensive.

The other memorable remark was briefer: "Herb, I want you to be my successor as director of the Radiation Laboratory." He was fifty-six at the time, young enough that retirement must have seemed far away, and superficially healthy and energetic enough that anyone who knew him only casually would have been surprised at his even thinking about it. At the same time, his chronic colitis was getting worse (I know this as much from his biography as from my memory), and so perhaps he was more aware than most that things cannot go on forever unchanged.

Pondering all that in retrospect, I feel he was thinking of a time still some years off, at the very least, and not only some months, as it turned out to be. In any event, when his health did seriously deteriorate a few months later, he named his brother-in-law, Edwin McMillan, to be acting director, and Ed in turn naturally took over when Ernest died shortly afterward.

Lawrence at Geneva

The underlying cause of Lawrence's death was his chronic colitis. A crisis in this illness occurred in the setting of the Conference of Experts that opened in Geneva on July 1, 1958. The purpose of the conference was to examine the scientific facts relevant to monitoring a ban on all nuclear weapons tests. The conferees were Americans, Russians, and a few others from countries allied to one or the other of the superpowers. Ernest was invited to be a member of the American group, and he, like everyone else, thought the matter was of the highest importance.

Lawrence was put on the delegation at the insistence of Lewis Strauss. Strauss was strongly anti-Soviet, anti-Communist, and anti–test ban. He also wanted to be sure that someone would be there who could be relied on to block any real chance of a nuclear test ban. Lawrence's record was such that Strauss thought he could count on him for that purpose.

Strauss seems to have had some last-minute doubts about Ernest's filling that role properly. Shortly before Ernest left for Geneva, Strauss sent him a letter in which he said, "No matter how eminent the Russian scientists are or how persuasive, never let yourself forget they are the envoys of men who are cold blooded murderers. Deal with them with reserve."[6] And, indeed, Strauss may have been right in these last-minute doubts. According to Harold Brown, who was also there, Lawrence took the purpose of the conference very seriously. During a period when the Western group was worried that the Russians might simply quit the conference, the Americans prepared what they called "break statements," which were to be delivered in such an event. In one drafted by Lawrence, he made a strong plea for continuing the talks, reminding the Soviets of the international nature of science and the necessity to avoid nuclear war, appealing to them to rise above narrow, nationalistic considerations, and noting that Nobel Prize winners sat on both sides of the table. Lawrence was definitely moving away from his previous, totally uncritical view of accelerators; maybe he was doing the same with nuclear weapons.

Even before Ernest left home to attend the conference, he was feeling worse than usual; but, despite the importuning of friends, he was determined to go anyway. Once he was there, a head cold, hard work, frustrating sessions, and long hours took their toll. He gave up before the conference completed its work, and returned to California, exhausted. He immediately entered Stanford University Hospital. The attending physicians did what they could, but his condition continued to deteriorate, and he died on August 27, 1958, shortly after his fifty-seventh birthday.

Sedov

I was in Amsterdam, at an international conference on astronautics, when I read in the *International Herald Tribune* that Ernest had died. I recalled his remark about wanting me to succeed him, but I knew there was no way that could happen just then, and it seemed equally unlikely for the future. Other important and exciting matters were pressing in on me from all directions, I was much engaged with another, even more exciting new frontier—space—and so I put nuclear physics and the Radiation Laboratory off in a quiet corner of my mind.

The conference was taking place less than a year after the first Sputnik, and even though the United States had by then put up some very modest satellites of its own, the Russians, naturally enough, were the center of attention, and they loved it. The head of their delegation was one Leonid Sedov, an academician who obviously knew a lot about the Soviet program but clearly was not in charge of it. The name of the man who actually was, Sergei Korolev, was still a high-level state secret, and so, unhappily and most unfairly for him, he could not be there in Holland to bask in the world's adulation.

My only opportunity to meet Sedov came during a recess in the formal meetings. He and I both happened to visit the Rijksmuseum that day, and we encountered each other in a small gallery where several large Rembrandts were displayed. He spoke only Russian and German, and I spoke neither of those; fortunately, Wernher von Braun was there, too, and he was obviously pleased to serve as our interpreter. I asked Sedov a few polite questions, getting no more than one-word answers to most of them, and he evinced no curiosity or particular interest in either ARPA or its chief scientist. Finally, I said something about the moon that provoked him into saying, "We should send Khrushchev and Eisenhower to the moon." At least, that's what von Braun said he said.

Another Russian, who seemed to be there just for the purpose of monitoring Sedov, said in English, "Professor Sedov means that if they could look back at us from the moon, it would improve their perspectives on our problems." Maybe so.

Who's in Charge?

Late in November of my first year in Washington, everything seemed to be crowding in on me: work, the usual bureaucratic struggles, testifying, normal family obligations, and now, in addition, getting ready for Christmas. At our family supper one day, I casually remarked, "If I can find out who's in charge, I will arrange to have Christmas postponed this year."

Cynthia, then seven, was appalled. Her face clouded up and tears got ready to flow. Rachel, nine, older and wiser, saved the day: "Don't worry, Cynthia; no one's in charge." I hadn't realized it was so obvious. And after only six months in our nation's capital at that!

CHAPTER 8

Eighty Thousand Projects

(1958–1961)

An Invitation

SHORTLY before Christmas 1958 Secretary of Defense McElroy called me into his office. "The president and I," he said, "would like you to be the director of defense research and engineering."

He was referring to the new post whose establishment was the single most important element in the Defense Reorganization Act of 1958. That act had become law some four months earlier, yet the post had remained vacant ever since. Like many others in the Pentagon, I was curious about who would fill the position, but I neither sought the job nor considered myself a potential candidate.

Despite a year in Washington, I was still naive about lots of things. I did not know that most "presidential appointees" never see the president, except perhaps at a large reception held for the purpose. I therefore answered Secretary McElroy's invitation by saying, "Fine, I'll talk with the president about it as soon as he wishes."

Without batting an eyelash, McElroy smiled, turned around to face the table behind his desk, picked up the white telephone, and called the president. After a few moments, he turned back and said, "He will see you tomorrow morning at eight."

The next morning President Eisenhower repeated the invitation. Commenting on how long the position had been vacant, he said, "You were my choice from the beginning, but they [in the Pentagon] had wanted someone older and more distinguished." I had already thought about it overnight, so I accepted immediately.

The president then told me that before the nomination could be made public, he had to clear it with the Republican leaders in the House and Senate. He added, "I wish you were a young Republican; it would be easier."

I said, defensively, "Mister President, my wife and my father are Republicans."

He slapped his thigh, laughed, and said, "That's a new political concept, absolution by association."

The next day, Sybil and I and the children drove up to Rochester to spend Christmas with my parents and my sister, Helen Koch, and her family. I told everyone about my meeting with the president and this sudden turn in my life. My mother's first reaction was "What about me? I'm a Republican, too!"

On December 30, 1958, in the secretary of defense's conference room, I was sworn in, at a private ceremony attended by my wife and children.

A few weeks later Sybil and I attended a reception at the White House. When we reached the president, I said, "Mister President, I would like you to meet my Republican wife."

According to Sybil's recollection of the event, Eisenhower, without any hesitation, said, "Mrs. York, I'm surprised such a charming and lovely young woman hasn't persuaded her husband to become a Republican." She replied, "Mister President, you know my husband. The real wonder is that I am not a Democrat."

There are, of course, other ways of describing those events. General John B. Medaris's book *Countdown for Decision* put it this way:

After the law was passed that reorganized (again) the top structure of the Defense Department, and in particular provided for the now extremely powerful post of Deputy Secretary of Defense for Research and Engineering [*sic*], quite a few months passed without any sign of an appointment to that post. In a casual conversation with Bill Holaday one day I asked him why the post had not been filled, since it was obviously considered a very urgent matter. His answer was a classic. "That's easy," he said. "Every man who is smart enough to do that job well is much too smart to accept it." A few weeks later Dr. Herbert F. York was appointed.[1]

Just as the creation of ARPA had been McElroy's short-term answer to the problems revealed by Sputnik, the establishment of the Office of the Director of Defense Research and Engineering (ODDR & E) was his long-term solution. In brief, the head of the office—the director of defense research and engineering—would rank with the secretaries of the military services and above the other assistant secretaries of defense. His purview would take in all "research, development, test, and evaluation" (RDT & E) programs and projects in all parts of the Department of Defense, with no exceptions. His authority and responsibility would include the power to "approve, disapprove or modify all programs and projects" falling within his purview. In addition, he would advise the secretary of defense on the acquisition of all types of high-technology equipment.

Seven men had served with differing titles as the Pentagon's chief of R & D before me. Four were chairmen of the Research and Development Board during the Truman administration—Vannevar Bush, William Webster, Karl T. Compton, and Walter Whitman. The other three were the assistant secretaries of defense for R & D during the pre-Sputnik years of the Eisenhower administration, Don Quarles, Clifford Furnas, and Paul Foote. There were many detailed differences between the positions, in those earlier times and in my day, but the most important by far was the great increase in its authority. My predecessors had had only the responsibility of advising the secretary of defense in such matters, but I now had full authority over appropriations and expenditures. Anyone with experience in a large bureaucracy knows that "the power of the purse" is just about all the power there is. The Defense Reorganization Act of 1958 now gave it, for the first time, to the Office of the Secretary of Defense's chief of research and engineering.

Scope

The scope of the job was enormous. I once estimated that about eighty thousand projects fell within my purview. They ranged from the development of better shoes for foot soldiers and improved means for preserving field rations to the then brand-new lasers and the most sophisticated electronic devices for detecting or confusing enemy weapons. They included the army's research activities on the Greenland icecap, the Air Force's wind research station atop Mount Washington, in New Hampshire, and the Navy's explorations in Antarctica and at the bottom of the sea. There were research projects to advance human health conducted at such diverse locales as the Walter Reed Hospital in Washington and the Center for Tropical Diseases in Cairo. And there were other projects to produce weapons that could spread nonlethal but temporarily incapacitating diseases among whole populations. In the dimension of secrecy, the programs ran the gamut from those in basic research in which the goal was to publish the results as widely as possible to projects that in one or two cases were so sensitive that within OSD only the secretary, the deputy secretary, and I were fully aware of their scope and purpose. In terms of money, the programs ranged in annual cost from a few thousand dollars to well over a hundred million dollars each.

In a word, the charter for my new office said I was responsible for *everything* going on in the defense establishment that involved research, development, test, and evaluation.

One might suppose that a simple, straightforward word like *everything* would be unambiguous, but it was not. On the one hand, my charter said that I was in charge of all RDT & E in all elements of the Defense Department, subject only to the authority of the secretary of defense himself. On the other hand, the charter of Roy Johnson, the director of ARPA and my immediate boss in my previous job, said that he was in charge of all work sponsored by ARPA and that he reported directly to the secretary of defense. It took a little while and a bit of fancy footwork to work out what some saw as a contradiction in those charters, but we did. On behalf of the secretary, I "approved, disapproved, or modified" all ARPA projects in exactly the way that I did those of the three military services. At the same time, the director of ARPA, like the service secretaries, took the initiative in developing the elements of his program and, as before, reported directly to the secretary of defense on all matters having to do with personnel, program administration, and the like. For the first several months, some members of Congress and the press persisted in asking each of us which one of us was "really in charge." We patiently repeated the relevant parts of our charters in a way that avoided "putting down" the other. Eventually the questioners got bored with the matter.

Staff: Old and New

I inherited the staff of my immediate predecessor, Assistant Secretary Paul Foote, plus a few quasi-independent officers, including the director of guided missiles. They consisted of some one hundred civil servants organized in a number of separate "offices," each headed by an "office director" and each dealing with a particular grouping of related technologies. Thus there was an Office of Aeronautics, an Office of Electronics, and so on. Most of the people were reasonably well informed about the technologies within their realm, but some were not. More important, it had been a long time since most of them had been actively engaged in doing research and development work or in directly supervising it. Taken as a whole, they were not up to handling the increased responsibility and authority inherent in the reorganization of 1958.

Civil service regulations prevented me from freely reorganizing the office. In particular, I could not promote or demote people in order to rearrange who was in charge of what. I could not get rid of deadwood and replace them by others better informed about the newest elements of modern science and technology.

I quickly decided that I had to find a way to finesse this problem. I created an entirely new set of officials whom I called assistant directors of defense research and engineering. I placed them one step higher than the office directors and gave them responsibilities defined by problem areas rather than by technologies. The problem areas I selected for such special treatment were strategic warfare, tactical warfare, air defense (including missile defense), naval systems, and intelligence. In addition to the assistant directors dealing with these specific areas, there was a clear need for a new deputy director to work across the full range of my new responsibilities.

I found only one of these new assistants, Hector Skifter, in the staff I inherited from Paul Foote. He was on leave from his position as president of the Airborne Instruments Laboratory—a private electronics firm—to serve temporarily as a special assistant to work out a program for developing a defense against ballistic missiles. He agreed to stay on briefly with me as assistant director for air defense.

I looked outside the Pentagon for the others. To recruit them, I proceeded in a fashion parallel to the one we had used nine months earlier in organizing the technical staff of ARPA. I called two meetings of aerospace and electronics industry executives and there explained our plans and needs. I asked them to nominate bright and energetic people in their companies to serve in the various new positions, and many of them did so. As a result, six new senior staff assistants joined us within the next few months, and several more came in the course of the next year.

Howard Wilcox became my first deputy director. He had just previously held the number two technical position at the Naval Weapons Laboratory at China Lake (Inyokern), California. Howard and I had gotten to know each other some years earlier when we both were new assistant professors of physics at Berkeley. He helped greatly in getting the new office going, but he left within the year to become a senior R & D official at the General Motors Corporation. That job had first been offered to me by Lawrence Hafstad, a senior vice-president at GM and longtime friend of Ernest Lawrence. The proffered salary, including bonus, was literally ten times my government pay, but I was so engrossed in what I was doing that I had no difficulty turning it down. When asked if I could suggest someone else, I gave Howie's name, and he accepted soon afterward.

I then named John H. Rubel to be my principal deputy. He had come from Hughes Aircraft Corporation in the first wave of new recruits to serve as assistant director for strategic warfare. Johnny was bright, energetic, and dedicated. We worked very closely together on all aspects of the job for the remainder of my tenure. His wry sense of humor helped pull us through some difficult moments. After I left the Pentagon, John stayed on for several more years to serve under my successor, Harold Brown. Eventually he moved back to southern California to become a vice-president of Litton Industries. After only a few years there, he abandoned defense work altogether. Since I was also back in California by then, we kept in touch until he retired completely and moved to New Mexico.

The other early change in staff was the substitution of Jack Ruina for Hector Skifter as assistant director for air defense. Before joining me, Jack worked in the Office of the Assistant Secretary of the Air Force for R & D. His responsibilities there were such that I quickly came to know and respect his technical knowledge and good judgment. Before that he had been a professor of electrical engineering at the University of Illinois. As good luck would have it, I worked closely with Jack not only during our joint tenure in ODDR & E but on a number of interesting future occasions as well.

The Yorks and the Ruinas also became close family friends. When their third and last child was born, soon after Jack joined my staff, they named her Rachel, inspired at least in part by the name of our own older daughter.

The AFPC and a First Look at Indochina

The Armed Forces Policy Council, or AFPC, was the inner cabinet of the secretary of defense. Its original members were the secretary and deputy secretary of defense, the secretaries of the Army, Navy, and Air Force, and the five members of the Joint Chiefs of Staff. The Defense Reorganization Act of 1958 included a provision that the new DDR & E was also to be a member, the first time the scientific side of the Pentagon was represented in such a high-level body.

Being a member of the AFPC afforded me a unique view of the whole world, especially of those events relating to national security. Some of the most interesting meetings I recall involved the precursors of the Vietnam War.

Near the end of the Eisenhower administration, in the late 1950s, we were much concerned about the course of events in what had been French Indochina. From this side of the historical divide, marked by our ignominious withdrawal from Saigon in 1975, it may seem strange, but the principal focus of our attention and concern in 1959 and 1960 was on Laos, not on North or South Vietnam. Gradually a picture emerged in which we saw Laos as the main route for future Chinese expansion in Southeast Asia. Historically China had not been expansionist, but it was easy to interpret her lively alliance with Russian and her behavior in Korea as signaling a change. We were wrong, but we had good reasons for being so. One was our own stupid action several years before in eliminating all the knowledgeable "old China hands" in a fit of political anguish over the question "Who lost China?" Equally important was the policy of supersecrecy both Russia and China used to hide everything they did. We were, in sum, mainly wrong because of ignorance, although surely a touch of paranoia was there too.

On top of that, Laos had for several years been in a confused state of civil war involving what Khrushchev once called "those three crazy princes." Laos had a long and undefendable border with China. On large-scale maps that ignored mountains, swamps, and jungles, the country appeared to be the route for any military move by China southward toward Thailand, Vietnam, Malaysia, and Burma. In each of those countries there were also Communist-inspired rebellions with Chinese connections. The outlook in the region seemed generally gloomy.

At one memorable AFPC meeting, an intelligence officer specializing in Laos briefed us. He said that if we were serious about helping the kingdom withstand the various internal and external aggressions facing it, we first had to teach nationalism and patriotism to the Laotian people. Only a minority of the people of Laos were aware they lived in a country by that name; outside the capital only a minority had ever heard of the king of Laos.

I was stunned. I decided then and there that the differences between the political cultures of the United States and Laos were so great that we could never effectively intervene. We could never find enough Americans who understood the situation well enough to be able to do anything useful.

Later, when the focus of attention shifted to Vietnam, I felt the same way. True enough, the cultural gap between Vietnam and the United States is not as large as that between us and Laos, but it was still too wide to allow us to intervene effectively in the internal struggles of that country. Later, during the Johnson administration, when the early military assistance program turned into full-scale war, I continued to feel that way. I learned new details and heard more explanations and rationalizations about why we were there, but I never learned anything that made me change my mind about the ultimate futility of our attempts to set things straight in that unfamiliar place.

Unlike some other Americans, I never believed that Ho Chi Minh was a demigod or that the North Vietnamese were in any sense right or justified in *their* intervention in the south. But I did believe that nothing we could do would make any real difference in the end—nothing, that is, except delay the time and increase the suffering before the local forces and trends could work themselves out.

Rationalizing the Space Program

During the course of my tenure as DDR & E, my colleagues and I made thousands of decisions involving many billions of dollars. I have selected four to serve as examples of the problems we faced and the actions we took.

The first involved the final rationalization of the American space program. As McElroy had hoped, the creation of ARPA had done much to resolve the confusion and disorder in the U.S. space program. Previously we had a collection of programs replete with unnecessary duplication. Often they consisted of activities determined more by the demands of interservice rivalry than by national need. Now we had just two distinct programs. One was made up of military space activities, directed by ARPA and designed to meet specific military objectives. The other, under NASA, was designed to promote the exploration of space and to create certain civilian-oriented satellite systems.

The form and organization of the program, however, retained some bizarre elements. I concluded that if these were not eliminated, new problems would arise and again distort the program's content and impede its execution.

The specific matter that forced me to focus attention on the situation was the program for the development of the Saturn IB. The Saturn IB was a new large booster whose first stage was to be powered by eight rocket engines, each of the type used for the Atlas missile, all simultaneously operating in parallel. With such a large first stage and additional upper stages, the Saturn IB would be able to loft more than forty thousand pounds into orbit around the earth, far more than any other American (or Soviet) booster. The Saturn IB was basically an Army idea that came up before NASA was fully under way, and ARPA had assigned the responsibility for developing it back to the von Braun team at the Army Ballistic Missile Agency.

There was wide agreement that launchers of this size were needed for an aggressive space exploration program. There was, however, no agreement on their role in the military space program. Roy Johnson and others in ARPA insisted that such boosters would be needed one day in the military space program, but they were unable to come up with specifics. My principal assistants, including John Rubel, and the PSAC firmly believed there was no legitimate military requirement for such a booster in the then foreseeable future.

These arguments exposed two major defects in the organization of the overall U.S. program. First, neither the Army Ballistic Missile Agency, which had the technical responsibility for building the Saturn IB, nor ARPA, which had the administrative responsibility for it, had a mission requiring it. Second, NASA, which had the responsibility for the exploration of space, manned and unmanned, had no existing programs for building the boosters needed for such a mission.

I proposed the obvious solution. First, transfer the authority (and the money) for the development of the Saturn IB and other large rockets from ARPA to NASA. And second, transfer the von Braun team from the Army to NASA. The second part of this solution was precisely what Glennan had tried and failed to achieve the year before. He still believed that the transfer made sense but was reluctant to reopen the matter unless he was assured in advance that this time things would come out right.

Both ARPA and the Army strongly opposed this solution. As before, Secretary Brucker and General Medaris charged that breaking up the Army missile team would gravely harm the national interest. In addition, they contended that there were real military requirements for such large boosters. They claimed it was only lack of imagination on the part of me and my colleagues that led us to conclude otherwise.

ARPA also saw such large rockets as the key to its future. Roy Johnson and George Sutton—then ARPA's chief scientist—strongly argued for retaining the responsibility for them in the Department of Defense.

Air Force reactions to my proposals were mixed. They, too, flatly disagreed with my contention that there was no military requirement for such a large rocket in the foreseeable future. They were, however, positively delighted with an action that would eliminate or reduce the role of the Army and ARPA in space. On balance, the latter factor proved to be more important, and the Air Force supported my overall conclusions. So did Air Force General Nathan Twining, then chairman of the Joint Chiefs of Staff.

Wernher von Braun was also equivocal about the matter. I met with him several times while I was developing these ideas. It was easy to discuss the issues in a calm and rational manner so long as I made clear my belief that there was a real national need for bigger rockets even though there was no specific military requirement. During our last meeting on this subject, he told me, "All I really want is a rich uncle." Keith Glennan's diary records von Braun's telling him exactly the same thing, perhaps even on the same day.

Wernher had had his eye on the stars from the days of his youth, and *anything* that furthered that goal was welcome and all right with him. In the 1930s Hitler was interested in rockets for use as a "secret weapon" in his forthcoming war against all Europe, and von Braun did his best to build the terror weapon history knows as the V–2. After the war, in the 1950s, the U.S. Army helped him move his dreams forward, but if its ability to do so was about to diminish, he would be pleased to join whoever else could supply the money. Some people regard von Braun's unwavering dedication to the grand dream of space flight as heroic and farsighted. Others cannot overlook the grotesque means and unprincipled behavior he used to realize his dreams. I am among the latter, but in this instance I was glad to exploit his willingness to go, without argument, wherever the money was.

On October 21, 1959, a group including McElroy, Glennan, Kistiakowsky, and I met with President Eisenhower in the Oval Office. I presented my rationale for transferring both the big booster program and the von Braun team to NASA. Everyone agreed.

As we left, Secretary Brucker was sitting alone outside in the waiting area. I watched him go in to make his pitch for preserving the status quo. The president listened to him, but the matter was closed.

The decision to transfer von Braun and the Saturn IB to NASA carried along several other such programs, including the Nova engine. Out of all this eventually came the great Saturn V booster and the Apollo lunar exploration system.

In my view this final reorganization of the U.S. space program was the key to its future success. In any event, it has stood the test of time for twenty-five years now without any further major adjustment. I regard it as the single most important act of my tenure in the Pentagon.

Antiballistic Missiles

In the early 1950s American intelligence discovered a major Soviet effort to develop an intercontinental ballistic missile. In 1954 the United States instituted a similar program of its own. Almost immediately, air defense specialists began to study means for intercepting such missiles.

By 1956 the Army had generated a plan to develop and deploy an antiballistic missile (ABM) system capable, it was claimed, of intercepting Soviet ballistic missile warheads as they reentered the atmosphere on their way to their targets. Powerful radars would first detect an attacking missile warhead and determine its course, and then a high-thrust rocket would loft a nuclear warhead into its path and destroy it.

Overall direction of the program was assigned to General Medaris and the technical team at Huntsville, headed by von Braun. The overall system contractor was the Bell Laboratories. The Douglas Aircraft Corporation was selected to develop the interceptor missile itself, called the Nike-Zeus.

By 1958 the Army was proposing to spend big money to deploy the Nike-Zeus ABM system at appropriate locations throughout North America. The secretary of defense turned for advice in the matter to a special review committee chaired by Hector Skifter. The two other members were John Klotz, one of William Holaday's assistants, and I, then still in ARPA. We concluded that a full-scale, high-priority program to develop and deploy such a system should be undertaken.

At the same time, the U.S. defense establishment became concerned about the possible development of an ABM system by the Soviets. A

committee chaired by William Bradley studied that possibility and uncovered a variety of technical means for deceiving, overwhelming, or
otherwise defeating any likely first-generation Soviet ABM system.
This, of course, raised doubts about the efficacy of our own Nike-Zeus
as well.

In the meantime, I had become the DDR & E. Because of these new
doubts, I instituted yet another review of the matter. By that time Jack
Ruina was the assistant director for air defense, so he organized and led
the review. We concluded that research and development should continue, but this time we recommended against any immediate deployment. The current Nike-Zeus design was vulnerable to relatively simple
countermeasures. A well-managed development program incorporating
some of the results of ARPA's Project Defender might evolve ways to
handle these countermeasures, and so it seemed worth pursuing one.
However, until effective means of coping with them could be found,
there was no point in going ahead with an enormously expensive deployment program. Doing so would not only waste money but also
severely interfere with the research that had to be done if we were to
have any hope of one day building a workable system.

At about the same time, PSAC also reviewed the matter and came to
similar conclusions. The secretary of defense and the president accepted our conclusions and decisions in the matter. Army Secretary
Brucker and General Medaris strongly opposed us.

As part of the continuing development effort, the Army had arranged
to have Zeus prototype equipment installed at Kwajalein Atoll, in the
mid-Pacific. The experimental plan, as we had approved it, called for the
Air Force to launch targets for testing this equipment from Vandenberg
Air Force Base, in California, using ICBM boosters. Suddenly I learned
that General Medaris proposed that the test targets be launched from
Johnston Island, also in the mid-Pacific. Since this was closer to Kwajalein than California was, the launch could be made with the Army's
Jupiter IRBM booster. Medaris supported his proposal with all sorts of
arguments about why this was a better way to do things. Ruina and I
examined the question closely and concluded that none of these claims
really made good sense. In keeping with my authority, I disapproved
this specific part of the Zeus test program.

The last Jupiters planned for deployment in Turkey and Italy were
about to come off the line at the Chrysler plant. The people there, of
course, had a great interest in keeping production going. Shutting down
the line would terminate the employment of thousands of persons in the
months immediately preceding the presidential election in 1960, and

Michigan was a key state. The White House therefore told Secretary
Gates and me to check with Vice-President Nixon, the presumed Republican presidential candidate, before doing anything so drastic. Nixon,
without a moment's hesitation, told us to do whatever was right in our
judgment without reference to politics.

At one point in this prolonged controversy, Secretary Brucker called
me to his office to tell me what he thought of my decisions on the ABM,
the Jupiter, and the Army's role in space. The Army's chief of staff, the
deputy chief, and the chief of R & D were all there, sitting at attention,
as was Richard Morse, the Army's civilian director of research. A colonel with a pen ostentatiously poised over a pad took up a position
behind me. General Medaris paced the floor. Brucker repeatedly tried
to threaten me by saying, "Just wait 'til the people hear what you're
trying to do; just wait 'til the Congress hears what you're trying to do."

I felt a bit overwhelmed at first, but a measure of personal vanity
sustained me. All the while the secretary threatened and scolded me,
a single thought kept circulating in my head: "He's the secretary of the
army, he's at the apex of his career, he's furious about what I'm doing,
but there's nothing the poor so-and-so can do that I care about, and he
knows it. If people here don't like what I'm doing, I can always go back
to the University of California." The only external evidence of his threat
was a small item that appeared in *Newsweek*'s "Periscope" column on
October 5, 1959.

HOUSE CLOAKROOM—Heavy pressure [was put on York by] Army Secretary
Wilbur Brucker and GOP congressmen from Brucker's home state of Michigan, to whom he appealed for help. These Republicans attacked York as
a "registered Democrat" and as a "young egghead—one of those scientists
trying to run the country." Their complaints reached [Deputy Secretary of
Defense] Gates.

The impasse between Brucker and me did in fact create a dilemma
for Tom Gates. He called me in, explained the matter, and with an
apologetic tone said he planned to ask George Kistiakowsky, then chairman of the PSAC, to look into the matter and advise him. Kisti established a panel to do so. The panel and Kisti supported my view, and the
Jupiter program, which probably should never have been started in the
first place, was at long last laid to rest.

Soon afterward General Medaris resigned from the Army and became
the president of the Lionel Corporation (which then made toy electric
trains). There his immediate boss was Board Chairman Roy M. Cohn,

RIGHT: HFY and sister Helen, 1945.

BELOW: Immediate postwar staff of Ernest Lawrence's Berkeley Laboratory between and around the pole pieces of the great 184-inch cyclotron, Fall 1945. Lawrence is sitting slightly to right of center, Herbert F. York just to left of center. Also future Nobel laureates Edwin McMillan *(front and right),* Emilio Segrè *(rear and right),* and Luis W. Alvarez *(rear and center).* (Photo: Lawrence Berkeley Laboratory, University of California)

HFY *(right)* with Lawrence at Eniwetok, 1954. (Photo: Courtesy of Lawrence Livermore National Laboratory)

ABOVE: In personal office of the Secretary of Defense just after being sworn in as DDR & E. *Left to right:* Sybil, Cynthia, HFY, Rachel, and David.

BELOW: One of the very first meetings of Eisenhower's Science Advisory Committee, Executive Office Building, December 1957. HFY at blackboard. At table, *clockwise from far left:* A. Hill, D. Bronk, E. Land, I. I. Rabi, R. Bacher, J.R. Killian (Chairman), J. Fisk, J. Wiesner, J. Zacharias, E. Piore, J. Doolittle, L. Berkner, H. Bethe *(farthest to right),* E. Purcell, H. Dryden, A. Waterman, G. B. Kistiakowsky. (Photo: Paul Shutzer, Life Magazine © 1958 Time Inc.)

Baltimore Sun

"RELAX, THEIR ROCKETS ARE JUST
TWICE AS BIG, THAT'S ALL"

LEFT: Cartoon from *The Baltimore Sun* and *Tim*
(October 1959) immediately after HFY gave a Pen
tagon press briefing saying that although Sovi
rockets were currently twice as big, the U.S. pro
gram was coming right along. (By Yardley an
reproduced by permission of *The Baltimore Sun*

BELOW: Briefing on the first SIOP, SAC headqua
ters, Omaha, 1960. *Left to right:* Col. Westber
Undersecretary of Air Force Joseph Charyk, DD
& E HFY, Deputy DDR & E John Rubel, and Mil
tary Aide Robert Holtoner.

RIGHT: Lawrence Livermore Laboratory directors, early 1960s. *Left to
right:* HFY, Harold Brown, and Edward Teller. (Photo: Lawrence
Berkeley Laboratory, University of
California)

HFY baring his soul about ABM before the Senate Arms Services Committee, 1969. (Photo: The Bettman Archive)

RIGHT: Peter Kapitza's home, Moscow, 1975. *Left to right:* HFY, Peter and Anna Kapitza. Fake headlines proclaim Kapitza winning bet from HFY. (Photo: Sergei Kapitza)

BELOW: HFY *(left)* with Keith Glennan (first head of NASA) atop first space shuttle, Palmdale, CA, 1975. (Photo: Courtesy of the Space Transportation Systems Division, Rockwell International Corporation)

ABOVE: At one of the (very) informal sessions during CTB negotiations, Geneva, 1979. *From left:* HFY, Gerald Johnson, and Andronik M. Petrosyants, the chief Soviet negotiator.

BELOW: The first five chief campus officers of UCSD in sequence. *From left:* Roger Revelle, HFY, John Galbraith, William McGill, and William McElroy, 1981. (Photo: University of California, San Diego)

Graduation at UCSD, 1971. HFY's older daughter graduating at the only formal commencement exercise ever presided over by HFY.

HFY's parents, Herbert F. and Nellie E. (Lang) York, in their early eighties. (Photo: Anne L. Bergamis)

HFY and wife Sybil bicycling along the Pacific shore near their home, late 1970s. (Photo: Wallace Litwin)

the same Cohn who had been one of the notorious Senator Joseph McCarthy's two chief aides.

Shortly after his resignation he also wrote *Countdown for Decision*, where he gave his version of much of what I have recounted above. He charged that there were a number of serious deficiencies in the decision-making structure of the Department of Defense. I ranked high among them.

At the time of the events described above, I judged the ABM program only in terms of technical feasibility and cost. Later I discovered profound connections between the search for an effective missile defense, the dynamics of the arms race overall, and the need to pursue political solutions to our national security dilemma. But all that is a story for later chapters.

Mach 3 Airplanes

During the early 1950s the technology of aircraft structures and jet propulsion reached a stage at which it became possible to build aircraft capable of flying long distances at three times the speed of sound, or Mach 3. At the same time Soviet progress in air defense raised doubts about the future ability of the current generation of subsonic bombers to penetrate to targets deep inside the USSR.

This combination of new capabilities and new perceptions gave rise to an Air Force plan to develop a Mach 3 bomber, then called the B–70, and a Mach 3 interceptor, the F–108.

The plan to develop these two aircraft resulted in prolonged and occasionally bitter arguments. Proponents contended that a supersonic bomber would be more effective in surprising enemy surveillance and detection systems and better able to outrun defensive weapons sent against it. It could also reach "time urgent" targets hours earlier than current long-range bombers, mostly B–47s and B–52s. The opponents held that the capability of Soviet defenses was overstated and that even if it wasn't, there were less expensive means for overcoming them. Moreover, ballistic missiles would be entering the strategic inventory long before the B–70 and would provide a more appropriate answer to the need for an "urgent" response where it was essential. In addition, the opponents claimed that the cost and time estimates for producing such a bomber were far off the mark.

George Kistiakowsky and the PSAC opposed development of both the B–70 and the F–108. Secretary of Defense McElroy was inclined to support the Air Force view. I recall his saying, "If I was minister of defense of Vietnam, I wouldn't support such a program. But I'm secretary of defense of the United States, the richest nation in the world and the leader of the West, and if we don't do it no one will, so I'm for it."

Some will regard McElroy's reasoning as simplistic or chauvinistic, but it really was us or nobody, at least nobody in the West. Mach 3 flight was new and different. We could not be sure whether it would work out, whether it would be useful. The arguments on each side were too uncertain and too closely balanced. It seemed reasonable and prudent to investigate further. In any event, right or wrong, I so concluded at the time. However, we didn't need two projects to investigate the problems and possibilities; one, either the bomber or the interceptor, would do.

I therefore told General Thomas White, the Air Force chief of staff, that I could rationally support the development of one such aircraft to explore this wholly new flight regime, but not two. Since the question of which one should have first priority was a purely military matter, I asked him to pick just one in return for my promise to support his choice. He pondered the matter and a few days later called to say he picked the bomber. This is the sort of decision that leaves no paper trace. To my knowledge both ends of this decision were handled orally.

Some months later General White and I both attended a meeting with the president to settle several major defense budget issues that were still unresolved. Secretary McElroy and other high Defense Department and Budget Office officials were also there. At one point Eisenhower pointed his forefinger straight at me and firmly said, "The only reason I'm supporting the B–70 is that *you* said it's a good idea." General White, across the table, stared hard at me. I avoided eye contact with anyone except the president and mumbled something unintelligible and noncommittal, and we moved on to the next topic. In retrospect, it was not one of my finest hours, but given what we knew and could know, I think what we did was not unreasonable.

The B–70 project went ahead for the next couple of years more or less as General White and the air staff wanted. Then, when Robert McNamara became secretary of defense two years later, he reviewed the project again and found it wanting. Further work had confirmed at least some of the opponents' arguments. As a result, the project was canceled in the mid-1960s. As usual in cases where the issue is so important and there is so much to say on each side, the matter didn't end there. The proposal to build a Mach 3 bomber was resurrected on a number of future occasions, and the B–1, a later version of the B–70, was deployed in the 1980s.

This matter of the B–70 and McElroy's remark about it illustrate one of the dilemmas top-level defense decision makers often face. On the one hand, a negative decision in such a matter has a greater degree of finality than it would in most other large institutions. If the director of research of General Motors says no to a good idea, someone else can bring it up in Ford or Chrysler. But when the director of R & D in the Pentagon says no, there is no place else to take it, and a potentially good idea may be quashed forever. On the other hand, a positive decision about something as expensive as the B–70 necessarily has high opportunity costs. Contrary to a common view, the defense budget is not the simple sum of the costs of a collection of programs and projects judged to be worthwhile. Saying yes to the B–70 necessarily meant excluding other projects totaling roughly the same cost. Moreover, the nature of the budget process is such that it is generally impossible to know just what the excluded opportunities are.

The Politics of Boron Hydride

Early in the Eisenhower administration the powers that be in aviation technology concluded that boron hydride, a noxious volatile liquid, showed promise for being a superior fuel for jet aircraft. In order both to investigate the method for producing the material and to determine its utility as a fuel, the Air Force and the Navy each decided to build plants for producing it, one at Muskogee, Oklahoma, and one near Niagara Falls, New York. Each plant used a somewhat different chemical process.

By the time I arrived in the Pentagon, further work had raised doubts about the promise of this new fuel. Even so, we decided to continue the project until we had enough boron hydride in hand for a fair test. We concluded, however, that just one of the plants would be adequate for the purpose. The question then became which one to shut down. From a technical point of view, it did not matter; the estimated costs and time were essentially the same for each. The quickest way to start saving the taxpayers money would be to toss a coin, but the politics of the situation did not permit that inexpensive solution.

Both Muskogee and the Niagara region were economically depressed areas. We needed reasons that would stand up in a political court. A coin toss, or its moral equivalent, would not do. I decided to order a study of the exact cost of each of the two processes. I fully expected the difference would be substantially less than the uncertainty in the cost of either one, but an arithmetical difference, however small, would let us make a politically viable decision.

While the cost study was still under way, Governor James H. Edmondson of Oklahoma and that state's entire congressional delegation, save only Senator Robert S. Kerr, came to my office to "discuss the matter." A dozen individuals lined the walls while the governor spoke. "We in Oklahoma," he said, "stand behind whatever is right and necessary for the defense of the country, but consider this one very carefully, young man." James H. Wakelin, Jr., assistant secretary of the Navy for R & D, was in the room in order to provide a friendly presence, but I nevertheless felt extremely lonely. I assured them I would indeed study the matter very carefully.

The New York delegation had more clout. Instead of coming to the Pentagon, they summoned Secretary of Defense Thomas Gates and me to the Capitol Building. Most of the delegation was there, including both senators, Jacob Javits and Kenneth Keating. They told us the same thing: "New York supports whatever is right and necessary for defense, but consider this one very carefully."

Some weeks later the review committee reported that the Muskogee plant would produce boron hydride for a slightly lower cost, and so we closed down the other. Within the next few years it became evident we really didn't need either one, and the survivor of that earlier review followed the other into oblivion.

The making of decisions like the foregoing requires, ideally, prodigious amounts of information. In the real world, given time restraints and the limitations of actual people, there is never enough information to do everything right. Experience and intuition, of necessity, play a big role.

Most of the information I worked with flowed in to me in my office. It came from staff and from the world at large in the form of reports, briefings, meetings with individuals, conferences, phone calls, newspaper items, televisions clips, and occasionally even books. To get more and to understand better, I also traveled to the various centers of action and thinking outside Washington. Two of these on-site inspections were especially instructive: one to the North American Air Defense Command, in Colorado Springs, and one to the Strategic Air Command, in Omaha.

Visit to NORAD: Launch on Warning

The responsibility for the defense of the United States and Canada against air and missile attack is in the hands of NORAD, the North American Air Defense Command. Its headquarters is near Colorado Springs, and the commander's staff consists of both Americans and Canadians. Its main activities and on-duty personnel are now located inside Cheyenne Mountain, but when I was in the Pentagon, that deep underground center was still in the planning stages.

I visited NORAD in my capacity as DDR & E sometime in 1960. I met with the commander, U.S. General Laurence S. Kuter, and his senior assistants and listened to an extended briefing about their activities and plans. After the formal part of the presentation, General Kuter added some personal thoughts about a particular warning system called BMEWS ("be-muse"), short for Ballistic Missile Early Warning System. Then still under construction, it eventually comprised three enormous radars, one near Thule, Greenland, one near Fairbanks, Alaska, and one at Flyingdales, England, plus the associated computing and communications systems. Because of their far-forward location, we hoped to get warning of an attack fifteen minutes before the enemy warheads reached their targets. The other promising means for getting such an advance warning was the Midas satellite surveillance system, then still in the early stages of development.

General Kuter told me that we had to complete BMEWS as soon as possible, and he urged that we expand it in order to create a highly redundant capability at each site: "We must have an absolutely reliable early warning of a missile attack." Basically, I agreed.

All would have been well if he had stopped there, but he didn't. In words I can't precisely recall, he went on to say that we had to have this redundancy and the resulting high level of reliability so that, when we finally connected the warning system directly to the launch button of our own ICBMs, there would be no false alarms.

I was astonished. I told him flatly that we would not automate our response, that we would not connect the warning system directly to the launch button. We would not, in sum, go to a "launch on warning" strategy. We would especially not go to one that did not have the president in the decision-making loop.

Kuter coldly replied, "In that case, we might as well surrender now."

I told him I believed that was not the only, and certainly not the proper, alternative.

This was my first direct encounter with the concept of launch on warning. Years earlier, as a member of the von Neumann committee, I had endorsed the requirement that the Atlas be built so that it could be launched on only fifteen minutes' notice. That requirement implied that we might indeed launch it within the period available from radar warning systems. This NORAD visit, however, was the first occasion that I had to face up to that concept in a concrete form.

Clearly, this is another of the dilemmas we constantly encounter in our national security strategy. From a technical point of view, launch on warning is the surest and cheapest way of assuring retaliation and reinforcing deterrence. It is also the most dangerous. On the one hand, it is cheaper and surer than the provision of active defenses, such as ABMs, or the provision of passive defenses, such as superstrong silos, or mobility, or deception, or any other known means for protecting our forces. On the other hand, if it ever fails in a way that produces a false but credible alarm, it may bring about the end of civilization. All the other means for assuring retaliation depend on techniques for riding out an attack. If they failed in part, our retaliation would be less complete than it would otherwise be, but at least such retaliation as we did get off would be for real cause.

I have discussed this matter with a number of very senior civilian officials since that conversation with General Kuter, and I am happy to report that none of them looked at the problem the way he did. They seemed as repelled by the notion as I was. It has often been suggested, but it has never, to my knowledge, been implemented.

Visit to SAC: The Single Integrated Operational Plan

In 1960 I visited the headquarters of the Strategic Air Command (SAC) at Offutt Air Force Base, near Omaha, Nebraska. John Rubel and Joseph Charyk, then undersecretary of the Air Force, were with me. We were there to be briefed on the SIOP, or Single Integrated Operational Plan. In 1961 I returned for the same purpose, then in the company of Robert McNamara, the new secretary of defense.

The creation of an integrated plan for strategic attack, the SIOP, had been ordered by Secretary of Defense Gates less than a year before my first visit. Prior to that time the Air Force and the Navy had each developed independent plans for strategic strikes. Years later, when I asked

Tom Gates why he had called for the creation of a single plan, he said, *"You* and Arleigh Burke [the chief of naval operations] told me we needed it." I don't recall that, but it could be true.

The briefing room at Omaha was deep underground. It had an unusually high ceiling, and a huge map of Europe and Asia largely covered one wall. A mechanical arrangement made it possible to drop successive huge transparencies over the map.

General Thomas Power, the SAC commander, personally gave most of the briefing on both occasions. The SIOP had been prepared by a group of officers from each of the services, but Power, because of his status, had a special influence on the process.

The briefing started with a description of an attack on Soviet bomber and missile bases and progressed to attacks on other nuclear and strategic systems. It then took in command and communications centers and finally moved to other military and industrial targets, mostly in or near Soviet population centers. In the main, long-range bombers carried out these attacks. In certain peripheral areas carrier-based aircraft also participated. At that time only a few Atlases, Jupiters, Thors, and Polarises were actually on station and ready, and they played only a secondary role in the attack.

As the briefing progressed, the large transparencies came down one by one. They showed the various areas of destruction expected at each stage of the attack. Toward the end it seemed that the purpose was simply to strip-mine much of the USSR. The total megatonnage of our stockpile was at its all-time maximum. That first SIOP made use of nearly a million times as much explosive power as was used at Hiroshima, perhaps five thousand times that used in all of World War II. Since then the destructive power contained in our stockpile of nuclear weapons has fallen to less than one-fourth of what it was then, but it is still enormous by any ordinary standard.

One of the last transparencies showed where the radioactive fallout would come down if the attack took place on a typical day. Many heavily populated regions of the USSR would be subjected to radiation levels exceeding those causing death within days or a few weeks.

The same transparency also showed a nearly lethal radiation level at Helsinki, Finland. At this point General Power turned to us and said, "Gentlemen, I must point out that this is the dose that some damn fool who went outdoors and looked up at the sky for two days would receive."

His statement was scientifically accurate; the mere act of staying indoors can reduce the radiation exposure by a factor of three or more. But the notion that it was the victims in Helsinki who were the "damn fools" in this situation struck deep. John Rubel and I talked it over on the way home and on other occasions thereafter. That casual but absurd remark is, I came to think, an accurate measure of the whole idea. And yet, as long as we depend primarily on the threat of mutual assured destruction for maintaining the peace, how else could it be?

I have many memories from those days in OSD, many of them delightful, but two of the most vivid are that remark by General Power and the earlier discussion of launch on warning by General Kuter. These two statements unintentionally made it crystal clear there is something seriously wrong, and at bottom absurd, about maintaining peace through mutually assured destruction, but they do nothing to indicate the way out. Unfortunately, that is pretty typical of most criticisms of the arms race, whether these criticisms are intentional or, as in the two instances cited here, accidental.

An Operational Decision

Generally, I dealt with long-range issues. Only rarely did I become involved in operational decisions. One such instance began with a telephone call soon after I arrived at my desk one morning. William Franke, the secretary of the Navy, was on the line. "You're the secretary of defense, and we've got a problem," he said.

Secretary of Defense Gates and Deputy Secretary James Douglas were both in Canada that day, so I was, indeed, the senior official on duty in the Office of the Secretary of Defense.

Franke explained that Navy and Air Force officials were at an impasse concerning a proposed launch from the Pacific Missile Range. The Navy was in overall charge of the range, including range safety. The Air Force made most of the launches. On that day the Air Force planned to launch a new satellite into a nearly polar orbit.

Satellites and satellite launchings were still in their infancy, and engineers calculated that a launch straight to the south would have less than an even chance of success. This particular satellite was so heavy that a launch somewhat east of south would be necessary if the odds were to become favorable. In that event the satellite would get a tiny additional push from the eastward rotation of the earth, and, though very small, that extra kick would substantially improve the odds of success.

The launch trajectory Air Force officials wanted passed directly over a small county park at Jalama Beach, northwest of Santa Barbara. The Navy's safety officer said that wouldn't do, and the range commander backed him. That, then, was the impasse. The Air Force said the launch path must be slightly east of south, and the Navy said it must not be.

Air Force Vice Chief of Staff Curtis LeMay made the case for the launch. It really was an important experiment, and the case for urgency made good sense to me.

Navy Secretary Franke sent aides to explain the potential danger to anyone in the county park. The odds of anyone's being injured or killed were exceedingly small, but not zero. In this case, as in many others like it, very small absolute measures of danger do not provide decision makers with much guidance, even if they are numerically correct. In order to convert such estimates into go-no-go decisions, it is necessary to compare them to something more familiar.

During the course of the morning, it occurred to me that delaying the launch would mean temporarily increasing the automobile travel on the roads in and out of the base. A quick estimate, based on well-known statistics about deaths per mile for automobile travel, easily showed that the increase in the odds of someone's being killed in this way were very much greater than the odds that any debris from the launch would hit someone in the park.

This calculation helped me put the whole matter into a perspective I could handle. I ordered the launch to go ahead.

A Very Special Meeting of the National Security Council

In the spring of 1960 I made a calculation of the probable outcome of an attack by Soviet ICBMs on our strategic forces at various times in the near future. I assumed total surprise and used only the official CIA estimates for the numbers, accuracy, destructive power, and reliability of Soviet missiles. The estimates of Soviet capability were reduced from their earlier "missile gap" values, but they remained formidable. I had doubts about some of the figures, but I set them aside for the purpose of this calculation.

Our retaliatory forces then consisted of long-range bombers and ICBMs based in North America, plus Thors and Jupiters based in Europe. Polaris missiles were not scheduled to enter the force until late 1961.

Given all these initial assumptions, my calculations showed that for a period beginning early in 1961 and lasting for many months the Soviets could hypothetically reduce our retaliatory forces to zero in a surprise attack. I didn't call it that, but the situation was identical to the one that in later years would be referred to as the "window of vulnerability."

I also worked out a straightforward means for mitigating the problem. If we were to speed up the BMEWS construction, move the deployment of the first two Polaris submarines forward six months, and arrange to put some of our bombers on air alert, the problem indicated by my calculations would be solved. With those changes, at no time could a Soviet attack bring our retaliatory forces down to zero. All this, of course, assumed that the CIA's estimates were right. Years later we learned that the estimates of Soviet force I used were still too high. There was therefore no such "window," but I could not know that at the time.

I went over these calculations with John Rubel. Together we prepared charts delineating them and briefed the secretary and others in OSD about our conclusions. We also briefed a full meeting of the Joint Chiefs of Staff. The chiefs took them seriously and urged me to bring these results to the attention of the president and the National Security Council. It was arranged that I should do so at an NSC meeting scheduled for the morning of May 5, 1960, to be held as usual in the Cabinet Room.

The afternoon before the meeting someone on the White House staff called and told me that instead of going directly to the White House the next morning, I should report to the Pentagon helicopter pad and bring my briefing charts with me.

I did as directed. Herbert ("Pete") Scoville, then deputy director of the CIA, met me at the pad. We flew off toward the Blue Ridge Mountains of Virginia and landed near the entrance to one of the president's special remote underground command posts. Shortly thereafter the president came in another helicopter and the secretaries of defense and state in a third. Only after the meeting did I learn that the regular members of the NSC, excepting only the president himself, had not been notified of the change in location until six o'clock in the morning of the day it was held.

Tom Gates later told me that he had left home that morning without any identification. When he arrived at the Marine Helicopter Station in Washington, where he had been told to report, the guard refused to let him enter until Acting Secretary of State Douglas Dillon vouched for him. It had been a genuine "fire drill," in which most of the principals were taken completely by surprise. I am not aware of another such instance.

Despite the unusual nature of the meeting, it proceeded in straightforward fashion. I gave a brief report of my calculations, which those present took seriously. Out of that meeting eventually came a plan to accelerate BMEWS and Polaris, and to arrange to place a fraction of our B-52s on air alert at such time as a future estimate might confirm the need.

Heart Attack

On Sunday morning, August 7, 1960, I awoke with the symptoms of heart attack in full flower. My left elbow ached; I was yellow, sweating profusely, and extremely agitated.

Two days earlier I had returned from an arduous trip to the West. Shortly before starting home, I came down with a severe sore throat and flu. I had my own airplane, and Sybil was with me, but I was pretty sick and uncomfortable when I finally arrived back in Washington. On Saturday morning a doctor met me at the airport and treated me for a strep throat.

Later I learned that the upper-respiratory infection I came home with had led to pericarditis (inflammation of the muscles surrounding the heart) and that it, in turn, had somehow induced my heart attack.

Sybil managed to reach General George Brown (then Secretary Gates's military aide and later chairman of the JCS) on the telephone. He arranged to have me admitted to Walter Reed Hospital. Our next-door neighbor Colonel James Lovelace drove Sybil and me there in his station wagon.

On arrival I received all sorts of attention and special tests. My symptoms got worse over the next several days. In addition to my heart problem, I developed a severe allergic reaction to the penicillin they were giving me for my throat infection. That, and the anticlotting medicine I was also taking, led to two internal hemorrhages, one in the kidney and one in the bowel. The latter brought my peristalsis to a halt, and I had to receive emergency treatment for that. All in all, I was a mess.

The whole affair was harder on Sybil than on me. Fortunately, she received timely support. John and Dorothy Rubel picked up the children and took them off for a brief holiday at Virginia Beach. Tom Gates saw Sybil frequently and told her he didn't want to hear reports on how I was doing from anyone but her. Other colleagues and friends extended their best wishes to both of us. The hospital staff, from the commanding general down to the orderlies, did what they could to bolster her morale.

After a week I started to get better, and everything slowly but steadily improved from then on. I was in the hospital for six weeks altogether.

They say every cloud has a silver lining. In my case it was all the special attention I received.

Harold Brown sent me a telegram saying, "Must you be precocious in everything you do?" Jerry Johnson brought the good wishes of the Livermore Laboratory. My father came down to Washington and, after first seeing me, paid a visit to the secretary of defense. As he reported it, while he was there a military attaché from the British embassy came in, bowed several times, and told him the queen sent her best wishes for my speedy recovery. My father often exaggerated, but maybe it was all true. Even the bows.

Tom Gates, George Kistiakowsky, and Benny Schriever were among my early visitors. Benny brought me a piece of the shroud of the parachute used to slow the reentry of the *Discoverer 13* satellite so that it could be snatched out of the air high over the Pacific. *Discoverer 13* was the first success in that program after a long series of failures—the first object of any kind to be recovered from space. I was cheered by that news.

The high points were two visits by the president. On the day of the first, Eisenhower had come to visit his granddaughter, then also in the hospital. He stopped by to see me on his way out. At the time I was still pretty sick and highly drugged, so he did most of the talking. He described his experience with heart attacks and said he believed he would not have suffered the first one (in Colorado) if he had had a "nightcap" that evening.

Eisenhower visited again three weeks later. I was much improved and had moved into the presidential suite, a special wing of six or so rooms set aside for convalescing VIPs. He had come in to see Vice-President Nixon, then a patient in the same suite. Again he stopped in to see me. This time I was alert and in good spirits. We spent half an hour or so gossiping about people we both knew but didn't like. It was delightful.

All this was during the presidential campaign of 1960. Nixon, the Republican nominee, had banged his knee on a car door while out on the hustings. The wound proved slow to heal, and so he was brought to the hospital for further treatment. The doctors thought that he, too, might be allergic to penicillin, and tests related to that problem extended his stay. Shortly after he was released, he had his first television debate with John Kennedy. The pallor he acquired while in the hospital showed and may have influenced the outcome.

On one Sunday late in my stay, Sybil, our three children, and I were all invited over to Nixon's room to say hello. Pat Nixon and their two daughters were also there. The next day was the first day of school, and so all the children were dressed in their new school clothes. The vice-president and I were in pajamas, and his leg was held in a raised position by a sling-like affair. Nixon tried to get our son, David, to talk about sports, but he wasn't particularly successful.

Other Nixon visitors also stopped by to see me on their way out. Nelson Rockefeller stepped in briefly, slapped a fist against the open palm of the other hand, and said, "Get well, guy!" I had met with him several times before, twice in connection with civil defense. ("We need it to stiffen the backbone of the American people," he had said.)

On the day the Senate adjourned, Lyndon Johnson and Everett Dirksen, the majority and minority leaders, respectively, came in to pay their respects to the vice-president, the Senate's formal presiding officer. He informed them that I was next door. I had testified frequently at hearings each of them had attended, so they were well aware of who I was and why I was in the hospital. On their way out they both stopped by to tell me about their own, personal experiences with heart attacks.

Yet another future president, Gerald Ford, was involved in my heart attack. He was the ranking minority member of the Defense Subcommittee of the House Appropriations Committee, and I met him often in that context. (I thought he was an especially effective member.) By chance, we lived only a few blocks apart in Alexandria and had the same milkman. While I was in the hospital, this milkman carried the news of my progress from Sybil to Betty Ford along with the day's dairy products.

Work went on in the office as usual during that period, in which John Rubel served as acting director. At one point he approved an Air Force program for the development of Saint, a satellite interceptor system. I had opposed it earlier, as had Eisenhower, but for reasons still not clear to me, John and other high authorities decided to let it go through at that time. After only a year or so, the program proved to be technologically premature and was abandoned. Also during that period, William H. Martin and Bernon F. Mitchell, two high-level mathematicians specializing in matters related to cryptology, suddenly defected to the USSR. They had been employed by the National Security Agency, a very important element of the U.S. intelligence community. Since the NSA was a part of the Department of Defense, its research program came under my jurisdiction. Rubel took a lot of flak as a result of their defections, and I was glad to be out of the way of it at the time.

Just before I returned to work, I made a train trip on the California Zephyr to Berkeley to explore what might be there for me to do if I were to return in the near future. The coming election would inevitably bring changes, even if Nixon were elected, and my heart attack seemed to call for changes in my life-style. I had been working eleven-hour days, with frequent evening receptions and speeches, and half days on Saturdays. I had every reason to believe I could not resume that pace. I concluded I should leave the government at the end of the Eisenhower administration. Nothing was decided during my visit to Berkeley, but a few weeks after I returned to Washington, Clark Kerr, the president of the university, called to ask if I would be interested in being the first chancellor of the new campus at San Diego. I told him I would. I would probably have returned to California the next year for the reasons given, but that clinched it.

CHAPTER 9

Reflection and Transition

(November 1960–May 1961)

WHEN John Kennedy won the 1960 election, we all became what politicians call lame ducks. Some find the lame duck's situation sad. They see it as the last gasp of a dying era, and they don't expect to be involved in the rebirth that will inevitably follow. I found it stimulating.

For the first time since I had come to Washington, I did not have to devote my whole attention to problems requiring immediate resolution. Or, as we more commonly put it, I didn't have to spend all my time "putting out fires." Now I had a real chance to reflect on what we had done and where it was leading us. The recent reminder that I was mortal contributed to a more philosophical attitude as well.

Eisenhower's Strategic Legacy

Our strategic forces and the policies governing their acquisition and use had both undergone truly revolutionary changes in the course of the Eisenhower administration. Since then all further changes in force composition, policy, and strategy have been evolutionary and gradual.

At the beginning of the Eisenhower administration, the U.S. strategic force consisted of 1,200 medium-range bombers on active status plus another 800 in reserve. By the end of that administration, the United States had fully developed plans for building a "strategic triad" of long-range offensive forces. This triad consisted of a mix of three very different types of weapons: intercontinental ballistic missiles, submarine-launched ballistic missiles, and long-range bombers. The idea was that, faced with so much variety, an enemy could hope neither to make a successful preemptive attack against us nor to defend against our retaliation.

By the end of the Eisenhower period, we had made firm plans and commitments for the deployment of about 1,075 ICBMs (805 Minutemen plus 270 Atlases and Titans). Twenty-five years later there still are just over 1,000. At the end of 1960 we had a total of 29 ballistic missile submarines at least partially committed and in various degrees of construction, and there were plans for building a total of 45 in all. In 1986 there were 40. And finally, at the end of the Eisenhower years we were gradually eliminating medium-range bombers (mostly B–47s) and moving toward a force of approximately 500 long-range bombers (mostly B-52s). These carried a variety of nuclear munitions, including an air-launched cruise missile (Hound Dog) capable of reaching well ahead of the bombers themselves in order to attack heavily defended targets. Twenty-five years later there are about 300 such aircraft, each carrying a variety of modern "stand-off" weapons, the current descendants of that old Hound Dog. All told, at the end of the Eisenhower administration we had plans, largely backed by solid commitments, for a strategic nuclear delivery force consisting of about 2,400 vehicles, just slightly more than we had in the mid-1980s, a quarter of a century later.

In 1953 our stockpile of nuclear weapons totaled about 1,200. By 1961 this figure had grown to more than 30,000. Today it is about 25,000. The remarkable thing about these and all the other numbers cited above is how much they changed during the Eisenhower administration and how little they changed since. And it isn't just numbers.

At the beginning of the Eisenhower administration, the authorities were hopeful that they could build air defenses capable of defending North America. We vigorously pursued the development of the means for doing so. These included radar warning networks, surface-to-air missiles of several kinds, and interceptor aircraft armed with a variety of antiair weapons. We also elaborated ideas and developed plans for vast civil defense programs. By the end of the Eisenhower administration, we concluded that we did not then know how to build a defense against missiles. We also decided, in effect, to stop extending our air defense system and to let what we had wither away. In sum, we decided to protect ourselves solely with the threat of nuclear retaliation. That policy has continued ever since.

Eisenhower, of course, supported and authorized all of the development and deployment programs listed above. Privately, he considered the numbers of offensive weapons excessive, but they were the best compromise he could work out, especially given some Democrats' strident complaints about the missile gap. More important, however, he believed that weapons were not enough by themselves and that the quest for nuclear peace must be bolstered by diplomacy and negotiations of various kinds. He explored a number of possibilities—"atoms for peace," "open skies," eliminating the threat of surprise attack, and a nuclear test ban. By the time he left office, the International Atomic Energy Agency (IAEA) had become a reality, and a nuclear test moratorium was in place. The goal of the IAEA was to prevent the proliferation of nuclear weapons while promoting the broadest-possible use of nuclear electric power. The test moratorium was intended as a first step toward wider and more important forms of arms limitation. Both succeeded, though not to the extent we had hoped. The current limited test ban and the other limitations on weapons that have been elaborated since then all derived directly from those first, modest successes.

Thus the three major elements that make up the current nuclear situation all assumed their present shape in the Eisenhower administration. To summarize, these are (1) the number and types of weapons making up our strategic nuclear forces, including the concept of the triad and its implementation; (2) the abandonment of any serious attempt to build either active defenses or civil defense, and the concomitant acceptance of a policy of maintaining nuclear peace through the threat of massive retaliation; and (3) the initiation of a search for political measures, including arms control, as a means for reinforcing and extending the quest for peace. In each of these areas the Eisenhower administration saw revolutionary changes. Since then, all further developments have been evolutionary. (In 1983, President Reagan initiated a program, quickly dubbed Star Wars, whose basic purpose was to reverse number 2 above and diminish the importance of number 3. If he were to achieve these ends, it would bring about a new strategic revolution, but I am certain he will not.)

None of the facts and figures describing our strategic forces resulted from a careful, formal analysis based upon agreed theoretical principles. The characteristics of the weapons themselves were determined very largely by the technological possibilities. The strategic policy of massive retaliation was seen as the only way of coping with the enormous manpower available to the Sino-Soviet bloc. The original numbers of strategic delivery systems derived mainly from a series of compromises between World War II bomber generals and various budget officials. The generals, whose plans for strategic attack derived from their experience in the war, always wanted more than they currently had. The various budget officers had their own, independent rationale for restraining them. The result was that as early as 1954 we all assumed there would be a thousand ICBMs, and that very round number, so arbitrarily arrived at, has persisted for more than thirty years. The phrases used to rationalize all these policies and plans—mutual assured destruction, graduated response, nuclear sufficiency, limited options—evolved much further than either the basic underlying strategy or the forces themselves.

The only large changes since the Eisenhower years have been in the external situation. There were only three nuclear states then. Now seven possess nuclear weapons, but still only five flaunt them.* More important, Soviet nuclear forces were then modest in size and relatively primitive in form. Now, for all practical purposes, Soviet nuclear forces are fully equivalent to our own. We have made some superficial changes in our forces and policies as a result of these external changes, but at bottom they are the same as they were then. And so are the frightful dilemmas and paradoxes that flow from them.

Kennedy Reconsiders

In February 1961, only a few weeks after he became president, Kennedy called a meeting to prepare his first budget and plans for our strategic nuclear forces. It was attended by a number of the new senior officials—including Robert McNamara, secretary of defense; Charles J. Hitch, the defense comptroller; and Jerome Wiesner, the science adviser. I was there also. We went over a number of major items, one by one. We changed some details, but the main result was a slight net reduction from the program Eisenhower had proposed. This was quite remarkable. Kennedy had campaigned on a platform criticizing Eisenhower (and Nixon) for allowing a "missile gap" to develop. Now, when he finally

---

*The five that flaunt them are the United States, the Soviet Union, the United Kingdom, France, and China. The two who probably have them but never openly boast about them or threaten to use them are India and Israel.

had a chance to do something concrete about it, the actual result was a small net reduction in our nuclear delivery forces.

Eisenhower had left a plan for the deployment of 805 Minuteman ICBMs, starting in 1963. Of these, 200 were to be placed on railroad trains so that they could be protected against a surprise attack by being moved around. McNamara advised Kennedy to keep the total number of missiles the same but to cancel the plan for putting some on rails. He also suggested that the production facilities be expanded so that the rate, but not the total number, could be increased. Kennedy approved.

Eisenhower also left a plan for the deployment of 90 Titan II ICBMs. Each of these delivered a nuclear weapon more than ten times as powerful as the Minuteman warhead. Of these 90, only 54 were fully committed in terms of financing. Kennedy, on McNamara's recommendation, approved the 54 but canceled the rest. Similarly, Eisenhower had left a plan for producing 45 submarines for launching Polaris SLBMs. Kennedy cut this total back to 41, but ordered the production rate doubled so that they would be available sooner. Eisenhower also left a plan for continuing the production of B-52 bombers indefinitely, at the rate of a few per month. McNamara recommended closing production down as soon as possible, and Kennedy approved that too.

A few other, lesser matters were also considered at that meeting. In nearly all cases the result was a cancellation or cutback of programs started by the preceding administration (including the B-70 and, later, the Skybolt). Obviously, Kennedy no longer believed there was any missile gap. When he and McNamara finally had the opportunity to see all the data and assume full responsibility for the American defense program, they reached the same conclusions we had come to earlier. (Later, after many more studies and analyses, the number of Minutemen was increased and the Atlases were eliminated from the force, thus keeping the number of ICBMs constant at one thousand, where it has remained for more than a quarter of a century.)

Some versions of folk history say that Kennedy expanded our strategic forces. The facts are just the reverse.

A Meeting with John J. McCloy

Toward the end of the period of relaxation and reflection between Kennedy's election and his inauguration, I received a call from John J. McCloy, who asked to see me. In early January, Kennedy had appointed him to be his special adviser on arms control and disarmament, and he was making a round of visits to persons in the outgoing administration who he had reason to believe could contribute in this regard. McCloy was an excellent choice for the task. Most Defense Department officials get nervous when someone approaches them to talk about arms control, but McCloy had a record and personality that dispelled such concerns. During the war he had been assistant secretary for war, and afterward he had served as high commissioner for Germany. In civilian life he was a banker. He had a ready smile, a steady gaze, and an air of confidence that said he was open but serious about the subject at hand.

Preparing for that meeting with the new president's emissary led me to crystallize my thinking. I organized my thoughts around three basic principles, each derived from my experiences of the last several years: (1) defense of the population is impossible in the nuclear era, (2) our national security dilemma has no technical solution, and (3) our only real hope for the long run lies in working out a political solution.[1]

The advent of nuclear weapons totally changed the prospects for air (and missile) defense. During World War II strategic bombers delivered chemical explosives on enemy cities and factories. It took thousands of bombers making repeated raids over a long time to achieve the required level of damage. A bomber attrition rate of 10 percent per raid was sufficient to blunt such a prolonged attack. Pilots, even very brave ones, could not continue indefinitely in the face of such odds. By 1960 the odds had completely reversed. With nuclear weapons, attrition rates of 90 percent will not be enough to prevent catastrophic damage. If ten bombs are sent against a city, and only one gets through, that is enough to destroy the city. Whereas 10 percent *attrition* was enough before, 10 percent *penetration* is enough now.

Moreover, it seemed to me the a priori odds strongly favored the offense. The offense could pick the time and targets to suit its purposes. The top command could wait, if necessary, until it was satisfied that all was ready, and then attack. The defense, on the other hand, had to respond at the time and place chosen by the offense. It always had to be in a state of perfect readiness, never knowing until the last moment when something was going to happen. Many of the principal targets the offensive missiles were aimed at were large and soft, and all were fixed. The targets for the defensive missiles were all small, tough, and fast moving. They could also be easily mimicked by decoys.

The recent historical record confirmed this projection. Whenever during the preceding fifteen years the Soviets introduced new or improved air defenses, we had no difficulty discovering ways to penetrate them. There was no reason to think the future would be any different.

Conceivably, a breakthrough favoring defense might come along one day. The odds of that happening, however, were so small that all serious strategic planning had to be based on the premise that it would not. In sum, I concluded that a *defense of the population was and very probably would remain impossible in the nuclear era.*

Our nuclear strategy, and the objective situation underlying it, created an awful dilemma. Ever since the advent of nuclear weapons, our national military power, as measured by the damage we could inflict on an enemy, had been steadily increasing. At the same time our national security, as measured by the damage that could be inflicted on us, had been steadily decreasing. This unhappy result came about not because of anything we failed to do; it happened simply because the Soviets successfully exploited the same general pool of basic science and technology that we had. The Soviets were in the same dilemma. The only defense either of us had was the threat to wreak an unacceptable level of revenge. Neither of us possessed any other means for stopping an attack. In the Eisenhower era we called this "the threat of massive retaliation." Now we call it "mutual assured destruction," or MAD. In testimony given two years after I met with McCloy, I said,

[T]he problem posed to both sides by this *dilemma of steadily increasing military power and steadily decreasing national security has no technical solution.* If we continue to look for solutions only in the area of science and technology the result will be a steady and inexorable worsening of the situation. I am optimistic that there is a solution to this dilemma; I am pessimistic only insofar as I believe there is no solution to be found within the areas of science and technology. (Emphasis added)[2]

These words were spoken in support of the Limited Test Ban Treaty, but I had developed the ideas behind them for my meeting with McCloy, and I meant them to apply to a search for political solutions generally, not just in arms limitation treaties or test bans. Adequate weapons and a proper measure of military preparedness were, I believed, necessary to preserve the peace, but they were not enough. The quest for nuclear peace had in the long run to be based mainly on political solutions. Weapons and armies could serve to keep the situation stable and thus provide the necessary time, but a system resting on the threat of mutual suicide could not be expected to work forever. The slow but steady spread of nuclear weapons to other countries only underlined the peril and reinforced the need to look elsewhere. It seemed to me that *our only real hope for the long run lay in working out a political solution.*

The foregoing are the views I developed in the winter of 1960–61, when, as luck would have it, I had both the time and the stimulus to spell them out. Since then I have refined them in the light of new developments, but they have remained basically the same down to the present. As a result, ever since that time I have worked on both sides of the national security equation. On the one hand, I have continued to contribute to maintaining of an adequate level of military preparedness. On the other, I have done what I could to promote the search for and development of political solutions of all kinds, especially those involving arms control. In my mind the two sides of the security equation are inextricably linked. In making decisions to develop and deploy the weapons needed to maintain a stable balance, we must take into account the way such actions will affect the nuclear arms race. And conversely, when working out plans for controlling or eliminating nuclear arms, we must bear in mind how the resulting action will affect the "correlation of forces"—to use the Soviet term. Most important, in all cases we must base our thinking on the facts as they are in the real world, not on how we might wish them to be. Fear and hatred do not constitute an adequate basis for planning our national security programs and policies, but neither does wishful thinking. Most people find it natural and convenient—and sometimes morally required—to work on just one side of the problem or the other; either to support preparedness and build new weapons or to seek to eliminate existing ones. Given my long history of involvement—some might say complicity—in creating the nuclear weapons world we all now must live in, I have felt obliged to maintain an active interest in and involvement with both sides of the problem.

McNamara Calls

In the middle of that last Eisenhower December, Robert McNamara, the secretary of defense designate, called me at my home one evening. Harold Brown happened to be in town that day, and he and I were off for supper in a Chinese restaurant out on Connecticut Avenue. Sybil called me there and gave me McNamara's number. I returned his call; he asked me to drop in as soon as I could. Harold and I finished eating quickly, and I sent him off somewhere while I dropped in on the secretary designate at his hotel.

McNamara invited me to stay on indefinitely in the new administration. Though flattered and tempted, I told him no—I planned to return soon to the University of California to take on an important new post there. He then asked me to stay on for at least a few months to help with the transition and, more important, to give him plenty of time to find a suitable successor. I agreed to do so.

Nixon Visits

Just a few days before the Eisenhower administration ended, Vice-President Nixon, the defeated presidential candidate, came over to the Pentagon for a good-bye luncheon. Secretary Gates hosted it, and a few other senior civilian officials, including me, attended. After lunch Nixon made a little speech about how he intended to try again. He was confident he would succeed on a second try. Most of us there didn't think that was very likely.

Even before Nixon finished saying his final good-byes, Jim Wakelin and I excused ourselves to go down the hall for a meeting called by Secretary Designate McNamara. Of those at the luncheon, we were the only two who would be staying on with the new team. The future service secretaries were also at the McNamara meeting: John Connally for the Navy, Elvis Stahr for the Army, and Eugene Zuckert for the Air Force. McNamara devoted much of the time to explaining to the new service secretaries that he wanted them to be his emissaries to the services and not vice versa. I remember thinking, this new man may be a great management expert, but he has a lot to learn about the facts of life in the Pentagon. Eventually, things worked out about halfway between what he wanted and what I expected.

Secretary of Defense ad Interim

On inauguration day I joined Tom Gates and one or two others in his office at around eleven o'clock. We watched the preliminary ceremonies and the gathering of the crowd at the Capitol for the main event. A few minutes before twelve, Tom left to go to a farewell luncheon for Eisenhower at one of the city's private clubs.

At exactly noon Kennedy became president of the United States. As the senior holdover in the department, I became secretary of defense ad interim at the same moment. Theoretically I would remain so until

McNamara or someone else senior to me could be confirmed by the Senate and sworn in. No one knew for sure how long that might take.

In recent years the president has been constantly accompanied by an aide carrying a case (commonly called the football) containing all the codes and other data necessary to enable the president to order the use of nuclear weapons by communicating directly with field commanders. We did not handle it that way in 1961. Then, the secretary of defense was responsible for getting the nuclear machine ready to go into action when the president so ordered. Tradition, not the Constitution, required that the senior officer at the Pentagon be a civilian. For the time being that was me. Decisions about future policies and plans could wait for a new secretary to be sworn in. Only emergencies like war needed someone in the post continuously, without any gaps. I thought of myself as the national duty officer while I sat there at the secretary's desk—the one General Pershing had used during World War I—watching the rest of the inaugural ceremonies.

In preparation for my few days as interim secretary, General Lyman Lemnitzer, chairman of the Joint Chiefs of Staff, briefed me in detail about how to go about raising the level of alert and how to prepare for the release of nuclear weapons in Europe or anywhere else. A special red telephone was installed in my bedroom at home. In addition to a regular ring, a large red light on top would flash when it wanted attention. It connected to only one place: the War Room, in the bowels of the Pentagon. I was also given a beeper to alert me and a special telephone number I could dial on any public telephone for calling into the War Room if necessary. It was a very serious matter, and I took it that way. I still remember that special telephone number. I suppose they've changed it since then.

The day after the inauguration, I decided to go directly to the War Room to see what, if anything, was going on in the world I ought to know about. When I knocked on the door, a major opened it a crack and asked me what I wanted.

"I'm the acting secretary of defense," I said.

"Just a minute," he said, and gently closed the door in my face.

Moments later a colonel came and ushered me in with a flourish. I asked about the places in the world where we were keeping a special "watch," as they called it. One of the two places then kept under constant attention was the Congo Republic (now Zaire), where a rebellion in a mineral-rich province, Katanga, had been under way for some time. The other was Laos, where that peculiar and decidedly un-Western state of confusion and rebellion persisted. Nothing special was going on in either place as far as our people knew. Vietnam was not yet in our sights; that would come only with the new president.

From there I went directly to the defense secretary's office. No one was there, but stacks of working papers lay on the desk. The new secretary had jumped the starting gun, but I wasn't about to argue about it. I then went down the hall to my regular office. I had invited John Foster—one of my colleagues in founding the Livermore Laboratory and soon to become its fourth director—to meet me there that day, and he was just about due. When he came, we talked for a while, and then I asked him if he would like to see the working office of the secretary of defense. He said yes, so we went down there and entered through a back door off the secretary's conference room. At that moment McNamara, Roswell Gilpatric (the new deputy secretary), and General Lemnitzer were huddled together on the far side of the room. When we entered, they looked up, startled. I was equally surprised to find them there.

"If anyone calls and asks for the secretary of defense, tell them I will be at home," I said.

Everyone chuckled politely, and Johnny and I left for home to join Sybil for lunch. My days of special glory were over.

After a week or so, Sybil asked me to tell them to come and take their red telephone out of our bedroom. I did so, but they replied, "Now that it is there, we would rather leave it. Who knows when you might be in that situation again." It remained there until I left Washington permanently, some four months later.

Ruina. ARPA. OK. RSM.

My first act of actual business with McNamara concerned the appointment of a new director for ARPA. The incumbent was General Austin ("Cy") Betts. He had recently been invited to become the AEC's director of military applications, a job he very much wanted. It was my responsibility to nominate his replacement, and I chose Jack Ruina. In addition to being widely knowledgeable about defense technology generally, he was a specialist in air and missile defense matters, which constituted the most important element of ARPA's program.

I presented his name to McNamara and urged that he appoint him to that post. He already knew something about Jack and agreed on the spot. He then took a small piece of notepaper and wrote on it, "Ruina. ARPA. OK. RSM."

"I don't need that," I said.

"I like to do business this way," he said.

"Yes, sir," I said, and took the piece of paper. I passed it on to Jack, who still has it among his memorabilia.

SIOP II

Very early in the new administration, McNamara took key members of his new team out to Omaha for a briefing on the SIOP (Single Integrated Operational Plan) and other related matters by the SAC commander and his staff. Besides the secretary himself the visitors included Roswell Gilpatric, General Lemnitzer, and me. It was, of course, my second exposure to the SIOP. Those who were hearing it all for the first time were just as impressed, awed, and even stunned as I had been the first time I heard it, less than a year before.

On the way back to Washington, McNamara and I had a private chat in which he outlined some of his thinking on the subject. He had in mind some substantial cutbacks from our existing strategic plans. Among other things, he spoke about keeping further production of B-52 bombers to the smallest number consistent with existing contractual commitments.

Shortly after returning from the Omaha trip, McNamara ordered a review of the nuclear stockpile. By that time Gerald Johnson had become the new assistant for atomic energy. It fell to him and Charles Hitch, the new comptroller, to carry out the study. The net result of that review and of McNamara's visit to SAC headquarters was a very large (nearly 50 percent) unilateral, but little-heralded, cut in stockpile megatonnage.

Harold Brown Takes Over

During those early weeks of 1961, I took on a number of other special studies at Bob McNamara's request, but none of them was as important as nominating my successor. I consulted widely in the matter. I met with Kistiakowsky, Killian, Wiesner, Fisk, Ramo, and a number of others like them. I developed a list of thirteen names and provided a brief paragraph of comments on each one. I took the list to McNamara and explained to him that the names were in alphabetical order. That automatically put Harold Brown's name at the top, but I went on to say he was in fact my first choice. McNamara had never met Harold personally, but Gilpatric, his deputy, already knew and thought well of him. Bob asked me to bring Harold in to meet him the next time he was in town. That turned out to be just a few days later. Harold and I went in together to see Bob, who offered Harold the job on the spot. Harold said he would like to do something like that one day, but he thought perhaps he was still too young for the post. McNamara said opportunities like this don't usually come twice. I believe that is correct in most cases, but probably not in this one.

I spent the following hour or so explaining to Harold why he should take it on. He accepted the next day.

Departure and Arrival

In early May I hosted a cocktail party at Andrews Air Force Base to introduce Harold and Colene to some of the people with whom he would be working. After the party was over, I watched my chauffeur drive Harold off in what had up to that moment been my official car. Harold sat in the right-hand rear seat with his left arm thrown up on the back. He looked as though he belonged there. For me, it was an especially poignant moment. The most intense period of my life had just ended.

We remained in Alexandria until school let out in June. Sybil and I arranged to rent the house (might we come back some day?) and prepared to drive to San Diego with Rachel and Cynthia in our station wagon. David had already left by train—with his turtles—to spend the summer in California.

We took a northerly route through interesting places none of us had seen before: the Wisconsin Dells, the Badlands and the Black Hills in South Dakota, the Devil's Tower and Yellowstone Park in Wyoming, and the Craters of the Moon in Idaho. We tried to stop early every afternoon either in a county park with a swimming pool or at some other place that would amuse us all and break the monotony of driving. That plan took us to some delightful examples of American exotica. One was the Corn Palace, a building apparently made entirely of corncobs, in Mitchell, South Dakota. Modest but appealing, corny but a source of local pride, it turned out to be the sort of place you write home about.

Three weeks after we left Virginia, we arrived at our new home: University House, La Jolla, California.

CHAPTER 10

At the University of California, San Diego

(Since 1961)

FROM the 1940s through 1960 my life had progressed along a single path. That path had many sharp and surprising twists and turns, but at any one time I was usually engaged in only one major activity. From 1961 to 1976 my career took on a very different pattern. Throughout that period I was typically engaged in three rather separate sets of activities. One was at the University of California, San Diego, where I served in a variety of administrative and academic capacities. These are described in this chapter. A second set of activities involved a continuation of my prior government service, mostly in the form of further advisory committee activities. These are presented in the next chapter. The third set of activities involved an expanding pattern of public actions, such as writing, speaking, and working with various public interest groups. These are presented in chapter 12.

By 1960 it was inevitable that the University of California would establish a general campus at San Diego. Demography alone made it necessary. The state of California continued its rapid growth; the fraction of its population that was of college age was still tending upward and so was the fraction of college-age people who actually wanted to go to college. Even before Sputnik gave its special push, authorities in California started to elaborate a plan for expanding all publicly supported elements of higher education in the state.

San Diego was the third-largest city in California, and, of the big three, it was growing the fastest. Local interests of various kinds looked with favor on the establishment of a UC campus in the area. It would, they thought, reinforce their own hopes and plans for growth and a more exciting future. The San Diego Chamber of Commerce, the press, and local high-tech industry all supported the idea. The General Atomic Corporation, then the most dynamic of the high-tech industries in town, took a leading role in promoting a new campus and made a special grant to the university to help in getting things moving.

Roger Revelle and the Origins of UCSD

But most important in determining the future of the enterprise were Roger Revelle and his colleagues at the Scripps Institution of Oceanography. Located in La Jolla, an elegant beach town just inside the northern limits of the city of San Diego, SIO had long been an important element of the University of California. Founded in 1912 by William Ritter, it became the world's premier oceanographic research institution. Roger joined its staff in 1931 as a research assistant in oceanography. Since 1950 he had been its director. Under his leadership it continued to grow steadily in both numbers and quality.

Sputnik spurred growth in higher education and research generally. Roger and his colleagues were caught up in the general exuberance of the times and sought ways to expand their horizons. Their first concrete success was the establishment of the School of Science and Engineering on the SIO campus in La Jolla in 1958, with Revelle as its director. From the very beginning the idea was to establish a school of the highest quality in which faculty and students were engaged in doing research at the frontiers of knowledge.

Roger and his colleagues made a special effort to recruit the best scientists in the country. The first to join the new school—Harold Urey (a Nobel laureate in chemistry), Maria Mayer (soon to be one in physics), Joseph Mayer, James Arnold, David Bonner, S. J. Singer, and Keith Bruckner among them—in their turn recruited others with similar talents and hopes. By 1960 the new School of Science and Engineering was well under way and ready to serve as the nucleus for a further expansion into a general campus of the university.

One important individual opposed the establishment of a general campus in La Jolla. He was Edwin Pauley, longtime chairman of the Board of Regents of the university. He was a wealthy oilman and a high-level operator in Democratic party politics at both the state and the national levels. He knew how to wage effective bureaucratic and political warfare, and he had become fully accustomed to getting his way in arguments with people he considered to be his subordinates. In my earlier role as director at Livermore, I had come to know him and to understand the way he regarded the university. In sum, he loved it, supported it, and thought it the greatest in the world. He wanted it to continue to be the greatest, but in time he developed ever greater confidence in his personal judgments about what was necessary to keep it that way. As a result of his very long service and record of success in getting his way, he seemed (to me) to believe he had a special right to be the chairman of its board. Sometimes, I thought, he behaved as if he owned the university.

I have never fully understood why Pauley opposed the building of a campus in La Jolla, but it was obvious that he did. Naturally enough, since Roger Revelle was the strongest promoter and most effective spokesman for the idea, the two of them clashed head-on.

The net result of all these trends and struggles was predictable. The regents, at the urging of President Clark Kerr, decided in November 1960 to establish a general campus at the La Jolla site. The general plan for establishing it and the guiding principles for its initial development were to be as Roger had elaborated them. At the same time the regents, under Chairman Pauley's leadership, made it clear that they would not appoint Roger as the first chancellor of the new campus. Roger and his colleagues were bitterly disappointed at this final turn of events.

First Chancellor

In November 1960, shortly after the meeting of the Board of Regents at which it was decided to establish a general campus in La Jolla, Clark Kerr telephoned to ask if I would be interested in becoming its first chancellor. I said yes. The following February, after yet another meeting of the regents, he called to say the board had approved my appointment.

As one local historian put it, "The Regents decision was widely discussed both privately and publicly." Given the expectations of many at Scripps and in San Diego, it is no surprise that "the campus and the community were therefore shocked when the Regents announced that they had selected Herbert York for the position."[1] And the *El Cajon Valley Times,* a suburban San Diego newspaper, ran an editorial asking, "Why did the Regents roam so far and come up with a chancellor from such an unlikely spot as the Pentagon?"[2]

I knew and understood the general nature of the university and its overall plans for growth and expansion, and I wholeheartedly embraced them. I agreed to take on the new responsibility on July 1, 1961. I knew virtually nothing about the various struggles that had recently taken place over the issue of the establishment of the new campus. Nor did I know of the specific ideas and hopes for UCSD—the University of California, San Diego—that the people at La Jolla had developed.

During the spring I made several trips to La Jolla and Berkeley and received a number of visitors from the new campus in my Washington office. I soon learned about the struggles that had taken place and the personal disappointments that had resulted. Obviously I faced a situation fraught with possible embarrassments and pitfalls. Roger was magnificent. He did everything he could to ease my way, as did most of his colleagues. A few of them, however, made it quite clear they had wished for something very different.

Roger explained his ideas and his hopes. I liked them and accepted them virtually in their entirety. Roger was concerned above all with assuring the quality of the faculty and the vigor of the research program. He had two particular ideas for doing so. First, he proposed to initiate the general campus with a research-oriented faculty plus the appropriate complement of graduate student research assistants. Together they would get a program of research and graduate education under way, and only then would undergraduate education be undertaken. And second, in doing their recruiting, the La Jolla people intended to seize targets of opportunity rather than fill positions as dictated by a predetermined table of organization. These two procedures, Roger thought, would assure the creation of a first-rate new university. Fortunately, Clark Kerr agreed with Roger's ideas and provided the funds necessary to give them life. I, and others after me, followed this basic plan. It turned out to work just as the pioneers at La Jolla hoped. By most formal measures—memberships in academies, research grants awarded, and the like—UCSD became arguably the most successful of the new universities founded after World War II.

Soon after I arrived at UCSD, Roger took a leave of absence and went off to Washington to be the resident science adviser to Secretary of the Interior Stewart Udall. He did so, I think, partly to give me a freer hand at La Jolla and partly to salve his feelings.

The next several years were very busy. I worked with the various faculty committees to develop and carry out plans for the further expansion of the faculty. We already had strong departments in oceanography, physics, chemistry, and biology, and we continued to enlarge and strengthen them. We found and brought in the initial cadres needed to create new departments: mathematics, literature, linguistics, philosophy, aerospace and mechanical engineering sciences, and psychology. We added new graduate programs and students as quickly as we could, and we laid out plans for admitting the first undergraduates in the fall of 1964. New buildings were constructed on newly acquired lands northeast of SIO, and plans for still more were elaborated. We undertook the initial planning for a medical school and established a faculty committee to search for its dean and other faculty. At the same time I started negotiations with San Diego County authorities, looking toward the acquisition of the County Hospital as a clinical teaching facility.

"San Diego Mother Wins Nobel Physics Prize"

One November morning in 1963 our daughters were involved in an automobile accident. They were moving slowly when another car suddenly came down an intersecting street and hit them broadside. The second car had almost managed to stop, but not quite. There were no serious injuries except for a sliver of glass that struck Cynthia's eye. It just barely failed to penetrate her cornea. Our family doctor removed it, but we anxiously awaited further tests.

The next day the morning radio carried the news that Maria Goeppert Mayer, a member of our physics department, had won a share of the 1963 Nobel Prize in physics for her pioneering work in nuclear structure. Later that day the *San Diego Evening Tribune* carried a delightful headline: "SAN DIEGO MOTHER WINS NOBEL PHYSICS PRIZE." All of us on the campus were enormously pleased at her selection for this honor. Those of us who were physicists knew it was richly deserved.

When I arrived in my office that morning, I thought of calling Maria to congratulate her, but I thought her really close friends would probably all be phoning her just then, so I decided to delay.

While I was still hesitating and wondering what to do, Maria called me. She said she had heard about Cynthia's accident and wanted to know just how things were working out. I told her what we knew—that it had been a very close call but that apparently everything was going to be all right. Before we hung up, I congratulated her on winning the prize.

Not My Cup of Tea

Participating in the building of a new university was exciting, novel, and worthwhile. But after about two years it nonetheless became clear to me that it was not, as the English would say, my cup of tea.

There were two reasons for this. First, I had been spoiled by the very special—indeed, unique—excitement of a position at the top of the national security establishment in Washington. Like many successful high-level bureaucrats, I had contracted a mild form of Potomac fever. In many cases it strikes its victims with such force that they cannot leave Washington. Many departing high officials search out jobs in Washington law offices, think tanks, research institutions, and the like and wait for another turn in the whirl at the top. Others accomplish the same thing by setting up consulting firms or making independent arrangements for keeping busy and involved in national affairs.

I had a less virulent form of the disease. I had no difficulty leaving the capital. Sybil and I were both very happy to get back to California—she was born in San Francisco—and I have never in the years since yearned to move my personal headquarters back to Washington again. I did, however, maintain an abiding and keen interest in what was going on in Washington, and I eagerly accepted opportunities to consult or otherwise involve myself in national affairs. When I did so, I usually found that, in substance, the issues involved were much more interesting than those that necessarily engaged my attention in La Jolla. I wished I could expand such activities, but my duties as chancellor at UCSD, as I saw them, precluded my doing so.

The second reason was mainly a matter of style. In my previous executive positions I had direct authority over and responsibility for the central activities of the institutions I headed. At Livermore I assumed primary responsibility for the recruitment of scientific staff and for the formulation and execution of the laboratory program. I dealt directly with higher authorities in Washington in working out the operating budget, developing the facilities plan, and formulating the test program. Later, when I was director of defense research and engineering, it was much the same. I worked out the main elements of the program and I sold my plans and ideas directly to higher authorities in the White House, the Pentagon, and the Congress. When they approved my plans, I instructed lower echelons how to carry them out. In all cases I consulted my colleagues widely. I carefully considered the advice they gave me, but I never thought of myself as being formally obliged to follow it. If something went badly wrong in those jobs, I knew it was my head that would roll and I behaved accordingly.

At UCSD, as on all other UC campuses, things were totally different. The most interesting matters of substance fell under the authority of the faculty, not the chancellor. Both the content and the form of the educational program are under the control of departmental faculties and campus committees. The recruitment and the promotion of faculty, while nominally under the authority of the chancellor, are in fact almost entirely controlled by faculty committees. The chancellor is in charge of relations with the world at large, including raising money from both public and private sources. He directly supervises only such matters as parking, accounting, purchasing, on-campus housing, and the construction of new facilities (but even then only after they have been approved by a faculty committee).

I believe that this is an effective arrangement, producing excellent results. As a member of the faculty of the university, I fully supported it, but it was very different from what I had become accustomed to. In sum, I approved of the system, with its deep and broad delegations of authority, but I didn't enjoy my role in it.

In the fall of 1963, at age forty-one, I finally came to realize that I did not want to spend the next quarter of a century as the chief executive of a university campus. At some time I would surely leave my post, and I decided that it would be better to do so sooner than later. I knew I would be letting a number of good people down, and I didn't at all like that aspect of it, but I determined to resign nonetheless.

Shortly after informing Clark Kerr in early November 1963, I called a special, early-morning meeting of the department chairman and academic deans. As I left my office for the meeting, I remarked to my secretary, "I don't look forward to headlines saying 'YORK QUITS.' I hope something else happens to cover it up."

I told the faculty of my intentions. I gave my recent heart attack and some follow-up symptoms as the main reason for resigning. That was partly true: I did fear that I could not count on enough energy to do all I really wanted to do. In particular, I was concerned that the extra responsibilities of being the chief representative of the campus to the world at large were more than I wished to carry.

When I returned to my office after the meeting, my secretary told me the radio was saying the president had been shot in Dallas. It was November 22, 1963. The news of my resignation was lost deep in the back pages of that evening's papers.

Not long after that, the San Diego city manager asked me where I would be going. I told him nowhere; I planned to stay right here as a professor. He expressed great surprise. He said he could not imagine stepping down from the city manager's post to work, for example, in the park department. It would simply be impossible to do so. I explained that life in the university was different. The outside world may regard the chancellor as being at the top of the heap, but the faculty themselves know that the position of professor is the highest and noblest in the university. I would therefore not be facing the same kind of "status problem" that he would encounter under parallel circumstances.

Even in those relatively tranquil days, the search for a new chancellor took a long time. It was only in November 1964, a year after I had resigned and a few months after the first class of undergraduates had been admitted, that John S. Galbraith finally succeeded me as chancellor at UCSD. He had arrived at UCSD nearly a year earlier to serve as vice-chancellor for academic affairs. He was from the start the logical candidate to replace me, but the university committees had to reach that conclusion on their own.

Back to Physics

I went off on a brief holiday after Galbraith took over, and then I joined the physics department as a professor. In doing so, I was attempting to get back on a career track I had left fourteen years before. At that time I had abandoned the Berkeley faculty to become director at Livermore. Then came Washington and the chancellorship at San Diego. Now, in the spring of 1965, I found myself trying to pick up the threads of that earlier career.

Things worked out better than I had expected. At first I taught only upper-division courses in physics: "Electricity and Magnetism" and "Modern Physics," including nuclear physics and quantum mechanics. It felt good to be thinking about those topics again, and I truly enjoyed the studying I had to do to teach those subjects to a group of bright students. I also took on the responsibility for one of our senior laboratories. It was outfitted to provide students with the opportunity to repeat certain relatively simple, but recent, basic experiments. And, of course, it let me bring myself up to date by going over some recent work I had missed while busily engaged elsewhere.

I was, happily, able to cope adequately with this delightful mix of old and familiar plus new and unfamiliar material. It soon became evident, however, that I could not seriously compete with the bright young people who were moving along uninterrupted career tracks. After about two years of such activities, I was therefore ready to return to midlevel university administration. That would give me a better opportunity to perform services of real value to the university while still leaving me with enough time and energy for part-time participation in the national security world. As a first step in that new direction, I served as chairman of the physics department for the next fifteen months.

Graduate Dean and Acting Chancellor

In 1968, four years after becoming chancellor, John Galbraith resigned and returned to his faculty position at UCLA. William J. McGill, one of the founding members of our psychology department and then chairman of the Faculty Senate, succeeded Galbraith. Shortly after McGill took over, he made a number of changes in the top levels of his administration. As a result, several important positions opened up, and after a few months he invited me to become graduate dean. By that time Richard Nixon had become president of the United States. He wielded the proverbial "new broom" with special vigor, and some of my richest and most interesting Washington connections were cut off as a result. I thus had more nervous energy than usual to spend at UCSD and was pleased to accept McGill's proposal.

Eighteen months into his term, McGill resigned in order to become president of his alma mater, Columbia University. The year was 1969, and the student rebellion in America and the Western world was in full swing. Some of the more strident students were demanding that university administrators everywhere stop the war in Southeast Asia. When they all proved unwilling or unable to do that, the students engaged in acts designed to force them to take action. That in turn aroused the general public and its political leaders. Everywhere they found it convenient to condemn both the actions and the inaction of university officials. In our case these problems and their consequences made it very hard to find a successor to McGill who was at once willing and able to do the job and acceptable to the highest authorities—especially when among those highest authorities was one Ronald Reagan, then governor of California and ex officio president of the university's Board of Regents.

When, after six more months, Bill finally left with no replacement yet in sight, it was plausible for me to be appointed acting chancellor. I was the next-ranking member of the staff, I knew where all the dead bodies were buried, so to speak, and I had made it clear I was not a candidate for the job myself. It was easier to appoint me on an acting basis than any of the other senior officers, some of whom were, in fact, interested in the top position.

It took even longer than usual to find a replacement for McGill. Not only did the general political situation delay the process, but a false start in our search stretched it out further. As a result, I held the post that second time around for almost two years. My service as chancellor for two terms at the same campus separated by a six-year interval may be unique in the annals of American academe. I thought of my situation as being similar to that of Grover Cleveland, the only man to serve two separate terms as president of the United States.

To my surprise I enjoyed the second, overtly temporary, term as chancellor much more than I had the first. The campus was more interesting than it had been earlier. There was a wide spectrum of departments, and a full complement of students, both undergraduates and graduates, some six thousand in all. All sorts of student activities, including intercollegiate sports, were under way. Some of the more obnoxious types of student rebels were still evident; by and large, though, the problems they represented were winding down, and the future looked promising and bright.

I have many pleasant memories from that period, but perhaps the single most enjoyable event occurred at the graduation ceremony of June 1971. My older daughter, Rachel, was one of the graduating seniors. As chancellor, I was the presiding officer but did not actually pass out the diplomas. The provosts of the individual colleges did that. When Rachel's turn came, she hurried across the stage, fearful that I might do something unseemly, such as rush over to kiss her. I knew she didn't want me to, so I didn't, but we exchanged a big hug immediately after the ceremony was over.

(Our other children were also in college at about the same time, but they went elsewhere. David went to UC Davis during the worst and most stressful period of student unrest. He also found that formal college work at UCD was not his cup of tea. He tried several other schools later, but he never made it all the way to graduation. Cynthia went first to UCLA. After dropping out for a couple of years, again partly as a result of the student unrest, she returned and finished a B.S. in zoology at Berkeley and then went on to get a D.V.M. degree at Davis in 1981.)

Finally, William McElroy, the director of the National Science Foundation, was appointed chancellor. He and his wife and two dogs arrived in the San Diego airport in late January 1972. Sybil and I picked them all up in our station wagon and drove them to University House in La Jolla. The next day we left for a month-long drive through Mexico, all the way to the Yucatán Peninsula and back. It was the first step in a year's sabbatical leave, my first ever.

Institute on Global Conflict and Cooperation

When I returned to work a year later, I did not go back either to the central administration or to teaching physics. With the support of the new chancellor and other colleagues, I set up an independent academic unit called the Program on Science, Technology, and Public Affairs. For the next few years the program consisted of myself, an occasional visiting assistant professor, and one research assistant, usually a graduate student in history. Together we developed a small set of courses dealing with such topics as the nuclear arms race and the world's space programs. With the help of a grant from the Ford Foundation, we also initiated a research program designed to explore the history and causes of the arms race. Through this new academic unit I was able to focus my energies within the university on precisely those topics that had long constituted my major intellectual interest. For the first time in many years, the work I was doing inside the university and the work I was doing outside meshed and reinforced each other. Much later, in 1981, a happy conjunction of two factors made it possible for me to expand this activity significantly.

One factor was my return to the campus after another four-year period of full-time work for the government (see chapters 13 and 14). Once again I found myself back home, institutionally speaking, and pondering how best to combine my university life with my permanent interest in peace and security issues.

The other factor rose out of a circumstance unique to the University of California. Every five years, including the year 1981, the university and the federal government renegotiate the contract under which the Regents of the University take on the responsibility for managing the Livermore and Los Alamos laboratories. Not surprisingly, many faculty members and students hold this relationship to be inappropriate or worse. As a result, a wide-ranging review of the situation takes place at many levels, including those of the president's office and the Board of Regents. In the 1981 review President David Saxon concluded that, yes, it was right and necessary that the university continue to be responsible for operating the nuclear laboratories, but because we did so we should also expand our involvement in peace and security affairs so as to include other, broader and more political studies of the issues involved.

Governor Edmund G. ("Jerry") Brown, Jr., was an ex officio member of the Board of Regents. After reviewing the situation, he concluded that, no, it was neither right nor necessary that the university continue to be responsible for operating the nuclear laboratories, but, given that he could not persuade a majority of the regents that he was right, then we should at least expand our involvement in peace and security affairs so as and so on and so on. Thus, the governor and the president, starting from opposite conclusions about the propriety of operating the nuclear laboratories, came to identical conclusions about the necessity for expanding our involvement in peace and security issues.

The net result was a decision to establish the statewide Institute on Global Conflict and Cooperation, whose program was to promote academic study of peace and security issues on all campuses of the university. I was ready, interested, and available, and in the summer of 1982 I was appointed acting director and, later, director of the new institute. The staff of the older Program on Science, Technology, and Public Affairs became the initial staff of the new enterprise. The institute has since then received growing support from the regents, the state, and various foundations. My primary assistants in this new enterprise were G. Allen Greb, a historian, and James Skelly, a sociologist. Greb had been with me for many years, first as a graduate student research assistant and later as a postdoctoral researcher, and has helped me greatly in getting the history right in the books and papers I have written since the mid 1970s.

CHAPTER 11

Advising Washington

(1961–1969)

Creating the Arms Control and Disarmament Agency

O NLY a month after I moved to La Jolla, I found myself back in Washington testifying in behalf of President Kennedy's plan to create the U.S. Arms Control and Disarmament Agency (ACDA). During the 1960 presidential campaign a Democratic party study committee had recommended that such an organization be established. Candidate Kennedy incorporated the idea into his platform, and now he was making good on it.

In my testimony I first presented the pertinent biographical information and then asserted,

> Uncontrolled arms races have a habit of leading to war, and if the global war that this modern arms race is leading to happens, the words "victory and defeat" will not be applicable afterwards. The only words that would make any sense are "complete and utter disaster, catastrophe."
> There is no question that there would be potentially grave dangers in a

careless or willy-nilly disarmament program. In the worst case, the end might even well be the same as the end in an uncontrolled arms race. But I believe the risk that would be incurred in not attempting to find some alternative path or solution is much greater than the risk that would be incurred in a careful and thoughtful attempt to achieve some measure of disarmament or arms control.[1]

The proposal became law later that year. The first director was William C. Foster, formerly deputy secretary of defense at the end of the Truman administration. The first deputy director was Adrian ("Butch") Fisher, a Tennessee lawyer with an endless supply of backwoods jokes and homilies. He habitually used them to make points with the Russians, but they in turn never quite knew what he was driving at, except that he clearly meant well.

The Arms Control Act of 1961 also called for the creation of the General Advisory Committee (GAC) to work with both the president and the agency director. Because of the politically delicate nature of arms control and disarmament, the Congress insisted that its members be appointed by the president with the advice and consent of the Senate. They feared that otherwise the committee and the process might somehow be taken over by "woolly-headed" types. Senators opposing arms control were afraid such people would "give away the store." Senators favoring arms control were afraid they would give the process a bad name and cause the public to draw back from it.

John McCloy, who had been Kennedy's special assistant in the area, was named chairman of the GAC. I became one of the members, and so did some other longtime friends and colleagues, including George Kistiakowsky, Trevor Gardner, I. I. Rabi, and General Thomas White (now retired).* I was chosen because I was thought to be both an expert on nuclear weapons and interested in pursuing arms control as an essential element of national security policy. Kistiakowsky and Rabi had similar reputations in this regard.

Our committee brought together a wide spectrum of views. One example of this spread involved B-47 bombers. The United States was decommissioning B-47s as fast as it added ICBMs to its arsenal. At first we mothballed the airplanes, but it soon became evident that we should simply destroy them. Someone proposed that we do so in a big public

---

*The other members of the first GAC were Roger Blough, of the U.S. Steel corporation; the Reverend Edward Conway, S.J.; John Cowles, of the *Minneapolis Star and Tribune;* Robert Lovett, a former secretary of defense; Dean McGee, of Kerr-McGee Oil; Ralph McGill, of the *Atlanta Constitution;* James Perkins, of the Carnegie Corporation; and Herman Phleger, a San Francisco attorney.

bonfire celebrating the event. Two of the GAC members, representing opposite political extremes, opposed the idea.

"No. It would be phony and misleading," said Rabi, noting that we were replacing them with something better.

"No. We might need them again," said Dean McGee.

We also reviewed related programs in other agencies, particularly the Defense Department and the CIA. One was Project Vela, a program I had been instrumental in starting when I was in ARPA. It was in essence a collection of technical devices and activities whose purpose was to monitor nuclear testing in all environments, including underground and in outer space.

One of those instruments was the so-called Vela satellite, designed to detect nuclear explosions in both space and the atmosphere. In the space case, it did so by detecting the gamma rays emitted during nuclear explosions. As a happy by-product, the Vela satellite led to a whole new science: gamma-ray astronomy.

In the atmospheric case, the Vela satellite detected nuclear explosions by observing the intense light produced during the fireball stage of the explosion. Years later, in 1979, when I was in Geneva negotiating a test ban treaty with the British and the Soviets, one of these satellites detected a peculiar, intense light flash over the ocean south of Africa. The light signal was similar to, but not identical with, that emitted by a nuclear explosion. It proved to be unique in the twenty-year history of the satellite. No other data corroborating a test at that time and place have ever turned up. Almost certainly it was a false alarm, but we could not know that when it was first reported. It became, for a while, the focus of much of our informal discussion in Geneva.

The two topics that interested me the most in those early days of the ACDA were the nuclear test ban and the proposals to eliminate, or limit, antiballistic missiles, or ABMs.

The Partial Nuclear Test Ban

The ACDA and its GAC took up their work shortly after the Eisenhower-Khrushchev nuclear test moratorium had broken down, in the summer of 1961. The causes of this breakdown go back to December 1959. At that time Eisenhower, piqued over delays in the negotiations intended to convert the moratorium into a formal treaty, announced that the United States was no longer bound by it but would not resume testing without giving notice. A week later, in January 1960, Khrushchev announced that in that case the USSR also ceased to be bound by the moratorium but that it would not resume testing unless the West did so first. A few months later the French conducted their first nuclear test, in North Africa, and Khrushchev promptly condemned it as testing by the West. Even so, it wasn't until September 1, 1961, following yet another Berlin crisis, that the Soviets actually began, on only two days' notice, a new series of nuclear weapons tests, this time in the Arctic.

I recall feeling that this test series confirmed my contention that the Soviets had not been cheating during the moratorium. When they finally decided to test, they did so openly—not, perhaps, because of any moral restraints, but because it was really the only practical way to go about it, even then with just the partially effective first-generation Vela system in place. However, some of those who had all along contended the Soviets were cheating on the moratorium said they wouldn't have been able to conduct such a huge series of tests without some earlier hidden explosions.* I remain convinced of the correctness of my original position.

The resumption of Soviet testing was followed by the resumption of U.S. testing. These events stimulated arms control advocates everywhere to redouble their efforts to produce a formal treaty banning nuclear tests.

The main stumbling block continued to be the problem of monitoring underground tests. Given the technology then available, these were much more difficult to monitor than tests in the atmosphere or other open media.

We had in place a worldwide network of seismic stations (earthquake detectors), which could detect most underground tests in the USSR but which could not distinguish them from earthquakes of similar energy, and these occurred by the hundreds in the USSR every year. In order to discriminate between earthquakes and tests, we said, we needed the right to conduct on-site inspections whenever we detected a suspicious event. Soon the general argument focused on a specific issue: How many "mandatory" on-site inspections were needed per year, and how and by whom would they be managed and conducted?

After much discussion the U.S. arms control authorities concluded that seven mandatory inspections per year were the least we could live with. The Soviet response continued to be that none were necessary. Briefly a ray of hope appeared. At one point Khrushchev seemed to be saying he had changed his mind and would accept three. Sometime after

*Edward Teller and Senator Thomas Dodd were two such.

that, Harold Brown, then DDR & E, said maybe five would be enough. Kennedy publicly corrected Harold, saying no, the number was seven. Perhaps we could have struck a compromise between three and seven, but before that proposition could be tested, the Soviets returned to their prior position that none were needed.

My personal guess is that no compromise was really possible. I believe Khrushchev's "three" may have been given without the full endorsement of his colleagues in the Politburo and would not have survived his dismissal, or any serious negotiation to that end even if he had not been fired.

Faced with this impasse, the ACDA in 1962 produced two draft treaties, one eliminating all nuclear tests everywhere and the other banning all tests except those that took place underground, in the one medium that could not be reliably monitored. In 1963 the latter version was successfully negotiated by Averell Harriman and a team of experts from the ACDA.

Support for a test ban had been coming from two distinct groups: first, those who were primarily concerned about radioactive fallout and its harmful effects on human health and genetics; second, those who were primarily concerned about the connection between nuclear testing and the nuclear arms race. By eliminating tests in the atmosphere, the Limited Test Ban Treaty of 1963 effectively satisfied the people in the first category. Those in the second continued to push for a complete ban, but they did not have enough weight to do so now that the environmentalists were satisfied and had dropped out. Government efforts to achieve a comprehensive test ban continued until 1981, including a period of two years in 1979–81, when I was the U.S. chief negotiator (see chapter 14). We came close at times during those eighteen years, but we never quite made it.

In 1981 President Reagan determined that a comprehensive test ban was not in the best interests of the United States. Since then certain public interest groups have continued to push for it, but within the government the matter has been dropped.

Limiting ABM

To my knowledge, the first high government official to propose and seriously study an international agreement to limit ABMs (antiballistic missiles) was Jack Ruina, then director of ARPA. He started from a half joking personal remark made by Jerome Wiesner, then Kennedy's science adviser. Jerry had said something to the effect that the only reason our people wanted to build an ABM was that the Soviets were building one. At the time the Soviets were installing an ABM system—named the Galosh by NATO authorities—around Moscow, and Khrushchev boasted about how good it was. He claimed it could shoot a fly out of the sky, and to prove his point he reminded us of the well-known and very annoying series of Soviet "firsts" in space.

Following up on Wiesner's remark, Ruina explored the possibility of a formal agreement to ban, or limit, such weapons. As Jack saw it, the current situation, in which no ABMs were deployed on either side, had brought about "a curious and unprecedented stability," deriving from two factors. First, the military balance was insensitive to the number and kind of offensive weapons in the arsenals of each country so long as they were invulnerable; second, the danger that either side would miscalculate the consequences of a nuclear attack was minimized. The introduction of ABMs by either or both sides would change that by introducing new, important, but incalculable changes in the strategic relationship. These uncertainties, in turn, could lead both to an arms race instability—that is, to an unrestrained series of attempts by each side to cope with the worst-possible case presented by the other side—and to instability at a time of crisis that could raise the pressure to go first.[2]

When he had the idea well formulated, he presented it to his boss, Harold Brown. Harold didn't think much of the idea, but instead of rejecting it outright he advised Jack to take it to Deputy Secretary of Defense Gilpatric, who would "probably like it." As Harold predicted, Gilpatric found it interesting, and the notion of banning ABMs took root at the top of the defense establishment.

In 1964, not long after leaving ARPA, Ruina presented the idea orally at a meeting of Pugwash conference, a meeting of specialists from both East and West concerned about where the nuclear arms race was taking us. After Jack's presentation the head of the Soviet delegation approached him and said there must have been something wrong with the translation. He explained that he actually heard the interpreter say Jack proposed to limit *defensive* weapons! Jack said yes, that is exactly what he proposed. The Russian then asked for a written paper on the subject. That evening Ruina and Murray Gell-Mann, a Nobel laureate in physics who received most of his education in defense matters through the Jason group, drafted a paper to submit to the conference the next morning. The Soviets still considered it a strange notion but agreed to think more about it.

The idea of limiting defenses seemed strange—indeed, even per-verse—not only to the Russians when they first heard about it but to most members of our own defense establishment as well. Eventually, however, many high officials in both the United States and the USSR, including Secretary of Defense McNamara, accepted the idea that limit-ing ABM could provide an effective damper on the arms race.

At the same time as he was trying to hold back ABM, McNamara was promoting a technical device called MIRV, for multiple independently targeted reentry vehicles.

Bombers had always been able to deliver more than one bomb on more than one target. The first missiles, however, were able to deliver only one warhead—or reentry vehicle, as it was usually called—on a given target. In the early 1960s the development of a new device called a "post boost vehicle," or "bus"—originally designed for making multi-satellite launches—made it possible for a single missile to loft multiple independently guided reentry vehicles, each aimed at a different target.

McNamara liked MIRV because it helped him solve two difficult, basically political problems at once. First, it helped him resist proposals from the military to increase the number of missiles. In the mid-1960s the Soviets finally did produce ICBMs at the rate anticipated back in the "missile gap" days, and some American strategists urged that we in-crease our strategic forces in response. MIRV made it possible to in-crease the number of warheads without increasing the number of mis-siles.

Second, MIRV was, as McNamara saw it, the final clincher in the argument against ABM. By providing each offensive missile with many warheads, one could easily saturate, or exhaust, any of the ABM sys-tems then being considered. MIRV, in essence, made it possible to arm the decoys, thus forcing the defense to shoot at everything that was thrown against it. At first the ACDA supported MIRV for the same reasons McNamara did.

Others, however, saw that MIRV had a darker side. By making it possible for each missile on one side to attack more than one missile on the other side, the introduction of MIRV would eventually make a preemptive strike look more promising, and therefore more likely, in a crisis situation. This problem was recognized early on by a number of analysts,* but as usual in human affairs—individual or collective—the short-term considerations overrode the long-term ones.

---

*Ivan Sellin and Morton Halperin in the OSD, Herbert Scoville and George Rathjens in the ACDA, and some in the JASON Summer Study Group.

In January 1967 McNamara carried the debate about ABM into the Cabinet Room. He arranged a meeting at which, in addition to the president, there were present all past and current special assistants to the president for science and technology (Killian, Kistiakowsky, Wiesner, and Donald Hornig) and all past and current DDR & E (myself, Harold Brown, and John Foster). We were asked the simple question that must be faced after all the complicated *if*'s, *and*'s, and *but*'s have been discussed: "Will it work and should it be deployed?" The outside experts all gave the same answer: "No. There is no prospect of its defending our people against a Soviet missile attack." McNamara said he would speak for the current Pentagon officials. To no one's surprise, he agreed with us outsiders. No one there contradicted him. It was my impression that Harold did in fact agree with him and that Johnny and the chiefs did not, but none of them were invited to give their views during that meeting.

In June 1967 Premier Aleksei Kosygin of the Soviet Union visited the United Nations headquarters in New York. Lyndon Johnson arranged to meet with him at Glassboro State College, in New Jersey, a point roughly halfway between New York and Washington. Relations between the two countries were especially poor at the time, and it took subtle maneuvering to arrange even such a mini-summit. McNamara went along and in a separate meeting with Kosygin tried to persuade him that deploying an ABM system would do nothing except stimulate the arms race. Kosygin, who very likely had never heard the idea before, replied as most people do when they first hear it: "Defense missiles don't kill people; they protect people. So why ban them?"

Despite these first reactions by the Soviets, American officials continued to push the idea. Other Americans, such as those private citizens engaged in the Pugwash movement or in similar enterprises, did what they could to promote the idea in unofficial meetings with Soviet counterparts.

Later that year Lyndon Johnson became concerned about a possible political battle over a hypothetical "ABM gap." The presidential campaign was only a year off, and Johnson expected to be in it. He therefore ordered McNamara to prepare to build a thin ABM system. In a speech given in San Francisco, McNamara reiterated his belief that we could not build an ABM system capable of protecting us from a Russian attack. Even so, he said, a decision had been made to build a thin ABM system able to cope with a hypothetical Chinese missile attack, which, by definition, would be light and uncomplicated. In making the announcement, he also warned us, "The danger in deploying this relatively light and reliable Chinese-oriented ABM system is going to be that pressures will develop to expand it into a heavy Soviet-oriented ABM system." The record of the events that followed shows that this prediction was quite right.

When Nixon succeeded Johnson as president, he picked up the idea of deploying an ABM and expanded it just as McNamara had predicted. Opposition to the idea, however, never ceased, and eventually the efforts of the opponents paid off in the ABM Treaty of 1972. I continued to be much involved in the actions leading up to that treaty, but not through the GAC, from which I resigned—as custom demanded—in 1969, when Nixon became president. More on all this later.

The PSAC Again

According to Jerome Wiesner, a proposal to appoint me to the PSAC for a four-year term beginning January 1964 was on Kennedy's desk when he was assassinated. In that, as in most other matters during his first year in office, Lyndon Johnson was true to his promise to "continue" what the slain president had started. I was pleased to accept. The invitation came only weeks after my resignation as chancellor, and I looked forward to spending a substantial effort on this new assignment.

It turned out to be very different from what I had anticipated. The relations between the president and the PSAC, particularly with its chairman, Donald Hornig, were very different from those that had prevailed in the Killian and Kistiakowsky era. A little golden age had come and gone in the span of only seven years.

Two meetings of the committee with President Johnson illustrate this point perfectly. The first took place soon after I rejoined the group. The president was open, cordial, and, above all, optimistic. He said, "You just tell me what it is I should do. Don't you worry about how to get it done. That's my job and I'll take care of it." Three years later, toward the end of his term (and mine), we had another such meeting. He started that one out by saying, "You people just come in here and tell me what I ought to do. You never stop to think how hard it is for me to do it, and you never take the time to help me with it."

Lyndon Johnson made it clear that there were two things he especially wanted from us. One was to tell him what he could do to make things better for "Grandma." The other was how to win the war in Vietnam. By "Grandma" he meant the deserving underprivileged in general. In the area of higher education, for example, he was every bit as interested in the junior colleges of the land as in the Harvards and the UCSDs from which all of us came, and he challenged us to pay some attention to these other places. And, of course, as the war consumed him more and more, our failure to help him win it contributed to his disenchantment with us and our kind.

This failure on our part was not for lack of trying. We had long briefings at every other meeting on the course of the war. We all became painfully familiar with the Ho Chi Minh Trail connecting North Vietnam, via Laos and Cambodia—supposedly neutral and independent states—to South Vietnam. We heard all there was to know about the American effort to interdict the supplies and soldiers coming down the trail, and we would have helped if we could. A steady stream of officers brought maps splotched with various colors, supposedly showing who controlled what areas in South Vietnam itself. We did contribute some ideas designed to improve the situation, but none of them ever seemed to do much good.

We heard largely the same stories about "light at the end of the tunnel" as the public did. The big difference was that we could pry further and question primary sources in the matter. When we did so, we found that the answers were no more useful than the publicly available stories. Although many of the higher brass believed they knew what was going on over there, it was evident that they did not. I often harked back to my days at the Pentagon a few years earlier. I recalled how badly informed we were about that unfamiliar place and how poorly we understood what information we had. Everything I heard during my four years on the PSAC confirmed what I learned during the Eisenhower years: we simply did not belong there. As Eisenhower and others had made clear, the United States should not fight a land war in Asia. I was convinced that we would not in the end prevail and, worse, that our attempt to do so would only prolong the war and lead to still more misery, destruction, and death.

As a result, I became disaffected with Lyndon Johnson and the war. I think about half the PSAC members felt the same way, and half continued to hope for the best and to have faith in the wisdom of their leaders. I considered resigning but told myself it was *my* government and country as much as it was *theirs*, and so I opted to retain whatever influence over events I might still have.

President Johnson knew that many on the PSAC disapproved his conduct in Southeast Asia. Moreover, we were the only inside group that had such people in it. If we had been political experts, if we had been people selected and recruited because of our political acumen, that would have been intolerable. He would have had to discharge us for being wrong and stupid. But we were recruited on the basis of different talents, and so he could brush off our disagreement with his political actions as naive and ignore this defect in our outlook.

It works out that way in the USSR also, only more so. I recall a conversation with Georgi Arbatov, then director of the Institute for U.S.A. and Canada Studies and, more important, a member of the Central Committee of the Communist party of the Soviet Union. It was about Peter Kapitza, the unofficial dean of Soviet science. Peter had recently said something gently critical about a Soviet policy. Arbatov, commenting on that, said, "Peter is a wonderful scientist, but he is hopelessly naive about politics." Khrushchev, in his memoirs, reported saying the same thing to Sakharov, but in that instance to the man's face. If the objects of these remarks had been in a high position because of expertise in political matters, the Soviet state would have found it necessary to take action against them. However, since they were scientists, Soviet politicians could simply declare them to be politically naive and let them get away with these idiosyncrasies. (Eventually, of course, the Soviet state did find it necessary to act against Sakharov, but it tolerated his political eccentricity for many years before finally exiling him to Gorki. The new 1987-style "glasnost", however, has made it possible to tolerate him once again.)

The most important tasks I personally performed for the PSAC in that second term were services as vice-chairman for two years (1965–66), as chairman of its nominating committee, and as chairman of the special Panel on International Technical Cooperation and Assistance. This last involved study of U.S. technical assistance to the Third World, both directly and through international organizations. It was a very interesting task, which took me on some great journeys to remote parts of Peru and Colombia, but it had no direct connection with the quest for national security, and I will refrain from discussing it further here.

Nonproliferation

I also served on an especially interesting ad hoc committee during this period. Its subject was nuclear proliferation. The Chinese exploded their first atomic bomb on October 16, 1964, shortly before this new group was convened, and the French test program, started in 1960, was moving ahead. Organized in November 1964, the committee issued its report only three months later.

Early in 1964 the French proposed to buy an advanced American electronic computer and install it at their basic research station near Saclas. Would it be used only in support of basic research or in support of nuclear weapons development, even though the center for such work was located somewhere else? That question stimulated the National Security Council to call for a review of the nuclear weapons proliferation question.

The ad hoc committee established to do so was chaired by Roswell Gilpatric, who had just recently resigned from his post as deputy secretary of defense. It included a wide spectrum of other experts, all with substantial experience in national security affairs. I was among them, and so were a number of old friends and colleagues, including George Kistiakowsky and John McCloy.

Our meetings were briefed by government officials from the Atomic Energy Commission and elsewhere. We eventually came up with a number of potentially useful, though perhaps not very surprising, observations and recommendations. As a basis for our recommendations, we agreed on four major points:

First, the spread of nuclear weapons poses an increasingly grave threat to the security of the United States.

Second, the world is fast approaching a point of no return in the prospects of controlling the spread of nuclear weapons.

Third, success in preventing the future spread of nuclear weapons requires a concerted and intensified effort.

Fourth, a major effort on our part has promise of success in halting or retarding the spread of nuclear weapons.[3]

We then recommended three actions that directly confronted the problem. In brief, these were the negotiation of a near-universal nonproliferation agreement, the negotiation of a comprehensive test ban, and the establishment of nuclear free zones in Latin America, Africa, and the Israel-UAR region.

More important, I think, we concluded that we would not get very far in controlling the spread of nuclear weapons so long as the superpowers were engaged in an unrestrained arms race. We therefore recommended three initiatives we felt would "reduce tensions between the United States and the Soviet Union and create an atmosphere conducive to wide acceptance of restraints on nuclear proliferation":

(1) A verified fissile materials production cutoff for weapons purposes, to be established by treaty. . . .

(2) A verified strategic delivery vehicle freeze coupled with significant agreed reductions (e.g. 30%) in strategic force levels, to be established by treaty.

(3) An 18- to 24-month halt in the construction of new ABM or ICBM launchers, to be accomplished by reciprocal Executive action based on unilateral verification capabilities.[4]

A Meeting with LBJ Produces Unexpected Results

We presented our results to the president in a meeting in the Cabinet Room on January 21, 1965. It was the very first day Lyndon Johnson was in office in his own right.

For some reason, the president was in a sour mood. He started the meeting off by saying, "I want to thank you all for taking time off from the golf course to come in and help me with this important problem."

Nearly everyone there smiled as if to say, "Thank you, Mr. President."

There was one exception: George Kistiakowsky. He replied, "Mr. President, I didn't come here from the golf course. I came from my laboratory at Harvard, where I will return this evening in order to meet with a graduate student whom I otherwise would have seen this morning." Perhaps only a scientist could have gotten cleanly away with such a remark. If a politician had said that to a sitting president, he would have been considered impolitic and slightly daft. But George was a scientist, an expert in an area remote from pure politics, and could be forgiven for simply being naive. In any event, the president merely said, "Oh, George, you know I didn't mean it."

At that point we should have moved on to the business of the day, but it was not to be. Alfred Gruenther, formerly supreme Allied commander, Europe (SACEUR), and then president of the American Red Cross, made another totally unexpected intervention.

"Mr. President, did you see that ad in the newspaper where those literature professors tried to tell you how to conduct your affairs in Vietnam?"

It turned out that the president had indeed seen it and some others like it. He let us know in plain language what he thought about such suggestions. When we finally got around to the main subject, all the steam had gone out of the meeting, and I have no particular recollection of how things went after that.

I have seen a number of other such advertisements and have often pondered their effects. Many of them, including the one Al Gruenther brought up, were addressed directly to the president.

If the purpose of the ad was to tell the commander in chief things he didn't know and to get him to change his mind as a result, it obviously failed. If anything, it stiffened his views and pushed his feet deeper into the concrete. He knew for sure that those presumptuous professors did not know nearly as much about the situation as he and his advisers did.

If, however, its purpose was to influence the politician Johnson, then it may have been successful. That ad, along with many similar ones, helped persuade him that important elements of the public were becoming increasingly unhappy with the way things were going. That surely contributed to his 1968 decision not to run for reelection.

Aerospace and IDA

Ever since I left full-time employment in the Pentagon in 1961, I have maintained a close working relationship with two special national security organizations: the Aerospace Corporation and the Institute for Defense Analyses (IDA). Both are not-for-profit corporations known as FFCRCs, federally funded contract research centers. Each works mainly for one primary customer: Aerospace, for the Department of the Air Force; IDA, for the Office of the Secretary of Defense, including the Office of the Joint Chiefs of Staff.

The Aerospace Corporation was founded in 1960, but its roots go back to 1954. The Air Force was then just in the earliest stages of initiating a "highest priority" program to develop long-range missiles (ICBMs and IRBMs) and space boosters. At first the newly established Ramo-Wooldridge Corporation simply provided the Air Force with the analysis and advice it needed to get these programs going. Soon, however, the new corporation decided to make and sell missile-related hardware as well. That was, and still is, where the real money is.

Ramo-Wooldridge tried to keep these two activities separate from each other, but it was never able to do so to the satisfaction of the other aerospace corporations with which it had to deal. In essence, these other corporations charged that the necessarily intimate connections between the Air Force and the analytical and systems engineering side of R-W gave its manufacturing side an unfair competitive advantage. The Air Force, too, was never fully satisfied with the dual personality of the corporation. At one memorable meeting of the von Neumann committee, Trevor Gardner in a great many well-chosen words read the riot act to Simon Ramo. Ramo sat stoically through it and afterward made a few changes in the arrangements.

The changes were, however, not enough to satisfy the critics. The Air Force concluded it had to start over from scratch, and so it established the wholly new, entirely independent, not-for-profit Aerospace Corporation, with its own board of trustees. The function of the board followed the norm: to review the corporation's work, to make sure it was what the Air Force needed and wanted, to hire and fire the president, and to be ultimately responsible for the company's property and funds.

Many of the first cadres of employees transferred over to the new corporation from STL. Ivan Getting, then a vice-president of the Raytheon Corporation, was selected to be the first president. Getting had worked at the MIT Radiation Laboratory during the war and later served as chief scientist of the Air Force.

The board was made up of persons who had distinguished records in national security, including a number of past (and future) officials. One of them was Harold Brown, then director of the Livermore Laboratory. Before the corporation was a year old, Kennedy became president. Five of the members of the Aerospace board were named to high posts in the new administration, among them Harold Brown, who replaced me in the Pentagon.* Naturally enough, I replaced Harold Brown on the board and have remained on it ever since.

The function of the new corporation was to provide the general systems engineering and technical direction the Air Force needed in the management of its space programs. By joining the Aerospace board immediately after leaving the Pentagon, I was able to continue my relationship with all these programs and their successors, albeit with a very different degree of personal authority. I regarded all of those programs as being both very interesting and very important. Not only did they support our national defense objectives in the usual sense—by serving as elements in our military-preparedness posture—but some of them played essential roles in our arms control and disarmament efforts as well.

Being a member of the Aerospace board also made it easy for me to continue some of the personal relationships I had earlier developed under very different circumstances. Among those with whom I served overlapping terms on the board were Benny Schriever, Jimmy Doolittle,

*The others were Roswell Gilpatric, who became deputy secretary of defense, William C. Foster, who was appointed director of the ACDA, Jerome Wiesner, who became Kennedy's science adviser, and Najeeb Halaby, who became the head of the Federal Aviation Administration.

Joseph Platt (from my University of Rochester days), Gerald R. Ford (who had been the ranking minority member of the House Appropriations Committee during my years in the Pentagon), and Ed Huddleson, a San Francisco attorney whom Sybil and I first met in the 1950s while hiking the long trail down from Merced Lake to Yosemite Valley.

My relationship with IDA has in many ways been similar to that with Aerospace. From its beginning in March 1956 until June 1968, the members of the IDA corporation were themselves other corporations—specifically, a group of universities, including my own University of California. This relationship would, it was supposed, make it easier to arrange for faculty members to come to Washington on a temporary basis. During the early 1960s I occasionally stood in for Clark Kerr, who, as president of the University of California, was an ex officio member of the board.

In the late 1960s, actions of the more strident students at the member universities made a change in this arrangement advisable. Not only did the students demand that their presidents stop the war in Vietnam; they also demanded an end to all working relationships with the "war machine"—including, quite specifically, IDA. As a result, a new board was created, consisting of individual persons rather than universities. At that point I was elected a full member of the board of trustees, a position I have retained ever since.

IDA, like Aerospace, provided me with the opportunity to continue to be engaged, though less intensively, with many of the projects I had had a hand in starting when I was a Defense Department official. Among the most interesting was the Jason group, the permanent successor to ARPA's Project 137.

Jason

For the first fourteen years of its life, Jason—whose creation was the final net result of Project 137—operated as a division of IDA. Since then Jason has been successively a division of the Stanford Research Institute and the Mitre Corporation.

My involvement in starting Jason in the first place, combined with my continuing membership on the IDA board, made it natural for me to participate in many of Jason's activities, including its summer studies, even though I did not fit the standard profile of a Jason member. Many of the chiefs and leaders of Jason have been friends from my early Berkeley days: Keith Brueckner, Marvin Goldberger, Harold Lewis,

Kenneth Watson, and William Nierenberg. Many other Jasons, includ-ing Dick Garwin, Sid Drell, and Freeman Dyson, are people with whom I have had other long working relationships.

In their summer studies, as in the predecessor Project 137, the Jasons continued to work on problems connecting the most advanced ideas and results in the physical sciences with current problems of defense.

Jason pioneered the work in beam weapons of all kinds. It studied a wide variety of strategic defense issues, ranging from basing modes (as for the MX) to the interaction between nuclear explosions and detection systems. More recently, it has reviewed essentially all of the technical questions relevant to President Reagan's Star Wars proposal.

Nicholas Christofilos was a member of the group until his death, and the Jasons reviewed and expanded some of his far-out ideas. Among these were both the Argus experiments and "Sanguine" (originally "Trombone"), a proposal for constructing a very low frequency radio system for communicating with totally submerged submarines, includ-ing those carrying strategic missiles. In one of its versions Sanguine would have used the entire electric power grid of the state of Wisconsin as its broadcasting antenna. The system had to be located in a well-watered state because it required that the soil under the grid be a fairly good electrical conductor.

Jason also did pioneering work in arms control. One of the earliest instances involved MIRV. In the 1964 Jason summer study, a group chaired by Jack Ruina and including Dyson and Gell-Mann examined the possible impact of new technologies on national security. MIRV was among them. The group concluded that its introduction, combined with foreseeable improvements in accuracy, would create a situation in which striking first could confer—or seem to confer—a substantial, per-haps decisive, advantage. The group was right on target; these develop-ments were precisely what led to the "window of vulnerability" debate of the late seventies and early eighties.

The most controversial of Jason's many projects involved the "elec-tronic battlefield" in Vietnam. The basic idea, which from the start received strong support from Secretary McNamara, called for installing a variety of special sensors in the jungles of Vietnam. The sensors would detect and report the presence of people or vehicles in the jungles and swamps of that unfortunate country. The main purpose was to deny the protection of natural cover to attacking enemy soldiers or infiltrating guerrillas. Many organizations were involved in the affair, but Jason was one of the most central.

Jason's role in the project became known to the public. Since many students and professors were actively hostile to the war in Vietnam, and since nearly all Jasons were also college professors, a very dicey situation developed. Many Jasons, particularly those at Columbia University, were hassled and picketed by their students and colleagues. Others, including Sid Drell, were prevented from speaking at European universities, even on subjects having no relation to defense work. In addition, a few of the Jasons themselves became disaffected with the war and dropped out of the group. Some announced publicly that they were doing so; others simply stopped participating.

I, too, felt pressure—from both friends and my own conscience—to resign from Jason. I believed that the war was a bad mistake, that our cause was hopeless, and that by continuing to fight we would only prolong the misery and increase the death and destruction. I did not, however, in any sense condone the North Vietnamese actions, as did many others on campuses and elsewhere, nor did I think it was a moral issue except in the general sense that all wars, especially modern ones, involve important moral questions and deep ethical contradictions.

More important, and despite my almost total lack of empathy with the main action going on at the moment, I continued to believe that the defense of the United States—and thus of the West—was a most worthy goal, and I determined to continue all my remaining relationships with the defense establishment, including Jason. The United States had more serious security problems than just those in Southeast Asia, and I continued to do what I could to help cope with them.

Many loyal and patriotic people did otherwise. George Kistiakowsky, Manhattan Project worker and science adviser to presidents, decided it was too much for him. As a result, he publicly refused to have anything to do with the American defense establishment for the rest of his life. Some other colleagues also dropped out but without making any public statement. They simply ended their participation and declined any further invitations to give advice. My Pentagon deputy John Rubel was in this group. In so behaving, they joined another group of veterans of defense science and technology—including Philip Morrison, Victor Weisskopf, Robert Wilson, and many other Manhattan Project physicists who much earlier, in the very first postwar years, decided they had done enough, or more than enough, of that kind of work.

End of an Era

In November 1968 Richard Nixon, on that second try he promised us he would make, was elected president. As custom required, we on the ACDA's General Advisory Committee submitted our resignations to the new president. I rather hoped he wouldn't accept mine—or most of the others'—but that was not to be. Only John McCloy continued, and he not as chairman but just as a member.

The year before, my term on the PSAC had run out. Now I was off the GAC as well. For the first time since I joined the Air Force Science Advisory Board in 1953, sixteen years earlier, I had no formal, direct connection to the highest levels of national security policymakers.

I continued on the boards of IDA and Aerospace. I also could call on my remaining friends in the upper reaches of the Pentagon—John Foster was one of the few to be held over—but it wasn't the same.

Partly because of that profound change, and partly because the generally bad situation seemed to call for it, I turned to working with public interest groups, writing, and doing other things that people usually call lobbying. I had done a little of each of those before, but now I would for a while do them much more intensely.

CHAPTER 12

On the Outside Looking in

(1969–1976)

ABM Again

Ｐ RESIDENT JOHNSON'S 1967 decision to deploy a light, "anti-Chinese" missile defense focused public attention on the ABM issue. Previously, the debate had been carried out by and among experts and insiders. Now the Congress, the press, and the general public took an active part in it.

The Army began to seek sites for the deployment of the system all around the country. Army teams briefed citizen groups about their plans. In effect, they told people that now, at long last, they would be defended against a Soviet missile attack. Many reacted very differently from the way the Army expected. They believed that siting ABMs in their neighborhood, far from protecting it, made it a prime target.

The last big public arms control action had been over the test ban issue in the late 1950s and very early 1960s. With the signing of the Limited Test Ban Treaty in 1963, most activists lost interest. Public interest groups became increasingly quiescent and, in some cases, moribund. The ABM controversy brought new life to some of them. As a result, a stream of letters from these groups and from ordinary citizens once again began to flow to the Congress.

Before the issue could be resolved, Nixon replaced Johnson as president. He proved to be even more bullish on ABM than Johnson. It soon became clear that a thin, "anti-Chinese" ABM was regarded by many of its supporters simply as a foot in the door, a means for getting started on the deployment of a thick, expensive, anti-Soviet ABM without admitting it.

I had long been deeply involved in this issue. Now, however, rather than continuing to do so as an official or high-level adviser, I would turn to testifying as an outside expert before congressional committees, by writing, and by participating generally in the activities of certain public interest groups, particularly the Federation of American Scientists.

On July 23, 1968, Hans Bethe, George Kistiakowsky, Jerome Wiesner, and I sent a telegram to Senator John Sherman Cooper, a Republican of Kentucky, which said in part, "We believe that it would be wise to delay this [ABM] deployment for a year."

When Senator Richard Russell, a Democrat from Georgia and chairman of the Senate Armed Services Committee, saw this telegram, he said,

> These scientists, every time a bill comes before the Senate, send a telegram saying this will not add to our defense. But at no time has any of them even asked to appear before the Committee. Not a single senator has ever asked one of them to appear. But year after year they send in this telegram when the bill is before the Senate.[1]

To my knowledge, the senator's remarks were incorrect—I had never before sent such a telegram—but they surely produced results. The Federation of American Scientists formally requested—on its own initiative—that the signers of the telegram be invited to testify, and several senators got in touch with us to explore our willingness to do so.

The net result was that on March 11, 1969, less than two months after the inauguration of Richard Nixon, I was invited to testify before the Subcommittee on International Organizations and Disarmament of the Senate Foreign Relations Committee.

The hearing took place in a large room in the Senate Office Building. Some hundreds of spectators and a large contingent of reporters were present. TV cameramen from all the networks recorded the events for later replay on the evening news.

After saying that the ABM system then planned was very easily countered by a variety of devices and tactics, I turned to the relationship between ABM deployment and arms control:

> [P]erhaps the worst arms control implication of the ABM is the possibility that the people and the Congress would be deceived into believing that at long last we are on the track of a technical solution to the dilemma of the steady decrease in our national security which has accompanied the steady increase in our military power over the last two decades. Such a false hope is extremely dangerous if it diverts any of us from searching for a solution in the only place where it may be found; in a political search for peace combined with arms control and disarmament measures.[2]

(The arguments that surrounded President Reagan's 1983 Star Wars proposal make it clear that my remarks on this matter were relevant not only in that 1969 context but in the present and, probably, in the indefinite future as well. Reagan, at least in large part, regarded Star Wars as a unilateral alternative to the—to him, unreliable—process of negotiating the arms balance with the Soviets. He and many of his supporters apparently believed that technology could substitute for diplomacy and negotiation as a means for saving us from "assured destruction" by the Russians.)

I summarized my testimony as follows:

> 1. Because of certain intrinsic disadvantages of the defense, and because of certain fundamental design problems, I doubt the capability of either the Sentinel system or the hard-point defense ABM to accomplish its task, whether or not it ultimately "works" on a test range.
> 2. I believe the deployment of any ABM would in the long run almost always result in further acceleration of the arms race. An exception would be in the case of the deployment of an ABM as a carefully integrated part of a major move in the direction of arms control and disarmament.
> 3. One result of the arms race is that, as our military power increases our national security decreases. I believe this basic situation would not be improved by deployment of any ABM.
> 4. Another result of the arms race is that the power to make certain life-and-death decisions is inexorably passing from statesmen and politicians to more narrowly focussed technicians, and from human beings to machines. An ABM deployment would speed up this process.[3]

James Killian and George Kistiakowsky testified similarly at the same hearing. Afterward the three of us dropped in on Henry Kissinger, then

Nixon's national security adviser, in his White House office. We presented our arguments and suggested serious further study by an *ad hoc* panel of scientists attached to the White House. Kissinger made it clear that he—and the president—needed no further help in the matter. His parting remark, however, was something like "Most of those people opposing ABM oppose everything defense does; if we give in on this, they will just demand more."[4]

Six weeks later I testified in the same vein before the Senate Armed Services Committee. In the short interval between these two committee meetings, the administration had changed its story. Previously the proposal had been to deploy the "Sentinel" ABM, a thin system intended to defend our cities against a Chinese or other smaller and less sophisticated missile attack. Now, suddenly, we were faced with the "Safeguard" ABM, a system whose purpose was to protect our offensive forces—Minuteman and Titan—in their silos against a surprise, preemptive, all-out attack by the Soviets. The name and purpose of the ABM had both been changed, but the equipment remained the same. To be sure, this new objective was technically simpler because only those warheads heading for impact within, say, two thousand feet of their well-protected targets had to be intercepted. There were, however, alternative ways to assure the survival of the retaliatory forces—mobility, deception, proliferation in numbers, and superhardening—ways that seemed more promising and much cheaper.

Six weeks after the Senate Armed Services hearing, I appeared before the House Committee on Appropriations Subcommittee on Defense Appropriations. The nature of that occasion was very different. This time I was there not on my own but as a representative of the FAS, the Federation of American Scientists. Of the public interest groups that participated in the 1968–70 ABM debate, the FAS played the most effective role.

The federation was founded in 1945 as one of several closely allied organizations made up largely of Manhattan Project veterans concerned about the impending nuclear arms race. I was then a graduate student at Berkeley. There was no active chapter in the region, and Ernest Lawrence discouraged those of us in his lab from involving ourselves in such diversions. As a result, I then knew and cared little about such organizations.

In 1969 our common interest in opposing the deployment of ABM brought me and the federation together in a common cause. Jeremy Stone, then a part-time staffer in the FAS Washington office, maneuvered my election as chairman of the FAS. After that was done, I helped arrange Jeremy's employment as full-time executive director. At the time there was nowhere near enough money in the till to pay him for a full year. It was a case of either allowing the slow withering of the organization to continue or taking a chance that Stone could make an aggressive new membership drive and fund-raising campaign work. We chose the latter course, and Jeremy succeeded brilliantly in pulling it off. The FAS has flourished ever since.

I was not the only organizational spokesman to appear before the House subcommittee that day. Jackie Robinson, the first black American to break into major league baseball, and the Reverend Harry C. Applewhite were also there to testify against the ABM, both as representatives of the United Church of Christ.

The hearing was held in a very small room in the Capitol Building. There was space for only the members of the committee plus the current witnesses. The six members present sat at attention with their eyes and ears open, but their minds were obviously somewhere else. After I finished reading my prepared statement, I said, as usual, that I would be pleased to try to answer any questions. For the first time in my long experience as a witness, there were very few on substance. All they really wanted to know about was the nature of the FAS and who and what it pretended to represent.

I was unprepared for such a cool and indifferent reception. Several of the members of the subcommittee were people whom I had dealt with regularly and intimately back in my Pentagon days. Now they hardly noticed me. Uncomfortable though it was, the experience taught me a lot. An invited witness is one thing; a witness who forces his way in, however politely, is quite another. In the first case the committee members really listen, very often for the right reasons; in the other they are simply performing a political duty, and their minds are not really engaged. In this last hearing, I could have been recounting my last summer's vacation for all the difference the actual words made.

Even so, such events can matter. When enough of them occur in a short time, their very numbers reinforce each other, and they can influence the course of events. It is, however, only the acts as such, and not their detailed substance, that matter. If an expert wishes merely to be counted as being on the right side, he can use a large variety of means to force his way into a committee hearing and into the *Congressional Record.* If an expert wants his ideas to matter, however, he must wait, or arrange, for a genuine invitation.

On July 16 I made a fourth appearance, this time before the Senate Foreign Relations Committee. In this instance, as in all others except in

the case of the House subcommittee, I was there at the specificic invitation of individual senators. To be sure, Stone and the FAS had worked
behind the scenes with the Senate staffers in developing the list of
witnesses, but I was there on my own account and not as a spokesman
for others. This is one of those distinctions that do make a difference.

In August 1969 the Senate vote on the bill to deploy the ABM resulted
in a 50–50 tie, which was resolved only by Vice-President Agnew's
tie-breaking aye vote. The margin was so small that, in effect, this vote
brought the plans for large-scale deployment to a halt.

This near-miss invigorated the opponents of ABM and disheartened
its proponents. The final result was a plan calling for the limited—and,
as it turned out, brief—deployment of a modest number of ABMs near
Grand Forks, South Dakota. Given their range, they could, in theory,
provide some protection for the Minuteman forces deployed in that
region.

(In January 1976, after it had been operational for less than a year,
Congress decided not to provide further support, and even that lone,
small system was decommissioned. Since then, the United States has
had no active ballistic missile defenses deployed anywhere.)

The debate over ABM continued even after the Strategic Arms Limitation Talks (SALT) got under way in late 1969. On August 3, 1970, I again
testified before the Senate Foreign Relations Committee on ABM, MIRV,
and arms control. On this occasion I made additional points about some
serious problems that had been bothering me for a long time: launch on
warning, decisions by computers, and preprogrammed presidents.

> The ABM is a low confidence system. The expressions of confidence in
> it by those who support it are bound to give way to a more realistic
> appraisal after it is deployed. When that happens, the defense establish-
> ment will turn in accordance with the precepts of "worst plausible case"
> analysis to other methods of insuring the survival of the Minuteman. Of the
> various possibilities, the surest, quickest and cheapest, is simply to adopt
> the Launch on Warning Doctrine. . . .
> This [launch on warning] method of coping with the problem had been
> in people's minds since the beginning of the missile program, [but] I find
> [it] completely unsatisfactory. The time in which the decision to launch
> must be made varies from just a few minutes up to perhaps twenty minutes,
> depending on the nature of the attack and the details of our warning
> system, communications system, and our command and control system.
> *This time is so short that the decision to launch our missiles must be made*
> *either by computer, by a pre-programmed President, or some pre-*
> *programmed delegate of the President.* There will be no time to stop and
> think about what the signals mean or to check to see whether they might

somehow be false alarms. The decision will have to be made on the basis of electronic signals, electronically analyzed, *in accordance with a plan worked out long before by apolitical analysts in an antiseptic and unreal atmosphere.* In effect, not even the President, let alone the Congress, would really be a party to the ultimate decision to end civilization. (Emphasis added)[5]

These extremely serious problems first came into my mind with force during my 1960 visit to General Kuter at NORAD. My interest in them was reinforced strongly by the 1969–70 debate over ABM and MIRV. Reagan's 1983 Star Wars proposal, with its emphasis on boost-phase intercept (that is, intercept during the first few minutes after Soviet missiles leave their silos), brought them up again with special force. The requirements for automated decisions are in that last case far more demanding, and therefore far more dangerous, than in the earlier ones.

Reagan's Star Wars

I was as surprised as anyone by President Reagan's notorious "Star Wars" speech, and it took me some time to get my thoughts about it in order. To understand the matter, I had to divide it into three parts: first, the general issue of strategic defense; second, technical issues; and third, the special political ramifications of Reagan's very idiosyncratic approach to the matter.

With regard to the first, I had always supported research and development intended to explore the possibility of achieving a defense against strategic nuclear attack on the United States. Christofilos's exuberant scheme was one such, ARPA's Project Defender was another, and the Army's Nike-Zeus R & D program was yet another. (It was the deployment of Nike-Zeus that I opposed.) I had believed earlier, and in 1983 I still believed, that if we could really build an effective defense we should do so. In short, a world in which the emphasis was on defense, rather than on offense, would be safer and saner. Unfortunately, whenever I had examined the situation closely, I had found the technology then proposed for the task to be wanting in the extreme. More important, I concluded that a poor, ineffective system would be worse than no system at all. It would, in effect, do nothing but stimulate an expansion of the other side's offensive forces, and that the end would leave us worse off than we were before.

Had technology progressed far enough in the intervening years that by 1983 a workable missile defense was in reach? I was open-minded on the subject. There had been great progress in many relevant areas, particularly in the technology of data processing, and that last might well hold the key to success. Many groups with whom I had close contacts studied the problem: Jason, IDA, Aerospace, and the Fletcher panel.* I followed their work in detail. Within six months I had to conclude once again that adequate technology was still not in sight.

Back in the late 1950s and again in the early 1970s, when similar proposals came up, it always turned out that relatively cheap and effective means for overcoming the defenses were readily available to the offense. In 1983 it was no different. All of the new ideas, especially those involving the intercepting of enemy missiles in space, were either well beyond the foreseeable state of the art or easily defeated by counter-measures, or both. The only exception was terminal defense, that is, defense based on the ground in the vicinity of the targets to be defended. It was possible, I thought, that we were approaching the time when that could be made to work; unfortunately, the main attention of the strategic defense program office (SDIO) was on the project's more exotic elements.

Even more important, the newly proposed space-based systems required even higher levels of automation and higher degrees of delegation of authority from people to machines. And this time the decision-making machines would be in orbit and thus even farther removed from human control.

No, I concluded, the new technology is no more promising now than the old was in its day, and if we move to deploy it the likely result will be a reaction by the Soviets that will simply make an already dangerous situation worse. As before, however, I continued to support a vigorous R & D effort, in the hope that maybe one day something useful would at last come out of it.

What about the political ramifications of the whole affair? Aye, there was the real rub. Many in the Reagan administration, including Reagan himself much of the time, did not believe that negotiations with the Soviets could lead to a genuinely useful result. Indeed, if one believed that the central and controlling characteristic of the Soviet Union is that it is an "evil empire" whose leaders will "lie and use deceit" whenever

---

*Set up by the White House and the Defense Department specifically to study the matter following the president's speech, it was chaired by James Fletcher, twice administrator of NASA.

it suits them, how could negotiations over such difficult and vital matters benefit us? Edward Teller, Secretary of Defense Caspar Weinberger, and many other key advisers saw Star Wars as a way out of the morass the "arms controllers" of past administrations had gotten us into. If we could effectively defend ourselves against attack, we would not need to negotiate with them—we could go it alone.

The vain hope of finding a technical solution to our nation's security dilemma remained alive and healthy. Its cost was not so much in the money wasted on it as in the way it diverted attention and nervous energy from the only promising longer-term solutions, those involving primarily political and diplomatic processes.

And there, indeed, lay the tragedy of Reykjavik. Both Gorbachev and Reagan gave far too much weight to the SDI (Strategic Defense Initiative, the Reagan administration's preferred name for Star Wars) in allowing it to dominate the outcome. Neither was able to see the SDI for what it really is: a very long-term research program based far more on hope than on promise.

Here, in brief, is another of the conundrums of the nuclear era. It is surely true, as President Reagan said, that a world in which we all had "mutually assured survival" would be better than one with mutually assured destruction. It is also true, as Premier Kosygin had said years before, that defensive weapons do not kill people; it is offensive weapons that do. But aside from technologists with a financial or other personal stake in the program, whom in the main did we find promoting it with the greatest vigor? Was it those well known as peace activists or arms control advocates? No, it was those best known either for their permanent hostility to negotiations and other diplomatic approaches or for their promotion of many other weapons systems, most of them clearly offensive in nature. For most of the active political promoters of the Star Wars program, the discovery that nuclear deterrence through the threat of assured destruction was flawed or immoral came quite late and at a rather convenient time.

International Public Interest Groups

During the Nixon and Ford administrations, I worked actively with several public interest groups that operated at the international level: the Pugwash movement, the Dartmouth conferences, and the American Committee for East-West Accord. Their general objectives were similar: bridging the East-West gap by bringing together people from each side who were "well connected" at home. On the American side this usually meant former government officials and high-level advisers, current business or academic executives, distinguished scientists, and the like. At least, that was the ideal. On the Soviet side it usually meant members and officers of the Soviet Academy of Sciences and its research institutes and, more rarely, members of the Central Committee of the Communist party or the Supreme Soviet.

The Pugwash Movement

The Magna Carta of the Pugwash movement is the Russell-Einstein manifesto of 1955. Drafted by Bertrand Russell and cosigned by Albert Einstein just before his death, it was written not long after the invention of the hydrogen bomb and says in part,

> In the tragic situation which confronts humanity, we feel that scientists should assemble in conference to appraise the perils that have arisen as a result of the development of weapons of mass destruction, and to discuss a [means for resolving it]. . . .
> We appeal, as human beings, to human beings: remember your humanity, and forget the rest. If you can do so, the way lies open to a new Paradise; if you cannot, there lies before you the risk of universal death.[6]

The first conference to examine these problems and discuss possible solutions was held in Pugwash, Nova Scotia, July 7–10, 1957. Pugwash was the birthplace of Cyrus Eaton, then president of the Chesapeake and Ohio Railroad and a man very interested in international understanding. He held views analogous to those expressed in the Russell-Einstein manifesto, and his providing financial support for the initial conference was a way to promote them. The first conference was attended by twenty-two people from ten countries. All but one of them were scientists.

The Soviet group consisted of three members: Alexander M. Kuzin, Academician Alexander V. Topchiev, and Academician Dmitri Skobeltsyn (the man I had met when he visited the 60-inch cyclotron more than ten years before). Vladimir Pavlichenko served as secretary and interpreter to the Soviet delegation. Pavlichenko became well known to a generation of official and unofficial U.S. negotiators as the KGB's point man in this area. (He appears as Smirnov in a fictionalized version of the SALT II talks, *Geneva Accord,* by John Whitman, the CIA representative on the U.S. delegation.) Among the Americans at Pugwash were Paul Doty, a Harvard chemist; Leo Szilard; and Victor Weisskopf.

The conference concluded that the Russell-Einstein manifesto was correct in its assessment of the dangers inherent in the current situation. Agreeing that tensions should be reduced and the arms race ended, it suggested, "The prompt suspension of nuclear bomb tests could be a good first step for this purpose."[7] Since then a conference has been held at least once every year, sometimes in Eastern Europe, sometimes in the West, and occasionally in the Third World.

Pugwash at Sochi

Although I had been invited earlier, the first conference I was able to attend was the nineteenth, held on October 22–29, 1969, at Sochi, a resort city on the Black Sea, in southern Russia. I had never been to the USSR before, and the fact it was being held there made the idea of participating all the more attractive to me.

The American group of ten or so scientists included Jack Ruina, Paul Doty, and George Rathjens, all experts in the technological side of national security. It also included Roger Revelle, then director of the Center for Population Studies at Harvard University. Roger had long been involved in North-South issues—including agriculture, food, and, of course, population—and this conference was to look into some of those issues as well.

The Soviet delegation comprised some twenty persons, including Georgi Arbatov, Mikhail Millionshchikov, Lev Artsimovich, Vasily Emelyanov, and Ludmilla Gvishiani.

Arbatov was head of the Institute of U.S.A. Studies (it later inserted "and Canada" in its name). As he put it to me at the time, his job was to explain "you and your government to my government." He was also a member of a special policy group called the auditing committee, a body that conducted a policy audit of government agencies on behalf of the Central Committee. He advanced steadily in rank and eventually became a full member of both the Central Committee and the Supreme Soviet. During the Reagan-Gorbachev summits of 1985 and 1986, and the preparations for them, he was much in evidence, especially on American TV, as perhaps the most acerbic of the Soviet commentators.

The Sochi conference provided my first opportunity to meet Arbatov. In subsequent years I met him often in very different places and came to know him quite well.

Millionshchikov and Artsimovich were both full members of the Soviet Academy of Science. Millionshchikov was one of the academy's
vice-presidents and, for a time, also chairman of the Supreme Soviet of
the Russian Republic. He won a Stalin Prize for his scientific work.
Artsimovich, a leading figure at the Kurchatov Institute in Moscow, was
the inventor of the Tokamak, perhaps the most promising of all the many
versions of fusion energy reactors. He received the Lenin Prize for his
work. Both men had been involved in Pugwash for some years, both died
just a few years after the Sochi meeting, and both were memorialized
on Soviet postage stamps.

Vasily Emelyanov was a metallurgist who built tanks during World
War II. As soon as it was over, he produced and assembled the various
special materials needed to build the first Soviet nuclear reactor. He,
too, received a Stalin Prize for his work in those areas. He was the only
Soviet at the meeting whom I already knew since he had been a member
of that first group of Soviets who visited Lawrence's laboratory in 1956.
I had also seen him in Washington at official meetings once or twice
after that.

Emelyanov was a great storyteller. At another Pugwash conference
a few years later, he described his introduction to the nuclear program
to me.

"Beria [the head of the secret police] phoned me in Kiev, where I
happened to be at the time, and told me Stalin wanted me in his office
the next day." In slow, delightfully accented English he added, "You
know, that could be either very good or very bad, but there was nothing
you could do about it."

He made it to Moscow as ordered, and Stalin told him to report to
Kurchatov, then just putting together the large-scale project that produced both the first Soviet reactor and the first Soviet bomb. He eventually worked his way up to be head of the Soviet civilian reactor program.
By the time of the Sochi conference, however, he had already somehow
been eased out of that position by Andronik Petrosyants, the man who
was my opposite number in the nuclear test ban negotiations in 1979–80.

Vasily Emelyanov also served for a number of years as the Soviet
ambassador to the International Atomic Energy Agency in Vienna.
While in that post, V. Molotov, formerly Stalin's foreign minister, served
as his assistant in a remarkable reversal of ranks.

At yet another Pugwash meeting, ten years later, Vasily told me that
he had recently chanced upon Molotov in a drugstore in the fancy Arbat
section of Moscow. After exchanging pleasantries, Molotov asked
Emelyanov what he was doing these days.

"Working on nuclear arms control," he replied.

Molotov looked surprised and said, "Do you still believe in that?"

Ludmilla Gvishiani was Premier Alexei Kosygin's daughter and a historian on the staff of Arbatov's institute. When I asked her what historical issues she specialized in, she said it was the American and other Western interventions in the Soviet civil war. Her husband, Gherman Gvishiani, was for many years the head of the State Committee for Science and Technology. Like many of the Soviets at the conference, Ludmilla also fit the notion I had in mind when I used the phrase "well connected."

The conference's work extended over five days. Most of the time was devoted to the preparation of reports for presentation at the final plenary session. Five working groups covered a wide spectrum of issues: measures for terminating current military conflicts; European security; reduction and elimination of nuclear weapons and delivery systems; biological and chemical weapons; and science and developing countries.

I was in Working Group 3, cochaired by Arbatov and Rathjens and dealing with the "reduction and elimination of nuclear weapons and delivery systems." Our report warned that another substantial escalation of the arms race was in prospect. It concluded that "early negotiation of an agreement to limit strategic arms is of highest priority, and that indeed the urgency is particularly great with respect to deployment of ABM and MIRV and the testing of the latter."[8]

Shortly after the conference convened, Washington and Moscow jointly announced plans to begin talks on strategic arms limitations (SALT) at Helsinki on November 17. On the day before the announcement, Arbatov made a point of telling me that some important news would be coming out of Moscow very soon. When the announcement came, he made sure I knew that was what he had been referring to. He was, I believe, genuinely pleased and excited by it, but he also took advantage of the occasion to let us know he was one of the insiders who heard about such things before they became public.

Halfway through the conference, we took a day off for a trip by bus to Pitsunda, a beach resort in Soviet Georgia. There we stopped off at a large hotel for lunch on a delightful veranda.

After lunch I remained alone at a table with Lord Philip Noel-Baker, a member of the British group. Philip, then eighty, had spent his entire life working on peace issues. In 1959 he was awarded the Nobel Peace Prize for his efforts. Our conversation turned naturally to his experiences as a peace activist. He told me about his introduction to the field when, as a young man, he had served first as secretary to the British delegation to the Paris peace conference that established the League of Nations at the end of World War I and then as a member of the League's Secretariat (1919–22). He participated in a number of other disarmament conferences between the wars. After World War II he served briefly in Prime Minister Atlee's cabinet as secretary of state for air. While he was in that post, the British government made its decision to build its own atomic bomb. Later he often expressed regret over not having done more to oppose that action. After leaving the government, he continued to be a disarmament and peace activist.

At one point during our discussion, he referred to the great irony he saw in the Antarctic Treaty, signed in 1959 and designed to prevent the militarization of that remote and icy continent. "At the same time as we were banning nuclear weapons in Antarctica," he noted, "we were putting seven thousand of them in Europe. It should have been the other way around!"

I was fascinated and inspired by that conversation with Noel-Baker. He had been working on behalf of international law, peace, and disarmament for more than fifty years. He had participated in one false start after another, yet he remained sanguine and eager to try again. I found his hope and his optimism infectious. In the years since, my thoughts have often returned to that conversation by the Black Sea.

I last saw Noel-Baker in 1983, at a Pugwash meeting held in Banff, Canada. By then he was well over ninety and had become quite feeble. When it came time for him to address the conference, he found it difficult to walk to the podium. At first he spoke very slowly, and his voice was thin and reedy. When he got going, however, and proclaimed "peace and disarmament" as "ideas whose time have finally come," his voice picked up strength, his eyes shone bright, and the decades dropped away.

Pugwash at Sinaia

The only other Pugwash meeting I attended in Eastern Europe was held in Romania in 1973. Sybil and Rachel were both with me. I learned nothing novel or important about international security or peace at that conference, but a great deal about Eastern Europe. It was less a large, single, revealed truth than a collection of minor events and discoveries that added up to something more than just the sum of its parts.

The first of these discoveries occurred just as we arrived. Antiaircraft guns and troops were ostentatiously deployed all over the Bucharest airport. It was quite obvious the show was intended not for us Americans but for the Soviets, those fraternal Warsaw Pact allies of the Romanians. I have flown in and out of a lot of national capitals in my day but have never seen anything else like it. I was impressed by the deliberate exhibition of internal strife and struggle.

The conference itself took place in Sinaia, an attractive town about a hundred miles northwest of Bucharest and just inside the foothills of the Carpathian Mountains. As usual, the conference directors arranged to have a recreational outing halfway through the program. It consisted of a trip back to Bucharest for a buffet reception at a government palace and a brief meeting with Nicolae Ceausescu, head of both the Communist party and the government.

The group traveled to Bucharest on several buses. We were escorted the whole way by policemen on motorcycles, their sirens often going full blast. The weather was adequate—a little warm, but clear and good for sight-seeing. For most of the way we traveled on a major highway leading straight across a flat, open plain. About halfway to our destination we pulled up short and stopped at a railway crossing. Moments before we arrived, the gateman had lowered the traffic barrier. No train was in sight, but the gate remained down, and traffic of all sorts—trucks, buses, and animal-drawn wagons—formed long lines on both sides. Nearly an hour went by before a small train showed up in the distance and slowly crossed the highway. After it was gone, the gateman let us all pass. Evidently his orders were to lower the barrier when the train was due and to raise it only after it had finally passed by, whenever that might be. The other East Europeans on the bus were annoyed at the delay, but seemed to regard it as natural. I took it as a measure of the efficiency of centralized planning.

The food at the reception was excellent and the setting impressive. Ceausescu met with us in groups of eight or ten. A question I asked stimulated him to comment on the arms race in general. "We have been conducting serious disarmament negotiations for more than fifteen years," he said, "and during that time the rate of spending on arms has tripled; we've got to do better than that." I said I thought so too. He then added that he had recently seen the Hollywood movie *Planet of the Apes.* In it mankind destroys itself, and the position at the top of the evolutionary ladder is taken over by apes. He said it was an accurate allegory of what awaited us if we didn't find a way out of the current mess. Unlike most other East European political figures, he did not go on to lay the blame for that mess on the West.

When the reception was over, we boarded the buses to return to Sinaia. After we were all in our seats, the buses continued simply to sit there without moving. Although it was evening, it was still quite warm, and the air in the buses was stifling. Everyone became restive; it had been a long day, and we had a long ride ahead of us. Suddenly Arbatov, who had been sitting a few rows behind Sybil and me, got up and stomped to the front. As he passed us he said in loud, clear English, "I'm going to explain this problem to the driver in plain Communist language." I was baffled; I knew why he was annoyed, but why did he say what he did so loudly and in English? True, English remains the lingua franca in the non-Slavic parts of Eastern Europe, so Arbatov's stern lecture to the driver did have to be in English, but he didn't have to announce it to us in advance.

Some Romanian students were also present at the conference, and our daughter Rachel became friendly with one of them. Rachel had been reading Solzhenitsyn's *First Circle,* and at one point she, naturally enough, mentioned Stalin. Her Romanian friend immediately let her know that those bad things people said about Stalin were lies. Many young East Europeans, especially those in Russia itself, do not want to believe bad things about Stalin, and so they don't.

At lunch one day I had a long and enjoyable conversation with a Bulgarian economist. Apropos of nothing in particular, I remarked that the Balkans used to be thought of as a hotbed of trouble, and I asked how things were these days in that regard.

His reply was classic: "The best way to explain the current situation to you is to note that today there are five fraternal socialist states in the Balkans, but our best relations are with Greece."

Greece at the time was ruled by the so-called junta of colonels, the most repressive of the postwar Greek regimes. Perhaps that special character made it especially easy for the Bulgarian regime to get along with them.

I did not draw any grand conclusion from these vignettes, but I did get a clear impression of Eastern Europe as a troubled place, where the people were in general dissatisfied with the political situation. It is not easy to determine the exact weight of this reality on the larger scale of East-West confrontation, but it is surely of critical importance, and we must find a better way than we have so far to take it into account. The Bulgarian people seem genuinely fond of Russia, but otherwise the Warsaw Pact has no real cohesiveness.

Peter Kapitza

The most interesting Russian I met during this period was Peter Kapitza. Like many Russians born and educated before the October Revolution (1917), he was much more open and less reserved than those who came later. From 1921 to 1934 he lived in England, where he worked with Ernest Rutherford at the Cavendish Laboratory. He frequently returned to Russia for his vacations. On one such trip, in 1934, Stalin ordered him to remain in the USSR to participate in the development of science there. With the help of Rutherford and other scientific leaders, Kapitza sought to persuade Stalin to let him return to England. When, after about a year, it became evident that this would not happen, Peter arranged for his wife, Anna, and their two England-born sons to join him in Moscow. He became director of the Institute of Physical Problems, located not far from the center of the city. An English-style country house was built right in the middle of the institute grounds to serve as the family residence. In the years that followed he became the unofficial dean of Soviet physics.

I first met Kapitza during a visit to Arbatov's institute in 1971. Even before my arrival I had asked Arbatov to arrange such a meeting. Sybil and Rachel were with me, and the Kapitzas invited Arbatov and us to lunch. Two or three other personal friends of the Kapitzas also were there. It was a fine, grand house, with a large, bright dining room off the living room. The exceptionally large dining table was, evidently, always set for sixteen or so persons. Peter sat at one end and Anna at the other, and the guests were distributed along the sides.

I asked Peter about the period of his exile from Moscow. As I already understood it, he had in 1945 or 1946 had an argument with Beria—chief of both the KGB and the nuclear weapons program—over the proper use of his laboratory in that program. When Kapitza declined to do what Beria thought he should, he was exiled to his dacha, just outside Moscow, and forbidden to come into the city and his laboratory. Rather naively, I asked him how that episode in his life came to its end.

Before Peter could reply, Anna rose from her chair and in a loud, firm voice said, "It was the greatest event in the history of Russia—Stalin died."

I imagined I could hear the microphones reverberating in the walls, and I was sure I felt Arbatov, sitting just to my left, cringe. Peter added something about its having been not so bad for him after all, and he began a discussion of the works of James Fenimore Cooper, one of his favorite authors. He said he probably was more familiar with Cooper's work than I was, and I had to admit he was right. He went on to say, "We Russians read much more and more critically than you Americans do." He added that civilization and culture were two quite different things: the Americans were civilized because they had cars and other machin. s, but the Russians were cultured because they read so much. At that point Rachel asked why, if the Russians were so cultured, the government had to control what they read. Arbatov interrupted to explain that it was precisely because they took what they read so seriously that the government had to make sure they read only what was true. When Rachel then mentioned Solzhenitsyn's works, Arbatov said *Cancer Ward* was simply a miserable book about an unpleasant disease.

The next time I met Peter was at a Pugwash conference in Aulanko, Finland. It was September 1973, and rumors about improper and illegal behavior on the part of Vice-President Spiro Agnew were just beginning to circulate. Kapitza, one of the few Russians who had easy access to the foreign press, followed the Agnew case closely. (He subscribed to *US News & World Report*. He said he preferred it to other U.S. news magazines because it published long direct quotations. He added he did not want reporters interpreting for him the original comments of others.)

He bet me a bottle of champagne that Agnew would not finish his term. We both knew that such an event would be unprecedented. I concluded the precedent was so firm, and the American political system so solid, that such an event could not happen. Kapitza was not inhibited by such confidence in our system.

When that bet was agreed, Peter said, "And Nixon will not finish his term, either." At the time there were only the first glimmerings of trouble in Nixon's case. I was certain a bet on this second notion would provide a good way to cover the chance he would win the other one, so I responded by wagering *two* bottles of champagne on it. Trudy Weiss, Leo Szilard's widow, was also at the symposium, and she agreed to be the official witness to our bets.

A month later, on October 10, Robert Hutchins, president of the Center for the Study of Democratic Institutions, and I had an appointment to see Henry Kissinger in his State Department office at 5 P.M. (The occasion of our being in Washington together was the Third Pacem in Terris Conference.) We waited one hour, and then another. Finally an aide came and told us the secretary was indefinitely detained at the White House. The newspapers the next day announced Agnew's resignation. Kissinger, as secretary of state, was the person to whom the formal papers of resignation were being submitted at the very moment we sat there cooling our heels.

Ten months after that, on August 8, 1974, Nixon also resigned.

In September 1974 I attended yet another Pugwash conference, this time in Baden, near Vienna. Kapitza was also there. I offered to go out and buy three bottles of his favorite champagne. He told me not to do it; it was too much bother to transport them back to Moscow. He asked me to think of some easier (for him) way of paying off my bet. For the time being I set the matter aside.

A year or so later, just before a trip to Moscow with the American Committee for East-West Accord, I arranged to have a dozen copies of the *San Diego Transcript* printed with a special fake headline: KAPITZA WINS BET, YORK HUMILIATED.

His winning that bet was not just a fluke; he really did possess acute insight.

The last time I saw Kapitza was in Switzerland, in 1979. He was visiting the European Council for Nuclear Research, CERN, at Geneva, as a special honored guest on the occasion of his eighty-fifth birthday, and he was staying with friends in nearby Lausanne. The Brezhnev period was clearly coming to an end sometime soon, and so I naturally turned our conversation to speculation about what would come next.

In essence he told me, "Our leaders after the revolution were very smart men, but they had no education, and they acted in the way you would expect from such people. Our current generation of leaders are educated, but narrowly, in engineering and technology. They are, therefore, better governors than their predecessors. The next generation of leaders will be broadly educated, in the humanities and arts as well as technology. When they take over, you will see that the government in Russia will be as good as yours."

Whether Peter was right in this last prediction remains to be seen. I didn't make any bets on it, but I believed he had a much better basis for his estimate than anyone else I knew.

A Dartmouth Conference in Riga

The Dartmouth conferences, named after the site of the first one, are another continuing series of private East-West meetings intended to contribute to understanding and defusing the antagonisms that divide us so harshly.

The only meeting of this group I attended was held in Jurmala, near Riga, Latvia, in 1977. Among the other Americans were Norman Cousins, Paul Doty, and David Rockefeller. The Soviet group included the usual bunch—Arbatov, his chief deputies, Vitali Zhurkin and Mikhail Milstein, and Georgi Zhukov, political editor of *Pravda*. Some others, including a few Latvians, were new to me.

Of all the visits I have made to the USSR, the one to Riga was the most unreal, the most like a visit to Alice's Wonderland.

C ir agenda included a meeting with the prime minister of the Latvian SSR. After welcoming us all—including the visiting Russians—to his republic, he gave us a short history lesson in which he explained how the Red Army had annexed Latvia in order to rescue the people from their rapacious bourgeois leaders and had brought them the great gift of socialism. I was appalled.

Later we went on an excursion to a delightful small outdoor museum. Among the old homes and other buildings that had been preserved was a handsome wooden church. In its rear loft was an old organ that still functioned. Norman Cousins sat down at it and played a few bars of religious music. I wondered when that had last happened.

Rita Hauser, an international lawyer and a member of the board of the American Jewish Congress, was another member of our group. She raised questions about the trial of Anatoly Shcharansky, then still some months in the future. Arbatov assured us there was nothing to worry about; Shcharansky would surely get a fair trial. Rita pointed out that no one tried under the statutes involved had ever been found not guilty. I watched Arbatov literally blanch, but he made no further comments.

A few months later Shcharansky was found guilty and sentenced to ten years in prison.

An Interim Conclusion

Many of these visits, the one to Latvia especially, helped me better appreciate one of the great paradoxes of our time.

On the one hand, we must, through official negotiations as well as private consultations, work out a modus vivendi with the Russians. There is no other option. Oppenheimer's analogy of the two scorpions in the bottle that will either live or die together is apt. The number and kinds of nuclear weapons that exist and might be used at the climax of a war between us really do suffice, as the peace activists are wont to say, to kill all of us thirty times over and to create such a situation that Western civilization could not be rebuilt, no matter how much advance planning was done.

On the other hand, it is clear that the Soviet Union is not just "some other state" with which we happen to have an "antagonistic relationship" that can be explained solely on the basis of certain historical events, important as they may be. The Soviet Union really is different from Western countries—in fact, from all other ones as well. Stalin, in the words of his heirs, was a paranoid tyrant, one of history's worst despots. The current regime, while different in many details, remains basically the same in its form. Worse, today's leaders still try to explain away Stalin and his "excesses" and strive mightily and successfully to keep the truth about him and his deeds from the Russian people. The Soviet Union is the only modern state that so thoroughly denies its recent history and so distrusts its people that it controls absolutely all the information they receive. The Soviet government, in sum, is not just one more alternative way of organizing society and the economy. It is different in kind, not just in degree, and we have to take that unhappy fact fully into account when dealing with the Soviet Union.

There is nonetheless, as Kapitza believed, room for real hope. The West, only a little more than a century ago, bought, sold, and used human slaves and killed aborigines in order to seize their lands and other treasures. We have successfully evolved away from such practices. The Russians can similarly evolve away from their present, totalitarian format. We should help them do so when and where we can, and we should allow them the necessary time and space. But we must not, as some would have us do, act as if their evolution away from totalitarianism had already happened or as if it were a sure thing.

In the meantime relations and negotiations must be built on a careful and conservative approach that places special emphasis on finding and exploiting areas of genuine, long-term mutual self-interest and on the unilateral verifiability of any specific agreements.

Private organizations, although never really popular with official Washington, clearly have a role in all this. Just as clearly, this role depends on the external circumstances. During the Stalin years, though many people tried such approaches, nothing worked. During the Khrushchev years, when the official channels were beginning to open up but were still very weak, Pugwash and other conferences contributed significantly to international understanding. Later, when the official channels really opened up and formal negotiations were being carried out in a number of disparate arenas, the informal channels played a diminished role. (The Reagan years have been so confused in this respect that I cannot yet assess the balance.)

Another Lesson

On one of my trips to the Soviet Union, I had a fascinating conversation with a young Russian who had never been out of the country. We were alone, well removed from buildings and other people. Suddenly he said, "You may think I am a dinosaur, but you must understand there isn't going to be a revolution in this country. If a Soviet citizen wants to improve things, he must join the Communist party and work to make things better from the inside."

I didn't think he was a dinosaur, and I agreed with the thrust of his remark. Indeed, there isn't going to be a revolution in any of the major powers, not in the USSR, not in China, not in the United States, Britain, or France. In such a circumstance, if a person wants to help resolve a serious structural dilemma like the nuclear arms race, the best way to do so is by joining the mainstream, the establishment, or, in the Russian case, "the party." Dissidents and outsiders can also at times influence the course of events but not as much as those who join the mainstream can.

Sometimes I hear persons who identify themselves as "peace activists" proudly boast that they are outsiders, and thus free from the sins of the dominant culture and politics. For people who cannot, for whatever reason, join the mainstream, being dissident activists may well be the most effective and satisfying thing to do. But when they recommend the same outsider path to college-age people, I have to disagree. In my view, young, adaptable persons are best advised to join the mainstream. The older people already there may have lots of warts and biases, but new people with fresh perspectives can and do influence the course of events. Persuasion, persistence, and patience are more powerful tools than placards. Serious study, including a real attempt to understand how things got the way they are, will produce better results than protest songs.

It is, of course, true that in the American system major social and political changes often develop out of the confrontation of persons and groups advocating contrary ideas. In such a system, dissenters, whistleblowers, and other social rebels play an essential role. However, it is almost never true that a ripe new idea is pushed only by a few active outsiders and unanimously opposed by those in the mainstream. Well before a new idea matures, the mainstream will itself become divided on the matter, and insiders as well as outsiders will be searching for ways to introduce the changes the new ideas call for. And when they finally succeed, it will be the insiders who work out the details and who control and elaborate all the other actions that, in the end, are necessary to make the changes effective. Thus, even in those cases in which dissidents play an essential role, and revolutionary situations aside, it is the insiders who ultimately determine the shape, extent, and effectiveness of the final result.

Signs of a Change

Late in 1975 I received an invitation to a small cocktail reception from a local Democratic group. The words JIMMY CARTER were written in large, bright red letters across the top of the sheet. I had never heard of him, and I did not bother to attend.

A year later he was elected president. By that time I was aware he had been a member of the Trilateral Commission and had, through that connection, become acquainted with several of my old friends and colleagues, including Harold Brown and Cyrus Vance.

In December 1976, following the election, I made a trip to Europe to visit some of the University of California's education abroad centers. (I was the UCSD faculty adviser for the program.) From there I went on to Jerusalem, where we also had one, and thence to Hong Kong, where we had a center at the Chinese University, at which Rachel was one of the students. Sybil also came to Hong Kong, but directly from California. In addition to the expected joys of Christmas in Hong Kong with our daughter, we also experienced two special surprises.

One was meeting John Williams, a Welsh student, then traveling around the world gathering data for a thesis on worker participation in factory management. Just weeks before we arrived, he and Rachel had met in a pub where she was a waitress. When we got there, she informed us that he was someone special. We all had tea on Christmas Eve in the lobby of the Peninsula Hotel. The scene was grand and the company delightful. Nine months later they were married at the registry in Cardiff, Wales, and the following New Year's Eve they went through a second wedding ceremony at our home in La Jolla, for the benefit of ourselves and our family friends.

The other special surprise turned up in the *South China Morning Post.* "President-elect Jimmy Carter," it said, "has appointed Harold Brown to be his Secretary of Defense."

When I got home, shortly after New Year's Day, I called Harold in Pasadena to congratulate him and wish him well.

Another round of unexpected adventures awaited us all. In the course of the year, I would return to full-time participation in national security affairs, Rachel and John would marry, and Cynthia would enter the veterinary school at UC Davis.

CHAPTER 13

Washington Once More

(1977–1978)

I SHOWED UP at Harold Brown's office a day or two after he became secretary of defense. He was reading a thick briefing book presenting the insiders' view of the history of his office and the permanent staff's ideas about the secretary's functions. He was more elated than I can recall ever seeing him. It was evident that he would throw himself into the job with an energy and intensity that few others can bring to such responsibilities. I told him I wanted to help in whatever way I could. The result was another four years of full-time work on national security problems at the highest levels.

Both the form and the content of my contributions evolved over the four years. At first I worked as a direct consultant to Harold and his new DDR & E, William Perry, on issues having to do both with high-technology armaments and with arms control. At the end I served as chief U.S. negotiator at the Comprehensive Test Ban talks in Geneva and otherwise dealt almost exclusively with arms control issues.

Changes since the Last Time

My last direct involvement in national security affairs at the highest levels had been during the Johnson administration, eight years before. To put it simply, the strategic balance at that earlier time was characterized by very substantial American superiority in both the quality and the quantity of high-technology armaments.

The qualitative superiority was the more obvious. In the 1960s a string of American successes in space made it clear that the Russian priority in launching the first Sputnik had been a historical accident, a flash in the pan, not a true measure of the relative positions of the two countries. We had a similar advantage in computers. In both design and applications we were way ahead, and it seemed clear that lead would persist indefinitely. There was every reason to believe that we had a similar edge in nuclear explosives and most other key technologies.

Eight years later, when Carter became president, we were still qualitatively ahead in all important areas of technology. In many important applications, however, the Soviets were narrowing the gap. They did so not by matching us in sophistication but by designing around the problem, by finding alternatives that were less elegant but, even so, entirely adequate for the job at hand. For example, perhaps they couldn't guide their missiles quite so accurately, but they provided them with more powerful warheads and thus achieved equal—or even greater—destructive power. They used the same general approach successfully in many other areas.

Quantitatively, the picture differed substantially. At the end of the Johnson administration, the United States still had more nuclear explosives, more long-range bombers, and more land-based and more sea-based missiles than the Russians. In all those categories, however, the Russians were even then busily engaged in a long-term program of steady expansion, while we were holding the size of our forces essentially constant. Eight years later they had indeed caught up with us in numbers and, for all we could then tell, were planning to surpass us.

There was nothing surprising or uniquely sinister in the actions that brought about this change. After the 1962 Cuban missile crisis, many Soviet officials were quoted as saying, "You will never do that to us again." When the Politburo fired Khrushchev and replaced him with Brezhnev, part of the deal evidently was a promise by the latter to achieve strategic parity (at least) with the Americans. And that is just what happened.

The Soviet strategic force in 1980 was essentially the mirror image of what any reasonable Soviet analyst working in 1964 would have predicted the U.S. force to be in the 1980s. The total number of Soviet strategic nuclear delivery vehicles in 1980 was approximately twenty-five hundred, a number equal to those we had had in 1964 plus the number we were then building, and the total size and power of their 1980 nuclear stockpile was also comparable to what we had had at that earlier date. In the meantime, however, we had decommissioned certain old delivery systems and cut back our nuclear stockpile in terms both of numbers (by 25 percent) and total explosive power (by 70 percent).

Many politically hawkish analysts have charged that the "massive" Soviet nuclear buildup of the sixties and seventies was "unprecedented" and "unexplainable." It was clearly neither. The Soviet buildup led to a force whose size in 1980 (as measured by either the number of delivery systems or the megatonnage) was the same size as the one we had in the early sixties, but it took the Soviets more than twice as long to build it. The American nuclear buildup of 1954–64 remains the fastest and the biggest ever, and it will probably never be matched.

The achievement by the Soviets of a strategic nuclear force at least equal to ours in terms of what it could do, if not in its sophistication, came about because the Soviets exploited in the sixties and seventies the same pool of technology we had so successfully exploited earlier. Nothing we could have done could have prevented this result. In particular, it was complete nonsense to blame this change in the relative balance on "arms control," as some sought to do.

Certain inactions on our part did, however, abet the process. In brief, Lyndon Johnson and Richard Nixon both largely financed the war in Vietnam not by sacrificing butter to buy guns but by cutting back on strategic R & D and other high-technology investments. By the end of that war, spending on strategic forces stood at only a fraction of its former level by any measure: in constant dollars, as a fraction of the GNP, or as a fraction of total defense expenditures.

Some argued that the reversal in the quantitative balance and the narrowing of our lead in technology did not matter. In essence, they said that since we could "already kill all the Russians thirty times over" it didn't matter if the Soviet level of overkill was higher than ours.

That notion might have been correct if our main purpose had in fact been to threaten to kill as many Russians as possible, but that wasn't and never has been true. Our purposes for maintaining strategic nuclear forces were, first, to deter nuclear war and other major aggressive acts and, second, if deterrence should somehow fail, to destroy as much as possible of the enemy's military forces, particularly their nuclear components. For these purposes the absolute and the relative numbers do indeed count. States are deterred by being threatened with unacceptable levels of damage in retaliation. Larger forces reinforce this threat better than smaller ones do, logical or not, like it or not. And in the event deterrence fails, the targets that must be hit include all the military forces of the other side. Altogether, these make up a target list that includes a great deal more than just a few hundred cities and a thousand silos. Moreover, our forces must be adequate for this purpose after absorbing a first strike. Their initial, preattack numbers must therefore be large enough that the expected survivors pose an adequate threat. All of these considerations point to numbers much larger than those needed just to destroy Soviet cities.

This underscored for me two more of the great dilemmas of our time. The first concerns making a choice between two very different nuclear strategies. The "minimum deterrence" strategy calls for the deliberate targeting of cities. This strategy minimizes the size of the forces because there are only so many cities to be hit. For that reason many self-identified peace activists recommend it. The other strategy calls for striking military-industrial targets only and for avoiding purely civilian targets as much as possible. This strategy maximizes the sizes of the forces because there is virtually no practical limit to targets of the type they are designed to strike. Advocates of peace through strength commonly favor it. Persons recommending either one of these strategies often glibly charge that those recommending the other are immoral. In either case, I believe, the number of casualties in an all-out war would be about the same, that is, somewhat more than 50 percent of the population. In the first case, however, this level of casualties would result on purpose, whereas in the second it would be, as the euphemistic jargon would put it, "unintended collateral damage."

The other dilemma can be stated more succinctly: larger nuclear forces strengthen deterrence and therefore make war less likely, while at the same time making the consequences of a failure of deterrence all the worse.

It is not as easy to choose between the alternatives in either of these dilemmas as the self-righteous persons at either extreme seem to believe.

In sum, when I returned to the Pentagon in 1977, I found that there had been important changes in the strategic balance since I had last worked there—and that these changes were unfavorable to us. A thorough review was clearly due, and I was pleased to participate in it. During the next two years I had the opportunity to work on a number of specific issues, the most important of which were the B-1 (a supersonic intercontinental bomber) and the MX (a new, very large ICBM).

The Case of the B-1

At the very beginning of his administration, Harold Brown decided to set up an *ad hoc* committee to study the B-1. The members were to be Ivan Selin, a former senior defense analyst, Paul Ignatius, a former secretary of the Navy, and I. The "sunshine laws," designed to promote more openness in government, were at their peak, and the establishment of a formal committee turned out to be very awkward and time-consuming. As a result, we performed the desired review as three independent consultants who met together frequently for briefings and discussions.

The question before us was whether this very expensive, modern, supersonic bomber was needed as a replacement for the aging B-52s that had made up the backbone of our strategic air force for almost twenty years. I started with a prejudice against the B-1. Many friends in and out of the defense establishment—Dick Garwin, Marvin Goldberger, and Jeremy Stone, to name only a few—had produced serious arguments against it, and I was inclined to believe them. As we examined the matter in detail, however, I discovered that the technical and tactical arguments for and against were more evenly balanced than I had thought.

In the end a more general consideration swung me over to supporting the B-1. As I indicated above, the strategic balance had been slowly but steadily deteriorating for more than a decade. I agreed with those who felt we had to address this situation and upgrade our strategic capability. There were only four real options for doing so, and for political reasons alone we had to pick up at least two of them. The four options were the B-1, the air-launched cruise missile (ALCM), the MX (a very large multiwarhead ballistic missile), and the adoption of a launch-on-warning strategy for our land-based missiles. In my view the ALCM and the B-1 were both much to be preferred to either the MX or launch on warning.

Unfortunately, the decision-making process, which is tied to the budget cycle, did not permit all four of these alternatives to be considered together and weighed against each other. Each was in a different phase of development, and so the system could not balance them against each other all at the same time. However, that didn't prevent me from doing so, and I reached my conclusions on that basis. To put it simply, launch on warning was much too dangerous, and the MX was a fatally flawed idea. The MX missile program called for building a very small number of very lucrative targets, precisely the wrong thing to do in a world where the ability to survive a surprise attack is crucial. That left the other two options, and I recommended that they both be pursued. Some of my outside friends thought I was crazy to support the B-1, but I was back inside, looking at these problems from the point of view of someone directly sharing in the responsibility for resolving them—even if only in a small way—and that no doubt affected my attitude.

I have made the switch from outside to inside—and vice versa—several times in my career, and each time I found that such issues looked different when I viewed them from the inside, in a shared responsibility mode, than when I viewed them from the outside, in a critic's or observer's mode. Back in 1957, before I went off to work for Killian in the White House, I had known well all the reasons for and benefits from nuclear testing, and so I always opposed proposals for a test ban. After I arrived in Washington, I had the opportunity to see the nuclear testing issue from a wide perspective, and I came to understand the benefits that a test ban could bring. After weighing these two sets of benefits against each other for a few months, I switched sides and became an advocate of a treaty to ban all nuclear tests. Edward Teller regarded that as an act of personal disloyalty and never forgave me for it.

Thus, while my general conclusions about the world have not changed with my status, some of my particular conclusions have. Perhaps that's wrong; perhaps my judgments about the details ought to be the same whether I am studying the problem from inside or outside, but I think not. Moreover, assuming that a difference in perspective ought occasionally to lead to different conclusions, I believe that when my conclusions do differ, those I reach when I am inside, being supported by a richer supply of information, are usually better than those I reach when I am outside. Persons who believe that the facts don't matter in such large-scale general problems, that such specialists "can't see the forests for the trees," or that bureaucrats are primarily concerned with protecting their careers will, perhaps, disagree.

The foregoing does *not* mean that one needs to be an insider or otherwise have access to classified information to make broad judgments about the nuclear arms race. The news columns and op-ed pages of the better newspapers and magazines contain enough information to support sound judgments about broad policy issues or candidates for public office. However, there is a level of detail involving questions whose resolution does require detailed and classified information not normally available. These questions, too, must be resolved by somebody while the broader issues are being dealt with; in general, only experts and insiders can do so. In this case the problem for the general public is somehow to see to it that the people selected to do so are sensible, sensitive, and competent. That is not easy in a democracy, and it is impossible under a totalitarian regime.

MX and Midgetman

The MX is a large, highly accurate, solid propellant ICBM with many (ten or so) nuclear warheads. It was first proposed by the Air Force in the late 1960s as a successor to the Minuteman system.

From the beginning much thought was devoted to the question of how to base the MX, but that important matter was never satisfactorily resolved. The reason is simple. The combination of many warheads and exceptional accuracy would make the MX the most menacing strategic weapon in the U.S. inventory. At the same time its relatively great size and consequent high cost meant there would be relatively few of them. It was inevitable, therefore, that the MX would constitute a high-priority target for the Soviets. That, in turn, meant that protecting it would be the highest-priority matter for us. Given the growing accuracy and power of Soviet warheads, silo basing of the kind used to protect Minuteman seemed inadequate.

Many alternatives were suggested, but none passed careful scrutiny. The alternatives included deep underground basing, mobility of various sorts (including the "racetrack system" favored by the Carter administration), and even the bizarre "dense pack" arrangement (favored, for a while, by the Reagan administration). Each of these basing modes proved to be either too expensive, too impractical, too uncertain, or otherwise undesirable.

I opposed the MX system from the day I first heard of it. The most important technical requirement for an ICBM is that it be able to survive a first strike against it. Land-based systems in which we put so many eggs in so few baskets, so to speak, clearly do not satisfy this requirement very well. The surest way to assure survival is to have large numbers of weapons, each of which must be attacked and destroyed individually. In general the smaller a missile, the cheaper; therefore, more of them can be bought for a given total budget. And not only is a smaller missile cheaper itself, but so are its peripherals—including transporter, launcher, silo, and other overhead and backup systems. The right size for an ICBM is therefore the smallest size that will do the job required. In the late 1950s the ICBM design that best fit these criteria was the Minuteman, and that is why we in the Eisenhower administration gave it priority over its larger and costlier predecessors, the Atlas and the Titan. By the 1970s technology had advanced so far that we could accomplish the Minuteman mission with a single-warhead missile weighing between one-third and one-half as much. The name of such an alternative became Midgetman.

Assuming that a successor to Minuteman was, in fact, needed, I favored Midgetman for that purpose from the beginning. One of the few papers I ever wrote as a participant in a Jason summer study (August 1978) discussed it and considered a basing system for it. In brief, I proposed a so-called MAPS, or multiple aim point system. In such a system, for example, a thousand Midgetmen would be shuttled around at random among a much larger number of small, cheap silos. When I circulated my paper to a somewhat broader audience, I discovered that several other analysts, including Paul Nitze and Albert Wohlstetter, were already thinking along similar lines.

The Air Force on more than one occasion considered and rejected such a system. On general grounds Air Force planners believed they needed a large, multiwarhead system in order to accomplish their mission. This notion was reinforced by their expectation that SALT-like agreements would continue to focus on, and limit, the total number of missiles rather than the capability of an individual missile.

The coming of the Brown administration in the Pentagon stimulated me to raise the question again. As part of my effort to do so, I presented an unclassified version of my ideas to an international security seminar at Harvard University. Many old friends were in the audience, including Jack Ruina, George Kistiakowsky, and Victor Weisskopf.

My ideas went over like a lead balloon. Most of those in the audience were (like me) advocates of arms control, and the idea of deploying a large number of Midgetmen in a MAPS deployment clashed with the mechanics of the current approach to it. It did not, however, run counter to the basic purposes of arms control. Indeed, compared with the plans for the MX, my proposal called for fewer and smaller warheads on many more missiles and thus was simultaneously less deadly and more survivable—both proper arms control objectives. But it did not fit the then fashionable versions of the mechanics of arms control (that is, limiting launchers) and that determined most people's attitudes toward it.

After the seminar Kistiakowsky was furious. His eyes flashed, and his face was red. "You have sold out to your friend Harold," he fumed.

George's disaffection with the defense establishment and defense policy was by then so complete that he opposed essentially all new strategic systems and the R & D behind them. I continued to feel that the right approach to the country's problems was to participate in picking and choosing among the possibilities. I hadn't sold out to anybody, but I did agree broadly with Harold's approach to defense policy, including its strategic elements.

Somewhat later I attended a meeting on the MX problem in Bill Perry's office. It was a Saturday morning, so the atmosphere was some-what more relaxed than on a regular business day. A dozen or so national security experts of various persuasions were there. Everyone agreed that there had to be some American response to the continuing buildup of Soviet strategic forces. A majority believed that the correct response was the MX missile. Dick Garwin and Sid Drell recommended, as an alternative, a small submarine carrying one or two large missiles externally. I alone spoke up for the Midgetman. Years later Bill Perry told me that both he and Harold were sympathetic to my ideas but that they considered it too late to make such a radical shift in the program.

About that same time I also presented my views on ICBMs to a subcommittee of the Air Force Science Advisory Board. At least two of the members said, in almost these words, "Even if the Air Force does go over to a single-warhead missile, the 'arms controllers' will continue to insist on the identical, low limit to the total number of missiles, and we will be stuck with insufficient firepower." In truth, the issues were so complex, and involved so many largely nonintersecting interest groups, that there was no way to have the MX-Midgetman trade-offs and the arms control issues considered in a single forum.

President Carter and Secretary Brown decided to continue with the MX even though there was no widely agreed-on scheme for basing it. One basing plan, the so-called racetrack system, emerged as the favorite. According to this plan, the MX missile would be placed on a large transporter and moved at random around a closed rail loop, or racetrack. Very strong, tunnel-like shelters would be located at intervals along the track. Sure enough, a few years later the Reagan administration rejected it, partly because it was considered impractical but mainly, I tend to think, because it had been invented during the Carter administration.

The ASAT Issue

The first Sputnik's 1957 flight around the world and over most countries established the precedent that overflight by innocent scientific satellites was legitimate and did not even require the giving of prior notice. Various international bodies, including the United Nations, sought to codify and extend this concept. These efforts met with some success. At no time, however, was the precedent extended to cover all types of satellites. From the very beginning the notion of illegitimate satellites—satellites that violated sovereignty and that therefore could be legitimately destroyed—was in the air. Indeed, for some years the question of the legitimacy of reconnaissance satellites remained open.[1] It was only in 1972, fifteen years after Sputnik, that references to the "national technical means of verification" (NTM) in the SALT I Treaty finally resolved the question in favor of the legitimacy of such satellites. And even then, strictly speaking, that treaty formally legitimized such satellites only if they were essential to, and used for, verification. It was therefore only natural that a lively interest in exploring the possibility of building antisatellites, or ASATs, should arise soon after satellites themselves came into being.

In the United States this interest led in 1960 to a proposal by the Air Force to develop the SAINT (*sa*tellite *int*ercepter) system. President Eisenhower took a dim view of the idea. The United States, he believed, would soon come to depend on satellites more than the Soviets did, and it was therefore not in our interest to initiate or promote the development of devices designed to destroy them. George Kistiakowsky in the White House and I in the Pentagon strongly supported the president's view. Later administrations confirmed these same ideas. As a result, full-scale development of a general-purpose ASAT was deferred for almost two decades in the United States.

In the early 1960s we did, however, find it necessary to deploy briefly a crude special-purpose ASAT. At that time the Soviets were deploying a huge rocket system clearly capable of placing large nuclear weapons in low orbits about the earth. With such a system the Soviets could launch warheads in a southerly direction and place them in low earth orbits passing over the South Pole. The rationale behind this strange system must have been the fact that most of our warning systems were oriented toward the north. An attack from the south therefore had a better chance to achieve surprise.

In response to this bizarre Soviet development, Secretary of Defense

McNamara in 1964 ordered the installation of an ASAT system on Johnston Island, in the mid-Pacific. Designated Project 437, its sole purpose was to intercept Soviet nuclear weapons in low earth orbits. It carried an atomic warhead and used the Thor missile as its booster. It could not have intercepted Soviet orbiting bombs in their first pass around the earth, but if they made multiple passes it could eventually do so.[2] When this threat failed to materialize, we decommissioned the Johnston Island system.

Unfortunately, the deliberate American moderation in this area was not reciprocated by the Soviets. In 1968 the Soviets initiated tests of a general-purpose ASAT. Through private channels—such as Pugwash—and through official channels as well, Americans tried in vain to persuade the Soviets not to take such a new and potentially dangerous step. The construction of ASATs and other space weapons might have been avoided for a long time if the Soviets had exercised self-restraint in this area, but they didn't.

The Soviet program was modest in size and proceeded in fits and starts. It was, however, as Khrushchev would have said in such a situation, a "bone in our throat." We could not ignore it indefinitely.

As a result, in 1977, the first year of the Carter administration, the president ordered, on Harold Brown's advice, the initiation of a three-pronged reply to the Soviet ASAT. One prong was an ASAT of our own. The second was an R & D program for finding means for defending our satellites against attack by their ASATs. The third was the start of negotiations designed to abolish ASATs altogether, thus making the first two prongs unnecessary.

The ASAT Negotiations

Harold Brown was well aware of my special interest in arms control issues, an interest that went back to my days with Eisenhower. In brief, he knew that while I fully supported the idea that the United States must maintain an adequate level of military force, including a nuclear component, I also believed that the national security establishment generally undervalued and underutilized arms control as an element of national security policy. He therefore drew me at the very beginning into the inner circle of those working on the problem of a negotiated prohibition of ASATs.

On the policy side those most directly involved were Walter Slocombe, a brilliant young attorney serving as deputy assistant secretary of defense for international affairs, and his assistant, Lynn Davis. On the technical side the man assigned to the task was Rear Admiral Ross Williams, the principal assistant to the deputy DDR & E for strategic and space systems.

Pentagon opinion was split on the question. The Air Force leaders, both military and civilian, generally supported a ban on ASATs. They believed that the United States benefited more from satellites than did the Soviet Union. A regime in which satellites could continue to function uninhibited and unthreatened was therefore to our advantage. They had substantial doubts about the verifiability of an ASAT ban and would not have accepted one that could not be verified. Assuming that this problem could somehow be resolved, though, they favored a ban.

Some in the Navy felt otherwise. They argued that the Soviet Ocean Reconnaissance Satellite posed a threat to U.S. operations at sea. We needed an ASAT system as one good means of dealing with that threat. Unfortunately, Ross Williams, the man designated by Bill Perry to work on the issue, was a partisan of the view to ban ASATs.

Some of the younger Air Force officers in the headquarters also were cool to a ban on ASATs. Enthusiastic about all varieties of satellites, space weapons, and space flight, they were opposed in principle to the erecting of artificial barriers by diplomats or politicians.

In sum, perhaps a majority of the interested people in the Pentagon accepted the idea of a ban on ASATs, but the opinion was far from unanimous.

As we explored the matter, we uncovered several major issues that blocked the development of really strong support for an ASAT ban. For one thing, the Soviets had already conducted at least a dozen ASAT tests against real targets in space, whereas we had not yet even initiated a serious development program. That difference was widely perceived as giving them a substantial advantage over us, which would have to be overcome somehow before any regime banning further work in the field could be put in place. I argued that our vastly greater ability to carry out computer simulations and our general lead in space technology more than made up for the modest experience their tests had provided, but I did not convince many others.

Another major issue involved the nature of ASAT technology. In brief, an ASAT system required a suitable launch vehicle, a means of assuring the rendezvous of the ASAT with its target, a means for destroying the target, and a system for commanding and controlling the whole process. Only one of these elements, the means for destroying the target, was unique to the ASAT system, but it was essentially trivial in its design and construction. All the other elements were common to many other space systems. Their development had been and would continue to be carried out in support of a host of other important and legal objectives, no matter what we did about ASATs. Was it really practical to ban one particular assemblage of these elements while we permitted the development of the elements themselves for these other purposes? In the future would it not be possible to assemble a reliable ASAT from existing subsystems and to ensure its reliability without testing?

This last issue tied in closely with the matter of verification. Even if we could assure ourselves that the Soviets had completely eliminated their existing capability, how could we be sure they didn't have stored away somewhere other units that could be quickly installed on rocket boosters built for some other legitimate purpose?

These issues were never resolved to everyone's satisfaction, but it was decided that we should undertake a negotiation anyway, in order to explore the range of possibilities and see where they might lead.

The Special Coordinating Committee, or SCC, was the standard mechanism for working out such matters during the Carter administration. Such committees were usually chaired by the president's special assistant for national security, Zbigniew Brzezinski. In this case the other members were the secretaries of state and defense, the chairman of the JCS, the directors of the CIA and the ACDA, the administrator of NASA, and the president's science adviser. Working with Walt Slocombe and the others, I helped develop the Defense Department position for consideration at the SCC meetings, and I occasionally attended the meetings themselves. They were held in the West Wing of the White House, in a tiny room specially selected to provide an acceptable reason for holding down attendance. Typically, eight or so principals sat around the table in the middle of the room, and eight to ten aides lined the walls.

Neither the Pentagon group nor the SCC was able to work out a detailed plan for eliminating ASATs, but the general goal was clear and had enough internal support to make exploratory negotiations with the Soviets worthwhile.

The American negotiating team was nominally headed by Paul Warnke. As head of the ACDA and U.S. ambassador to the SALT II talks and most other important arms control negotiations, he was a very busy man. In most cases, including this one, the work of actually planning and conducting the negotiation had to be turned over to deputies. Robert Buchheim became responsible for these functions in the ASAT talks.

Buchheim is an engineer who devoted much of his professional life to work at the Rand Corporation. He also served for a year as chief scientist of the Air Force. He worked for the ACDA during the Nixon and Ford years and was one of the few senior staff members held over on the Carter team. He started as deputy U.S. negotiator in the first round of ASAT talks, and immediately following that he was appointed chief negotiator, the position he continued to hold for the rest of the Carter administration. A stolid, taciturn, unflappable person with a caustic wit, and an ideological conservative who believed in both the need for and the possibility of negotiated controls over armaments, he made an excellent negotiator.

I became Harold Brown's representative on the delegation. Each of the other agencies whose heads made up the SCC also had representatives.

Stopover in Geneva

The first round of negotiations was scheduled to begin on June 8, 1978, in Helsinki. On the way I stopped off in Geneva to learn what was happening at the SALT II talks and the Comprehensive Test Ban (CTB) negotiations. These were well under way, having been given new life and vigor by President Carter. I had a good visit with the chief negotiator, Paul Warnke, but I spent most of my time with my old friend from Livermore days Gerald Johnson, then serving as Harold Brown's representative at both negotiations.

Jerry hosted a private luncheon so that I could meet privately with Alexander Shchukin, his opposite number on the Soviet SALT delegation. Shchukin, an engineer who had been involved somehow in the Soviet missile program, was one of the very few Soviet delegates who had direct technical knowledge about the subject of the negotiations. He understood spoken English but did not feel confident enough to speak it. He would reply only in Russian or in French. That meant interpreters were also present, one for each side. (Michael May, another old Livermore colleague, had served on the SALT delegation during the Ford years. As a native speaker of French, he had been able to have completely private, "walk in the woods" conversations with Shchukin.)

Shchukin, born in 1900, was seventy-eight when we met. Russian officials of that vintage differed from younger ones in two important ways. First, they were no longer bucking for advancement in the Soviet bureaucracy. Second, and probably more important, they had been raised and educated before the Stalin years, and their minds and their approach to other people were not so strongly colored by the mind-warping events of that dreadful period. Such persons were more relaxed, easier to talk with, and less reserved than their younger col-leagues. Of the Soviets I mentioned previously, Peter Kapitza and Vasily Emelyanov also fall into this category.

Our luncheon conversation ranged over a wide spectrum of topics, including their ASAT program.

"You must have known it would make trouble and that we would eventually have to respond. Why did you do it?" I asked.

His reply was classic. In essence, he said, "You know how it is. You have the same thing in your country. Some young, ambitious technicians get hold of an idea they believe is both practical and important, and they promote it and push it until finally the authorities let them go ahead with it." I believed him. The Soviet ASAT was less the result of an action-reaction mechanism, or a calculation of a military need, than a case of an interesting technology sold to a gullible and poorly informed leader-ship by aggressive salesmen. It happens often enough in the United States; how could it fail to happen in the Soviet Union?

It was all very interesting and encouraging. I had been part of the apparatus supporting our negotiating teams ever since Eisenhower got bilateral arms control negotiations going in 1958. This was, however, the first time I met a Russian official in the line of such duty. (My previous meetings with Russians in Pugwash and other conferences were always unofficial, and hence inherently quite different.) More important, the negotiations seemed to be getting somewhere. There was real promise of bringing the whole mad process of the arms race under control.

Helsinki

A few days later I was in Helsinki, ready to join in making a try in yet another dimension. I thought of our job as being to prevent the real "Star Wars." The movie by that name had recently been making the rounds, and so that seemed an appropriate way to think about it. Of course, I did not even dream that in only a few years another president would deliberately set in motion a program that would quickly—and rightly—be dubbed with that same nickname.

Our negotiating team in Helsinki consisted of about eight persons. The Soviet team was roughly the same size. It was headed by Ambassador Oleg Khlestov, a lawyer and a member of the collegium (governing committee) of the Soviet Foreign Ministry. Boris Mayorski, a younger man who often represented the Soviets at meetings of the UN Committee on Space in New York, was his deputy. We met on a rotating home-and-home basis in each other's embassies. Normally Buchheim presided over the American team. Warnke attended only briefly, but a private session between him and Khlestov, in a real Finnish sauna during one of his brief visits, provided the opportunity for a full exchange of views.

The negotiations lasted eight days. We held several plenary sessions, plus some less formal meetings of subgroups.

The plenary sessions followed the standard pattern. We all sat on one side of a long table and they on the other. Buchheim and his interpreter sat in the middle of our group, and Khlestov and his interpreter did the same on their side. Mayorski and I usually faced each other across the table. Each chief of delegation spoke exclusively in his native language. Normally, no one else, other than the interpreters, spoke at all.

The opening position of the Soviets was that they were not sure what this negotiation was all about. Carter had insisted on including a negotiation on ASATs, among other similar initiatives, and they had only agreed to meet with us to explore the matter. They had come, moreover, with no particular position on it. Indeed, they made it clear that they thought a self-respecting modern state needed an ASAT capability and that it was not at all self-evident that such weapons should be banned outright.

Why might a state need an ASAT? we asked. To defend itself against intrusions on its sovereignty from space, they replied. They never presented any specific examples, but they pointed out that it was not only we and they who had satellites. Third parties had them as well. The Soviets did, however, express interest in formulating rules that would protect innocent satellites against attack, molestation, or removal from orbit.

We brought up the problem their long, continuing ASAT test program created for us, but they did not at first even directly acknowledge its existence. Instead, they accused us of having an ASAT. To my surprise, they referred not to the recently decommissioned Johnston Island system but to the space shuttle. They implied we intended to use it to destroy or to capture and inspect their satellites, and they told us that must not happen.

I had a long private meeting in a small café with Boris Mayorski on this issue. I said the notion that we would bring an unknown satellite on board the shuttle was absurd. A strange satellite would commonly contain high-energy fuels and might be booby-trapped besides. The shuttle was too expensive and the lives of its crew too precious for such a rash act. I thought I had him convinced.

A day or two later we met again, this time at our embassy. Boris picked up a NASA brochure that happened to be lying on a table. It was a typical sales promotion piece, designed to sell the American public and the Congress on the value and utility of the shuttle for a whole host of purposes. It had a two-page centerfold featuring a shuttle in flight. A long arm with a great claw was reaching out to grab a small sphere with a large red question mark inscribed on it. At a quick glance the red question mark looked like a hammer and sickle.

"See!?" he said.

We went back to square one on this issue.

Why were they so hostile to the shuttle? Why did they insist it was really an ASAT and not the innocent transportation system, or space truck, that we claimed it was?

The reason, simply stated, was that American technology was capable of building the space shuttle at that time and Soviet technology was not. Despite their early, flashy lead, as seemingly demonstrated by the first Sputnik, we had long since surpassed them in space technology. The shuttle only emphasized that fact. They couldn't build one and we could, and they didn't like it.

I found it especially interesting to meet and observe the Soviet delegates. One vital fact about them, I thought, was that there was no overlap between these official Russians and those I had met at unofficial conferences on similar subjects. Later on, when I met many more such officials in Geneva, I continued to find this to be generally true. The only exception, oddly enough, involved the KGB. At least two of the KGB officers I met at official conferences also showed up at the unofficial ones. Moreover, not only was there no other overlap between the official and unofficial Soviets, but with only two, easily explained exceptions (Arbatov and Kapitza) the official Soviet negotiators seemed not even to be aware of their countrymen who were involved in the Pugwash conferences or in others like them.

It was very different with the Americans. Some who in one era were at a Pugwash or a Dartmouth conference were on the official delegations in another. Beyond that, many of those on the official delegations were well acquainted with at least some of those engaged in the unofficial contacts, and vice versa. I took this difference between the American and Soviet delegations to be both important in itself and indicative of the extreme compartmentalization existing in the USSR.

The Soviet delegation in Helsinki included an army general whom I found fascinating. He seemed to have been selected for his role by Hollywood central casting. He was short and stocky and had pale blue eyes set in a perfectly round Slavic face. A fringe of short sandy hair surrounded a thin spot on the top of his head. When he sat opposite us at the conference table, he seemed to be very nervous. It was as though he had never been this close to the enemy before and was very uncomfortable about it. At informal gatherings—receptions and luncheons—we tried to get him to talk by the usual means: asking questions about what he had done during the "great patriotic war" and the like. Nothing seemed to work. At one point I asked him if he had ever been abroad before. "Czechoslovakia," he replied. I wanted to ask him if that was on the occasion of their 1968 invasion of that hapless country, but I didn't. Not all Soviet generals I have met were like him, but he wasn't entirely atypical either.

Toward the end of that first round of talks, Mayorski and I were given the job of jointly preparing a final communiqué. We found it hard to agree on language. The publicly stated American purpose in being there was to discuss what to do about ASATs, but the Soviets would not even agree to the use of that word in our report. Part of the difficulty was that I was new at this game. I simply wanted to tell the world what we had been doing. Eventually I caught on to the spirit of the affair. The final result was a classic, brief piece of obfuscation. Here, in its entirety, is the substantive part of our joint report to the world on our eight days of negotiation:

> Delegations of the US and the USSR held consultations in Helsinki from June 8 through June 16, 1978, to discuss questions in connection with limiting certain activities directed against space objects and incompatible with peaceful relations between states, including the means and systems for conducting such activities. The consultations were of a preliminary nature, and enabled each side to understand better the views of the other on these questions.[3]

Despite our differences, we discovered enough mutual interest in the matter to make further exploration worthwhile. To allow us enough time at home to discuss the various questions in our bureaucracies, we tentatively scheduled the next meeting for six months later, in the winter of

1978–79. We agreed that it ought to be possible to find some place more suitable for a meeting at that time of the year than Finland. We considered a number of southerly locales but could not find one where each of us had suitable meeting places and adequate communications facilities. Eventually we settled on Bern. That isn't exactly tropical, but it isn't subarctic either.

Before the second session took place, Paul Warnke resigned from all his positions. He had become fed up with what he regarded as inadequate support from the White House. In brief, Paul felt that Brzezinski took an unnecessarily hard line in dealing with the Russians on arms control and that the president failed to back him adequately in the unavoidable arguments he had with Zbig and with other agency heads.

As one result of Warnke's resignation, Buchheim became the U.S. chief negotiator on ASATs. I was about to be named deputy when a different and more interesting opportunity suddenly intervened and removed me from the delegation altogether. (More on this in the next chapter.)

Only two more negotiating rounds were held. The second, in Bern, began January 23, 1979, and lasted three weeks. The third, in Vienna, ran from April 23 to June 17. In these later rounds the two sides made real progress toward a common understanding of the issues. The outlines of some possible agreements limiting the development, deployment, and use of ASATs began to emerge from the mists. Before much more could be done, however, first the entire SALT process ran into trouble and then the grim events in Tehran and Afghanistan burst onto the world scene. Further negotiations on this difficult subject became pointless.

Later, during the Reagan administration, the Soviets repeatedly urged resumption of negotiations in this area. They apparently even stood down their ASAT test program as a carrot. At first the United States declined to resume serious negotiations. Later we agreed to include this issue among those to be discussed at Geneva, when the Strategic Arms Reduction Talks, or START talks, resumed there in 1985. (As of this writing, there has been no useful result.) In the meantime the Soviets have continued to maintain a small deployment of operational ASATs, and the United States has proceeded very slowly and fitfully with the development of an ASAT of its own.

A Personal Aside on Deterrence

One of the personal joys of the Helsinki negotiations was that they provided Sybil and me a delightful opportunity to renew our friendship with Jorma and Irya Miettinen. Jorma was a professor of radiochemistry at the University of Helsinki, an adviser on nuclear matters to the Finnish Foreign Office and UN delegation, and an active member of the Pugwash movement. We had come to know both of them quite well in that last connection.

Jorma was also a veteran of the two Finno-Russian wars of 1939–44. At Pugwash conferences and in private conversation, he represented a point of view that was at once officially neutral insofar as the cold war was concerned, realistic, and warmly pro-Western in its social and political dimension.

He also helped me further clarify my thinking on the psychological dimension of deterrence. "The reason Finland is independent and Estonia, Latvia, and the others are not," he told me, "is that the Russians know for certain that we will fight." It's not the size of the forces so much as the will to use them that counts most—or, at least, comes first—in deterrence.

Meeting with the Secretary

During the Carter years I had many opportunities to meet with Harold Brown in his office. These meetings usually took place on Saturday afternoons, often after his return from a period of hard exercise or swimming in the Pentagon gym. His calendar was usually free at such times, and the exercise made him more relaxed than usual. He normally wore a sweatsuit or some other casual gear.

Our discussions ranged very widely but involved mainly technical issues. We talked about the B-1, the MX, cruise missiles, launch on warning, strategic and nuclear policy, NATO, China, SALT, the test ban, satellites and ASATs, technical intelligence, and the notorious Presidential Directive (PD) 59.* We never discussed the ill-fated Tehran

---

*PD-59 came out very late in the Carter administration. It dealt with some of the details of how a nuclear war might actually be fought should deterrence fail. Its primary thrust involved limiting such a war to the lowest-possible level of intensity and damage, but many "doves" nonetheless opposed it, because they felt any such efforts only made nuclear war more "thinkable" and hence more likely. The ideas in it had been around for

rescue operation, either before or after it happened. He regarded that as a purely operational matter, completely outside my purview. And he never gossiped about such things as what the president or other high officials said to him except when his telling me what they thought was directly necessary in my own work on national security issues. Harold was always staunchly loyal to his boss and colleagues and never, to my knowledge, careless or casual in the way he treated a confidential relationship.

I enjoyed those meetings very much. I learned a great deal from them and used them to present my views on all sorts of subjects. I think Harold must have found them useful, too, even though he had a vast network of other advice and opinion at his beck and call.

After finishing the business part of our discussion, we often continued on with talk about personal things, especially our families. Sybil and I first met Colene soon after she and Harold started dating, and we knew Deborah and Ellen from the time they were babies. Harold knew my children just as well, and he still vividly remembered my midnight call asking him to baby-sit for Rachel and David while Cynthia was being born. Now the children were all grown and launched on lives and careers of their own, and we traded the most recent news of them.

From that close and personal perspective, it was easy to see how difficult Harold's job was, how heavy the burdens could become, and with what great dedication and seriousness he tackled them. On more than one occasion I failed to criticize or comment negatively on something he had done or said, solely because I could not bring myself to add another straw to his load. I remember and regret several such instances.

---

some time and had most recently appeared in the open in Secretary Brown's annual posture statements, but raising the matter to the level of a presidential directive focused special attention, and wrath, on them. People on both sides of the general issue accused the president and Brzezinski of having issued the directive when they had solely in order to prove that they were "tough and realistic" in the course of a political campaign in which they were accused of being soft and timid.

CHAPTER 14

The Comprehensive
Test Ban Negotiations

(1977–1981)

Before Carter

SINCE the bombing of Hiroshima all American presidents had actively sought means to contain, stop, and reverse the nuclear arms race. Jimmy Carter differed from his predecessors not in kind but only in degree. He tried harder than they and explored the broadest set of possibilities. In one of modern history's all too common ironies, he accomplished the least. Events over which he had little control ultimately prevented him from adding very much to the limitations already worked out and put into place by the efforts of Eisenhower, Kennedy, Johnson, Nixon, and Ford.

The idea of a nuclear test ban as a first step in containing the arms race emerged in the mid-1950s. The first concrete accomplishment was the nuclear test moratorium of 1958–61, achieved under the leadership of Eisenhower and Khrushchev (see chapter 6). The purpose of the moratorium was to provide a political climate suitable for working out a formal treaty permanently banning such tests. Tripartite negotiations to this end, including the United Kingdom as well as the United States and the Soviet Union, were in almost continuous session from October 31, 1958, to January 19, 1962. Internal disputes among the Americans studying the issues in Washington, combined with some hard-nosed attitudes on the part of the Soviets in Geneva, delayed the negotiation of a treaty. Finally, in 1961, the sudden resumption of nuclear testing by the Soviets brought the whole process to a total, but temporary, halt.

The dangers demonstrated by the 1962 Cuban missile crisis inspired Kennedy, Khrushchev, and Prime Minister Harold Macmillan of Britain to make another try. As before, the single most difficult issue was the monitoring of underground tests. Small nuclear tests made seismic signals much like those generated by earthquakes, and the latter were very common in the USSR. American specialists could not agree even among themselves, much less with the Soviets, on the means and prospects for coping with this problem.

Tripartite negotiations in Moscow in 1963, led on our side by Ambassador Averell Harriman, achieved a treaty banning all tests except those underground. In addition to banning tests "in the atmosphere, in outer space, and under water," the treaty pledged the parties to continue to seek "to achieve the discontinuance of all test explosions for all time" and "to continue negotiations to that end." In order to be sure of getting the support needed for ratification by the Senate, President Kennedy agreed to support a vigorous program of nuclear weapons development, including whatever underground tests were necessary to that end.

During the Johnson administration two additional major multilateral arms control treaties were elaborated. One, the Outer Space Treaty, banned the deployment of "nuclear weapons or any other kind of weapons of mass destruction" in space or on "celestial bodies." The other, the Treaty on the Nonproliferation of Nuclear Weapons, was designed to prevent the spread of nuclear weapons to states that did not already possess them. Its own preamble recalled the pledge in the preamble of the Limited Test Ban Treaty calling for a comprehensive ban. More important, Article 6 of the Nonproliferation Treaty called on the parties to "pursue negotiations in good faith on effective measures relating to the cessation of the nuclear arms race at an early date and to nuclear disarmament."

Richard Nixon, in addition to the more important SALT I Treaty, also directed the negotiation of a treaty setting the upper limit on the permissible size of underground explosions at 150 kilotons, more than twelve times the power of the Hiroshima bomb. Called the Threshold Test Ban

Treaty (TTBT), it was signed by Brezhnev and Nixon in July 1974, only a month before the latter's resignation.

Gerald Ford placed highest priority on continuing the SALT process, but he also managed to add one more treaty to those governing nuclear tests. Known as the Peaceful Nuclear Explosions Treaty (PNET), it was signed by Brezhnev and Ford in 1976. It is, in effect, a supplement to the TTBT, designed to eliminate the possibility that certain allowed "peaceful nuclear explosions" might be used as a cover for weapons tests exceeding the 150-kiloton limit. Like his predecessors, Ford in principle supported the goal of a comprehensive test ban treaty, but he did not conduct negotiations to that end. As he later put it, "You can only handle so many things on your plate at one time, and a test ban was not our highest arms control priority."[1] Like Johnson and Nixon before him and Carter after him, Ford put the highest priority on limiting, and ultimately reducing, the number and types of strategic weapons—that is, on the SALT process. Ford's summit meeting with Brezhnev in 1974 was devoted to this process, and so were the talks that took place under his direction at Geneva in 1975 and 1976.

First White House Review

Arms control is, as Paul Warnke once noted, an unnatural act. A new president must therefore always review the situation very carefully before proceeding. This was especially true for Carter, who was widely known to be eager to move in this area. Such a review provides the new president and those of his key associates who are inexperienced in the matter with the knowledge necessary for making sensible decisions. It also serves a more political purpose by helping to assure those who have substantial doubts about arms control that their concerns will at least be heard.

As usual, the review, or "interagency study," involved people from several different agencies and levels of government. In addition to the White House staff, these included the Departments of State and Defense, the Energy Research and Development Agency (which at that time funded the work of the nuclear laboratories), the ACDA, the CIA, the Joint Chiefs of Staff, and the Defense Nuclear Agency. The group's initial report, known as PRM-16 (Presidential Review Memorandum No. 16), confirmed Carter's intuition and led him to take the further steps necessary to set in motion the trilateral Comprehensive Test Ban negotiations of 1977–80.

The interagency study did not end the review process. Further studies to explore and elucidate the problems inherent in the negotiations themselves continued in and among the same agencies. It was my good fortune to be involved in two of them, one in the White House and one in the Pentagon.

The principal White House study was directed by Carter's science adviser, Frank Press, a geophysicist from MIT. Frank assembled a panel of experts including Hans Bethe, Richard Garwin, Carson Mark, W. K. H. Panofsky, Jack Ruina, and me. In addition, the two nuclear laboratory directors, Harold Agnew of Los Alamos and Roger Batzel of Livermore, sat regularly with the panel.

By that time, spring 1977, the argument over the utility of a test ban had come down to making a judgment about the relative value of two quite different factors, one of which weighed in on each side.

The main argument in favor of a test ban was that it was a necessary element of our nonproliferation policy. The Nonproliferation Treaty of 1970 called on the nuclear weapons powers to negotiate in good faith to end the nuclear arms race, and that was widely interpreted to require a comprehensive test ban as an early step. In 1975 the first quinquennial review of the nonproliferation regime focused major attention on this point. To be sure, nuclear proliferation had proceeded much more slowly than had originally been expected, but this situation could change quickly. A change was especially likely if the superpowers continued to engage in "vertical proliferation," a phrase meaning the development and deployment of ever more varieties of nuclear weapons in their own arsenals.

The main argument against a test ban revolved around the issue of stockpile reliability. Nuclear weapons experts pointed out that these devices were built of both chemically active and radioactive materials, which steadily undergo changes that can adversely effect their performance. Occasional full-scale nuclear tests would be necessary in order to assure that old weapons still worked. Even rebuilt weapons would inevitably include small, supposedly harmless changes in their manufacture, and these, too, would have to be subjected to full-scale tests to assure performance. Opponents of a test ban also argued that we needed to continue testing in order to build safer and more secure bombs, to develop bombs properly optimized for new delivery systems, and to learn more about weapons effects. Perhaps more important, continued testing was said to be needed in order to preserve a cadre of weapons design experts at the laboratories. In the absence of an experimental program, the experts would gradually move into more dynamic areas; when and if we ever needed them again, it would take a long time to reassemble or regenerate them. The Soviet laboratories, it was argued, would not suffer the same kind of loss in a test ban environment.

We studied the problem of stockpile reliability thoroughly and, except for the lab directors, decided that the nuclear establishment's worries were exaggerated. In brief, we concluded that regular inspections and nonnuclear tests of stockpiled bombs would uncover most such problems and provide solutions to them. Moreover, the laboratories could, if they tried, find ways around those that might remain. Agnew and Batzel disagreed. The in-house staffs in the Department of Energy and the Defense Nuclear Agency concurred with the laboratory directors, and the higher authorities in those agencies accepted their advice in the matter. The Joint Chiefs of Staff, whose nuclear arm is the Defense Nuclear Agency, also accepted the conclusions of the working-level experts immediately responsible for such matters. They really had no other choice.

Secretary of Energy James Schlesinger also felt that Carter was making a serious error in pushing ahead with a comprehensive test ban. Schlesinger had previously been chairman of the AEC, director of the CIA, and secretary of defense, and his views were based on his experiences in those posts. In an attempt to dissuade Carter, he arranged to have the president meet with Agnew and Batzel so that they could explain to him why further tests were needed.

This direct intervention by the laboratory directors at the highest level eventually caused quite a stir in the University of California, a stir that persisted for many years. The regents of the University managed the laboratories, and the directors were responsible to them through the university president. Most faculty members favored a test ban. In addition, a long series of faculty consultations had shown that roughly half of the faculty felt the university should not be operating the labs. It was therefore no surprise that many faculty reacted negatively when they learned about what they regarded as unwarranted political intervention by persons who were, ostensibly, spokesmen for the university.

I believe that the lab directors acted responsibly and properly. The president of the United States can consult with whomever he wishes. The consultants, in turn, are morally bound to tell him the truth as they see it. And that is exactly the way it happened. I, and many other members of the faculty, disagreed with the lab directors both on the facts and on their policy implications, but that was beside the point. I knew them both very well, and I had no doubt they told the president the truth as they saw it. I cannot fault them for having done so.

Harold Agnew has reported that the president took their arguments seriously. Others in a position to know say that Carter was not, in fact, persuaded by the substance of their arguments. He did, however, come to understand that the opposition to a test ban was deeper and stronger than he had realized. Pressing hard for a test ban could interfere with related objectives, particularly with SALT II. Carter therefore adjusted his priorities so that a comprehensive test ban would not come up for Senate ratification before SALT II could. He did not otherwise modify his drive for a comprehensive test ban. Everything I know confirms this second view, and not Agnew's, of this matter.

The other technical issue that absorbed our attention involved the threshold for detecting and identifying nuclear explosions in the Soviet Union. The same majority considered the threshold was low enough that we could detect any test explosion that could be of real use to the Soviets. The Department of Energy and laboratory representatives again disagreed.

In sum, the Press panel reconfirmed Carter's intuitive view that a comprehensive test ban was in our national interest and could be adequately monitored, and it reinforced his determination to proceed with negotiations.

An initial bilateral U.S.-Soviet meeting on the subject was held in Washington in July 1977. In October, trilateral negotiations among the British, the Soviets, and the Americans were initiated in Geneva. Paul Warnke, also simultaneously the director of the ACDA and the chief U.S. representative at most other arms control negotiations, headed the American team.

First OSD Review

Shortly after the Press panel started its review, I also began to work closely but informally with several individuals and groups charged with reviewing these same issues in the Pentagon. Among them were David McGiffert, assistant secretary of defense for international security affairs, and two of his aides, Walter Slocombe and Lynn Davis, all of whom were newly nominated to their posts by Harold Brown. Another was James Wade, a longtime high-level member of the Defense Department planning bureaucracy and a specialist in nuclear affairs. The new appointees all supported the president's quest for a CTB. Wade opposed it, and so did everyone else—civilian as well as military—on the nuclear side of the Pentagon.

I spent a lot of time working with Wade. Despite our differences over fundamentals, we were able to make joint studies of certain details of a test ban. Among other things we examined possible alternatives that might accomplish the same objective but be generally more acceptable in the Pentagon. These included threshold test bans limiting explosions to very low yields, in the kiloton range and even below. We also looked at various quota systems that might limit the number of tests per year to some very low number, perhaps just one. Such a regime might provide enough tests to handle the stockpile reliability problem while slowing the rate down so much that a serious nuclear arms race would no longer be possible. To put it differently, a very low limit would in effect put an end to so-called vertical proliferation.

None of the alternatives I could think of were of much interest to either the proponents or the opponents of a CTB. Those who believed testing was essential regarded them as totally inadequate for their requirements. Those who believed a test ban was the keystone for further progress in arms control felt the same. There were, it seemed, no in-between solutions. It had to be either a total comprehensive test ban or nothing. In this situation Harold Brown and those he had appointed to high positions in the Pentagon supported the president's objectives. Most of the military, including the Joint Chiefs of Staff and, essentially, the entire permanent civilian nuclear staff, opposed it openly and strongly.

I often discussed these issues privately with Harold, usually on Saturday afternoons, just after I had met with Wade. At one such meeting he asked me for my private view of a letter that had recently been addressed to the president by Dick Garwin, Carson Mark, and Norris Bradbury and made public by Senator Edward Kennedy.

That letter discussed the matter of stockpile reliability. In it the authors wrote that the key question to be answered was the following:

> Can the continued operability of our stockpile of nuclear weapons be assured without future nuclear testing? That is, without attempting or allowing *improvement* in performance, reductions in maintenance cost and the like, are there non-nuclear inspection and correction programs which will prevent the degradation of the reliability of stockpiled weapons?[2]

Garwin, Bradbury, and Mark answered their question with an unequivocal yes.

The three authors were well qualified to discuss the matter. Bradbury had been the director of Los Alamos for more than twenty-five years following World War II. Mark had been head of the laboratory's Theoretical Division for the same period of time, and Garwin was Garwin—an outstanding expert on many aspects of military technology, including nuclear weapons.

In my commentary on their letter, I first wrote that I agreed with the technical judgment presented there, but I immediately added that that did not settle the issue. What ultimately mattered was what the top leadership of our national security apparatus concluded and not what a small minority of former scientific leaders (myself included) might think. And my review of the situation made it clear that the "leadership does not have confidence in a stockpile in a hypothetical future in which testing has been banned for many years, and it is also clear that no amount of persuasion from the outside world would convert it from its current position."

Even if a CTB could somehow be put in place, I felt, it would not be politically stable:

> In my experience, the U.S. national security establishment, both the part currently in government and that just outside, is too high strung and nervous to live contentedly with a CTB. Horror stories would thrive in a CTB environment and agitation within the executive branch and in the general political arena would be widespread and constant. . . .
>
> I continue to believe that a CTB is in the best interests of the United States and the world, but I have doubts about the advisability of achieving a comprehensive test ban in a single step. . . . I am inclined to favor an intermediate step consisting of a simultaneous limit on yield (say 10KT) and on testing rate (say one or two per year) coupled with forthright presidential statement to the effect that we have stopped developing new nuclear weapons but we must from time to time conduct proof tests in order to assure the condition of our current stockpile. . . .

A Call from George Seignious

In late 1978 Paul Warnke, frustrated by the loss of too many arguments to Brzezinski, resigned from his posts as director of the ACDA and chief U.S. negotiator in several different arms control forums, including the CTB talks. George Seignious, a retired Army general, replaced him in his role as director, but not in any of the others.

Shortly after New Year 1979 Seignious telephoned to invite me to become the chief U.S. negotiator at the CTB talks. I was taken completely by surprise. I knew, of course, that the post was open, but I had not the slightest notion that I might be asked to fill it. When he added that if I accepted I would be given the title of ambassador, I could not immediately reply. My mind was suddenly flooded by the recollection of the time when, forty-one years before, I, then still in high school, had written to my congressman telling him I wanted to be an ambassador when I grew up and asking for his advice on how to go about it. I couldn't possibly have turned the post down.

When I got a grip on myself, I said I very probably would accept but should check with Sybil first. No other consideration—no conflicting duties at UCSD, for example—could possibly have led me to turn this proposition down. I put aside the doubts I had expressed to Harold only a few months before and once again prepared to sally forth in pursuit of a comprehensive test ban. Twenty years earlier Eisenhower had first persuaded me this was a good idea. If Carter now thought so, too, I was ready to give it my best. As I recall those moments, it all seems like a corny bit of melodrama, but that's the way it really was.

A few days later I was in Washington to prepare myself for the next round of negotiations, scheduled to begin only a few weeks later. I first visited Harold Brown. I told him I supposed this whole thing was his doing. He replied that the idea of my appointment had come up at one of the regular weekly lunch meetings he held with Secretary of State Vance and National Security Adviser Brzezinski. I then asked whether the decision was unanimous. Harold said, "No, I was against it, but the other two insisted." So much for an impolitic question and its answer.

I also visited the ACDA leadership and those on the White House staff—David Aaron and John Marcum—with whom I would be working directly. Some of the ACDA staffers expressed concern over my letter to Harold Brown in which I pointed out the inevitable military opposition to a CTB. I reassured them that I had, as they knew, long supported a CTB and still did. The military would, I said, continue to believe that a CTB would interfere with military preparedness, and the president had to take that into account. However, if this president—like his predecessors—determined that the political benefits overrode the technical drawbacks, I was more than willing to help him achieve his goals.

The Negotiating Team

Except for myself, the American CTB negotiating team consisted of persons carried over from Warnke's time. Happily for me, and for the good of the country, my old friend Gerald Johnson, who had been Warnke's deputy and Harold Brown's personal representative, agreed to stay in that position. Jerry was also a senior member of the SALT II negotiating team, the only person then serving on both delegations simultaneously.

The senior representative of ACDA (in theory, I represented the president, not the agency) was Alan Neidle, a professional Foreign Service officer and longtime tiller in the arms control vineyard. His zeal for success sometimes made him difficult to deal with, and the military and Energy Department representatives wanted him off the delegation. I decided I needed his experience, so I arranged for him to stay on for the next round.

General Edward Giller, USAF retired, represented the Joint Chiefs of Staff. Earlier, he had been the Energy Department representative on the interagency group that produced PRM-16. His bosses were against a test ban, and General Giller reflected their views accurately. This situation did, of course, carry the seeds of potential trouble, but Ed and I were old personal friends and had no difficulty in developing a good working relationship despite this fundamental difference. (When I was director of Livermore, Ed Giller was a young officer dealing with nuclear matters at the Air Force Special Weapons Center. We met then, and our careers crisscrossed in the ensuing years.)

Warren Heckrotte was one of several representatives of the Department of Energy. A fellow physics student at Berkeley many years before, he later joined the Livermore staff when I was director. While on the staff there, he became involved in nuclear test limitation questions as an adviser to the Department of Energy and the ACDA. In the early 1960s he served as a member of the U.S. team on the Eighteen Nation Disarmament Committee, and in the 1970s he was in Moscow when both the TTBT and the PNET were completed. All told, Warren has had more experience on negotiating teams than anyone else I know. He favored nuclear arms control in general but had some reservations about the practicality of a comprehensive ban on testing.

The British Delegation

Ambassador John Edmonds was head of the British delegation to the tripartite negotiations when I joined them.* Originally a naval officer, he had been able to transfer laterally to the Foreign Service when the British made drastic reductions in their navy after the Suez crisis of 1956. Later he also served as a diplomat at NATO headquarters, so he well understood the military and technical factors that called for nuclear tests as well as the political benefits to be gained from a ban on them. He was friendly, serious, pro-American, and typically English in his personal style, and we quickly developed a warm and lasting relationship. At first, Edmonds's deputy was Dennis Fakley, a nuclear weapons expert from the Ministry of Defense. Fakley was later replaced by Michael Warner, a senior civil service administrator in the same ministry.

The delegation also included several technical experts associated with the nuclear weapons establishment. Most were well known to the Americans who had been in similar work, and I had met several of them myself in that connection long before I had become involved in the negotiations.

The Soviet Delegation

Andronik Melkhonovitch Petrosyants was the head of the Soviet delegation.† The highest-ranking Armenian in the Soviet central government, he held the concurrent position back home of chairman of the State Committee for the Utilization of Nuclear Energy. His colleagues explained that his role in Moscow was equivalent to that of "an under secretary in your government" and that he preferred to be called chairman rather than ambassador. His responsibilities in this regard occasionally brought him into direct contact with the Soviet Politburo and with leaders of civil nuclear programs throughout the Soviet international system.

*Sir Percy Cradock headed the British team when the negotiations started. At the end of 1977 he left to become ambassador in Beijing. Up to that time Edmonds had been his deputy.
†Morokhov was the first head of the Soviet delegation. At the same time he was also Petrosyants's deputy back in Moscow at the State Committee for the Utilization of Nuclear Energy.

Short, balding, and already in his seventies, Chairman Petrosyants approached his job with considerable energy. He now and then showed a flare of temper, after which he would put on a wry smile and say something like "You know how it is; we southern peoples are very temperamental." (He still headed the civil nuclear program when the Chernobyl accident occurred, in 1986. I spotted him on a televised news conference that followed that disaster. He remained as feisty as he had been six years before.) He spoke only Russian, Armenian, and German. I could follow "diplomatic Russian" to a modest degree but could not make small talk in it, so he and I never had a conversation except through an interpreter. On rare occasions when we might meet without an interpreter present, I would comment on the weather in French, and he would do the same in German. That worked, but it probably didn't move the world forward very much.

Roland Makhmudovitch Timerbaev was the deputy head of the Soviet delegation. Half Russian and half Bashkir, he was a professional Foreign Service officer, dealing mainly with American and UN affairs, especially disarmament. His name was wonderfully contradictory. His mother had named him Roland after the medieval hero who kept the Moors out of France, his patronymic made him one of the sons of Muhammad, and the Timer in his surname came from the same root as that of Tamerlane, the scourge of Central Asia. He was well educated and spoke nearly perfect English. He knew a great deal about the facts and ideals of American politics and demonstrated a great curiosity to know even more. (As of this writing, he is deputy chief Soviet representative to the United Nations.)

Roland was an avid reader of the *International Herald Tribune,* and he occasionally quizzed me about the details of stories he read there. That newspaper also carried Art Buchwald's columns, and Timerbaev, like me, had been a Buchwald fan for years. All I needed to do was say, "Remember the one about Sidney in Santo Domingo?" and we would both laugh heartily. Roland would then name one of his own favorites, and we would both laugh again.

Colonel Boris Tarasov was the third-ranking member of the Soviet delegation. He was from the Defense Ministry and spoke only Russian as far as I knew. He got along well enough with his opposite number in our delegation, Ed Giller, but I can scarcely recall his saying anything at informal gatherings, even when nearly everyone else managed to loosen up a bit.

The Soviet team also included a number of technical experts who came and went according to the topics under discussion. They were usually either from the State Committee for the Utilization of Nuclear Energy, the Ministry of Defense, or the Academy of Science's Institute on Geophysics.

There were also, I believe, at least two KGB men on the Soviet delegation in my day. One was, in keeping with the common practice, the secretary of the delegation, the man we would call if we wanted to make contact at a time not otherwise prearranged. The other was Peter Pogodin, their chief interpreter. Peter prided himself on being able to write what he thought was passable English doggerel. It usually was crude, sometimes racist and anti-Chinese. Years later I ran into Pogodin again, at a Pugwash meeting in Bjorkliden, Sweden, in 1984. He showed up there unexpectedly, in addition to Pavlichenko, the KGB man who normally had that duty.

Instructions from Home

The delegations in Geneva were all on very short leashes. We had some local maneuvering room with regard to tactics and scheduling, but in general Washington, London, and Moscow controlled the substance of our discussions tightly. I could, of course, try to influence the substance of our negotiating position, but I did so not by working things out with my colleagues in Geneva but by dealing with higher headquarters via telex and scrambler telephone. Indeed, I was really effective in this regard only when I was back in Washington, between rounds. Then I could meet directly with the two "backstopping" groups, one chaired by John Marcum of the White House staff, and the other by Admiral Thomas Davies, the ACDA's assistant director for multilateral negotiations. In addition to these "working level" committees, the Cabinet-level Special Consultative Committee (SCC) would meet when problems appropriate to it arose, typically once during each recess. If I was in Washington at the time, I would join that meeting.

The SCC meetings were usually attended by the top officials of the agencies involved. Most of the members fully supported the president's goals. Two of them—General David Jones, chairman of the JCS, and Secretary of Energy James Schlesinger—openly did not. They deemed the test ban a bad idea. Anything that worked to slow the negotiations or prevent or constrain their outcome was a step in the right direction. I did what I could to moderate this opposition.

On one memorable occasion I met with the chiefs as a body in their headquarters in the Pentagon. All of those at the table except me wore four stars and so, it seemed, did their aides. I knew they were to a man opposed to the undertaking I represented. They were courteous, and I had met and come to know several of them before, but even so it was for me a tense time. Down deep I was a patriotic country boy. (My father, though never preachy about it, had repeatedly told me never to let the flag touch the ground.) I simply couldn't feel happy or relaxed face to face with our top military leaders while representing a course of action they all felt was not in our national interest. I had similar meetings with Energy Department officials, not including the secretary. In that case they were all people of a sort I was more accustomed to dealing with, and so their obvious hostility to my purpose was much less unsettling. In both instances I tried to explain why I thought the president's objective—to end all nuclear tests for all time—was in our national interest. I also looked for any modifications in our approach that might achieve nearly the same purpose but be less unacceptable to those with whom I was meeting. As in my earlier, similar attempt working with James Wade in OSD, I found no useful compromises.

As a result of these differences among the principals, the SCC itself often ended its meetings without being able to agree on a specific set of instructions to the delegation. When that happened, the various options and opinions would be taken by Brzezinski directly to the president. Carter would resolve them then and there on his own. Since Brzezinski himself was not really interested in a CTB, it is not surprising that this process often produced instructions I did not find particularly useful.

Locale and Schedule

The negotiations all took place in Geneva. Typically, the delegations would spend six weeks there, meeting with each other, and then return to their capitals for another six weeks. There we digested what had happened and worked with home officials on the development of instructions and tactics for the next round.

Our delegation made its headquarters on the Rue de Lausanne, a little over a mile from the place where the waters of Lake Geneva flow out into the Rhône. The building was called The Botanique, for a typically delightful and perfectly manicured Swiss garden park just across the street. The Geneva headquarters of the UN were only two blocks away, and many other world organizations were housed in the vicinity. The U.S. SALT delegation occupied the two floors above us; the U.S. delegation to the standing consultative commission and the U.S. ambassador to the international trade commissions were on floors below us. The ground floor was occupied by a lamp shop, which never seemed to have customers. Except for that, access to the building was controlled by Marine guards. Geneva might be a city dedicated to peace, but U.S. missions everywhere seemed to be fair game for terrorists. We could not be sure we were different.

Our Marines always wore their brightly colored uniforms inside our building, but not on the street, where doing so was prohibited by Swiss law. Their changing room was right next to my office, and occasionally they forgot where they were and became a little boisterous and noisy, but I was glad they were around looking after us, so I never objected.

The British delegation was housed in an office building nearby. The Soviet CTB delegation made its headquarters in the main Soviet mission to the UN, a large, walled-off compound near the Palais des Nations. When I first arrived, it was guarded by young KGB men dressed in civvies, but some months later they all suddenly sprouted dark brown uniforms like those the border guards wear all over the USSR itself.

Form and Style

The international meetings among the three delegations came in many forms and styles. The plenary sessions were the most formal. They occurred once or twice a week, depending on how fast things were moving. They were held on a rotating basis in each of the three missions, the host of the day serving as overall chairman. The entire professional membership of the three delegations, up to fifty persons in all, sat around a large table. Small placards in front of each head of delegation identified us, not by our names but by our countries: United States of America, Union of Soviet Socialist Republics, or United Kingdom. Only the three ambassadors spoke at the plenary sessions, always in their own language, and in short paragraphs followed by a sequential translation by the speaker's own interpreter.

The style and form of these plenary sessions served as a powerful reminder that we were not there on our own or to express our individual opinions. We were there purely as representatives of our various chiefs of government, and it was their opinions alone that we were presenting. It took a little getting used to, but it obviously had to be that way. (Years later I watched Henry Kissinger respond to a press question in which he was asked whether Anatoly Dobrynin, the longtime Soviet ambassador in Washington, had been honest and sincere. Kissinger said he did not know about that, but Dobrynin had certainly always been "accurate" and that was what mattered. Whatever he himself might have thought, he always fully reflected his bosses' views, and that was essential for effective state-to-state communication.)

The statements we made at the plenary sessions were, in general, read from papers that had been carefully prepared in a collaborative effort within each delegation. It was during these preparatory sessions that all members of the delegation (at least in those of the United States and the United Kingdom) had a chance to speak their minds and present the views of their home agencies. Once the statement was finally agreed, however, it became the sole responsibility of the ambassador to present it and explain it. Only the agreements made at the plenary sessions had any status in the negotiations. Details usually were, of necessity, elaborated in smaller working groups, but until the reports of these groups were accepted at a plenary, they had no formal standing.

When a plenary session ended, those present split into two groups. One group was made up of the "heads of delegation" and the other of the rest of those present. The remainder customarily stayed on in the main meeting room, where they gathered in small, informal subgroups to chat, drink tea or coffee, and eat cookies and peanuts. The "heads of delegation" group typically included the three highest-ranking persons in each delegation plus their interpreters, a total of twelve in all. This group retired to more comfortable quarters, typically a smaller room with a number of easy chairs and sofas arranged around a coffee table. On the table were decanters of coffee, tea, and orange juice and bottles of alcoholic beverages appropriate to the host mission. In our case that meant no liquor at all if the meeting was in the morning and both scotch and bourbon if it was later in the day. (When I arrived on the scene, no alcohol was served at the U.S. mission at any time of day, but I changed that under gentle chiding from the British. They explained that this was the reason the informal postplenary sessions were so much shorter when they were held at the U.S. mission.)

These "heads of delegation" meetings were more relaxed than the plenaries, but the first round of conversation nevertheless consisted of comments and questions by the ambassadors only. After the opening, however, others could speak and bring up topics they were especially concerned about. These smaller sessions provided an opportunity for further clarifying issues that had come up in the plenary. They were also typically used for elaborating the working calendar for the period immediately ahead—including, above all, the dates for adjourning the current round and opening the following one. Even in that case we followed a particular pattern. The Soviets often let us know by various indirect means what adjournment date they preferred, but they never formally proposed one. They always left that for the Western delegations. There must have been some bureaucratic reason for that ritual, but I never learned what it was.

Working groups also operated in a more relaxed way, partly because they were smaller and partly because they dealt with narrower questions. Ritual and formality still played a role, however. In particular, the ambassadors were, as a practical matter, forbidden to attend. On one occasion when I hinted I would like to be present to hear some of the arguments, it was made clear that the other ambassadors would then have to come, too, and that this would guarantee that nothing would be accomplished.

Less formal meetings of various other kinds also played an important role in moving the negotiations along. One type consisted of a carefully programmed sequence of trilateral lunches and receptions. The lunches were typically attended only by the "heads of delegations," as defined above. The receptions were for all of the members of all delegations, secretaries and other staff included. In addition, there was a carefully integrated rotating series of bilateral lunches.

The trilateral lunches might start out a little stiffly, but in time they loosened up. Alcohol was the main reason for the relaxation, but food and environment played a role as well. They usually went on for about two hours. Toward the end we inevitably raised toasts to success and the ladies, the latter in deference to a Russian custom. We toasted our wives, our mothers, and the female interpreters present. These references to women were never lascivious, just a bit maudlin.

There was also plenty of good humor on those occasions. I recall one bilateral lunch at the Soviet mission particularly. When it was just us "superpowers" off by ourselves, the Russians became even more relaxed. After the basic inhibitions of everyone present had been well washed away, the conversation somehow turned to the topic of Stalin's speeches. One of the Americans remarked that the formal records of these speeches, as published in the daily press and elsewhere, were always punctuated with frequent parenthetical remarks. These would range from a simple "Hurrah, Hurrah!" on through "Standing ovation" and up to "Prolonged standing ovation, with thunderous applause." I became a little concerned with this choice of topic, but, to my surprise, everyone seemed to find the matter very funny. Finally, one of the Soviets remarked, "You forgot the highest level." After a moment's pause he supplied it: "All rise and sing the 'Internationale.' " Everyone laughed at the preposterousness of it all, and then we went on to some simpler subject, perhaps another toast to our wives and mothers.

I am not a heavy drinker in real life, and I used all sorts of stratagems to avoid drinking more than I could easily handle. I thought I succeeded in general, but some of the photos the Russians took at these affairs— and then gave me—indicated otherwise (see the photo section for an example).

There were other, even smaller and more private meetings. These included many one-on-one meetings between John Edmonds and me. In them we could almost entirely ignore the long leashes that otherwise bound us and have really frank discussions about the problems we faced. I also had several useful two-on-two meetings with the Soviets. These always involved Petrosyants and Timerbaev (acting as both deputy and interpreter) on their side and usually just Jerry Johnson and me on our side. They invariably took place in Chairman Petrosyants's rather modest room at the Epsom Hotel and were always accompanied by the usual vodka and brandy with peanuts and potato chips. They were franker and freer than any other talks I ever had with the chairman, but a substantial gulf always remained. The language barrier and, even more, the political and historical differences between us were simply too great. Those factors did not, I believe, hamper the negotiations in any important way, but they did affect our personal relationship. To help make up for that, I was on a few very delightful occasions able to meet privately with Roland Timerbaev.

When Petrosyants was in Geneva, diplomatic protocol prevented private meetings between Roland and me. However, on a number of occasions the chairman had to be back in Moscow in connection with his job as head of civilian nuclear energy development; when he was, Roland became acting head of delegation and we could properly meet. The language barrier disappeared, and the even greater privacy helped overcome the other barriers as well. Even then, however, we both carefully avoided certain forbidden subjects—such as how many seismic stations the British might be persuaded to settle for—but we had good and fairly open discussions about other matters of mutual interest, including topics not directly connected to the CTB.

International Athletics

There was yet another and higher level of relaxation and informality: international athletics. One such event was a strictly U.S.–U.K. affair: an evening volleyball match in a local school gymnasium. To our surprise the British team included two men unknown to us but said to be from the local British chauffeurs pool. They added a lot of talent to the British team, but we won anyway. John Edmonds and I served as team captains, and we both stayed in there doing our best almost the entire time. It was great sport, but not enough to give any long-term aerobic benefit. Herbert Okun, my deputy at the time, marched up and down the sidelines with a reversible sign saying "Go Brits" on one side and "Go Yanks" on the other. Soon thereafter, but probably not for that reason, Herb was named ambassador to East Germany. In announcing the news to me, he said he was about to become an ambassador to a "real country," not merely to "initials," as I was.

Another memorable occasion involved all three delegations in a game of lawn bowling at John Edmonds's residence. We broke up into two teams, with Americans, British, and Soviets on each. The only difficulty we encountered was Peter Pogodin's penchant for stepping over the line when it was his turn to bowl. Happily for the good of the world at large, his Soviet teammates usually called him on it first.

The last athletic event I can recall took place at my residence in Coppet. It was during the later hours of an evening reception. The air was pleasantly warm, and many of the guests were on the patio overlooking Lac Léman. A solid young American naval officer and a burly Soviet technologist, both fairly far into their cups, were engaged in a very serious arm-wrestling match. Some others had already tested each other out, but those prior matches all ended easily and quickly one way or the other without incident. This contest stretched out with neither party winning. The men's faces turned deep red, and the air grew tense. Each of them had little tolerance for what the other represented. Each acted as though he absolutely had to win, and the rest of us, I included, became tense as well. To make matters worse, they were using a table with a glass top, and anything could have happened. I turned away for a moment, and it all suddenly ended. I don't remember who won, but they both walked away from the scene led by others in their own groups.

These special international contests aside, most of my physical activity consisted of hiking in the Alps and along the lake. Sybil and I took as much advantage of those glorious opportunities as time permitted, but the call of duty prevented me from doing anywhere near as much of it as I wished.

The Treaty and the Separate Verification Agreement

The Comprehensive Test Ban treaty was intended to be universal, and all states would be urged to accede to it. It would go into effect, however, as soon as the first twenty signatures were obtained, provided these included those of the United States, the United Kingdom, and the Soviet Union.

The main focus of attention of the tripartite negotiations, as well as of the negotiations within the governments in Washington, London, and Moscow, was less on the CTB treaty itself—that was seen as a relatively easy matter—than on an ancillary document, the so-called Separate Verification Agreement (SVA). This separate agreement would govern the way each of the negotiating powers satisfied itself that the other two were complying with the treaty. Each negotiating power had a long history of conducting tests, and each was much more concerned about compliance by its negotiating partners than by the world at large. (Of course, it was really the United States and the United Kingdom on one side concerned about the Soviets on the other, and vice versa, but the treaty and the SVA were drafted as though all three were independent actors.) Thus, although we always spoke of our negotiations as being about the CTB treaty, they were, in fact, very largely devoted to the separate, though closely coupled, SVA.

The three negotiating parties were very well aware there were two other overt nuclear powers in the world—France and China. We all knew that they would eventually have to become full partners in any comprehensive agreement to ban tests. For the time being, however, we tacitly agreed we could usefully go ahead without them. The two superpowers alone possessed over 97 percent of all nuclear weapons, conducted the great majority of all tests, and otherwise dominated the military scene. If those two, with the British, could work something out, then that treaty, or some modification of it, ought eventually to prove attractive to the others.

In any event, political realities dictated our going ahead without France and China. They made it clear they would not participate if invited. Moreover, the negotiations were already very complex and difficult with just three parties. Adding two more, each with its own, very particular views, would have made the negotiations impossible. In sum, we three not only believed we could profitably go ahead without the other two; we also knew that doing so was both necessary and desirable. We were making a virtue of necessity, not an uncommon practice in the diplomatic world.

Substance

During the first two Carter years, the CTB negotiations moved forward rapidly. They came closer to a successful conclusion than ever before. By the time I became chief negotiator, in January 1979, virtually all the general agreements needed to complete the treaty had been worked out, but only about half of the details. Persons with more experience than I thought we should be able to finish the whole process in six more months if we had sufficient "political will" in back of us. I agreed with that estimate.

By the end of 1978, general agreements covering four key issues had been achieved. First, national seismic stations (NSS), designed to detect and identify nuclear explosions, would be emplaced on the territory of each of the three negotiating powers. Second, there would be a provision for on-site inspections (OSIs) in case of ambiguous or suspicious events. Third, the treaty would run for a finite period, before the end of which another conference would be held to determine how and whether to continue it. Fourth, for at least the initial treaty period, nuclear explosions for "peaceful" or "economic purposes" would be outlawed, along with all explosions for the purpose of testing nuclear weapons. The main task still to be accomplished when I arrived on the scene was that of working out the remaining half of the details.

The national seismic stations, or NSS, were an old idea. Originally conceived back in the 1960s, they were then called black boxes. Their principal element was a seismometer that would be buried in the ground at carefully selected places on the territories of the contracting powers. The NSS would be operated by personnel of the host nation and provided with electrical power and communications facilities necessary to keep them going continuously and to transmit the data they produced out to a central collecting point in a timely fashion. Each seismometer would also be provided with a special "authenticator"—in essence, a device based on cryptological principles that manipulated the data in such a way as to guarantee that they were unchanged in any way.

Early in 1978 a subcommittee to work out the technical characteristics of the seismometers was set up. The original American position concerning the manufacture of the NSS was that, once the technical characteristics had been agreed, it did not matter where they were actually made, provided they met those characteristics. We, of course, would supply the authenticating devices needed to assure the reliability of the data, but the rest of the device could be manufactured anywhere, even in Outer Mongolia, as one American diplomat once put it. Later, under pressure from the Joint Chiefs of Staff and the Department of Energy, Carter changed the U.S. position to insist that any NSS deployed in the USSR had to be entirely manufactured in the United States. The Soviets never absolutely rejected that change, but they never accepted it either. They simply said that was not how they saw it.

As a first step toward fixing the locations of the NSS, the parties on each side had handed over a list of the general, approximate locations it wanted on the territories of the other.* In the next step, the receiving side would select a precise location within each limited general area. To the surprise of all parties, the question of the number and the location of NSS on British territory turned out to be by far the most difficult of the three cases. Although we did not anticipate it at the time, this issue proved to be the most intractable of the many internal problems faced by the negotiators.

There was a similar impasse concerning data transmission. The Western view was that seismic data must be made available very promptly, preferably in real time. We proposed satellite data relay as the best means for doing so. Indeed, given the remote locations of many of the sites, it was the only possible means. The Soviets expressed reservations about letting such data out of their country without the opportunity to examine them first. As they saw it, that probably excluded the possibility of satellite transmission, even within the USSR. The Soviets seemed to believe that we would somehow use this system to transmit illegally obtained data out of their country. I never could figure out how they thought we might do that, but something was obviously bothering them in this regard.

At the end of 1980, when we finally adjourned the Carter round of negotiations for good, most of these NSS issues were still unresolved.

---

*Here and in many other places, I recount the events as if the British and Americans made up one side and the Soviets another. Things did not always work out that simply.

On-site inspections had been a matter of contention between the Soviets and ourselves for many years. As far back as the Eisenhower administration, we had proposed them and the Soviets had rejected them. We wanted a specific annual quota of mandatory inspections. Except for a brief interval during the middle Khrushchev years, when they apparently were ready to agree to a very small quota, the Soviets always said no. In 1976–77 both sides made significant concessions in the area. We agreed to drop both "mandatory" and "quota" from our description of the idea. The Soviets agreed to accept the notion of "voluntary" OSIs in case of genuinely suspicious or ambiguous events.

The compromise involved a hierarchy of challenges and responses. For example, we would be required to explain the origin of our suspicions, and they would be required to reply directly and concretely to them. If we were not satisfied with their reply, we would request an OSI. If they then refused, we would have a prima facie case for accusing them of a violation, and we could take that accusation and the data to the UN Security Council, or to the world at large, and otherwise act as we saw fit. It may seem that there is a big difference between *mandatory* and *voluntary* OSIs, but there really isn't. If the Soviets were to cheat, they would certainly never allow foreign inspectors to find the evidence, regardless of any agreements to the contrary.

At the time I took over the negotiations, the parties had agreed to establish the Joint Consultative Commission, or JCC, modeled after the Standing Consultative Commission established by SALT I. The JCC would handle all the questions arising at the time of a suspicious or ambiguous event and manage the arrangements for an OSI. Most of the details of an OSI had been worked out, but some questions remained, including the maximum delay that could occur before they undertook their work. More important, we had not been able to agree on the kind of information that could be used in support of a claim for an OSI. The Soviets were insisting on the use of seismic data only, and we wanted to be able to use more general information. (The original U.S. position, back in the 1960s, had been that seismic data alone would trigger an OSI. When we accepted the notion of voluntary OSIs in 1977, we argued that the basis for asking for an OSI should no longer be so limited and that other physical evidence could be used as well. The Soviets seemed to fear that we might go so far as to base our requests on mere rumors.) Nor could we completely agree on the details of the tools and instruments the inspectors could bring with them. Most of these matters were still unresolved two years later.

Carter's original position on the duration of the treaty was that it should be forever. There would be, of course, the usual termination-for-cause clause, but there would be no allowance for periodic reconsideration. The Soviets, on the other hand, said the duration should be only three years. At the end of that time, we would reconsider the whole thing, and one of the factors that could influence whether or not it would be extended would be continued testing by others, meaning by France and China. The United States continued to insist on "forever" and on leaving out any references, however indirect, to France and China.

In the meantime, on the U.S. side, both the Joint Chiefs and the Energy Department also objected to "forever" and favored a finite, short duration. Bowing to the pressure on his right, Carter accepted the notion of a finite duration but set it at five years. The Soviets were surprised but pleased. A few months later, again in response to internal pressures, Carter accepted the idea of a three-year duration but continued to reject the idea that continued testing by others should be referred to explicitly in the treaty text.

In similar fashion many of the details relating to the connection between the Separate Verification Agreement and the CTB itself still remained to be resolved at the end of 1978, and so did such things as the precise wording of the preamble. Along with a number of lesser issues, most of these also remained unresolved when Reagan was elected president.

The Case of the British Seismic Stations

When, at the end of 1978, the CTB negotiators were considering the question of where the seismic stations should be deployed, everyone focused on the Soviet and American cases. Would the Soviets accept enough sites? Would they accept the locations we needed, or would they try to keep us out of certain sensitive but necessary areas? Would they pick sites in the United States on the basis of a genuine need or for some mischievous purpose?

No one anticipated problems with the British in this regard. Therefore, when on a gray, snowy day in January 1979, on which the men who should have been putting sand on the icy roads were out on strike, the British Cabinet finally got around to considering the Soviet proposal in detail and summarily rejected it, we were all caught flat-footed.[3]

The most serious problem the British had with the Soviet proposal concerned the locations. They made up, in retrospect, a very strange list:

Eskdalemuir, Scotland
Aldabra Is.
Brunei, Borneo
Tarawa Is.
Pitcairn Is.
Malden Is.
Port Stanley, Falkland Is.
Egmont Is., Chagos Archipelago
Belize, Br. Honduras
Hong Kong[4]

The first location, Eskdalemuir, a seismically quiet site in the northern part of Great Britain, made sense. Almost all the other sites were impossible. They seemed to have been selected by someone in Moscow using an old atlas or perhaps a child's stamp album as a guide. They made little sense in the modern world.

Belize had been self-governing since 1964 and was about to become independent in 1981. Tarawa and Malden were to become constituent parts of the independent republic of Kiribati that very summer. The sultan of Brunei had long had total control over internal affairs, and by the end of 1983 his country would be totally independent. None of these five locations would be on British territory at the time a treaty went into effect.

The Falklands and Hong Kong were worse. They could be expected to remain British for some time, but in each case a neighboring power raised conflicting claims of sovereignty. One can only imagine the reactions of either the Argentines or the Chinese to the Russians' installing instruments in those places in order to detect nuclear explosions on the territory of guess what adjacent country. In sum, seven out of ten sites were inappropriate, and five were even illegal.

I personally thought the Falkland Islands site made a lot of sense. Situated on the South American continental shelf, they made a good location for monitoring any nuclear tests in Argentina and Brazil, both of which had pointedly refused to ratify the Nonproliferation Treaty. The British government, however, was already anticipating the sort of blowup that actually happened only a couple of years later. It was totally unwilling to discuss anything touching on the Falklands—no matter how noble the purpose—with anybody, not even with its closest allies, and certainly not with the Russians.

The selection of Pitcairn Island posed a special problem all its own. There were no good port facilities on the island, so getting a complicated device like an NSS onshore and installed promised to be a formidable task. At one point later in the negotiations, Ambassador Edmonds and I tried to joke with Chairman Petrosyants about the problem. The occasion was a reception at my residence, and the three of us were joined only by Peter Pogodin, acting as interpreter. Edmonds went on at length, with plenty of hand gestures, explaining how the three of us would have to wade ashore through the surf carrying all this apparatus in our bare hands. Petrosyants looked more and more perplexed. Finally he turned to Pogodin and said, "What is this *Pitcairn* they are talking about?"

After that question was duly translated, Edmonds expostulated, "It is one of the islands *you* selected for an NSS!" Petrosyants snorted and changed the subject.

But a highly peculiar set of locations was not the only problem. Cost was another. We still did not know what the price of an individual NSS would be, but a few million dollars seemed likely. When multiplied by ten that came to a pretty penny by British standards. Up to this point no one seemed to have thought much about that issue. The Foreign and Commonwealth Office, which managed the negotiations, was not accustomed to spending that kind of sum on that sort of project. It turned naturally to the Ministry of Defense. There the problem was intercepted by Victor Macklen, an artful bureaucrat who used it to bring further internal consideration of the issue to a near standstill.

Macklen had long been an important figure in British nuclear circles. At the time he was deputy chief scientist in the Ministry of Defense, and thus Dennis Fakley's immediate boss. Adamantly opposed to a test ban himself, he was in close touch with those Americans who also were, including General Giller and Donald Kerr. Kerr and Macklen were, in effect, part of a larger group of insiders dedicated to thwarting Carter's desire to negotiate a test ban. Others especially effective in this regard were Admiral Bob Monroe, the chief of the Defense Nuclear Agency; Julio Torres, one of Kerr's assistants; and the notorious Richard Perle, then still on Senator Henry Jackson's staff. Each was an experienced bureaucratic infighter; all were determined to stop any progress toward a test ban, no matter what their top national leaders might think or want. In this instance Macklen, with whatever help his American coconspirators were able to give him, used the NSS issue to develop opposition to the nine remote NSS within British defense circles. There the possibility of having to spend even a farthing on them was especially unwelcome. This opposition evidently played a role in persuading Prime Minister Callaghan on that gray January day to reject the Soviet list of sites.

This turn of events took all the delegations by surprise. I, of course, had just arrived on the scene of the negotiations themselves, so everything was new and, often, surprising to me. This development, quite obviously, amazed my experienced colleagues as well.

The Soviets, when we informed them a few weeks later, were even more astonished. Once they had caught their collective breath, they flatly rejected the British proposal that there be only one NSS on their territory. We supported the British position by pointing out what a small country the United Kingdom is, but the Soviets would have none of it. This is a political issue, they said, not a technical one, and so it must be resolved on the basis of an appropriate political principle. In this case that principle was clearly the principle of equality. Furthermore, in their technical judgment, no NSS were needed anywhere. The current deployment of seismographs all over the world was adequate for the job and did not need to be augmented. They understood, however, that the U.S. Senate would never ratify a treaty without NSS on Soviet territory, and so they were willing—for that basically political reason—to accept NSS as a condition for a CTB. In sum, they said, either there are ten stations in the USSR, ten in the United States, and ten in the United Kingdom or it's 1-1-1, or 0-0-0, but never, no never, 10-10-1.

To emphasize the seriousness of the issue, the Soviets went on to say there was no point in holding further discussions on the technical characteristics of the NSS until we could settle the matter of their number.

As soon as we understood just how serious the number issue was, we started to look for a suitable compromise. Perhaps if the British could be persuaded to come up to some other number—not ten, but more than one—the Soviets would come off their 10-10-10 stance.

But before we could even begin to work out a compromise, an additional complication intervened. The political situation in London made it necessary for Callaghan to call for new elections. Very quickly, I knew, London would become totally absorbed in these events. If anything was to be done, it had to be done fast. I decided to do something slightly out of line for a CTB ambassador. Instead of going through the ACDA bureaucracy, as was the norm, I sent an encrypted telegram explaining the situation directly to Secretary of State Vance. (All of the hundreds of daily telegrams from U.S. ambassadors to their home offices are addressed to the secretary of state, but he does not normally receive or read them unless certain extra words are added to their routing instructions. In this case, I used those extra words.)

I suggested that Vance intervene personally in the matter. He seemed willing, but the idea raised a storm of objections at both ideological extremes. The ACDA said, no, we should insist that Britain accept ten, just like the big boys. The Joint Chiefs of Staff and the Department of

Energy said, no, we should not suggest a compromise, because the British are right. It also quickly became clear that any suggestion that the United States supply the British with NSS free of charge would be fought tooth and nail by those who wanted no treaty at all.

This conjunction of arguments created an impasse within the U.S. government that was too hot for the working-level backstopping group to handle. The issue had to be considered by the Cabinet-level SCC before Vance could intervene with his British counterparts. That process would take much more time, and before it could happen, Britain had a new government, with Margaret Thatcher at its head.

Prime Minister Thatcher had been educated as a chemist. Like Jimmy Carter, who had a background in nuclear engineering, she felt she could personally understand the technical details of the test ban issue. On looking into them, she decided she was against it. Even before she took office, some opponents of the treaty, probably Victor Macklen and perhaps one of the American opponents as well, met with her and presented their side of the argument, which she accepted. Later, when the American and British negotiators finally had a chance formally to propose that she accept more than one NSS on British territory, her response was, in effect, "If one was good enough for Callaghan, one is certainly good enough for me." In essence, her government continued to follow the U.S. lead and to support the U.S. position that a CTB was in the Western interest, even though she personally had reservations about it. Whenever difficulties arose in the negotiations, however, she did nothing to help overcome them.

(In 1985, long after the end of the Carter round of negotiations, I had a chance to discuss this whole episode individually with Jimmy Carter and David Owen, the British foreign minister in the Callaghan government. They both firmly recollected that a compromise in which three NSS would be placed on British territory had been worked out. I was very surprised by that claim and said so. However, each man independently stuck to his story, though neither could recall further details. It seems possible, therefore, that in some completely private venue Vance and Carter had agreed to that idea, and then presented it to Owen, who also accepted it. But whatever may have been privately discussed and tentatively arranged, it had no official status whatsoever. Neither Edmonds nor I, despite much urging and prying, ever got a number from either of our headquarters different from one, even on a very informal or confidential basis.)

At the same time when I was trying to persuade the British to accept some number of NSS greater than one, I was doing my best to persuade

the Soviets that one was just right. On more than one occasion I noted
that the Soviet Union was a very large country and that at least ten
seismic stations would be needed to monitor events on its territory. The
United States is big, too, so ten stations are justified there as well. But
the United Kingdom is a comparatively small country, for which one
station surely suffices.

Petrosyants generally stuck to his argument that the matter was
purely political in nature and that my technical arguments were therefore irrelevant. Once, however, he replied directly to them.

"Da," he said proudly, holding his hands out in a wide gesture
confirming great size, *"Sovietskii Soyuz ogromnaya strana*—Yes, the
Soviet Union is a huge country."

Holding his hands somewhat closer together, he went on to say, "And,
the United States, too, is a big country."

Then he gestured even more broadly with both hands and waved his
ten fingers in all directions, adding, "But the British Empire is all over
the world!"

To personalize the whole affair, he said he was less concerned about
Ambassador Edmonds's testing his own bomb in some remote place,
than about Edmonds's allowing Ambassador York to test one of his on
British territory. That happened in the past, he noted, so why not again?

The matter of the British NSS remained unresolved for the rest of the
negotiations. The British position continued to be that one was enough.
The American position, as presented to the Soviets, was that the British
position made good sense. The American position, as presented to the
British, was that they ought to accept some small number of NSS on
overseas territories. The Soviet position was that the British and American positions were unacceptable and that they could not sensibly discuss anything else about seismic stations until that basic question was
resolved.

Other NSS Issues

During the next two years the Soviets made two exceptions to their
refusal to discuss the technical characteristics of the NSS. One instance
involved a visit by Soviet specialists to the Sandia Laboratory and other
U.S. institutions where our version of the NSS was being developed.

The invitation to the Soviets had originally been made in the fall of
1978, when Paul Warnke was still ambassador. When the Soviets finally
accepted it—some six months later, on my watch—I expressed my

pleasure. I immediately informed Washington, expecting the authorities there to proceed promptly with all the necessary arrangements. To my horror, Washington wired back instructing me, in effect, to hold on, to avoid making any final agreements about the visit, even regarding dates, until certain problems could be worked out. Bureaucratic opponents of a test ban had raised several eleventh-hour issues—including those of security and funding—and until these were resolved I was to do nothing more. The opponents were not concerned about the issues themselves; they simply wanted to delay or, if possible, stop the whole process.

I found myself in an extremely awkward position. On the one hand, I was telling the Soviets how pleased the United States was that they had finally accepted its invitation. On the other, I was declining to agree to any specific arrangements, even to the date we would accept them. "We are still working out the mechanics," I said on more than one occasion. "I will let you know about them as soon as I can."

I felt as precarious as a tightrope walker, but somehow we managed to bring off the visit in the summer of 1979. As Jerry Johnson often remarked, the most difficult times were when the Soviets unexpectedly said yes.

The other exception to their refusal to talk about technical characteristics came in 1980. To our surprise they suddenly agreed to discuss those of the down-hole components of the seismometers themselves, but still not those of any of the support equipment, including that needed to record or communicate the data. Additional experts from all three countries temporarily joined the negotiations. The academician Mikhail A. Sadovsky, a very distinguished Russian scientist and head of the Soviet Institute of Geophysics, was among them. In just a few weeks we were able to work things out to everyone's satisfaction. The agreement on those technical characteristics turned out to be the last substantive thing we accomplished.

Stopping Over in London . . .

Every time Sybil and I went to Geneva to start a new round, we stopped over in London. We did the same on our way back home six or so weeks later. Happily, Rachel and John were living in London at the time. They had a house in Islington, which, though typically small and narrow, had an extra room just right for us.

At least once during each round trip, I checked in at the Foreign and Commonwealth Office in Whitehall. Edmonds and his equivalent of a backstopping group were headquartered there. We used the opportunity to make certain the two Western parties understood each other's positions and purposes, especially on matters on which they differed somewhat.

I also occasionally met with officials in the Ministry of Defense, including Victor Macklen. The people there were obviously troubled—to put it mildly—by the whole affair, and I wanted to understand their position as well as I could. On one stopover General Giller exercised his nuclear connections and arranged for several of us Americans to visit Aldermaston, the site of the AWRE, the British Atomic Weapons Research Establishment. We were able to have a good discussion about the British experience during past moratoriums (including a long self-imposed one) and to learn more about their hopes and plans for future tests at the Nevada Test Site. The close cooperation between the American and the British nuclear establishments was manifest. As I saw it, it benefited both sides—but, of course, especially the junior partner, Britain.

That relationship had its origins in the Manhattan Project itself. After the war it fell off for a time to virtually nothing, and the two parties proceeded along separate ways. In the 1950s cooperation was reestablished, gradually and tentatively at first. In May 1957 I was invited to be one of two U.S. representatives to witness the first British thermonuclear test, staged out of Christmas Island and conducted over Malden Island, in the mid-Pacific. I estimated the yield from the fireball size and found it relatively modest. I wondered about the design, but my hosts were not allowed to tell me anything about it. Now in 1979, more than twenty years later, the relationship was more intimate. In an utterly different context, one presumably devoted to stopping nuclear tests rather than to promoting them, I finally got a close look at the details of the bomb itself. My yield estimate had been correct, but the design turned out to be more advanced than I had guessed.

Much of the work at Aldermaston at the time was devoted to the Chevaline program, whose purpose was to provide a suitable warhead for the British Poseidon submarines. Considered in the context of British military preparedness only, the people at the Ministry of Defense and the AWRE did indeed need more tests to achieve their objectives. Considered in the larger context of international security as a whole, the world—including Britain—needed to move away from its heavy dependence on nuclear weapons. From the point of view of those in the nuclear establishment, the first set of considerations was compelling.

From that of my new friends and colleagues in the Foreign Office, the second set was compelling. It was a microcosm of the situation in Washington, with only irrelevant differences in the details.

My frequent trips to London also allowed me to renew my close working relationship with Lord Solly Zuckerman. Solly, originally a zoologist, had become a major figure in British defense affairs during World War II. When I was working in the White House and Defense Department in the late 1950s and early 1960s, Solly served as chief science adviser to the Ministry of Defense; later he was adviser to the Cabinet as a whole. At that earlier time we saw each other often on official business, usually in Washington. Now, at the time of the CTB negotiations, he was in his seventies, formally retired from his principal government and university posts and living in Burnham Thorpe, in the northern part of East Anglia. Despite his formal retirement, he remained very active in London affairs. Not only did he participate in debates and other activities in the House of Lords, but, more important, he also maintained a place in the Cabinet Office in Whitehall. He strongly supported the push for a test ban and did what he could to overcome the opposition at No. 10 Downing Street and in the Ministry of Defense. To that end, he arranged for Sir Robert Armstrong, then newly appointed secretary of the Cabinet, to spend a weekend with me at Burnham Thorpe. Our joint purpose was to bring Sir Robert up to date on the negotiations and to make sure he fully understood the official American view of them. It was typical of Solly's approach to such problems—and, I believe, a successful and useful weekend.

Solly also was long (1955–84) head of the London zoo, a position he never fully relinquished, no matter what else he was doing. I took advantage of this side of him, too, and arranged for Cynthia, then a veterinary student at UC Davis, to spend two weeks working behind the scenes at the zoo. Solly was tied up when she first arrived, and planned to meet her at lunch toward the end of her stay. On the scheduled day Lord Mountbatten, last viceroy of India and Solly's longtime friend and close colleague, was assassinated by Irish terrorists. Cynthia lost that opportunity to meet Solly, and another never came. The long arm of terrorism reaches out and touches people in unexpected ways.

... and in Moscow

I wanted to visit Moscow, too, to see if there was anything I could do there to help clear the air and move the negotiations forward. That, however, was not as casually or as easily arranged as a stopover in London. I had to have a formal invitation. To get one, I regularly reported my visits to London to the Soviets. I boasted about how useful they were in moving things along and hinted that a visit to Moscow might do the same. In the summer of 1979, after several such hints, they extended an invitation to me for a visit by three U.S. officials and their wives. In June, Jerry and Mary Kay Johnson, Sybil and I, and John Marcum, my anchorman on the NSC staff, arrived in Moscow.

We first visited various elements of the State Committee for the Utilization of Nuclear Energy—Petrosyants's Moscow base—and the Geophysical Institute. That was very interesting, but not particularly relevant to our negotiations. We then made a side trip out to Obninsk, where we visited the "first-in-the-world" nuclear power plant and the underground seismic laboratory. There they showed us some of the seismic detection technology they had in mind for monitoring a test ban. The equipment was heavier and otherwise more crudely built than ours, but it did seem to measure seismic signals adequately, or nearly so.

The most important part of the trip was a brief visit with Georgi Kornienko, first deputy foreign minister and longtime expert on American affairs. He spoke excellent English, as did most of the other Soviets present, so no interpreters were needed. The meeting, however, did not go as I had hoped. Another of those pieces of bad luck in timing that have plagued the CTB for decades intervened.

Just weeks before our arrival in Moscow, the United States had detected an explosion at Semipalatinsk, in central Siberia, that appeared substantially to exceed the limits set by the Threshold Test Ban Treaty. That treaty was, unhappily, still unratified by the United States, but both sides had pledged to live within its restrictions. There were large uncertainties in our estimates of yields, and it was entirely possible that this recent one had not exceeded the limit, but it seemed to. At the last minute we received instructions to make the matter of this apparent violation the first order of business. We therefore opened our discussions by asking for more information about it. Kornienko smiled coldly and flatly denied they had exceeded the threshold then or at any other time.

He then added something we already knew. If we wanted to improve our ability to measure the power of such explosions, we could easily do so by ratifying the Threshold Test Ban Treaty. When we ratified, they would supply the additional geophysical data the treaty called for, and then perhaps we would be less prone to overstate the size of their explosions. We continued to speak past each other for a few more minutes, but to no result except to spoil whatever chance this visit might have provided for helping the CTB negotiations. In retrospect, I do not believe we could have accomplished very much in any event, but you never know, and it's always worth a try. We—or maybe the Russians—muffed that one.

Last Days in Geneva

As November 1980 approached, all of us, British and Soviets included, focused more and more attention on the forthcoming American presidential elections. Usually the incumbent—in this case Jimmy Carter—has a distinct advantage. This time, however, the negative impact of the ongoing crisis in Tehran began to make it look as though the challenger, Ronald Reagan, had a good chance to win.

In late October, a few weeks before the actual election, we obtained a videotape of the Reagan-Carter debate and arranged a private showing at the main U.S. mission to the UN offices in Geneva. Most of the British and the English-speaking Russians attended. They were not happy with what they saw. Obviously, Carter supported our efforts and could be expected to continue to do so. Almost as obviously, Reagan did not. Those who understood U.S. politics well—Edmonds and Timerbaev, in particular—felt that Reagan had won the debate and probably also the presidency. The future of the negotiations was in doubt, to say the least.

The elections were scheduled for November 5, just two days before the celebration of the anniversary of the Great October Revolution. The Russians wanted to be back in Moscow for that occasion. It is, I learned, a family holiday as well as a patriotic celebration, and it is accompanied by much partying and drinking. The Soviets therefore proposed that we adjourn the present round early enough for them to get back to Moscow for the festivities, and that meant before the U.S. election. I disagreed, saying we simply had to know how the U.S. election came out before we left Geneva. The Soviets put forth all sorts of arguments, including a plea that the academician Sadovsky, then a temporary member of the delegation, had to get back for his seventy-fifth birthday celebration with his family. Petrosyants also suggested we prepare two separate contingency plans for the future, one for each possible president. I insisted we needed to know the final outcome in order to focus our minds properly.

Petrosyants then made a Solomonic decision. Half the delegation would go home for the big party, himself and Sadovsky included, and the other half would stay in Geneva with Timerbaev as acting head. That satisfied me, so we all agreed and set adjournment for November 12.

The election made us all lame ducks, Soviets and British as well as Americans. Neither Edmonds nor Timerbaev wanted to believe it was over. I knew it was, certainly for me personally and very probably for all of us.

I had a number of private meetings during those last days with John and Roland. Roland said these negotiations may well have been our last chance for making a test ban treaty that would effectively reinforce the nonproliferation regime and thus prevent the nuclear genie from getting totally out of control. He was obviously sincere. I told him I agreed with him.

We had one last plenary, at which I announced my final instructions from Washington. I was to fix no date for resumption. That would be determined later through diplomatic channels.

Later never came.

The Many Causes of Failure

In retrospect it is clear that the failure of the Carter round of CTB negotiations was very overdetermined. Several major problems arose, any one of which would have assured failure by itself. Certain groupings of lesser problems could have had the same effect. All of the main problems were external to the negotiations; most of the lesser ones were intrinsic to them.

The intrinsic problems arose both at the international level—that is, in the form of differences between the negotiating parties—and at the national level, as differences within the various national bureaucracies. Among the most important problems at the international level were the matter of the number of seismic stations, differences over both the form and the content of on-site inspections, and arguments about the treaty review process and the eventual role of France and China in it. All of these problems could probably have been resolved eventually, but failure to do so for any of them would have resulted in no treaty.

In Washington, at the national level, the most important of the intrinsic problems was the continuing total opposition to any CTB by powerful elements in the military and in the upper reaches of the Department of Energy. In addition, real differences over important details among those who favored a test ban, or who were at least tolerant of one, hampered progress throughout Carter's presidency.

In London important elements of the Ministry of Defense and, after May 1979, the new prime minister, Margaret Thatcher, took a dim view of the whole idea. The arguments over the numbers of NSS and how they would be paid for only made things worse.

There may have been important unresolved differences in Moscow also. Soviet reluctance to accept certain of our requirements for on-site inspections seemed to reflect one such difference. The Politburo, led by Brezhnev, had evidently decided that OSIs were both necessary and tolerable. That historic breakthrough was surely not easily accepted by the secret police. As usual, direct evidence of such a difference was hidden very effectively, but it cannot be that the KGB officers threw their hats in the air and cheered when they received the news about the Politburo's decision. The best evidence of this was the repeatedly expressed concern that our hidden purpose was somehow to obtain what they always called "information not necessary for purposes of verification." In any event, even though the Soviet government had accepted OSI in principle at the start of the Carter round, Soviet negotiators continued to argue over essential details until the very end. As always, we wanted easier, quicker, and surer access, and they wanted more restrictions on what we could do.

It is probable that with sufficient "political will" in the three capitals, these internal problems could have been overcome eventually. But before that proposition could be tested, three major external events intervened. Any one by itself would have eroded the available political will below the level needed for success. With the occurrence of all three in quick succession, the chance for a successful outcome dropped to zero.

The first to appear was a collection of disputes and delays experienced in the SALT II negotiations being conducted at the same time. Some of these were matters intrinsic to SALT itself; others were the result of external events. The most important intrinsic arguments were those over Soviet data encryption and the Soviet Backfire bomber. While these were still on the table, Deng Xiaoping, the Chinese leader,

paid a state visit to Washington. The visit, which seemed to portend
further improvements in U.S.–China relations, annoyed the Soviets. As
long as news of Deng's visit was still reverberating in the world at large,
the Soviets stalled in Geneva. As a result, when SALT II was finally
signed in Vienna on June 18, 1979, it was already more than half a year
behind schedule.

Then, in August, just as Senate consideration of the treaty was about
to begin, Senator Frank Church suddenly raised the issue of a supposedly "new" battalion of Soviet troops in Cuba. It took months for
Washington to discover not only that the battalion had been there all
along but also that President Kennedy had known of it and implicitly
agreed to its presence. Before this tangle of errors could be unraveled,
two more disasters occurred.

The first was the capture of the American embassy in Tehran by a
band of "student" followers of Ayatollah Khomeini. The ayatollah had
recently become the only real power in Iran, and no one in Washington
knew how to deal with him. As the weeks and months wore on with no
resolution in sight, the image of the helpless giant being tormented by
the Lilliputians took hold. Any action anywhere that could possibly be
characterized as weak—or even accommodating—became unacceptable to more and larger segments of the U.S. body politic. Negotiating
with the Soviets, even in the absence of information linking events in
Tehran to Moscow, took on that color.

Important as this political link between events in Tehran and negotiations in Geneva may have been, the mechanical linkage was more so.
After the capture of the embassy, it became a practical impossibility to
get either the president or any Cabinet-level group, including the SCC,
to focus on the CTB negotiations or any other such side issue. The
bureaucratic opponents of the CTB were quick to take advantage of that
situation. They more and more often claimed that even minor questions
required Cabinet-level consideration. Since such consideration could
not be obtained, we American negotiators began to find it ever more
difficult to respond to even the smallest propositions or questions our
negotiating partners raised. Not only the political will to negotiate but
even the ability to do so, in the mechanical sense, was destroyed by the
events in Tehran.

As if all that had not been enough, the Soviets invaded Afghanistan
only seven weeks later. That disaster happened during our Christmas–
New Year recess. Before we went back to Geneva, the White House
instructed us to proceed very slowly with the negotiations and not to
engage in any overt social interactions with our Soviet counterparts. In

addition, I was ordered to open the next round of negotiations with a formal condemnation of the invasion before proceeding with the substance of our work. The British ambassador had parallel instructions. Since the same thing was happening in all other U.S.–Soviet diplomatic contacts, the Soviet CTB delegation was expecting it. They listened stone faced and said very little in reply, and we all then went on—albeit very slowly—with the main business at hand.

Other reactions by Carter also affected our negotiations, although not so directly. For one thing, he ordered tighter controls on the transfer of high technology to the Soviets. U.S. opponents of the CTB asserted that these expanded controls covered certain components of the seismic stations, and they tried to achieve yet more delay on the basis of that claim. More surprising, even the cancellation of the Olympics entered into our negotiations. During one of our semiformal "heads of delegation" meetings, Petrosyants suddenly proposed a toast to the Olympic Games. As an undiplomatic act, it deserved some sort of gold medal itself. God only knows what inspired him. Ambassador Edmonds, I, and the other Westerners present sat with our arms folded and scowled. All the Russians raised their glasses. Except for their leader, all of them were obviously sorely embarrassed by this unexpected turn of events. As they normally did in such cases, they stared with great determination at the floor or straight ahead at the opposite wall, carefully avoiding eye contact with any of us. I made some strongly negative comment, which I cannot remember, and we adjourned that meeting immediately thereafter.

Any one of these major developments alone would have doomed the CTB negotiations. It took some time for the seriousness of the problem with SALT II to become evident. When the embassy was first captured, we again could not know how long that miserable event would drag on. There thus remained, for a while, hope that the problems confronting us, external as well as internal, would be resolved in due time. But after the Soviet seizure of Kabul, it was obvious that all was lost.

I had to reflect on my own position in all this. Was there a point to going on, even in the face of such odds? Winston Churchill's one-liner "Jaw, jaw, jaw is better than waw, waw, waw" came to mind. Our government and, evidently, those of the United Kingdom and the USSR had clearly decided not to cut off all contacts. In particular, they intended to go on with the kind of exercise that engaged us. I easily concluded that continuing with the talks was clearly worth my personal time and effort. Talking is indeed better than many of the alternatives.

We took the restriction on social relations seriously. We no longer invited the Soviets to evening receptions, though we did maintain the custom of a rotating series of working lunches. Similarly, we declined invitations to come to their embassy to celebrate their various patriotic holidays.

I made one exception to the rule on socializing. When Timerbaev's wife, Nina, came to visit Geneva for a few weeks, I arranged for her and Sybil to have a quiet lunch at our residence in nearby Coppet. During my two years at the negotiations, she was the only Soviet wife who came to Switzerland. Most of the Americans, and many of the British, had their wives with them all of the time, but not the Soviets. Nina's visit, then, was a special and unusual occasion. In addition, she was a delightful person, with lots of verve and sparkle.

Sybil and Nina even talked about the Olympics, but not in the negative and provocative style of Petrosyants's toast. Nina and her working group back in Moscow had put in much overtime on peripheral activities intended to help make the games a success, and she had been looking forward to them as a bright and hopeful event. The withdrawal of the Americans was a major blow to those plans and hopes, and she was personally sad that it had happened. She did not, however, comment on whose fault it might have been.

What of the Future?

The most decisive of the factors causing the failure of the Carter round of CTB negotiations were all accidents peculiar to that time. If they had not happened, how would our negotiations have come out?

I am certain that with an adequate level of political will on the part of both Carter and Brezhnev, and despite the doubts of Thatcher, we could have achieved a treaty satisfactory to all three parties. Carter would have had to put down some of the more extreme demands of internal opponents of a CTB, including those relating to the treaty review process and the real-time reception of NSS data. Brezhnev would have had to accept basically our version of the on-site inspections. And both Brezhnev and Thatcher would have had to admit that there were numbers between one and ten, such as three. It would have required some hard work and some compromises, but it could have been done.

But what then? Would the treaty have been ratified? Aye, there's the rub! The Founding Fathers of our Republic were determined to avoid "entangling alliances," and they created machinery designed to assure just that. The most important and enduring element of this machinery is the requirement that treaty ratification be approved by a two-thirds vote of the Senate, the less representative of our two legislative bodies. That peculiarly American requirement kept us out of the League of Nations in 1919 and for fifty years blocked ratification of the 1925 convention outlawing chemical warfare. More generally, it has caused presidents to hesitate and lose opportunities on other occasions. It would, I fear, have blocked ratification of a CTB even if we had been able to elaborate one agreeable to the president in 1979 or 1980, and even if none of the external impediments had existed.

In retrospect my thirty years' experience with this issue tells me that probably at no time since the cold war started would the Joint Chiefs of Staff have endorsed—or even quietly acquiesced in—a comprehensive test ban, and, given that, no Senate would have assented to ratification.

The JCS and their allies in the nuclear community have used a number of arguments in opposing a CTB. Foremost among them are doubts about verification and the claimed need for tests to assure the continuing reliability of our stockpiled weapons. They believe what they say about those issues, but their real opposition is even more fundamental. In their view it simply makes no sense to halt weapons testing in a world where nuclear weapons are, and promise to remain, the cornerstone of our security policy. They are willing to accept a prohibition on the kind of tests that cause direct harm, such as tests in the atmosphere, but they see no sense in limiting tests that do not. They are, of course, strong supporters of our nonproliferation policy, but they do not agree with the claim that a CTB is essential to limiting further proliferation. The Joint Chiefs and the nuclear establishment do, in general, support arms control agreements that limit or modestly reduce the numbers of weapons or that restrict weapons altogether in certain areas, such as nuclear free zones. They will not, however, willingly endorse or acquiesce in restrictions on the tests needed to maintain readiness or to support the kind of modernization that is always under way in the military establishment.

In sum, however desirable a CTB may be, it seems not to be a promising option under current world conditions. Moreover, if another president were again to push hard for a CTB, doing so would, as it did in Carter's time, make it much more difficult for him to achieve other and, I think, more valuable forms of arms control, such as that involved in the SALT and the START negotiations.

After thirty years of actively working for a CTB, I have again been forced to conclude that one will be politically possible and stable only in a world in which the great powers are clearly and forcefully moving away from their current dependence on nuclear weapons. In a world in which strategic arms limitations and other nuclear restrictions were the order of the day, a CTB would not only be possible but even strongly reinforce those other actions. In a world like the one we currently have, however, a world without that precondition, a freestanding CTB is apparently not viable. (Nevertheless, I believe many other forms of arms control are currently possible, given a properly inspired and competent administration. I specifically include SALT-like limitations and reductions, the elimination of battlefield nuclear weapons, nuclear free zones in sensitive places, and the like. A CTB, uniquely among mainstream arms control proposals, draws an especially hostile response.)

In 1979 when President Carter invited me to be chief negotiator, I set such thoughts aside. The excitement of the opportunity and the hope that he could achieve controls on arms across a broad front combined to overcome my doubts, and I marched forth full of optimism. I would do it all over again under similar circumstances. Someday someone must succeed.

Wasn't it frustrating? Friends back home frequently ask that question. The answer to it is short and simple. Yes, it was, but working things out in the Washington bureaucracy was much more frustrating than dealing with the Russians.

Are they serious? It is seldom easy to decide exactly when the Soviets are serious and when they are engaged in political posturing. Even so, in the case of the CTB, I come down solidly on the side of concluding they were serious, certainly during the Carter years and most likely at other times as well. My long personal contacts with Kapitza, Emelyanov, Timerbaev, and Petrosyants and other high-ranking Soviets who dealt regularly and at length with the CTB and related subjects convinced me that these men, at least, were honestly in favor of stopping all nuclear tests, those of the USSR included. All of them had solid contacts with still higher authorities, sometimes even with members of the Politburo itself, and they therefore knew how the people at the top felt about the question. I believe the men I met would not have worked so hard and so long on the issue if they had not believed they had the backing of the top leaders.

That said, I must add that I do not know why the Politburo favored a CTB. Perhaps it was because its members were more concerned than we were about proliferation. They saw—correctly, I believe—a CTB as being a good as well as a necessary means for inhibiting proliferation. Perhaps, too, they felt they could not win a wide-open technological race with us in this field. Simply stopping the whole thing may have seemed better than allowing us to lead them and the rest of the world they knew not where.

But can we trust them? The simple answer to that persistent question is that we don't. The entire negotiating process is designed to create a situation in which the need for trust is replaced by adequate verification policies and procedures. These may depend on a certain amount of overt cooperation, but not on unsupported trust.

More basically, I hold that *trust* is a word that should be used only to describe the way one human being perceives what another says or does. States, or governments, may be made up of human beings, but the sum is an entirely different thing from the parts. Words invented to describe people and their behavior, including *trusting* and *trustworthy,* should not be applied to these other, nonhuman entities. To do so can be and often is grossly misleading.

In sum, no, we cannot trust the Soviet government, but not because it is made up of Communists and Russians. Our Founding Fathers long ago concluded that we individual citizens cannot simply "trust" our own government indefinitely either. That is why the Constitution they wrote restricts the powers of government and describes and reserves the rights of citizens.

Treaty writing and other state-to-state projects simply must take this—often unwelcome—fact into account.

CHAPTER 15

The Pope
and the Archbishop

The Physics Elders

I HAVE always been aware that the nuclear arms race has a moral, or ethical, dimension, but it has never been entirely clear to me how to incorporate that fact into personal or collective behavior. The words and deeds of my elders in physics and politics have been of some, but not decisive, help.

Shortly after the explosion at Hiroshima, Robert Oppenheimer wrote that in building the bomb "the physicists have known sin." Despite that and other remarks indicating a certain anguish, he continued to support the U.S. nuclear program in general, and he never said or implied that he would not participate in the Manhattan Project if he had to do it all over again. Most other project veterans behaved similarly. They had eagerly joined the project when we seemed to be in a race for the bomb with the Germans, and they were proud of the bomb's role in ending the war in the Pacific. They regretted the lives the bomb had cost, but they found that those it had saved more than made up for them. Later many of them were active in the campaign to contain the nuclear arms race, but that was inspired more by worries about the future than by regrets about the past.

What then did Oppenheimer mean by saying the physicists had known sin? I believe he meant simply that, in building the bomb, the physicists had come down from their ivory tower and joined the politicians and statesmen and others in doing those immediately harmful and regrettable acts that occasionally become necessary or unavoidable in the slow and often fitful march of civilization. As a result, they now shared in the task of determining what might be done next, but they were by no means solely responsible for it.

In 1949 Oppenheimer and his colleagues on the General Advisory Committee on atomic energy were called upon to consider the question of whether to go ahead with an urgent program to develop the hydrogen—or super—bomb. The Soviets had just exploded their first atomic bomb, and many American leaders were urging the development of the vastly more powerful hydrogen bomb as the answer to that event. The GAC's report on the matter concluded that the world would be better off if we could find some way, preferably involving Soviet cooperation, to avoid introducing this terrible new weapon into the world's arsenals: "We base our recommendation on our belief that the extreme dangers to mankind inherent in the proposal wholly outweigh any military advantage that could come from this development."[1]

For the GAC members Enrico Fermi and I. I. Rabi that was not strong enough. In an addendum to the report, they wrote, "It is clear that the use of such a weapon cannot be justified on any ethical ground which gives a human being a certain individuality and dignity even if he happens to be a resident of an enemy country." A few sentences further on they added, "It is necessarily an evil thing considered in any light."[2]

President Truman, on the nearly unanimous advice of his closest senior advisers, decided to go ahead with the development of the H-bomb. He and those advisers were aware of the opinions of the Oppenheimer committee and a handful of others to the contrary, but their own view of the world and the role of the Soviets and nuclear weapons in it prevailed.

And then what? Fermi and two of his students—Richard Garwin and Leona Marshall—joined the small group at Los Alamos then searching for the design breakthrough that would make the hydrogen bomb practical, and they made very important contributions to it. Rabi remained on the GAC and in other high advisory positions that dealt with nuclear weapons and similar high-tech issues. In 1953, after Oppenheimer's removal from the chairmanship of the GAC on grounds that he was a "security risk," Rabi replaced him as chairman. The explanation for the apparently contradictory behavior of Fermi and Rabi is straightforward. Both believed that in a democracy, once the system has considered an issue and reached a conclusion, the matter is, in the main, settled.

Fermi died soon after the successful development of the hydrogen bomb. Rabi continued to participate for many years at the highest levels of government. He and others with similar views—Hans Bethe, for instance—continued to speak out against expanding our dependency on nuclear weapons and in favor of negotiating controls over them; with very few exceptions, though, they never repudiated either the people or the institutions that promoted and built them.

There was an additional important twist to the Fermi-Rabi remarks about the ethical side of the H-bomb issue. I did not have access to the GAC report at the time it was written, but I did have the opportunity to gossip about it with both Ernest Lawrence and Edward Teller. Each of them thought, incorrectly but plausibly, that the GAC had reached its negative conclusions very largely on the basis of the political and ethical beliefs of its members and had distorted its technical arguments in order to seduce others into reaching the same conclusions. More precisely, Lawrence and Teller felt that the whole sorry affair was Oppenheimer's doing. They regarded him as particularly persuasive and believed he had somehow led the whole committee to warp its technical analysis in order to support his own moral and political conclusions. Since the members of the GAC had no special standing in the field of morality, these critics rejected the entire report and urged others to do the same. A couple of years later, when I got to know Lewis Strauss, another one of the principals in the H-bomb decision, I found that he saw the GAC report in the same light, and so did many other high officials privy to it. In sum, in the eyes of many people the introduction of ethical arguments into the GAC report definitely undermined whatever effectiveness it might otherwise have had.

Yet another informative event occurred in the mid-1950s. Edward Teller and Linus Pauling debated on TV the morality of exposing the world's population to the radioactive fallout then being produced by above-ground nuclear weapons tests. Pauling said the resulting nuclear radiation would cause cancers in many unsuspecting individuals all over the world. It would mutate the genes, and thus the progeny, of others. Both of these effects were obviously bad in themselves, and therefore it was morally wrong to conduct tests known to produce them. Teller countered by noting that a nuclear war would kill and damage a great many more people than fallout from tests would. Furthermore, he said, the testing of nuclear weapons was essential to maintaining peace, defending civilization, and preserving freedom, and therefore the greater good was served by continued testing. The two men agreed that killing people was wrong and had to be avoided as much as possible, but they disagreed entirely about the optimal means for reaching this end. Most of the arguments over nuclear weapons and nuclear war contain similar contradictions. People on both sides agree on the basic moral premises, but they differ greatly over the mechanics of how best to fulfill them. What seemed to be a moral issue at first sight was often something quite different and, indeed, even in a different dimension.

In 1958 yet another circumstance shed light on these issues. Both Eisenhower and Khrushchev were at that time seeking ways to ban all further nuclear tests. Their main motivation was the belief that doing so would help contain the arms race and avert an even more dangerous situation than the one then prevailing. They were also concerned about fallout, but that was a lesser matter. As part of the campaign to promote this goal, the Soviet government permitted (or encouraged?) the publication of a book entitled *Soviet Scientists on the Danger of Nuclear Tests.*[3] It was a collection of essays by individual authors, many of whom contributed diatribes on the dangers of American testing and other American actions. One chapter, by Andrei Sakharov, then a leading figure in the Soviet nuclear weapons program, was more thoughtful and did not focus on the United States. In it Sakharov wrote,

> Another widespread argument (used to justify testing) . . . is that the progress of civilization and the development of technology lead to loss of human life. A common example used is automobile accidents. But the analogy here is neither exact nor justified. Motor transport improves the living conditions of the population, while accidents are the result of carelessness on the part of specific individuals who are held responsible. The distress due to testing, on the contrary, is an inevitable consequence of each explosion. It is the author's opinion that, ethically speaking, the only peculiarity of this problem is the total impunity of the crime (for in no concrete case can it be proved that the death of a person is caused by radiation) and also to the total defencelessness of future generations with respect to our actions.
>
> The cessation of test explosions will preserve the lives of hundreds of thousands of people and will have a still greater indirect effect by helping to lessen international tension and to reduce the possibility of a nuclear war—the greatest danger of our age.[4]

At the time Sakharov was not yet known outside of Soviet scientific circles, and his remarks went unnoticed in the West. Working in the

White House and the Office of the Secretary of Defense, I was then in close touch with those in the intelligence community charged with analyzing Soviet nuclear and other technological developments. I never heard a single suggestion that there might be people inside the Soviet nuclear establishment who were pressing for moderation. In retrospect this seems astonishing, but the picture of the Soviet Union as being, in effect, a vast prison camp simply did not allow room for such an idea. Of course, one swallow does not make a summer, but we might have made slightly different and perhaps better policy decisions had we known about even one such voice. It was only years later that we learned that Sakharov had opposed the resumption of nuclear testing in 1961 and otherwise acted in a fashion fully consistent with the views expressed in that essay. Indeed, a few years after it was published, he met personally with Khrushchev in a vain attempt to stop the atmospheric testing of certain very large bombs—no doubt including the 58-megaton test of 1961. Both Khrushchev's memoirs and Sakharov's confirmed that, in effect, Khrushchev told Sakharov, "You are a brilliant physicist, but you do not understand politics. Politics are my responsibility. I know that the Americans only understand strength, and I conclude we must go ahead with the tests." Not long afterward Sakharov was eased out of the weapons program. In the 1970s he became an across-the-board dissident and, finally, an internal exile in Gorki.

In 1963 the issue of test fallout was largely resolved by the banishment of nearly all nuclear testing to underground caverns specially constructed for the purpose.

The Pope

When I was ambassador to the CTB negotiations in 1979–80, circumstances led me to see more of Victor Weisskopf than at any other time since he had left the University of Rochester in 1942. CERN, the Conseil Européen pour la Recherche Nucléaire, was also located near Geneva, and Viki had been one of its earliest and most admired directors. After stepping down as director to return to his professorship at MIT, he continued to maintain a summer residence nearby in France. This happy fact, plus my lifelong affection for him, led us and our wives to meet together for meals and conversation. Given my mission in Geneva, it was only natural for us to turn often to the nuclear problem.

Weisskopf had long been deeply concerned about where our nuclear weapons policies were taking us, and he had sought and seized opportunities to intervene in the matter. Recently, he had chanced upon an especially good one. He was elected to the Pontifical Academy of Science, and the new pope, John Paul II, to whom the academy reported, was also very concerned about nuclear war. Viki did what he could to reinforce the pope's views and to back him up in whatever actions they might lead him to take.

In the spring of 1980 the pope decided to accept an invitation to address the annual UNESCO conference in Paris. It would, he felt, provide him with a good platform for airing some of his views on nuclear weapons and nuclear war. A small subgroup of academy members, augmented by a few outside experts, was invited to come to Rome to help lay the groundwork for the speech. The group, eight in all, included Viki and several other academy members, plus Emilio Segrè, Carl Friedrich von Weizsäcker, and me. To say the least, the group was broadly ecumenical: four Catholics, two Jews, and two Protestants. The date I arrived in Rome is easy to remember: April 25, 1980, the day the failed attempt to rescue the hostages in Tehran was made. The press—and the local U.S. embassy—were totally preoccupied with that sad event.

We met for two days in the Vatican gardens and drew up a series of agreed background papers for the pope and his speech writers to use in preparing for the UNESCO speech. I drafted one that summarized arms control negotiations to date and suggested what might be done next. When we finished, we were invited to meet with the pope in his Vatican office. Each of us spoke in the language personally most convenient: English, French, Italian, and German. The pope responded to each of us in our language of choice.

At the beginning of the meeting, he seemed somewhat nervous. He faced a group of experts in a field about which he knew very little. He urgently wanted to talk with us about it, but, like any human being, he did not want to appear totally ignorant or say anything foolish. We were all tense, too, for our own reasons, but the tensions passed quickly as we each had our say.

From the pope's own words, from reports of what he had said elsewhere, and from his aides, a clear picture of his beliefs emerged. Nuclear war absolutely must not happen; no human beings anywhere should ever be the victims of nuclear mass slaughter, whether deliberate or incidental to some other objective. Self-defense, however, was in general legitimate and necessary; in particular, an adequate level of nuclear deterrence must be maintained, at least so long as no better alternative was within reach. On the one hand, he was deeply convinced that the present situation had to be radically changed. On the other, he was wary of the Russians for obvious reasons, and he did not favor large unilateral actions that could unbalance the strategic relationship and lead to rash and dangerous acts.

The pope had another, quite different problem on his mind. If he came out against mass nuclear murder, people would say, "Of course, what else would you expect?" If he said such and such a missile should not be deployed in such and such a place, because it would be strategically destabilizing, people would say, "What does he know about that?" Finding a useful middle ground between simply "pontificating" and pretending to have expertise he didn't have was for him, and for others in high positions, not easy. In fact, it was the flip side of the problem Fermi and Rabi created when they introduced ethical considerations into the debate over the hydrogen bomb. If the pope now pretended to have special strategic wisdom or technical expertise, he risked undermining his moral authority.

When, after a little more than an hour, we left the pope's office, Jacques Chirac, then mayor of Paris and later prime minister of France, was in the outer office awaiting his turn. The modern pope has more functions than Saint Peter ever dreamed of.

That evening I had supper with Viki and Emilio. We reminisced about the extraordinary events of the past three days. We all agreed that at one point we had heard John Paul II say (in French, we thought) that he felt as though the Holy Spirit had told him to become involved in the nuclear weapons problem: "It was so insistent that I think it was not only my conscience but the Holy Ghost."[5] One did not have to be a Catholic to be greatly moved when someone whom billions believe to be the vicar of Christ made a remark like that.

The UNESCO speech itself was something of a disappointment. Only the last few paragraphs dealt with the nuclear weapons problem, which even then was presented in rather stilted terms. The speech contained no clear sign of our briefing papers or conversations. Evidently the pope's speech writers had somehow managed to tone down his views for the occasion. Later, however, in other speeches in Rome and in Hiroshima, the pope warmed up to the subject, and I thought I did see some evidence of our efforts.

Weisskopf had more meetings on the same subject with the pope and the Pontifical Academy. He invited me to several of them, but my schedule never again permitted a replay of that fascinating—and, I hope, useful—event.

The Archbishop

Later that same year I arranged through Solly Zuckerman, who seemed to know everybody in Britain, to meet with the archbishop of Canterbury. I knew that he, too, was very much concerned about nuclear war, and my meeting with the pope encouraged me to think I might be of some help to him too. We met in Lambeth Palace, for centuries the official London residence of the archbishops of Canterbury. Sybil and a clerical aide, whom he referred to as his chaplain, were also present. Like the pope, he was planning some public speeches on the subject, including one before the American Association of Newspaper Editors the following spring. I reported on our earlier meeting with the pope and what we had concluded there, and I brought him up to date on my mission in Geneva. Afterward I remained in touch with his aide while the speech for the editors was being prepared. It did, I thought, reflect something of my meeting with him.

His approach to the problem was similar to the pope's. He, too, knew that nuclear war must not happen and believed in self-defense and the need for maintaining nuclear deterrence. He also saw the need for radical changes in the way we maintained the peace, but he did not favor great unilateral actions that would suddenly unbalance the strategic relationship. Again like the pope, he was puzzled about where to find the middle ground between saying the obvious and making arguments— perhaps wrong or foolish—in areas where he had no special knowledge.

As we parted, I asked if he would give me a signed photograph of himself that I could pass on to my parents, both lifelong loyal Episcopalians then in their late eighties. He graciously did so, and I proudly presented it to my parents a week or two thereafter. When they moved into very modest quarters in a nursing home about a year later, it was one of the few mementos they took along with them.

The Bishops' Letters

Following the renewal of interest in the nuclear question by their leader, the American, German, and French Catholic bishops' councils also took a long, serious look at the problem. In time each of them produced a "bishops' letter" on the subject. There were some differences among these groups—and within them—but they generally agreed on the main points. As I understand the American bishops' letter in particular, its three key points were as follows:[6] (1) "Under no circumstances may nuclear weapons or other instruments of mass slaughter be used for the purpose of destroying population centers or other predominately civilian targets. Retaliatory actions which would indiscriminately and disproportionately take many wholly innocent lives . . . must also be condemned." (2) The "deliberate initiation of nuclear war, on however restricted a scale," cannot be morally justified. (3) "In concert with the evaluation provided by Pope John Paul II, . . . a strictly limited moral acceptance of deterrence" is appropriate. (The conditions are that there be no immediately accessible effective alternative and that the governments be genuinely and actively engaged in seeking one.)

Most observers interpreted the proviso that the governments must search for a way out of the present strategy to mean that they must be seriously engaged in negotiating arms control. This solution does indeed receive special emphasis in the bishops' analysis of the issue. But is that the only, or even the best, way of complying with the bishops' moral injunction? Is it the optimal way of taking into account Fermi and Rabi's assertion that "the use of such a weapon cannot be justified on any ethical ground"?

My experiences have taught me that nuclear arms control and disarmament are means, not ends. The ends are avoiding nuclear war in the short run and abolishing all war in the long run. Arms control and disarmament negotiations and treaties can obviously help achieve these ends, but not by themselves.

There are three major means for averting nuclear war. The choice of which one to emphasize depends mainly on the time scale we have in mind. In order of expanding time scale, these means are, first, maintaining the strategic balance; second, promoting détente, containing antagonisms, and otherwise implementing peaceful coexistence; and third, creating a world political order in which war has no place.

The *strategic balance* is widely credited with being the basis for the peace that has prevailed among the major nuclear states since the beginning of the nuclear age. For those whose primary or sole concern is the immediate future, this approach is, it would seem, the most promising. It cannot be proved that the "nuclear balance of terror" is, in fact, the primary basis for the peace, but it is obvious that no major nation— either its leadership or its people—is willing to test this proposition by deliberately and unilaterally accepting a position of substantial inferiority. And maintaining the strategic balance means that for the immediate future, at least, we must continue our current arms deployment, procurement, and development programs roughly along present lines. The precise arms and policies selected for this purpose must, of course, be those that maximize stability and minimize any temptation ever to "go first" in a desperate crisis.

The primary role of arms control in the short term is to reinforce those elements of the balance that enhance stability and eliminate those that might encourage preemption or other rash and dangerous acts. Arms control negotiations can, if properly integrated with other elements of strategic policy, help cool antagonisms and calm fears by making it clear that neither side is seeking "superiority" or any other unacceptable advantage.

Promoting détente, containing antagonisms, and implementing peaceful coexistence provide the best hope for avoiding nuclear war and other large-scale conflicts for the intermediate future—that is, for the decades as far ahead as we can even dimly see. Experience tells us that such conditions are necessary if arms control and disarmament negotiations are to succeed. Conversely, such negotiations and the actions that flow from them are among the best means for promoting and reinforcing these conditions.

Creating a world political order in which war has no place seems to be the only reliable solution for the long run. Five thousand years of political and social evolution from the creation of the first city-states and theocracies have led us to our present situation. That situation is surely generally better than those that preceded it, except for one important defect. And that defect is awful: the current means for maintaining peace at the largest scale—the deterrence of global war through the threat of mutual assured destruction—openly risks the destruction of civilization if it fails. Therein lies the root of the long-term dilemma we face. Nuclear deterrence has worked in the sense that there have been no nuclear wars among the nuclear powers. Nor, for that matter, have there been any other kinds of wars directly among them. But no one believes that this can last indefinitely.

Many peace activists like to say, "War is obsolete." Would that it were, but the simple, empirical facts are otherwise. Conventional wars—that is, nonnuclear wars—have in recent decades been just as common as ever. And it is not merely that wars continue to happen; the participants still sometimes achieve objectives they could not have attained in any other way. The problem is not that war is really obsolete but that stubborn statesmen refuse to admit it; the problem is that war is not obsolete, though it surely must become so soon. The very real and legitimate fear is that one day one of these frequent "other wars" will somehow develop in such a way that the nuclear powers find themselves engaged in direct, head-to-head conflict. Then, when one side or the other becomes desperate, there is no telling what will happen next.

We must promote the further evolution of the world political system so that wars of all kinds truly do become obsolete. Only then will we be safe from the threat of nuclear war. Current relations between states are governed by very little law and absolutely no law enforcement. The relations are, in brief, anarchic and chaotic. The use of force is often the best, and sometimes even the only, means for solving severe problems between states. Somehow, law and order, analogous to that governing relations between individuals in free societies, must be introduced at the nation-state level.

Such a world is obviously some generations in the future, at the very least. In the meantime—while conventional war remains a plausible extension of "politics by other means"—we must make sure that small and conventional wars stay small and conventional.

Deliberate confrontation, bluster, striving for superiority, policies and strategies based mainly on hatred and fear—all these are counterproductive. Classical diplomacy enhanced by détente and arms control still appears to be the best means for taking us where we want to go for the immediate and intermediate future. Beyond that, something new and different is needed.

Nuclear weapons issues clearly do have a moral dimension, and proper consideration of this moral dimension does lead to some moral imperatives. But these imperatives are not best fulfilled by simply deploring nuclear war and reiterating the Ten Commandments. They are best served by making sure that political and social evolution continues, and continues in the right direction—toward a world in which social and economic justice exists within nations and peace, law, and order between them.

Where Do We Stand Now?

In 1945, right after the first two atomic bombs exploded over Japan and ended World War II, I and many of my seniors believed we had at last made war obsolete.

Sixteen years later, in the early 1960s, after I had finished my first tour in the Pentagon and had reflected on where we were going, I began to have to have serious doubts about our course. By the end of the 1960s, I was downright pessimistic about it.

By then there were five nuclear powers, and many more states seemed to be on the verge of joining them. The United States alone possessed some thirty thousand nuclear weapons and was rapidly building the means for delivering them to targets half a world away in half an hour. The Soviets appeared determined to match us, and it was evidently only a matter of time before they would. The advent of a Soviet nuclear threat seemed to portend the need to place some of our forces on a "hair-trigger" alert and even to adopt a "launch on warning" tactic in which either computers or, at best, preprogrammed officials would assume the authority for launching Armageddon. Worse, international attempts to control the growth and spread of nuclear weapons had either met with failure or produced results that were very modest alongside the great crescendo of the arms race itself. Still worse, war proved not to be obsolete. Wars continued to occur at more or less the same rate as before. To be sure, the hot ones were all off on the periphery somewhere, but even in Europe, with its hostile blocs and recurrent crises, war seemed to be a real possibility once again.

An article I wrote for *Life* magazine in 1970 presented my net assessment of the situation. After listing ways to "roll back" the arms race, I concluded by saying, "[U]nless we nerve ourselves to make the attempt, and make it soon, we are quite simply doomed."[7]

I was not alone in expressing such pessimism. Many other veterans of the Manhattan Project had done so well before I did. They commonly estimated that the art of building nuclear weapons would quickly spread to many nations, and they predicted that a spark somewhere would soon ignite the world's nuclear stockpiles.

Such gloomy thoughts and doomsday predictions were not confined to those concerned about the nuclear arms race in general. Others, more worried about Soviet weapons in particular, created their own choruses of doomsayers and warned about what could happen when the Soviets acquired enough weapons of their own. In numbers, these people at least equaled those concerned about nuclear weapons in general, and they certainly were more influential. Indeed, immediately after the first Soviet atomic bomb exploded, in 1949, those then in the government warned that the Soviets would soon be in a position to carry out a devastating—possibly decisive—surprise attack on us (with propeller-driven aircraft, no less). In 1957 the Gaither panel, whose report I had helped prepare, reaffirmed and updated such gloomy estimates.

In the late 1970s the leaders of this latter group, then largely outside the government, founded the Committee on the Present Danger. They again warned that the Russians would soon gain a decisive and exploit-

able advantage if we did not immediately mend our ways. More specifically, they warned us against President Carter's "fatally flawed" SALT
II Treaty and vigorously supported the election of Ronald Reagan.

In short, from the very beginning of the arms race, there have been
many doomsayers on both sides of the issue. To make matters all the
more confusing for the general public, many of the best-informed people
in the land were among them.

So, how do things look in 1987? I have moved partway back toward
my earlier optimism. On the one hand, I find that the strategy of peace
through nuclear deterrence is working and seems to be very stable. On
the other hand, however, it remains very dangerous: if deterrence
should fail for any reason, the use of only a fraction of the world's
nuclear stockpiles could permanently destroy Western civilization.

The United States long ago lost whatever usable nuclear advantage
it might once have had. And despite oft-repeated warnings to the contrary, the Soviets have never been able to attain one. Such warnings
were usually false alarms, and even those with some real basis were
answered by easy adjustments in our own defense programs.

In the late 1970s some claimed that the United States would face a
"window of vulnerability" in the early 1980s.* The notion was based on
the claim that a hypothetical vulnerability in only one leg of our triad—
in this case, land-based missiles—would create an exploitable advantage for the Russians. The idea is totally false; the reason for maintaining a triad of very different forces in the first place is to preclude such
a possibility, and the triad does that very well.

Oddly enough, the same notion appeared in reverse form only a few
years later. Then, many antinuclear activists opposed the MX missile
and a close relative, the submarine-launched D-5, on the ground that
their deployment would gravely threaten Soviet land-based missiles.
They went on to assert that this would give us a useful advantage over
the Soviets and that this in turn would provoke some unseemly reaction
on their part. The latter notion, put forward by people who in the main
ridiculed the earlier "window of vulnerability" claim, is also wrong for
the very same reason. The Soviets' ability to deter an American president from making a rash nuclear act, if one were ever to be so inclined,

---

*One of the main promoters of this idea was T. K. Jones, a Boeing analyst who later
became deputy undersecretary of defense in the Reagan administration. The idea was
adopted by many if not all of the leaders of the Committee on the Present Danger.

is not seriously undermined by a hypothetical threat to only one component of their strategic forces.

In sum, what was once called the "delicate balance of terror" has turned out to be very robust. It remains terrible in terms of its possible consequences, but it shows no more signs of becoming unhinged in the future than it showed in the past.

What about the problem of systems that have a "hair-trigger" mode, systems that must be constantly ready for sudden use and in which the authority to initiate a nuclear action may therefore be delegated to computers?

I encountered this issue in crystal clear form almost thirty years ago when General Kuter told me of some of the notions then in the wind for automatically launching our offensive missiles on warning. Even that, however, was not my first brush with the idea. In the early 1950s, as a member of the von Neumann committee, I had become aware that the Atlas had to be launchable on fifteen minutes' notice because that was the longest warning we could expect from the radars then being planned. And one of the features that helped sell the Minuteman in the late 1950s was that it could, as its name implied, be launched on only minutes' notice.

The notion of automated launch has continued to come up since then, but the highest authorities always shy away from it, and I do not now see any long-term trends likely to lead to its adoption. One possible exception would be the deployment of space-based intercept weapons, as in the Star Wars proposals. These would have to respond to an attack in such a short time (minutes or even seconds) that they would have to be controlled by an on-board computer to be effective. However, despite enormous fanfare on the part of their promoters and great fears on the part of their detractors, I do not expect to see such weapons deployed in the foreseeable future.

In short, dangerous notions about delegating to computers the authority to fire weapons will continue to be with us, but I believe if sensible people remain alert to it and oppose it whenever it arises, we will continue to avoid it.

Arms control has been a disappointment but not a failure. Large areas of the earth, including Latin America and Antarctica, remain free of nuclear weapons at least partly because of deliberate diplomatic efforts to keep them that way. Certain environments—outer space and the sea bottom—have been placed off limits for nuclear weapons. The deployment of the kind of strategic defenses that could lead to an arms race has so far been severely inhibited. Limits—to be sure, rather high ones—have been placed on offensive weapons. Nuclear weapons tests have been banned from environments where they would constitute a menace to health. Obviously more remains to be done in all these areas, but what has been accomplished is valuable and helps restrain the arms race and diminish the number of possible nuclear flash points.

The most successful, and arguably the most important, of all arms control policies have been those designed to limit the spread, or "proliferation," of nuclear weapons to additional states.

Despite almost universal expectations to the contrary, there are still only five overt nuclear powers, and the last state to become one, China, did so in 1964, a full generation ago. In the quarter of a century since that happened, only four others—India, Israel, Pakistan, and South Africa—have taken strong steps toward becoming nuclear powers, but none of them has yet built and deployed substantial, overt nuclear forces. This surprising but happy result must be credited to the combined antiproliferation policies and actions of the majority of the world's states. Together they created a network of unilateral, bilateral, and multilateral arrangements, all designed to inhibit the further proliferation of nuclear weapons. Among them are the International Atomic Energy Agency, created to support and monitor most of the world's nuclear energy programs, and a variety of bilateral trade agreements intended to prevent the diversion of nuclear power technology to the production of nuclear weapons. More important, the great majority of the world's nations have been persuaded to sign the Nonproliferation Treaty (NPT), in which the nuclear have-nots promise to remain that way and the nuclear haves promise not to help anyone else join them. The principal quid pro quo for a state's remaining nuclear weapons free is that its neighbors also agree to refrain from going nuclear.

While these arrangements may not have totally prevented proliferation (though there has in fact been none since the NPT went into force), they certainly have greatly inhibited it. No doubt other nuclear states will eventually join the current five, but here, too, I see no reason to expect things to get out of hand rapidly.

The paired notions that we must "do something" radical about either the "Soviet Threat" or the "Nuclear Arms Race" very soon or be doomed have been with us for more than forty years. So far they have always proved to be wrong, and I expect they will remain so for the foreseeable future. The maintenance of an adequate balance of power, including its nuclear component, combined with classical diplomatic actions designed to control arms and preserve the peace, has in fact bought us time. If we are wise enough, we will use it to find a way out of the grand nuclear dilemma.

Two great realities dominate the world scene. One is that the strategy of maintaining peace through the threat of mutual annihilation cannot work forever, no matter how stable it may currently be. The other is that finding an effective, moral, and permanent replacement for the current strategy will take serious effort and a long time, generations at least.

I recall once reading an old story in which a lazy gardener told his master, a statesman, that there was no reason to hurry in planting a certain tree, because it would in any event take a long time to grow tall. The statesman countered that that was all the more reason to get on with the job forthwith. Today's statesmen, and the people behind them, must do no less.

NOTES

Chapter 1

In preparing this chapter, I made extensive use of two books dealing with the larger events that engulfed me during this period. They are Richard G. Hewlett and Oscar E. Anderson, Jr., *The New World, 1939–1946*, vol. 1 of *A History of the United States Atomic Energy Commission* (University Park: Pennsylvania State University Press, 1962), and Herbert Childs, *An American Genius: The Life of Ernest Orlando Lawrence* (New York: Dutton, 1968).

1. Banesh Hoffman, *Albert Einstein, Creator and Rebel* (New York: Viking Press, 1972), 206.
2. Quoted in Childs, *American Genius*, 321.
3. Hewlett and Anderson, *New World*, 51.
4. Truman speech, quoted in *New York Times*, August 7, 1945, 1.
5. It was later published as Henry De Wolf Smyth, *Atomic Energy for Military Purposes* (Princeton: Princeton University Press, 1945).
6. Hirohito speech, quoted in *New York Times*, August 15, 1945, 3.
7. V. F. Weisskopf, *The Nuclear Arms Race: How to Survive the Next Forty Years*, paper no. 1, Niels Bohr Centennial Conference on the Challenge of Nuclear Armaments, University of Copenhagen, September 27–29, 1985.
8. Reagan news interview, March 29, 1983, quoted in *New York Times*, March 30, 1983, 14.

Chapter 2

For general background information I used Richard G. Hewlett and Francis Duncan, *The Atomic Shield*, vol. 2 of *A History of the United States Atomic Energy Commission* (University Park: Pennsylvania State University Press, 1969), and Herbert Childs, *An American Genius: The Life of Ernest Orlando Lawrence* (New York: Dutton, 1968).

1. J. Hadley, E. L. Kelly, C. E. Leith, E. Segrè, C. Wiegand, and H. F. York, "Angular Distribution of *n-p* Scattering with 90-Mev Neutrons," *Physical Review* 73 (1948): 1114–15.

2. Russell Bjorklund, Walter E. Crandall, Burton J. Moyer, and Herbert F. York, "High Energy Photons from Proton Nuclear Collisions," *Physical Review* 77 (1950): 213–18.

3. Herbert F. York, "Secondary Particles from Various Nuclei Bombarded with 90-Mev Neutrons," *Physical Review* 75 (1949): 1467.

Chapter 3

1. Churchill speech, Fulton, Mo., March 5, 1946. In *New York Times,* March 6, 1946, 4.

2. *Pravda,* February 17, 1950 (private translation). Brief coverage in *New York Times,* February 18, 1950.

3. J. Robert Oppenheimer, "Physicists in the Contemporary World," *Bulletin of Atomic Scientists* 4, no. 3 (March 1948): 66, and Herbert Childs, *An American Genius: The Life of Ernest Orlando Lawrence* (New York: Dutton, 1968), 405.

4. A more complete discussion of the GAC recommendations can be found in several places, including my earlier book *The Advisors: Oppenheimer, Teller, and the Superbomb* (San Francisco: W. H. Freeman, 1976), to which the complete GAC report is appended (pp. 152–57).

5. *New York Times,* February 1, 1950, 1.

6. For more on Fermi's famous question, see *Physics Today,* August 1985, 11–13.

7. Stanislaw M. Ulam, *Adventures of a Mathematician* (New York: Scribner's, 1976), 219.

8. Teller, "The Work of Many People," *Science* 121, no. 3139 (February 25, 1955): 267–75.

9. *In the Matter of J. Robert Oppenheimer: Transcript of Hearings Before Personnel Board* (Washington, D.C.: U.S. Government Printing Office, 1954), 81, 251.

Chapter 4

In preparing this chapter, I reread my own work in this area in order to remind myself what my more nearly contemporary views of these matters were: especially *The Advisors: Oppenheimer, Teller, and the Superbomb* (San Francisco: W. H. Freeman, 1976) and *Race to Oblivion* (New York: Simon and Schuster, 1969). I also consulted Edward Teller with Allen Brown, *The Legacy of Hiroshima* (Garden City, N.Y.: Doubleday, 1962), and an extensive news conference by Norris Bradbury, director of the Los Alamos Laboratory, September 24, 1954. In addition, I had the opportunity of perusing the Livermore Laboratory archives; unfortunately, very little has been retained from this period.

1. Teller, *Legacy of Hiroshima,* 54.

2. *In the Matter of J. Robert Oppenheimer: Transcript of Hearings Before Personnel Board* (Washington, D.C.: U.S. Government Printing Office, 1954), 248.

3. See Teller, *Legacy of Hiroshima,* 55, and James R. Shepley and Clay Blair, Jr., *The Hydrogen Bomb* (New York: Greenwood, 1954), 150. Teller's version of this episode is given in both books.

4. Shepley and Blair, *Hydrogen Bomb.*

5. I have discussed this matter at some length in *The Advisors.*

6. See *New York Times,* June 19, 25, and 27, 1957. In those three issues the three steps in the process described above can easily be seen.

Chapter 5

There is as yet no biography devoted solely to the life of John von Neumann, but I made use of two other books that contain long descriptions of von Neumann and his ideas: Steve J. Heims, *John von Neumann and Norbert Wiener: From Mathematics to the Technologies of Life and Death* (Cambridge: MIT Press, 1980), and Stanislaw M. Ulam, *Adventures of a Mathematician* (New York: Scribner's, 1976).

1. Theodore von Kármán with Lee Edson, *The Wind and Beyond* (Boston: Little, Brown, 1967).

2. Quoted in Fred Kaplan, *The Wizards of Armageddon* (New York: Simon and Schuster, 1983), 63.

3. Thomas A. Sturm, *The USAF Scientific Advisory Board: Its First Twenty Years* (USAF Historical Liaison Office, 1967), 61.

4. Quoted in *Newsweek,* July 29, 1985, 38.

5. This report, RW011-4, February 10, 1954, was downgraded to unclassified in 1966. It is on file at the USAF Historical Liaison Office.

6. Eugene M. Emme, ed., *A History of Rocket Technology* (Detroit: Wayne State University Press, 1964), contains a chapter written by Tokaty-Tokaev that gives a good idea what he knew and could tell us.

7. Gaither Panel Report NSC 5724, November 7, 1957 (reprinted 1976, Washington, D.C.: U.S. Government Printing Office).

Chapter 6

The three president's science advisers with whom I worked during this period have all written memoirs that provide extremely useful background material for further writing in this area: James R. Killian, *Sputnik, Scientists, and Eisenhower* (Cambridge: MIT Press, 1977), George B. Kistiakowsky, *A Scientist in the White House* (Cambridge: Harvard University Press, 1976), and Jerome B. Wiesner, *Where Science and Politics Meet* (New York: McGraw-Hill, 1965).

1. Personal communication from Scoville about 1969.

2. Dwight D. Eisenhower, *The White House Years,* vol. 2, *Waging Peace, 1956–1961* (Garden City, N.Y.: Doubleday, 1965), 224.

3. John B. Medaris with Arthur Gorden, *Countdown for Decision* (New York: Putnam, 1960), 156.

4. Memorandum George B. Kistiakowsky to James R. Killian, December 19, 1957, Dwight D. Eisenhower Presidential Library, Abilene, Kansas (DDE Library), White House Office, Office of the Special Assistant for Science and Technology: Records, Box 12 Missiles [Nov.-Dec. 1957] (1).

5. Memorandum James R. Killian to the President, December 28, 1957, DDE Library, Dwight D. Eisenhower Papers as President, Administration Series, Box 23 Killian, James R. (2).

6. Dwight D. Eisenhower, State of the Union Message, January 9, 1958, DDE Library, Dwight D. Eisenhower Papers as President, Speech Series, Box 24.

7. Memorandum of conversation of February 4, 1958 with the President, James R. Killian, George B. Kistiakowsky, Herbert F. York, and A. J. Goodpaster, February 6, 1958, Dwight D. Eisenhower Papers as President, Dwight D. Eisenhower Diary Series, Box 30 Staff Notes-February 1958.

8. From an address to the Conference to Plan a Strategy for Peace, June 3, 1960, published in Wiesner, *Where Science and Politics Meet,* 173.

9. Eisenhower, *Waging Peace,* 476.

10. Ibid., 543, 547.

11. Reagan, State of the Union Message, February 11, 1985.

Chapter 7

In addition to the president's science advisers' memoirs cited above, I also made use of Keith Glennan's unpublished diary, which may be found in the Smithsonian Institution's Space Museum, and of an as yet unpublished but thorough history of ARPA written by Lee Huff at the request of Steven Lukasik, then director of ARPA.

1. Ernest D. Courant, M. Stanley Livingston, and Hartland Snyder, "The Strong-Focusing Synchroton—A New High Energy Accelerator," *Physical Review* 88 (1952): 1190–96.

2. This and other quotations are from a statement prepared by Wheeler and Wigner, dated June 4, 1958.

3. Personal communication from Goldberger in 1985.

4. Dwight D. Eisenhower, State of the Union Message, January 9, 1958, DDE Library, Dwight D. Eisenhower Papers as President, Speech Series, Box 24.

5. Freeman Dyson, *Disturbing the Universe* (New York: Harper & Row, 1979).

6. Strauss to Lawrence, June 23, 1958, Ernest O. Lawrence Collection, Bancroft Library, University of California at Berkeley.

Chapter 8

1. John B. Medaris, *Countdown for Decision* (New York: Putnam, 1960), 251–52. Bill Holaday was the OSD Director of Guided Missiles.

Chapter 9

1. In order to be sure that what I write *here and now* really reflects what I thought *there and then,* I have freely quoted from several papers I wrote at the time. These are (1) testimony before the Senate Committee on Foreign Relations in support of the establishment of the ACDA, August 14–16, 1961; (2) testimony before the same committee in support of the Limited Test Ban Treaty, August 26, 1963; and (3) the article "National Security and the Nuclear Test Ban," written with Jerome Wiesner and published in *Scientific American,* October 1964, 27–35.

2. Herbert F. York, Hearings on Nuclear Test Ban Treaty, Senate Committee on Foreign Relations, August 26, 1963 (Washington, D.C.: U.S. Government Printing Office, 1963), 758ff.

Chapter 10

1. A Guide to the Roger Revelle Papers, MS Collection MC6, Archives of the Scripps Institution of Oceanography.

2. February 23, 1961.

Chapter 11

1. Herbert F. York, Hearings on Safeguard Ballistic Missile Defense System, Senate Committee on Foreign Relations, April 14–16, 1961 (Washington, D.C.: U.S. Government Printing Office, 1961), 162ff.

2. Adapted from the report of the Pugwash meeting held at Udaipur, January 27 to February 1, 1964, 232–34. Provided by J. Ruina.

3. These extracts are from a heavily censored copy of the 1964 report of the Gilpatrick Committee on Proliferation available at the National Security Council's staff office.

4. Ibid.

Chapter 12

1. The telegram and Senator Russell's comments are in the *Congressional Record.* 90th Congress, 2nd sess., 1968. Vol. 114, pt. 22, pp. 29175 and 29178.

2. Herbert F. York, Hearings, Subcommittee on International Organizations

and Disarmament of the Senate Committee on Foreign Relations, March 11, 1969 (Washington, D.C.: U.S. Government Printing Office, 1969).

3. Ibid.

4. James R. Killian, *Sputnik, Scientists, and Eisenhower* (Cambridge: MIT Press, 1977), 92.

5. Herbert F. York, Hearings, Subcommittee on Arms Control, International Law, and Organization of the Senate Committee on Foreign Relations, August 8, 1970 (Washington, D.C.: U.S. Government Printing Office, 1970), 58–117.

6. Quoted in Joseph Rotblat, *Pugwash—the First Ten Years: History of the Conferences of Science and World Affairs* (London: Heinemann, 1967), 77, 79.

7. Cited ibid., 84.

8. Quoted in Joseph Rotblat, *Scientists in the Quest for Peace: A History of the Pugwash Conference* (Cambridge: MIT Press, 1972), 323.

Chapter 13

1. See Gerald Steinberg, *Satellite Reconnaissance: The Role of Informal Bargaining* (New York: Praeger, 1983).

2. A discussion of this and other early U.S. and Soviet ASAT programs is in Paul Stares, *The Militarization of Space* (Ithaca: Cornell University Press, 1985).

3. Quoted in a press release from the historical files of the ACDA, Washington, D.C.

Chapter 14

I consulted several other memoirs and analyses of the Comprehensive Test Ban negotiations. For my purposes the most important were a chapter by John Edmonds (my British counterpart) in Josephine O'Conner Howe, ed., *Armed Peace: The Search for World Security* (New York: St. Martin's Press, 1984), and chapters by a number of seminar participants in Leon Sloss and M. Scott Davis, eds., *A Game for High Stakes: Lessons Learned in Negotiating with the Soviet Union* (Cambridge, Mass.: Ballinger, 1986). Also useful was a study by Roland Timerbaev, deputy chief of the Soviet negotiating team: *Problems of Verification* (Moscow: Nauka Publishers, 1984). In addition, I consulted two of my American colleagues, Warren Heckrotte and Gerald Johnson, about this matter.

1. Gerald R. Ford, comment in seminar at University of California, San Diego, February 5, 1986.

2. *Congressional Record.* 95th Cong., 2d sess., 1978. Vol. 124, pt. 20, pp. 26706–26707.

3. For another discussion of this problem, see the chapter by E. Giller in Ann Kerr, ed., *The Vela Program: A 25 Year Review* (Executive Graphic Services, 1985), 26–37.

4. Quoted from a working paper on NSS on U.S. and U.K. territory, DARPA/DirNMRO, U.S. Department of Defense, February 6, 1979, originally secret, declassified December 31, 1985.

Chapter 15

1. U.S. Atomic Energy Commission Document No. 349, quoted in my book *The Advisors: Oppenheimer, Teller, and the Superbomb* (San Francisco: W. H. Freeman, 1976), 156.

2. Quoted ibid., 158.

3. A. V. Lebedinsky, ed., *Soviet Scientists on the Danger of Nuclear Tests* (Moscow: Foreign Languages Publishing House, 1960), 48–49.

4. Ibid.

5. From a note I wrote that same evening.

6. The quoted sections below are taken from "The Challenge of Peace," a pastoral letter by the National Conference of Catholic Bishops, 1983. It was published in a supplement to the *Chicago Catholic,* June 24 and July 1, 1983.

7. Herbert F. York, "We *Can* Reverse the Arms Race: A 10-Point Plan," *Life,* December 11, 1970, 40–41.

Index